THE SAFETY OF ELDERLY DRIVERS

THE SAFETY OF ELDERLY DRIVERS

Yesterday's Young in Today's Traffic

J. Peter Rothe

With Contributions by

P. J. Cooper
and
B. de Vries

Foreword by
Joseph Gusfield

Transaction Publishers
New Brunswick (U.S.A.) and London (U.K.)

Library of Congress Catalog Number: 89-32158
ISBN: 0-88738-728-4
Printed in the United States of America

Library of Congress Cataloging-in-Publication Data
Rothe, John Peter, 1948-
The safety of elderly drivers : yesterday's young in today's traffic / J. Peter Rothe.
p. cm.
Bibliography p.
ISBN 0-88738-728-4
1. Aged automobile drivers. 2. Traffic safety. I. Title
TL152.3.R68 1989 89-32158
363.12′51—dc20 CIP

Contents

List of Tables

List of Figures

Foreword

Joseph Gusfield

For the past several years J. Peter Rothe and his associates, working with the Insurance Corporation of British Columbia, have produced a series of innovative studies of automobile driving and drivers. Using a combination of data types and methods of analysis they have studied youthful drivers, the accidents of young drivers, the use of safety belts, and now the elderly driver. Several features have been distinctive in their work. A careful and exhaustive exposition of the often voluminous literature is incorporated into research, which uses both conventional survey methods and, quite unique for the area of traffic safety, attempts through interviews to see the events of accidents and the activity of driving from the perspective of the drivers themselves. They interviewed young drivers to see what the auto and driving mean to them, and the place of driving in youthful life-styles. They interviewed seat belt users and nonusers to understand what the safety belt and its use signifies to them. This use of a phenomenological method opens up the study of traffic safety to wider understandings of what is involved in driving and in auto safety.

Those methods are equally characteristic of the present work. It moves away from the limits of the conventional display of the attributes of elderly drivers to consider elderly driving as a process in which the perception of the driver's own abilities and disabilities is connected with his or her adaptations to such perceptions. It gives the reader a sense of how the use of the auto and the possibility of its limited use with aging relates to changed activities and situations that aging and retirement bring.

In societies such as ours, the auto is a basic instrument of transportation. The environment of activities and physical structures has adapted to the widespread ownership of automobiles and its necessary accompaniment to membership and integration in modern life. The finding of other studies, which Rothe recognizes, has underscored both the adaptations and the risks of elderly driving. We have lower accident rates than other age groups because we drive less, but when we do drive, we have higher rates. To restrict or eliminate driving, however, is to move toward a less than full membership in this society, whose autocentrism permeates the physical and symbolic environment.

As one who celebrated his sixty-fifth birthday six months ago, I resonate to the stories of what the auto means and symbolizes in the lives of these respondents. They make their adaptations by how carefully they drive, when they drive, and where they drive. Some drive less, some not at all. They depend less on the auto and more on the kindness of friends and kin, on the schedules of public transportation, and on walking.

There is a sadness about these accounts, even though many aver that they have not changed; that they drive as well or better than they ever did. That sadness is itself a clue to much of what marks the discussion of elderly driving in this society.

In many ways the aging motorist has occupied a privileged position in the public discussion of auto safety. He or she has escaped the condemnation and attention given to the young driver and the drinker. The public is almost apologetic when renewed tests for licensure are required, or when the statistics of road accidents displayed unfavorably to those over sixty-five. The disapproving tone in the focus on youth expresses the mixed envy and fear that youth incurs among the middle-aged. The drinking driver is easily shunned and given the attribution of a criminal-like evil. These groups are portrayed as dangerous to others and secondarily to themselves. The elderly driver is treated with much more respect and sympathy. If we are the objects of concern, it is mixed with helpful amounts of concern *for* us even more than fear *of* us. Even the title of this volume, *The Safety of Elderly Drivers*, reflects this attitude. The public can perceive young people and drinkers as willfully evil, but the woes of aging are unconnected to moral failing.

A part of the sadness, which unhappily I can identify with, stems from the deep individualism which the automobile both reflects and occasions in contemporary life. Anyone gazing down on the modern freeway sees thousands of four-to-six-passenger vehicles, most of which contain one or two riders. In this automobilistic society, we have accustomed ourselves to the flexibility and spontaneity that individual ownership of the means of transportation both affords and costs.

This basic individualism is carried over as well to the research on the elderly and to policies of automobile usage. We take present alternatives to individual driving as given and search for how the elderly might adapt to their needs by their own changes. The focus is on the driver and not on the environment of transportation possibilities. It is here, however, that opportunities exist for innovative planning once we depart from the individual auto driver as our object of study.

There is much need for experimentation and creative thought to be given to new forms of "public" or group transportation more adapted to specific activities and purposes than is current public transport. The development in recent decades of planned housing developments, often of expensive, detached homes, indicates that collective ownership of such things as swimming pools, tennis courts, and even streets is not prevented by the individualist anathema toward collective and cooperative ventures. Quasi-public transportation, more local and particularistic, is by no means unthinkable or commercially unfeasible. The alternatives that stress the small communities of the elderly accentuate the isolation of the aged from the mainstream of neighborhood and public life.

Ours is an aging population and will come to require that our societies devote greater attention to developing new institutions and technologies that recognize this. Peter Rothe has done good service in widening the area of thinking about us.

Preface

This book is aimed at a diverse audience: traffic safety professionals, social and health science personnel, social service people, government policymakers, gerontologists, lay people actively involved with the elderly at the community level, and of course the elderly. Most of the information is fresh, based on the elderly people's experiences and points of view. We commissioned much of the data gathering to university personnel to retain rigorous empirical standards. The findings, however, were interpreted to enhance interest and relevance. They were written to provide the reader with optimal information in a spirit of imagination and originality.

The concept and structure of the manuscript is based on two powerful forces—knowledge and imagination. As Gorki wrote in his treatise "On Literature," knowledge reflects thinking through the faculty of cognition. It means to observe, compare, and study phenomena or, in our case, the facts of elderly social life. Imagination is also a way of thinking about people. It means to make more vivid, to attribute to the essential forces of human nature, qualities, meanings, feelings, and intentions.

By concentrating on knowledge and imagination, we refashioned some traditional ways of doing things—ways which we considered to be too rigidly structured and too narrow in focus. Although we were cognizant of the latest thinking and research on elderly drivers, we ventured beyond without sacrificing integrity. We observed, asked, reviewed, and listened. We did not just paraphrase what is already known.

A glance at the table of contents discloses that the treatment of topics strongly reflects knowledge and imagination. There is a logical order to their inclusion. We considered the social organization of elderly drivers according to statistical generalizations, survey definitions, daily life routines, and involvement in serious motor vehicle crashes. But we did not assume or overlook the researchers' contexts. They are vital ingredients for substantiating problem definition, research approach, and problem solution.

We invite the readers to think about or contemplate recommendations we felt were dignified and meaningful. They were not designed to degrade the elderly as compensatory victims, but rather to recognize their many strengths and build on them. None of us can escape the exigencies of the calendar, but all of us can learn to become more than what we are. This book follows through on that thought.

Acknowledgments

After a major research project is conceived, its development and growth can be traced to a number of individuals. First and foremost are the thousands of elderly drivers who participated in the data-gathering phase. I cannot mention them by name, but they know who they are. To them, many thanks.

Two creative colleagues, Peter Cooper and Brian de Vries, deserve special mention for contributing several chapters to the manuscript. Without their insight, this project would not have taken the form it did.

Data gathering is the most vital ingredient of any research project. For help in this area, I am grateful to Gloria Gutman, director, Gerontology Research Centre, Simon Fraser University, and her research associate, Steve Milstein. They were commissioned to interview the elderly. Ken Stoddart, Department of Anthropology and Sociology, University of British Columbia, organized and conducted the interviews with elderly drivers in accidents.

In the analysis phase, I am thankful to Mario Pinili and Sylvia Fockler. Their help contributed greatly in the production of numbers and tables.

Special mention must be made of the British Columbia Motor Vehicle Department. Staff cooperation and interest were vital to the successful completion of the study.

I thank the many behind-the-scenes people, such as the members of the word processing department who typed and retyped manuscripts and edited the text, and others who duplicated copies for cutting and pasting. They really maintained the organization of production.

1

Growing Older

> In short, enjoy the blessings of strength while you have it, and have no regrets when it has gone—any more than young men should regret the end of boyhood, or those approaching middle age lament the passing of youth. Life's course is invariable—nature has one path only, and you cannot travel along it more than once. Every stage of life has its own characteristics: boys are feeble, youth in their prime are aggressive, middle-aged men are dignified, old people are mature. Each one of these qualities is ordained by nature for harvesting in due season.
>
> (Cato the Elder on Old Age in Cicero, *Selected Works*)

Human beings grow older, a fact not considered to be a major breakthrough in thought. It is assumed, understood, and taken for granted. But as more of us are getting older, human aging is fast becoming more noticed. The biological and medical sciences, the social and behavioral sciences, engineering, civil rights, social welfare, economics, and philosophy are fields of endeavor where energies are being channeled to investigate the domain of aging.

A common assumption held by various disciplines is that chronological age equals biological function and mental ability. Deteriorating vision, hearing, coordination, reaction, and mental processing have become primary indices for defining old age—usually sixty-five years of age or older. The factors are considered a natural progression towards death. Biology is the driving force.

To illustrate what a biological conception of aging looks like in the literature, we include the following pronouncement by an Organization for Economic Co-operation and Development (OECD) research group. Members expressed aging as:

> . . . a biological process in which various mechanisms, which are not all very well known, cause the cells to deteriorate, leading with time to limitations of the functions of the cells. The different mechanisms cause the functional changes to take place at different speeds, but they are all presumed to be controlled by the permanent interaction of factors belonging to three distinct classes:
>
> a) the genetic characteristics of groups and, to a smaller extent, of individuals belonging to the same groups;

> b) the accidental circumstances at the level of the cell, in particular the accumulation of free intracellular radicals and endogenous somatic mutations;
> c) the pressure of the environment (infections, pollution, traumas, nutrition) which favour certain changes in the cells similar to the above-mentioned non-exogenous changes.
>
> Under the impacts of these factors, the cells accumulate a series of imperfections, at first subtle, but in the end, as they add up, having repercussions on the functioning of the cells, of the organs formed by them, and of the system interactions of the organs. The vulnerability of the living organism vis-à-vis the pressure of the environment increases with age and results in the growth with age in morbidity and risk factors [OECD 1985:15].

A more progressive view on human aging includes biological change within psychological and social contexts. As our bodies change, so do our attitudes towards self and other people. The philosophers Sartre, Heidegger, and Ortega, among others, wrote passionately that the mind is not separate from the body. We think through our physical being. As our physical appearances and views of self change, we expect other people to interact with us in relation to the changes.

To better understand the personal and social adjustments and readjustments that people experience as they grow older, more research is required. There is insufficient evidence concerning social and psychological variables that encompass aging. Too often research is initiated in which investigators regard aging as a pathological process, rather than a social continuum. Standards of comparisons are set arbitrarily. Judgments are made based on correlations. The results often suggest that the elderly are different from younger people. The difference is assumed to be negative.

To be normal requires a view of self as being normal. Abnormality encourages compensation, whereby officials attempt to improve the elderly people's lot in life, by making them more like normal young people. This compensatory perspective is followed by an attitude towards the elderly that hinges on burden. On the basis of a pathological outlook, the elderly are judged to be poorly equipped for carrying on normal functions in a society. Consequently, their independence may be restricted. Input from the elderly people on such matters is seldom asked.

A predominant activity that penetrates the elderly's mental, physical, and social skills is the operation of a motor vehicle. It includes health, reaction time, coordination, threshold of attention, and social tact. Also, driving is a central concern for compensatory interventions which may impact heavily on the elderly.

The Elderly as Drivers

Interest in the elderly as drivers reflects an awareness of the demographic trend. North Americans are living longer while simultaneously decreasing the birth rate. At the beginning of the twentieth century every twenty-fifth American (4 percent) was sixty-five and over. By 1980 they comprised over 11 percent of the population (Brotman 1980). It is projected that by the year 2050, the percentage will increase to 17.6 percent (Winter 1984).

The 1985 OECD Report on elderly road users describes a global picture on the population demographics:

> An examination of population data related to OECD countries highlights certain variations in the 65 plus age groups. Of the four regions represented in the OECD (North America, Asia, Europe, Oceania), the estimated percentage of the elderly is highest in the European communities (13 percent), followed by North America (11 percent), and is lowest in the Oceania region represented by Australia and New Zealand (9 percent) and the Asian region represented by Japan (9 percent). . . . This is a rather striking general feature of the total European population in contrast with populations in OECD countries in other regions [OECD 1985:21].

As the number of elderly citizens steadily increases, a greater pool of drivers with similar profiles evolves. Winter writes:

> It is that along with the population trends the proportion of older drivers has been steadily increasing. The automobile remains the way most adults satisfy their transportation needs. Between 1969 and 1978, the number of drivers' licenses per 100 population increased by three or more within each age group; however, among the age groups over 55, the increase was at least 10 licenses per 100 population (National Traffic Safety Administration, 1979). Presently, of the 141,832,000 licensed drivers in the United States, 25% are 55 and over. By the year 2000 the projection is 28%, by 2050, 39%. As stated, these figures support demographic trends and, as a larger and larger pool of older people join the traffic mix on the streets and highways, transportation safety officials are faced with a traffic profile and problems different from any previously addressed [Winter 1984:136].

Statistics Canada (1985) provided projections which are lower than those for the United States, but still they show an increasing trend. In 1981 the national percentage of people aged over sixty-five was 9.7 percent. A projected increase to 11.8 percent is expected for 1991. This will further increase to 13.6 percent by the year 2001. In British Columbia the trend is from 10.9 percent in 1981, to 12.7 percent in 1991, and 13.5 percent in 2001. Gutman et al. further noted that:

> The older population is itself aging. The proportion aged 80 and over within the 65 and over age group is growing and it is expected to continue rising sharply in the near future. In 1981, people aged 80 and over represented 19.6% of B.C.'s population aged 65 and over; by 2001, they are expected to comprise 26.4% of the elderly population [1986:03].

There is life in the numbers. More and more elderly people are becoming and staying actively involved in driving. Although drivers over the age of sixty-five have, as a whole, the lowest involvement in accidents of any age group, they are more likely to have a fatal accident than drivers between age thirty-five and sixty-four (Finesilver 1969). Furthermore, whenever researchers factor-in the estimated miles driven annually by different groups of people, the aging drivers show up as higher risk (Planek and Overend 1973; Burg 1967).

After a serious look at the present scenario of elderly drivers coupled with the fact that the North American population over sixty-five will increase markedly, especially in the numbers of the very old (over seventy-nine years of age), we can appreciate the profound implications for the roadway travel. Traffic safety policy will require major reevaluations, according to the trend of the times.

Researching the Elderly Drivers

So many research projects on elderly drivers support the assumption that just because investigators have identified "issues," "problems," or "determining factors," they have also captured their meanings for the elderly. It would be safer to state that researchers fashioned meanings out of their own beliefs and attitudes (Ryaff 1984). The elderly are seldom partners in the search for empirical detail on their lives.

Marshall (1987) advised future researchers to ascertain the extent to which all old people are alike, the ways in which some old people are alike, and the ways in which no elderly people are alike. In traffic terms we need to understand how all elderly people behave as drivers, how some elderly people behave as drivers in similar ways, and how individual elderly persons drive in unique ways. To do so we need to gather a variety of information such as: life accounts of people who have experienced injury-producing crashes and have developed personal outlooks on such events; behaviors, normal rules of behavior, and reasoning that elderly drivers use in their everyday lives and driving; and, classifications of variables and attitudes that relate to social behavior as defined by the elderly drivers and statistical constructions of motor vehicle crashes.

Marshall's suggestion that we give as much attention as possible to a social research approach which captures meaning was taken seriously. As we wrote concerning young drivers in 1987:

> It is a well accepted truism that the more perspectives brought to the study of young drivers, the more researchers "see" and the more they overcome the limitations (and encapsulation) of one perspective alone. A multiple perspective approach is preferred for identifying, defining and describing young drivers [Rothe 1987:2].

We have included a series of chapters that reflect a continuum of description, the aggregate of which is faithful to a philosophy of holism as a scheme for understanding and describing the reality of elderly drivers. At the outset, we closely reviewed the research context, or the well-worn routes researchers have travelled to investigate the phenomenon of elderly drivers. Two chapters are presented to give the reader an understanding of the conceptual boundary lines that have marked the research to date.

Chapter Two entails a broad description on important models and theories that impact studies on aging. We felt that it would be highly pretentious to offer a book on elderly drivers without first identifying the general framework of gerontology in which we are operating. To further explore the research context, we offer a review of the literature pertaining more directly to elderly drivers. Chapter Three outlines the empirical and theoretical building blocks that have been used to make sense of elderly drivers. Part of the description includes empirical and conceptual deadends that forced us to take detours in our research routes.

Following the presentation of the research context, we unfold our conceptual plan. It is similar to the design we employed in *Rethinking Young Drivers*. So, in Chapter Four we untangle the philosophical and conceptual grounds for the elderly driver presentation.

In Chapter Five we move to the construction of a statistical reality of elderly drivers. Through intense analysis of the Motor Vehicle Department data base and Insurance Corporation of British Columbia accident information, we produce a statistical picture of elderly drivers. Chapter Five is the launching pad for further deep-structure descriptions of factors identified in the numerical data.

Chapter Six sketches elderly driver trends based on the application of a questionnaire survey. We begin to reveal thoughts and attitudes that elderly drivers have on traffic-related issues.

The emerging trends arising from Chapter Six are further investigated in Chapter Seven. The elderly people's everyday lives are explored. Through small-group conversations we were able to arrive at a greater understanding of how elderly drivers normally behave and reason, and how their behavior and reasoning processes are attached to features of lifestyle, physical health, automobiles, and social relationships.

Moving evermore into the direction of personal meaning, we arrive at Chapter Eight. Here we include in-depth descriptions on elderly drivers who were victims of injury-producing motor vehicle accidents. For hundreds of hours we listened to elderly drivers explaining, in detail, their involvement in serious crashes.

Chapter Nine is designed to project the reader into the future. By reflecting on "what was yesterday" and "what is today," we provide scenarios of what may occur tomorrow, given the elderly driver's social, physical, economic, and political realities.

Finally, in Chapter Ten we summarize important aspects of our research and translate them into a series of recommendations.

Our major goal for serializing the chapters in the way described is to provide as full an understanding of elderly drivers as possible. We took great caution to avoid presenting elderly drivers as static, stereotyped automatons. Faithfulness to the phenomena was the primary objective for us. We therefore organized the book from a perspective that provides statistical reconstructions as accounted for by social constructions of reality.

References

Briggs, R.P. 1987. "Is Selective Screening of Older Drivers for Vision Feasible?" *Proceedings of the Human Factors Society*, 31st Annual Meeting.

Bromley, D.B. 1966. *The Psychology of Human Aging*. Hammondsworth, Middlesex, England: Penguin Books.

Brotman, H.B. 1980. *Every Ninth American*. Prepared for the Special Committee on Aging, United States Senate.

Burg, A. 1967. *The Relationship between Vision Test Scores on Driving Records: General Findings*. Report No. 67-24. Los Angeles: University of California, Department of Engineering.

FHWA. 1980. An Effect on Symbol Recognition. Report No. RD80/126. Washington, DC.

Finesilver, S.G. 1969. "The Older Driver—A Statistical Evaluation of Licensing and Accident Involvement in 30 States and the District of Columbia." Denver, CO: University of Denver College of Law.

Gutman, G., M.G. Gee, B.C. Bojanowski, and D. Moffet. 1986. *Fact Book on Aging in British Columbia*. Burnaby, B.C.: Gerontology Research Centre, Simon Fraser University.

Havighurst, R.J. 1957. "Personal and Social Adjustment in Retirement." In Donahue, Wilma, and C. Tibbits (Eds.), *The New Frontiers of Aging*. Ann Arbor, MI: University of Michigan Press.

Heran, A., and S.M. Chown. 1961. *Aging and the Semi-Skilled*. Medical Research Council Memo No. 40, London: H.M.S.O.

Marsh, B. 1960. "Aging and Driving." *Traffic Engineering*, 31(2), pp. 11-29.

Marshall, U.W. (Ed.). 1987. *Aging in Canada: Social Perspectives*. Markham, ON: Fitzhenry and Whiteside.

McFarland, R.A., S.G. Tune, and A. Welford. 1964. "On the Driving of Automobiles by Older People." *Journal of Gerontology*, 19(2): pp. 190-97.

McFarland, R.A., and R.G. Domey. 1958. "Experimental Studies of Night Vision as a Function of Age and Changes of Illumination." Highway Research Board Bulletin, (191), pp. 17-32.

Mourant, R.R. 1979. "Driving Performance of the Elderly." *Accident Analysis and Prevention*, Vol. 11, No. 4, pp. 247-338.

Munn, N.L. 1955. *Evaluation and Growth of Human Behavior*. Boston: Houghton Mifflin.

Norris, J.E. 1987. "Psychological Processes in the Development of Late-Life Social Identity." In Marshall, V. (Ed.), *Aging in Canada: Social Perspectives*. Markham, ON: Fitzhenry and Whiteside.

OECD and WHO. 1985. *Traffic Safety Of Elderly Road Users*. Paris: Organization for Economic Co-operation and Development.

Planek, T.W., and R.B. Overend. 1973. "Profile Of The Aging Driver." *Traffic Safety*, 73, pp. 9-10; 37-39.

Rothe, J.P. (Ed.). 1987. *Rethinking Young Drivers*. North Vancouver: Insurance Corporation of British Columbia.

Ryaff, Carol. 1984. "Personality Development from the Inside: The Subjective Experience of Change in Adulthood and Aging." In P.B. Baltes and O.G. Brim, Jr. (Eds.), *Life-Span Development and Behavior*, Vol. 6. Orlando, FL: Academic Press, pp. 244-80.

Scialfa, C.T., B. Lyman, D. Kline, and W. Kosnik. 1987. "Age Differences in Judgments of Vehicle Velocity and Distance." *Proceedings of the Human Factors Society*, 31st Annual Meeting.

Statistical Bulletin. 1984. April-June, pp. 8-15.

Statistics Canada. 1985. Population Projections for Canada, *Provinces and Territories 1984-2006*.

Winter, D.H. 1984. "Needs and Problems of Older Drivers and Pedestrians: An Exploratory Study with Teaching/Learning Implications." *Educational Gerontology*, 10, pp. 135-46.

Yanik, A.J. 1985. "What Accident Data Reveal About Elderly Drivers." *SAE Technical Paper Series 851688*, Warrendale, PA: SAE.

2

The Elderly Under the Conceptual Microscope

Brian de Vries

Four seasons fill the measure of the year;
There are four seasons in the mind of man:
He has his lusty Spring, when fancy clear
Takes in all beauty with an easy span:
He has his Summer, when luxuriously
Spring's honey'd cud of youthful thoughts he loves
To ruminate, and by such dreaming high
Is nearest unto heaven: quiet coves
His soul has in its Autumn, when his wings
He furleth close; contented so to look
On mists in idleness—to let fair things
Pass by unheeded as a threshold brook:
He has his Winter too of pale misfeature,
Or else he would forego his mortal nature.

(John Keats, *"The Human Seasons"*)

Social research does not occur in a vacuum. It is constructed on a heritage of collective perceptions and sense-making strategies that have evolved from the perennial search for information. It is like a map that researchers pass on to colleagues.

The first set of contour lines concerns broad interpretation devices used to make sense of the elderly. The aim of this chapter, therefore, is to present a range of theories, concepts, and models that are popular when discussing aging and later adulthood. Towards such an end, this chapter is organized into

---

Brian de Vries, SSHRC Post-doctoral Fellow, Gerontology Research Centre, Simon Fraser University, and Assistant Professor, School of Family and Nutritional Sciences, University of British Columbia; J. Thornton, Coordinator, Committee on Gerontology, Faculty of Graduate Studies, University of British Columbia.

three sections. The first section discusses models and metaphors of aging. It deals with current perspectives and assumptions in the aging literature, and how aging is conceptualized and defined by various disciplines and research perspectives. The second section presents a life-span perspective on aging. Rather than viewing age as the primary organizing variable, this perspective deals with issues (e.g., significant life events) and processes (e.g., social comparison) that attain their salience in the context of the life course. The third section highlights some of the methodological considerations that must be addressed when choosing an appropriate strategy for the study of age-related differences and the interpretation of existing research findings.

Metaphors of Aging

It is important at this point in the study of aging to understand the role of metaphors in the ways in which aging is thought about and construed. Howes (1962) has noted that "scientist, historian, poet, man in the street, all alike reply upon the metaphorical dimension of language for vividness, for clarity, for forming and expressing difficult concepts. The fact that language enables us to say or imply that one thing is like something else has been basic to our development of complicated ideas and concepts in all fields." We ought to become aware of these implicit metaphors because they provide a deeper understanding of the conceptualizations guiding research on aging.

A metaphor is a device of thought and speech which offers a way to "see," and to "speak" of, one thing in terms of another. According to Valle and van Eskartsberg (1981) a metaphor "takes us from the familiar to the unfamiliar and, speaking metaphorically, serves as a bridge." The use of metaphors expresses our perceptions about, and social constructions of, reality.

Metaphors about age and aging have their origins in the physical and mystical worlds. From the earliest of times, individuals, as observers and observed, have chronicled the coming and going of the seasons, the movement of the heavenly bodies, and the flow of their own births, lives and deaths. Over the centuries, metaphors have provided ways to describe and explain these events and processes that otherwise could only be imperfectly understood and conceptualized. Most of the present views of human development and aging have been derived from a predominantly "positivistic" (scientific) paradigm based on the root metaphors of a mechanistic (machine-like) and organismic ("whole" organism) world (Hultsch and Deutsch 1981). A contextualistic worldview in which the setting or context plays a seminal role has also developed from the symbolic interactionist paradigm. These three views or metaphors (mechanistic, organismic, contextualistic) offer different developmental paradigms to explain changes in behavior. Each view leads to data about how the body works but none of them readily tells us why it works the way it does and what it works for.

Perhaps the most common metaphor is the image describing aging as a process borrowed from the changing seasons to characterize changing physical appearances. "Metaphorically, everyone understands the connections between the seasons of the year and the season of the human life cycle" (Levinson et al. 1978:7). Another conceptualization of aging is associated with the "clock" metaphor—that is, being "on time" or "off time" in one's development—and the "time to reap, a time to sow" (Dowd 1980). Neugarten (1970) has given primacy to this idea and to scenarios of time in the flow of one's life.

The stage metaphor has been particularly powerful (especially in sociology) as a normative conceptualization of human development. Sheehy's *Passages* (1974) and Lowenthal et al.'s *Four Stages of Life* (1975) are examples of this "being on time" metaphor and of "establishing a stage" where one is when one is on time. "Actor" and "role" concepts are also imposed by this stage metaphor to explore normative ideas of behaviors, tasks, and expectations: life-span stages as a series of one act plays. The stage metaphor is striking: life is a stage—connoting scripts, scenarios, scenes, center stage, and back stage, costuming, masks, and make-believe, and of course the final curtain (Shakespeare, *As You Like It*, Act II, Scene vii; Brown 1977). All of this prescribes some synchronization of life events as if they follow some immutable pattern, and *aging* is the name of the script and the play. Aging as an "on time–on stage" metaphor of the life course and life-span development serves not only to rank people hierarchically, but it becomes the basis for prescribing, proscribing, and permitting various social roles.

The ultimate consequence of this is society's pretense that aging is intrinsically a mask that the individual wears. Prevailing paradigms in gerontology would suggest that problems (when they develop) have their causes and solutions largely in individual adaptations. Only recently has the scientific study of aging recognized the complex interaction between the person and the event, the organism and the environment. Old age is not a homogeneous category but a period significantly shaped and structured by and within socioeconomic classes within a specific historical context (Dowd 1980). We frequently lose sight of this in present time for those whose lives have been shaped by an extensive previous time.

Models of Aging

In an examination of the literature on aging, we need not look far in order to find claims of aging as degeneration: almost all bioscience models take the view that aging is a deteriorative or decremental process that functions to bring organisms closer to death (Birren and Stacey 1984). Handler (1960), for example, has said that "aging is the deterioration of a mature organism resulting from time-dependent, essentially irreversible changes intrinsic to all members of a species, such that with the passage of time, they become increasingly unable to cope with the stresses of the environment, thereby increasing the probability of death." Comfort (1956) defined aging as a "change in the behaviour of the organism with age, which leads to a decreased power of survival and adjustment." Inherent in such views is the assumption that aging is associated with a loss of vitality and capacity for self-repair and an increased probability of mortality (Birren and Stacey 1984).

The empirical foundations upon which such assumptions are based are readily found in the literature. Out of numerous analyses of measures of functional ability related to aging and stage of health, four functional parameters are frequently used: forced expiratory volume, lecithin/lysolecithin quotient, psychomotoric speed, and verbal capacity (Svanborg and Thornton 1986). Changes in these parameters in later life provide evidence of a loss of a functional reserve capacity. Horn and Donaldson (1980) reported that the following neurological changes occur between the ages of about twenty and sixty-five years: there is a decrease in brain weight of about 12 percent; there is a decrease, of up to 50 percent in some areas of the brain, in total number of functional neurons; there is a corresponding increase in the water content of the brain; there is a decrease in neuronal conduction rate; there is an increase in inert waste products (such as lipsofuscin) in the neuron cells, perhaps having a detrimental effect on cell motility; and, there is an increase in neurofibrillary tangles resulting in a loss of neuron function. This is no more than a partial list of neurological "age"— changes which, considered as a package or in conjunction with other more indirect evidence, support the hypothesis that there is deterioration in cognitive performance.

Memory is a cognitive activity that has received a great deal of scientific and popular attention: the feeling that one's ability to remember and to retrieve information is not as good as it used to be is practically a universal complaint among middle-aged and elderly persons (Poon 1985). It must be said that middle age is commonly defined as falling between ages thirty-five and sixty or sixty-five, with old age—in various forms—coming afterwards and young adulthood before. Cavanaugh et al. (1983), for example, asked young and elderly subjects to keep diaries of their experiences of memory failures. They found that older adults reported a greater number of memory failures and were more likely to be upset by such experiences. Memory failures included forgetting names, faces, objects, appointments, locations, routines, addresses, and phone numbers. Older adults reported more incidences of forgetting names, routines, and objects than younger adults. Memory failures occurred more frequently when the older adults were out of their normal routines (e.g., in novel situations or settings), or when they were required to remember information not used recently. Younger adults reported that most memory problems occurred when they were under stress (Poon 1985).

An important question to ask is whether the age-related memory deficits are due to deficiencies in learning new material or difficulties in the retrieval of material that has already been learned. Winn et al. (1976) provided a partial answer. They reported that older adults exhibit slower acquisition rates in tasks of paired-associate learning. Paired-associate learning is the term given to the technique when an individual is first presented with paired items and must then respond with one item—typically a word or syllable—when given the other item with which it has been paired. Poon (1985), countered this position in citing similar significant differences, as a function of age, in tasks of free recall, although it may be that poor recall performance is a by-product of faulty processing during information acquisition. Birren and Stacey (1984) suggested that evidence for a retrieval deficit can be found in the consistent finding that age differences in recognition are much smaller than those for recall, implying that the information is stored but cannot be accessed.

Perhaps a more basic and fundamental issue is one that addresses the methodology within which these research questions are posed and these research findings are derived. Smith (1980) reported that providing older persons with organizational techniques (e.g., mnemonics or memory-enhancing strategies), and/or semantic cues at the time of stimulus input minimizes age differences and improves performance. Smaller or no age differences have also been reported when the pacing of the experiment was modified to one more suitable to the subject (i.e., a self-paced versus an experimenter-paced condition), when sufficient practice, or time, was provided, or when the stimulus material was familiar to the subject (Poon 1985). Treat and Reese (1976), for example, found improved performance when subjects used self-provided versus experimenter-provided imageries. Furthermore, Barrett and Wright (1981) found that older subjects outperformed younger subjects in the recall of words more familiar to them and Gardner and Monge (1977) indicated that older adults tend to do better on tasks that have direct life relevance.

The point to be underlined here is that although there may be reliable age differences in memory task performance, the memory "deficits" evinced by the older subjects are not necessarily irreversible or attributable to some loss of cognitive functioning. That is, given the proper instructions, techniques, and methodologies, these age differences may be, at least, qualified and, at most, reversed. An area that is currently under investigation is metamemory (memory about memory) or knowledge actualization described as a functional or real-world memory that reflects a lifetime of education and experience. In contrast to the age differences found with respect to secondary memory (selecting and combining features and relating these to that which is already in memory), there were no age differences found in temporal or spatialknowledge acquisition. This was borne out by Perlmutter et al. (1980). Such knowledge is particularly important because it assists the individual in selecting strategies that will significantly enhance performance (Birren and Stacey 1984).

There are several issues of interest embodied in the preceding paragraphs: some will be discussed later in methodological issues, while others are of more immediate conceptual concern. For example, deficits in ability need to be understood in the context of competence-performance distinctions. Competence refers to what individuals can do under ideal conditions; performance refers to what individuals do under actual conditions (Reese and Rodeheaver 1985). Some of the research findings from the memory literature provide the basis for the position that age differences are really differences in performance and not competence, and perhaps can be attributed to characteristics of the task and not the individual. It is also the case, however, that performance may be the most relevant dependent variable when the question is phrased according to what individuals do as opposed to what individuals are capable of doing. The ways in which the questions are phrased necessarily affect the ways in which the answers are given. It should therefore be made clear at the outset which level of analysis is more appropriate and what is the concomitant best-suited interpretation.

Labouvie-Vief (1982) has drawn attention to this point. He stressed that much of what is usually characterized in terms of cognitive *deficits* in later life is perhaps better characterized in terms of cognitive *differences*: there is the anthropological realization that a group can be different without being deficient or inferior (Reese and Rodeheaver 1985). In such a light, aging may not reflect the loss of abilities, but rather the gain of other equally desirable abilities.

Okun (1976) suggests that one such ability that gains prominence in old age is cautiousness. Cautiousness is, in many ways, a post hoc explanation for observed performance differences between younger and older adults. It is inferred primarily on the basis of two measures: errors of omission and reaction time. Botwinick (1967) and others have found that, particularly in tasks of verbal learning, young adults tend to make more errors of commission (i.e., adding items to a list in tasks of serial recall) and older adults tend to make more errors of omission (i.e., deleting items from a list in tasks of serial recall). Leech and Witte (1971) found that when commission errors were reinforced, the rate of omission errors dropped significantly. In other words, by removing the sanctions associated with errors of commission for the older subjects, there is a reduction of omission. Omission errors, then, need not reflect associative learning difficulties or deficiencies in competence.

Reese and Rodeheaver (1985) wrote that "one of the best established findings in gerontological research is the slowing in the speed of responding and cognitive processing that occurs with age." Whether this is the result of a primary effect of aging and one beyond the individual's control or a deliberate, purposeful slowdown (based on a value of carefulness) is really a frame-of-reference issue. Both hypotheses appear equally tenable, defensible, and controversial (Salthouse and Somberg 1982).

Okun (1976) listed five "causes" of increased cautiousness in old age: physiological variables; rational variables (reflecting the hypotheses elucidated above); cultural variables (lowered self-esteem with increased age creating greater cautiousness to compensate for the elderly's perception of less competence); motivational changes (a decrease in achievement motivation, or an increase in fear of failure); and, generational or cohort differences (whereby cautiousness is stable within cohorts and varies between them). An alternative interpretation provided by Reese and Rodeheaver (1985) as well as Okun (1976) is that cautiousness does not increase. There is a decrease in risk-taking. Phrased in such a way, perhaps a more appropriate question to ask, is: "Why do young adults take more risks?" rather than "Why are older adults more cautious?" Where one chooses to put the emphasis is an indication of the implicit model of aging to which one adheres.

Cognitive deficits, or deficits in the act, process, or product of knowing and perceiving as a function of age, have also been reported in the literature on intelligence. Botwinick (1977), for example, concluded that after reviewing the available literature, there is a decline in intellectual ability. It is clearly part of the aging picture. Horn and Donaldson (1980) have reported decrements in such measures of intelligence as visual organization, common word analogies, as well as figural and inductive reasoning. These variables represent qualities of intelligence that are loosely tied to formal education and outside influences. This constellation of abilities has been labeled fluid intelligence (i.e., intelligence determined largely by maturation and/or physiological factors) and is "an outcome of . . . influences that directly affect the physiological structures and processes on which intellectual development is most fundamentally based" (Horn and Donaldson 1980:461).

In contrast to decrements in fluid intelligence over time, there is a body of literature showing increments in crystallized intelligence with age. Crystallized intelligence is another second-order factor referring to a universe of highly valued abilities systematically imparted to acculturation. Some of the abilities that exemplify crystallized intelligence are: verbal comprehension (the ability to decipher a written or spoken message and extract the main idea); experiential evaluation (the ability to use social conventions and the knowledge and nature of a culture in making decisions); formal reasoning (the ability to deal with problems in ways that are more or less formalized within a culture); and technical proficiency (the abilities invoked in everyday calculations) (Horn and Donaldson 1980). A more accurate characterization of intelligence in later life (or across the life span), then, is one of both decline and growth: decrements in abilities associated with fluid intelligence and increments in abilities associated with crystallized intelligence.

The aim of this discussion has been to demonstrate the less-than-perfect fit of the bioscience model of aging onto a selected summary of research issues and results from the psychological arena. That is, decline or decrement only partially represents the picture of aging; stability and growth are also key factors. To recognize the lack of correspondence is to be critical of the application of a biological model to an essentially behavioral analysis (memory, cautiousness, intelligence).

Lest one be swept away by such criticism, however, there are several issues that need to be addressed. For one thing, the literature on and our attitudes toward aging have been heavily weighted by the decline model as posited by bioscience. There are many factors that have contributed to this, not the least of which is the strength of the medical model within the scientific community. Psychology, and perhaps social science in general, has in the past apparently willingly embraced this model, perhaps in an effort to gain acceptance in the eyes of its "harder" scientific siblings. It is only through post hoc realizations (identity crises?) of inappropriate model-discipline fits that new and more adaptive models have been developed. It is also the case, however, that many articles and books in psychology have been written about aging without any reference to the definition that has guided the thinking of the authors. Birren and Cunningham (1985) suggested that there is a hierarchy in which biologists provide definitions of aging most often, psychologists rarely, and other social scientists almost never. As in elections and debates, the failure to support one position is often taken as support for another.

Birren and Cunningham (1985) observed that there is an assumption among biologists that they are studying the length of life of an organism. Aging and old age are associated with the nearness of death. Mortality rates are high for infants. They decline to a minimum at about age ten, and then rise progressively throughout the remainder of the life span (Birren and Cunningham 1985). However, it is our belief that "life" somehow involves more than the sum total of number of days lived. Just as it is irrational to assume that human organisms are immortal, it is unreasonable to assume that the quality of life is expressed in some pure temporal form. As Birren and Stacey (1984:1) said, "ultimately, it is not whether our heart and bones are strong but whether we derive a sense of meaning from a long life and are competent in dealing with an environment that challenges us with its changes." Biological health is a necessary, but not sufficient, condition for a meaningful, competent life. An exclusive focus on either the biological or the social/behavioral aspects of aging is essentially forcing a multidimensional topic into unidimensional space.

What is required, then, in an approach to the study of aging, is a recognition of both the decremental changes and the incremental functions that occur over the adult life span in biological, social, and psychological terms. Birren and Renner (1977:4) have offered the following general definition of aging for the behavioral sciences: "Aging refers to the regular changes that occur in mature genetically representative organisms living under representative environmental conditions." In describing "changes," we may refer to either increments or decrements; in describing "representative" organisms and conditions, we may focus on typical patterns and not rare genetic problems or unusual environmental conditions.

Just to muddy the waters a little further, there is also some discussion in the area of personality as to whether or not there are reliable changes of any sort across the life span. Neugarten (1970), for example, claimed that we all "know" personality changes with age, it is just that such changes are difficult to demonstrate. On the other hand, McCrae and Costa (1982) have reported that studies "have consistently shown little or no change with age in a wide variety of traits." Perhaps part of the disagreement rests in the ways in which stability and change are typically defined. For example, although an individual may repeatedly describe himself as a Canadian male, this does not necessarily mean that his conceptions of nationality and gender membership have remained stable. Such conceptions may change as a function of increased knowledge, exposure to incongruous exemplars, or significant events or experiences (e.g., international war/conflict, the women's movement, etc.).

A Life-Span Perspective

Adulthood, as a topic for developmental psychology, has largely been ignored (Gould 1972). Thomae (1979) has written that recent sections on developmental psychology in the *Annual Review of Psychology* have reported exclusively on child development. Furthermore, the American Psychological Association's journal *Developmental Psychology*, while sanctioning life-span issues, has focused almost entirely on child psychology. The basic premise seems to be that nothing much of psychological significance takes place during the adult years. This view is present, either implicitly or explicitly, in much of the developmental literature; for whenever there is talk of formative experiences and formative stages, the implication is that there is an early stage of high malleability followed by a stage of relative stability (Glenn 1980).

Life Beyond Adolescence

There are growing numbers of people who reject the child development view and have made substantial contributions to the area of adult development. Erik Erikson's (1968) work on the eight stages of life is probably the best known of these efforts. Erikson posited that: corresponding to the stages of psychosexual development, described by Freud, were psychosocial stages of ego development, in which the individuals had to establish new basic orientations to themselves and the social world; personality development continued throughout the whole life cycle; and each stage had both a positive and a negative component.

Of special interest to us are Erikson's latter three stages which, taken together, extend from late adolescence into late life. For example, Stage Six: intimacy versus isolation. The years roughly cover the period of courtship and early family life that extends from late adolescence until early middle age. Within this stage people establish a sense of intimacy with friends or a marriage partner (sharing and caring about another person without losing oneself in the process). Failure to achieve intimacy results in isolation, or being alone without someone with whom to share or about whom to care. Stage Seven represents middle age where it is generativity versus self-absorption. Generativity is the concern for others of future generations and a concern with the nature of society and the world in which those generations will live. Self-absorption or stagnation is a state in which personal needs and comforts are of predominant concern, much like Scrooge in Dickens' *A Christmas Carol*. Integrity versus despair is the eighth (last) stage or old age. It corresponds roughly to the period of time when the individual's major efforts are nearing completion and when there is time for reflection. Integrity arises from individuals' abilities to look back over their lives with satisfaction; despair is a retrospective characterized by missed opportunities and missed directions. A sense of despair at what might have been results.

Other authors and theorists have also offered insights into the thesis of adulthood as a dynamic period of life. Jacques (1977), for example, described the "mid-life" crisis as a painful confrontation with the inevitability of death and the finitude of time. Neugarten (1970, 1976) described the increased "interiority" with age: an inward-examination and an increasing dedication to a central core of values and beliefs. She has also described the changing time perspective in middle age, which causes individuals to stop counting "time since birth" and to begin to think of their lives in reference to "time yet to live," with an attendant reordering of life priorities. Gould (1972) delineated seven phases of adult life between the ages of sixteen and sixty on the basis of questionnaire and interview data from cross-sectional samples of psychiatric outpatients and middle-class adults. He described periods of existential self-examination and how autonomy waxes and wanes across the adult years.

While the efforts described in the foregoing paragraph may all be applauded for their "outreaching" emphasis on post-adolescent adulthood, in some ways they are subject to the same criticisms leveled earlier against developmental psychology. That is, developmental psychology may be criticized for what little it has to say on development following adolescence; the efforts described above may likewise be criticized for what little they have to say about adulthood beyond the age of sixty. The difference between a fifty-year-old person and a thirty-year-old person or, perhaps even more so, the difference between a thirty-year-old and a ten-year-old is well-recognized; the same twenty-year difference, however, between those who are eighty and those who are sixty is almost always overlooked. Neugarten (1970) distinguishes between the "young-old" (fifty to seventy-four) and the "old-old" (seventy-five and older). The young-old are characterized by better health, more education, relative affluence, and greater political activism (Ward 1982). There is also some recent discussion describing the so-called "middle-old." The point is that there is as much variability among older people as there is among younger people.

Units of Change

The extent to which individuals or individual attributes remain the same or change throughout the whole life course is of primary importance in life-span research. The ability to explain and predict the degree of stability and change across the life course has been recognized as a central problem of developmental analysis (Baltes et al. 1980); (Mortimer et al. 1982). A life-span perspective would be of little theoretical and practical significance if there were no demonstrable changes beyond adolescence. A question worth asking, then, is: "How does one characterize such change?" or, more topically phrased, "What are the parameters and pragmatics of a life-course perspective?" Although the provision of a comprehensive conceptual framework is outside the scope of this chapter (see Baltes 1979; Baltes and Schaie 1973; Thomae 1979, for more complete discussions of this issue), some comment on the meaning of "life-span" is warranted and relevant here.

Baltes (1979) said that "the term 'life-span' is not intended to imply that chronological age is the primary organizing variable rather, the primary focus is on processes that attain their salience in a life-span or life-course context." In fact, Baltes et al. (1977) cautioned that the goal of developmental research should be the identification of key behavior-change processes rather than age changes. They suggested that the current strong focus on age development is a major theoretical cost of a life-span orientation, for the age variable may be viewed as transient and therefore unproductive for theory construction. Hultsch and Plemons (1979), and others emphasized that there are many conceptions of development that go beyond the use of age as an important theoretical variable. Thus, the term "life-span" should not be understood as communicating a sole concern with age change. The major concern is with the processes and events that occur throughout life. Age changes and age-related explanations represent only one class of ontogenic change sequences (Baltes 1979).

Life Events

Brim and Ryaff (1980:368) claimed that the concept of life events is central to the field of life-span development: "life events are as integral to life-span developmental theory as are atoms and other lesser particles to physical theory." Although there is a potentially infinite number of life events—given the interactive nature of individuals and their environment—there is also a fairly reliably reproduced list of socially recognized and well-labeled normative life events. Retirement and widowhood are two such events of later life. It is important to note that these events are correlated with age but are not age-specific. That is, retirement and the death of a spouse may occur at virtually any point of the adult life span with varying degrees of probability. In fact, an analysis of the differential responses and reactions to these events as a function of age may prove to be an interesting and valuable field of inquiry. The following section, however, will examine retirement and widowhood with specific reference to some of the social and psychological issues and processes characteristic of later life.

Retirement

The sociopsychological impact of retirement upon individuals has been the focus of considerable theoretical and empirical attention in recent years. Most of this effort has been spent in the assessment of the loss of the work role on males, with very few valid insights on the impact of retirement on women. There is, however, significant debate regarding the effects of retirement: that is, is retirement best seen in terms of crisis or continuity? Persuasive and compelling arguments are available for both positions.

The crisis view (Blau 1956; Lopata 1973; Miller 1965) holds that work is a major source of social status, self-respect, and identity and is the major and culturally dominant role for males. Accordingly, severance from the work role results in a loss of self-respect and social status, in lowered morale and in an alleged crisis of identity. Blau (1956) wrote that retirement can be seen as a "roleless" role, a demotion in the work system accompanied by a decline in self-respect and an alteration of self-concept. Retirement signifies that one is old, useless, and no longer a vital, contributing member of the community (Thompson 1983).

Miller's position argues that leisure roles cannot provide the sense of identity formerly achieved through work. Leisure is only valid to the extent that it refreshes one for work. One cannot legitimately engage in leisure full time without undergoing some rethinking of self, or without experiencing the social stigma of inability to perform (Miller 1965). Just as Lopata (1973) wrote that the roles of wife and mother are the basic and important roles for adult women, Miller and others saw the role of "worker" or occupation as basic for men, providing the social substance by which other roles are maintained and coordinated. Work is considered crucial in structuring relationships and social interactions, serving as a fundamental link between individuals and society, conditioning lifestyles, and partaking in normal patterns (Friedman and Havighurst 1954). Occupational identity pervades all areas of a person's life, such that "the retired person finds himself without a role which would justify his social future" (Miller 1965:72).

The continuity theory elaborated in the work of Atchley (1971) and Bultena and Wood (1969), on the other hand, denies that an identity crisis is occasioned by retirement. Instead they claim that the adult identity is based on a variety of roles, only one of which is work.

Each person generally has several roles on which he stakes his identity. Work may be at or near the top, but not necessarily so. There simply is not the kind of homogeneous consensus on the value of work that would keep it at the top for everyone. In fact, the many systems of competing values in a complex society ensure that there will be a wide variety of self-values. Thus, the probability that retirement will lead to a complete identity breakdown is slight. There may be just as many people who rely on leisure pursuits for self-respect as there are who rely on work, particularly among those with unsatisfying jobs (Atchley 1971).

The crux of this alternative theory is identity continuity whereby the retired individual will continue to see himself as a railroader or teacher, even though he no longer plays the role (Lipman and Osgood 1982). Strauss et al. (1976) supported this proposition finding that many individuals keep their job identities after retirement. Moreover, successful adaptation to retirement is promoted by continuity in other phases of life, even when the work role is disrupted. Continuity theory assigns a great deal of importance to other, nonoccupational roles.

Lipman and Osgood (1982) claimed that the nature and meaning of work, leisure, and retirement are changing in North American society. Friedman and Orbach (1974) have concluded that work does not seem to take precedence over other life areas for most workers. Work is no longer a central life interest for men—it is a means to an end. Leisure is becoming legitimized, assuming a greater importance and credibility and is able to serve as a source of positive personal identity (Kaplan 1975). Correspondingly, retirement is assumed to no longer stand out as a negative event, but is seen as a further point along life's continuum with a different set of roles replacing former occupational ones. Lipman and Osgood (1982) suggested that as the concept of retirement becomes incorporated into the culture, the tendency to look upon work as a temporary part of life will increase. Furthermore, people tend to associate with others of the same age both on and off the job, creating a cohort of individuals who retire together, providing social and emotional support, and serving as relevant models (Atchley 1980).

Thus, for the interested researcher, whether or not retirement constitutes some crisis of identity is really a conceptual issue. Both positions appear equally defensible. At the very least, however, retirement presents itself as an opportunity for crisis. On a more idiographic or clinical level, whether or not retirement is experienced as a crisis by the individual may depend on several factors.

Attitudes toward retirement, for example, are not uniform and vary according to a number of individual characteristics. Ward (1982) reported that individuals at higher levels of income, education, and occupation tend to have more favorable attitudes toward retirement. Such relationships, however, obscure the more pragmatic concern that those with higher incomes can also expect greater financial security in retirement. Paradoxically, workers at higher educational and occupational levels also report that their work is more interesting, they are more committed to it and are, therefore, less inclined to retire. Thus, they retire later, as they often have the freedom to do so, even though their attitudes toward retirement may be more favorable (George 1980). Studies have also found that older workers are often less "accepting" of retirement and prefer a later retirement age (Ekerdt et al. 1980). That is, preferred retirement age was later among those who approached retirement. This study was cross-sectional; therefore, it remains unclear as to whether this is a cohort effort or a developmental shift.

Other studies have focused on adjustment to retirement. Satisfaction was found to be somewhat higher among the employed than among the retired, but this could be attributable to differences in health and income, which are themselves the major determinants of retirement satisfaction (George 1980). Strauss et al. (1976) reported on a sample of retirees, 83 percent of whom felt that a retired man was "treated with less respect," but only 15 percent felt that they were personally treated with less respect. Again, one is confronted with the powerful and pervasive influence of societal attitudes. Just as in menopause, perhaps the critical element here is not the objective experience of retirement, per se, but the effect of being labeled as "retired." Neugarten (1977), for example, has reported that most middle-aged women could point to gains or advantages when questioned about their experiences with menopause, but responded more negatively when the questions were phrased in more general terms (i.e., "women" as opposed to "yourself"). Grossman and Bart (1980) suggested that although middle age in general may not be a crisis for everyone, there are structural and cultural factors in our society that can increase the likelihood of a person's experiencing problems at middle age. Perhaps it is fair to say that it is the attitude toward, as opposed to the experience of, menopause or retirement that renders it a potentially negative event.

Blau (1956) discussed the relationship between age and age identification. For example, with a sample of seniors sixty years and older, Blau found that fully 60 percent of the respondents considered themselves middle-aged, and that people come to believe that others consider them as old only if they consider themselves old. She claimed that it is a shift in age identification that precedes and produces an increased awareness of, or changes in, the self and not vice versa. In examining the relationship between age, age identification, and employment status, Blau found that among those under seventy, less than one-fifth of those employed, but more than one-third of those retired, identified themselves as old. Among those who are seventy and over, 41 percent of those employed, but 68 percent of those retired, regarded themselves as old. Certainly, "old" is more than a state of mind, but these are interesting results, nonetheless. Blau (1956:200) stated that "retirement is a social pattern which implies an invidious judgment on the part of others in the society about the lack of fitness of old people . . . Thus, the retired individual is socially defined as old."

Several factors, then, operate to influence the perception, interpretation, and subsequent experience of retirement. In light of this, it is probably wrong to adopt any blanket position proclaiming that retirement either is or is not a crisis. Nevertheless, retirement is a salient, socially defined life marker which, at its very least, forces the individual to juggle around—add or delete—some of the various adjectives used in self-description.

Widowhood

Marriage is considered to be one of the major social relationships for both partners, but particularly for women. Lopata (1973) suggested several reasons why the process of marriage has an especially profound influence upon a wife. First, although socialized into individualistic personal identities, married women and mothers are expected to be oriented primarily toward family welfare. Second, the roles of wife and mother are considered the basic and important ones for adult women. Lopata's (1972) study showed that women rank the roles of worker, member of the community, and member of an organization (e.g., religious) very low in importance. Mother, wife, woman, housewife, daughter, grandmother, sister, neighbor, and friend were ranked higher. Gilligan's (1982) work on self and morality supports Lopata's thesis. Gilligan hypothesized that self and morality are intricately linked. The two distinct modes of moral judgment (i.e., justice, and care), are not only gender related but they are also related to modes of self-definition. Whereas men conceive of the self as separate and objective (i.e., in terms of justice) in relation to others, women conceive of the self as connected and attached in relation to others. The third reason given by Lopata is that the additional roles of husband and father do not produce an equivalent significant shift in the way men see their roles. Fourth, the reality constructed by a couple symbolically and through lifestyle tends to be built around the husband's occupational role outside of the home.

It is rare that both spouses die simultaneously. It is likely, therefore, that widowhood will be experienced by a large proportion of the adult population at some time, most typically in later life. It is also likely that this experience will be negative: that is, widowhood most often has negative consequences. For example, those who are widowed exhibit higher rates of mortality and suicide and rate their health more negatively (Riley and Foner 1968). Such results, however, must certainly be attenuated by the fact that those who are widowed are themselves typically older. This influences the higher rates of mortality and negative ratings of health. George (1980) suggested that because the role of spouse is usually such a pervasive aspect of identity, the widowed individual is likely to be stressed while she or he negotiates new roles and social statuses.

Symbolic interactionists such as Goffman (1967) and Mead (1934) contributed to the widowhood discussion. According to these authors, people's identities are formulated through social interaction involving symbolic definitions of the self, the other, and the situation. They become stabilized in long-term significant interactions (e.g., Goffman 1963, 1967). Therefore, changing the definition of the situation or removing the spouse from interaction with the self necessitates changing the definition of the self, and modifying, or reformulating, that identity. After all, as McCall and Simmons (1966) claimed, the married partners are not merely disjointed individuals but constitute a collective unit. Married people are invited to events not as persons but as couples. The dissolution of this unit by the death of a partner entails more than an alteration of behavior. It necessitates a change in the person's entire way of looking at the world.

Of particular interest to the discussion of widowhood and the elderly is the sex distribution in this age group. Statistics Canada (1979) reported that over seven out of every ten elderly men (sixty-five and older) are married and living with their wives, while not quite four out of every ten women are married and living with their husbands (given the combined facts that women have a longer life expectancy and tend to marry men older than themselves). (See Tables A-1 and A-2 in Appendix A for a general and more recent summary of the age structure, sex ratio, and marital status of the elderly population—i.e., age sixty-five and older—of British Columbia.) In other words, almost every other woman sixty-five or over is widowed. A widower, then, occupies a more atypical position relative to his peers than does an elderly married man. A widow, on the other hand, is in a less atypical position than her married counterpart. This supports Blau's (1961) proposition that men have more difficulty adjusting to widowhood than do women and encounter greater social isolation because of it. With widowhood being more unusual for men, a "society of widowers" (as a support group or for role models) is more difficult to achieve.

Since friends tend to be of the same sex and in a similar age group, a change in marital status places an individual in a deviant position among his age and sex peers. His interests and experiences, which differ from married people's, are likely to have an adverse effect. On the other hand, when widowhood becomes prevalent among others similarly located in the social structure, it is the married individual who occupies a deviant position and who, therefore, often sees less of his old friends (Blau 1961:438).

Thus, widowhood in later life presents a special challenge for the remaining spouse (especially the husband). Not only must the surviving individual struggle to regain a more separate, autonomous sense of self, but this struggle is often without the social support systems that are intact and available for younger groups.

These foregoing events have been presented to illustrate the dynamics involved in labeling and interpreting the death event. Life events offer the *opportunity* for a reexamination of self: how individuals give shape and meaning to their life course. Life events, however, are not neat and discrete independent variables or units of analysis. They may represent different things for different individuals as a function of any combination of factors associated with the individual, the society, and the event itself. Neugarten (1970) claimed that the salience of a life event lies in its timing. She suggested that individuals pass through a socially regulated cycle from birth to death, a succession of socially delineated age statuses in which there exists a prescribed timetable for the ordering of major life events.

According to Neugarten (1970), predictable on-time events are not unsettling when they arrive. They are anticipated and rehearsed, the grief work is completed, and the reconciliation is accomplished without shattering a sense of continuity. She suggested that it is the unanticipated, not the anticipated, that is likely to represent the traumatic event; or, as Brim and Ryaff (1980) wrote, it is not the birth of a child but the death of a child we should be studying.

As interesting and novel a concept as this notion of on-time/off-time is, an event is more than its temporal relativity. Costa and McCrae (1980) suggested that event reaction may just be the older adult's manifestation of a predisposition that endures from late adolescence. With reference to the male mid-life crisis, Costa and McCrae (1980) suggested that men going through this crisis period are not temporarily neurotic as Levinson et al. (1978) had suggested, but rather "neuroticism in adult men is likely to take the form of . . . job dissatisfaction, marital troubles, concern over failing health, and so on" (Levinson et al. 1978:84). These crises are more indications of a life-long history of adaptation.

There is undoubtedly merit in this view as well. The bottom line is the familiar person-by-situation interaction. Significant life events are valuable constructs insomuch as individuals view them as such. Self-concept has value in its relation to an individual's past (Gergen and Gergen 1983). It is an organizing factor as the individual recounts the story of his/her life. Although there may be considerable overlap and correlation between events as defined by psychologists or sociologists and those as defined by the individuals whose lives are of research interest, there need not be an isomorphic correspondence. The final word with respect to the significance of life events rests with the individual.

Existentialism offers an interesting variation on this perspective. Existential psychology disavows explanation linking early experiences to later behavior; rather, the view is that an individual's whole existence is a historical event. Dwelling in the world always means dwelling in a past, present, and future simultaneously. When something is recalled from the past, it means that existence at that time is open to the past. Individuals do not exist in the past, the past exists in the individuals. Similarly, when an individual looks forward to something in the future, it means that existence is open at that moment to the future. Ideally, existence should be open to all of one's past and all of one's future, as well as all of one's present.

Boss (1977) claimed that genetic explanations can only come to the fore after one understands the present phenomena in their own right. Motivational and genetic explanations are tautological. People may act today as they did yesterday, because they perceive that the present encounter has the same *meaning* as a past encounter. Repetition or habit is due to the meaning the act has in the present. Humans have no existence apart from the world, and the world has no existence apart from humans.

Social Relations

Friendship and Kinship

Social support in the form of friends and family is an interesting issue to examine in a life-span perspective. Across life, we can point to several junctures in life in which individuals might alter their perceptions of friends and family. Much has been written about adolescence and young adulthood, for example: a time of psychological and physiological maturity accompanied by new feelings, sensations, and desires, and a multitude of new ways of looking at, and thinking about, the world. Traditional psycholanalytic theory characterizes adolescence as a time when an individual encounters a reawakening of the family-romance problem of early childhood, which is resolved by seeking and finding a partner of the same generation (Elkind 1977). Friendships play an increasingly important role in socialization; peer groups teach acceptable norms for behavior (Donelson and Gullahorn 1977). As an individual disengages from his/her family, intimacy needs are met through friendships and dating relationships. Kon and Losenkov (1978) reported that adolescents rate their friends as more understanding than their parents or teachers, and they feel more comfortable with (and are more likely to confide in) a friend rather than parents or other adults.

On the other hand, little is written or known about the nature and the meaning of friendship in middle life. Brown (1981) suggested that the demands of, and competition at, work and familial responsibilities consume the greatest proportion of time of the mid-life adult. Little time remains for friends. Correspondingly, Shulman (1975) and Lowenthal et al. (1975) reported that middle-aged individuals claim to have fewer friends than either younger or older adults. It may well be, however, that intimacy needs are met by family members. Shulman (1975), for example, found that middle-aged respondents were more likely to confide in relatives than in friends.

Whereas the social trajectory of adolescence is outward, away from the family, in mid-life the inverse is true: familial concerns seem preponderant. It is a time when parents may be dying or experiencing diminishing health, so that they require assistance (financial, physical, psychological) from their middle-aged offspring. It is a time when children may be leaving home for work and/or families of their own (Brim 1976). Deutscher (1959) claimed that this postparental period precipitates a rediscovery of the personality of the marital partner as it has evolved during the period of child-rearing. It seems reasonable to propose that a great deal of cognitive activity and behavioral activity is directed toward the family and less toward friends.

There is a developing body of literature of the friendships and the social sphere of older adults, which is appropriate given the great promise held for the importance of friends in old age (Mancini 1980). Several researchers such as Adams (1971) and Butler and Lewis (1977) felt that there is a link between morale, life satisfaction, and enjoyment in the later years of life, and the interaction and maintenance of relationships with friends and intimates. Friendship is said to be an integral factor in the adjustment processes of older adults.

An older adult is supposedly better equipped to cope with the role of becoming "old" when interaction with friends and intimates is possible, or when friendship relations maintain role continuity (Blau 1973).

The friendships and interaction patterns of the elderly have some qualities unique to this period of life that warrant further discussion. After the family- and work-oriented period of mid-life, there is often an increase in the amount of contact with friends in the "young-old" stage of later life (Brown 1981; Lowenthal et al. 1975). Overall social networks, friendships, and frequency of interaction, however, all decline with age, as older individuals find themselves less able to maintain social contacts as a consequence of increased physical disabilities and decreased mobility (Riley and Foner 1968). The friends are vulnerable to infirmity or death, and may be unable to provide assistance or support. Furthermore, Philbad and Adams (1972) suggested that friendships are not independent of marital status.

The role of friends versus family in the life of an elderly person is a controversial issue. Blau (1973), for example, holds that an older person with a single good friend is better able to cope with old age than one with a dozen grandchildren but no friends. A competing point of view offered by Riley and Foner (1968) is that although friends play an important role, they are generally less important to older people than are children and other family members. The authors suggested that friends are more of a complement than a substitute for kinship associations. More recently, Wood and Robertson (1978) demonstrated that involvement with both family and friends accounts for significant proportions of variance in the measures of elderly people's life satisfaction. The contributions of friends, however, were significantly greater than that of grandchildren and other family representatives. In a review of the literature, Adams (1971) concluded that there is a positive relationship between social contacts and satisfaction. Of all the types of social relations and activities, friendship association appears most highly and consistently related to satisfaction.

As suggested by Wood and Robertson (1978) and Rosow (1970), perhaps the difference between family and friends is really the difference between obligation and choice. That is, the obligatory nature of the parent-offspring relationship may detract from the quality as the generations become estranged. In a different light, friends and family may serve differing functions. That is, friends may be the primary suppliers of comfort, support, and assistance to an ailing individual, but family (adult children and, to a lesser extent, other relatives), not friends, are the potential sources of financial aid. (See Tables A–3 and A–4 in Appendix A for a general summary of the urban/rural distribution and living arrangements of the elderly population in British Columbia.)

There is reason to assume, then, that various predictable junctures of the life course present individuals with the opportunity to change their perceptions and alter their understanding of their social world in general, and of friends and family in particular. Similarly, there is reason to assume that the life course presents individuals with various opportunities for reexaminations and reevaluations of the self.

Social Comparison

Suls and Mullen (1983), expanded upon Festinger's (1954) social comparison theory, which suggested that self-perception and self-evaluation are influenced by position in the life cycle. They posited three modes of evaluation that are operative throughout life: temporal conditions, comparisons with social-similar others, and comparisons with social-dissimilar others.

Preschoolers typically gauge their capabilities by comparing their present performances with past performances (i.e., temporal comparisons). The enormous increments in cognitive and physical skills of early childhood make these temporal comparisons especially satisfying. As this incremental pace tapers off, however, temporal comparisons begin to yield smaller measures of improvement, propelling children toward social comparison.

Young children use social comparison fairly indiscriminately. They compare themselves with both similar others and dissimilar others. As they acquire certain critical concepts (e.g., the discounting principle, a knowledge of the difference between performance and ability), they begin to compare themselves predominantly with similar others. They continue doing so through adolescence and much of adulthood.

During middle age, this process begins to change somewhat. Suls and Mullen (1983) suggested that, during this time, individuals strive for distinctiveness and uniqueness. They compare themselves with dissimilar others. "Furthermore, comparisons with dissimilar others are frequently encouraged and even imposed in the work place. It is not uncommon for middle-aged persons to find themselves competing with younger as well as older coworkers, competition frequently imposed by one's employers" (Suls and Mullen 1983:101).

It has been said that older individuals live in a contracting social world characterized by losses of social and interpersonal contacts, restricting social comparison (Riley and Foner 1968). As a result, the individual relies less on interpersonal comparisons and more on temporal comparisons: evaluations based on what one could do before versus what one can do now. This is representative of Erikson's final stage, integrity versus despair, during which individuals review their life to understand and accept it for what it has been and what it means.

Methodological Considerations

Cross-sectional and Longitudinal Designs

The two conventional designs used for the examination of an age-functional relation are the cross-sectional and longitudinal methods. The cross-sectional method compares different age groups at a single point in time; the longitudinal method follows the same persons through all age levels with repeated observations. The critical difference between the cross-sectional and the longitudinal designs lies in the use of independent sampling in the case of the former (i.e., different groups) and dependent sampling in the case of the latter (i.e., the same group). In both models, differences between the observations on the different samples are attributed to various levels of the age factor (Baltes 1968). There are costs and benefits attached to each of these models.

With respect to sampling, longitudinal designs almost always fail to meet the criteria of representativeness of a group to the general population (as a function of the repeated participation required of subjects). Cross-sectional samples usually fulfill this requirement (Baltes 1968). Correspondingly, although the different age groups of a longitudinal study are theoretically homogeneous, they become more heterogeneous over the course of the study due to dropouts or subject mortality. Furthermore, this dropout rate may be selective (i.e., not random) if there is a correlation between the dependent variable (the variable being measured) and the characteristics related to dropout. As a consequence, the longitudinal sample, as measured later in the experiment (or course of events) may no longer be comparable to the original sample. As Baltes (1968) reported, the sample may become progressively more biased in a positive direction. That is, age changes may result from changes in the composition of the population and not from changes within individual members of the population.

In contrast to selective dropout, there is the issue of selective survival. This phenomenon applies to longitudinal as well as to cross-sectional samples. The population change at issue here is selective to the extent that the survival rate is correlated with the measurement variables. Birren (1959), for example, proposed that survivors might have been taller or shorter, brighter or duller, happier or unhappier than their nonsurviving cohort. Recent research on mortality has demonstrated that not only is there a change in the original sample, but there may also be changes within individuals as a function of their approaching death.

Kleemeier (1962) and others reported an accelerated rate of change in behavior during the last few years before "natural" death. This is referred to as "terminal drop." The argument goes that as the age of a given cohort increases, so too does the proportion of individuals who are within a few years of death. It may be that these individuals exhibit significant drops in intellectual capacity that bring down the average for their cohorts—individuals from a similar year of birth (Suedfeld and Piedrahita 1984). Therefore, differences in intellectual functioning across several older-age cohorts might be attributed to the behavior of persons who do not survive the years following test administration. If we were to exclude these "high risk" subjects from the analysis, little or no change might be observed (Riegel and Riegel 1972:306-307).

This "terminal drop" hypothesis has something interesting to say about the proposed and cross-sectionally observed curvilinear relation between age and several measures of behavior and cognitive functioning. The mortality curve indicates an increasing frequency of death with increasing age. Older samples will therefore contain a higher proportion of persons who are in the process of terminal change. This accelerates or makes more extreme the rate of change for the group as a whole. Thus, although the means of these groups representing a cross-sectional slice of the life span may neatly fall into the pattern of an inverted "U," the rate of change would actually apply only to those in the older sample who are in the process of terminal change related to death. The actual longitudinal graph may perhaps be best represented by gradual decreasing degrees of growth, followed by a plateau or phase of stability, followed by a period of rapid decline in the time interval (about four years or less) immediately preceding death.

Cross-sectional designs are likely to miss such abrupt individual changes. Moreover, by comparing different age groups at a single point in time, the issue of generational (or cohort) effects gains prominence as a source of error to impair the internal validity of cross-sectional studies. Birren (1959) and others argued that samples differ not only with regard to age, but also with regard to the differences in the culture and the conditions under which age-homogeneous groups were reared. Education may be one such difference. (See Table A–5 in Appendix A for a general summary of the educational level attained by the elderly population of British Columbia.) Therefore, the results of cross-sectional studies should not be interpreted as pure age effects. Similarly, cohort effects serve as sources of error to impair the external validity or generalizability of longitudinal designs. Different cultures and social conditions may alter the developmental patterns demonstrated by one cohort. It is, therefore, difficult to generalize the results of longitudinal studies to other populations.

The longitudinal method is also subject to the problem of testing or practice effects, largely as a function of repeated measurement. The assumption usually made here is that repeated observations of the same sample have no effect on the dependent measure. Such an unlikely assumption is made more tenable by extending the time interval between observations or testing administrations. Nevertheless, the importance of testing effects as confounding variables should not be underestimated, since many longitudinal studies employ a high number of retests. Baltes (1968) reported that over a period of eighteen years, the majority of the subjects of the well-known Berkeley Growth Study were tested thirty-eight times.

A related point worthy of attention concerns the general concept of measurement equivalence. Baltes et al. (1977) asked some interesting questions about the issue. For example, if the average score of a group of persons on a particular test changes as they grow from ten to fifteen years of age, is it the persons themselves that change or is it what the test is measuring that has changed? Or is it both? Similarly, if a test of some personality dimension is given to a group of males and a group of females and a ten-point difference in mean scores is observed, does this mean that one sex has more of this particular trait than the other, that the accuracy of the measure is different for the two sexes, or that the test measures somewhat different attributes in the two sexes? This is a point reminiscent of the earlier discussion of cognitive functioning (and particularly memory) across various age groups. It was suggested that the difference between older and younger subjects on such tests may, in part, be a function of the relevance or, more broadly stated, measurement equivalence. What it means to be a Canadian male at one point in time may well differ from what it means at some later point, or for a different group or cohort.

Not one of the criticisms raised thus far with respect to these experimental designs has been sufficiently damning to inhibit or preclude their usage. Other factors such as economic considerations and desire for tenure also weigh heavily. Moreover, other strategies of data collection and data analysis have been proposed. Perhaps the major current alternative is the cross-sequential method in which independent groups are tested once at all cohort and age levels. The cross-sequential merges the cross-sectional and longitudinal methodologies. That is, in an age-by-year of birth matrix, the cross-sectional method studies the columns, the longitudinal method studies the rows, and the cross-sequential method studies the diagonals. The cross-sequential method attempts to correct, for the likelihood that researchers will generalize purely on the basis of age. The point is that being seventy years old is not an experience or event that holds perfectly overlapping meanings for all cohorts of seventy-year-olds over time.

Retrospective Accounts

A strategy that has recently reemerged in the literature has more of a phenomenological or hermeneutic nature and begins to account for the experiential effects of aging. It is simultaneously referred to as reminiscence

(Butler 1963), life review, or life history (Buhler and Massarik 1968), and autobiography (Allport 1955; Birren and Hedlund 1986). Although clinicians and social service caregivers have often extolled the positive benefits to be derived from the engagement in such processes, psychology (in general) has typically considered such study "unscientific" (Cameron 1972).

The use of information gleaned from sources such as autobiographical accounts, life reviews, and reminiscences has played an interesting and varied role in the history of psychology. Freud, after all, derived many of his seminal psychological constructs by listening to the life accounts and experiences of his patients. Hall (1922) and Murray (1938) also used diaries and autobiographies—in part, at least—as sources of information in the development of their theories of adult development and personality (Birren and Hedlund 1986). Allport (1942) made a strong plea for the continued use of personal documents in psychological research, much as Wrightsman did (1980). He claimed that they provide an inner view of the person not accessible through other methods of data collection.

Such a plea, however, did not thrust the personal document research enterprise to the forefront of psychology. There is little doubt, in this regard, that the climate created by behaviorism diminished the importance and usefulness of personal documents as sources of ideas and data about living, growing up, and growing old. For this reason, the publication of B. F. Skinner's autobiography itself may have elicited surprise, "that the crown prince of behaviorism would take his subjective experiences so seriously as to publish an account of them" (Birren and Hedlund 1986:3).

Perhaps major reasons for this reluctance and hesitance to accept and use autobiographical/retrospective data may be found in one of the often-cited methodological (and conceptual) "difficulties" in this area, and in the idiographic (or individualistic) approach in general. Nunnally (1978) said that the idiographists may be entirely correct, but if they are, it is a sad day for psychology. Idiography is an antiscience point of view: it discourages the search for general laws and instead encourages the description of particular phenomena. Implicit in such a view is the untenable suggestion that there are only general laws and not laws applying to particular cases, a criticism that, according to Runyan (1984), has been refuted by a proliferation of quantitative and experimental studies of the single case. Moreover, the suggestion that science, as a whole, is not concerned with the study of particulars summarily dismisses significant portions of endeavors in the areas of geology, astronomy, and evolutionary biology. These sciences are not concerned solely with general principles and processes, but also with such topics as the structure and evolution of this particular planet, the structure and origins of our solar system, and the particular sequence of species leading to the evolution of humans (Runyan 1984).

A related criticism of the idiographic approach revolves around the issue of generalizability. Holt (1962:398), for example, argued that "if every personality structure were as much a law unto itself as Allport implies, it would be impossible to gain useful information in this field; there would be no transfer from one case study to another." Such a view is based on the unwarranted assumption that the goal of psychology is the production of generalizations at the highest possible level of abstraction. There are, however, at least three different levels of abstraction relevant to the needs of the psychologist: namely, the levels of universals, groups, and individuals (Runyan 1984). Although these levels are partially independent of one another, there is also some transfer between them, and work on all three levels of analysis is necessary. To the cry, then, of "How can you generalize from that idiographic study?" the equally appropriate response is "How can you particularize from that group or population study to the individual?" (Runyan 1984).

Perhaps the major argument against the use of autobiographical and/or retrospective accounts as a data base or source has been the suspected lack of accuracy demonstrated by individuals as reporters of their own lives. Recent research, substantiated by a great deal of the eyewitness testimony literature, suggested that individuals have characteristic agendas for, or styles of, recollection. Kent (1985) demonstrated that patients' reports of acute pain obtained three months after a dental appointment are often substantially different from reports given immediately following the appointment. Anxious patients, in particular, report *more* pain at follow-up than they had previously. These findings are interpreted as consistent with the hypothesis that patients' memories of experienced pain are reconstructed over time in order to become consistent with their existing levels of anxiety or some other, pervasive organizing framework. Such subjectivity in reporting is only a problem or handicap for the researcher to the extent that the goal of investigation is an objective account of something in the past. Since psychologists are typically not historians in this sense (their aim is not to recreate the past, but rather understand the past from the perspective of the present), these characteristic biases or deceptions engaged in by individuals may be seen as signs of cognitive organization or glimpses of salient individual differences (Greenwald 1980). That is, the very reasons that make retrospective accounts of questionable validity from a simplistic and narrowly "objective" point of view render them especially valid and valuable from a "subjective" stance.

Thomae (1970) developed several postulates of human behavior which support the idea that the personal interpretation of experience is a primary factor in both behavioral and emotional reactions to life events. The first postulate states that "perception of change rather than objective change is related to behavioral change;" and the second is that "any change in the situation of the individual is perceived and evaluated in terms of the dominant concerns and expectations of the individual" (Thomae 1970:4). Similarly, the work of Cohen and Lazarus (1980) demonstrates that stress is appraised in terms of threat, loss, or challenge depending on how the individual *perceives* the immediate experience rather than on the objective characteristics of the situation. In other words, research supports the idea that the perception, and not the actual occurrence, serves as a stimulus for behavioral change. "Since individuals carry the history of past experiences with them continually, it may be more important when doing research on psychological aspects of development to understand the individual's interpretation of his or her experiences rather than to have objective information about these experiences" (Birren and Hedlund 1986:14-15). Concurring and expanding upon this point of view, Oresick et al. (1986:5) claimed that "the crucial information is not how many events occur, but what meaning they have for the subjects." Again, one is confronted with the executive function played by life events in an individual's history and life story.

Summary

Embedded in the foregoing sections of this chapter has been a "loose" structural analysis of the gerontology literature (models, metaphors, and perspectives on aging, and ways to operationalize these views), at least as seen through the eyes of social scientists. Attached to this "scaffolding" have been some of the important and frequently cited substantive issues (e.g., cognitive functioning, personality dimensions, perception of self and others) relevant to a discussion of aging and old age. An analysis of significant life events has been offered as a method of examining structure and substance as they interact across the individual's life span.

Some of the major points to be taken away from this discussion are itemized below and, in large measure, follow from each other.

1. The elderly are not a homogeneous group and aging is not a standardized experience. There is as much (if not more) variance in a population of older adults as there is in younger samples. There is similarly as much variance within one life span (cohort) as there is across life spans or cohorts.
2. There is no singular, linear model of aging that adequately captures the complexities of the aging process. Any model must simultaneously account for increments, decrements, and enduring patterns or consistencies.
3. The elderly as an age group are not an isolated pocket of individuals independent of their pasts or other age groups. Aging is a continuous experience necessitating a life-span perspective.
4. A life-span perspective is not meant to imply that age alone is the primary organizing variable; it is intended to provide a forum by which processes

which attain their salience across the life course may reasonably be discussed. Life events, for example, offer an alternative metric for the evaluation of different life situations.

5. A series of research strategies (all with their own benefits and drawbacks) exist for the examination of both individuals and individual performance across the life span.

References

Adams, D.L. 1971. "Correlates of Satisfaction among the Elderly." *The Gerontologist*, 11, pp. 64-68.

Allport, G.W. 1942. *The Use of Personal Documents in Psychological Science*. (Bull. 49). Social Science Research Council.

Allport, G.W. 1955. *Becoming*. New Haven, CT: Yale University Press.

Atchley, R.C. 1971. Retirement and Leisure Participation: Continuity or Crisis? *The Gerontologist*, 11, pp. 13-17.

Atchley, R.C. 1975. "Dimensions of Widowhood in Later Life." *The Gerontologist*, 15, pp. 167-78.

Atchley, R.C. 1976. "Social and Psychological Differences between Men and Women in Later Life." *Journal of Gerontology*, 31, pp. 204-11.

Atchley, R.C. 1980. *The Social Forces in Later Life* (4th ed.). Belmont, CA: Wadsworth.

Baltes, P.B. 1968. "Longitudinal and Cross-sectional Sequences in the Study of Age and Generation Effects." *Human Development*, 11, pp. 145-71.

Baltes, P.B. 1979. Life-Span Developmental Psychology: Some Converging Observations on History and Theory. In P.B. Baltes & O.G. Brim (Eds.), *Life-Span Development and Behavior*, Vol. 2. New York: Academic Press, pp. 255-79.

Baltes, P.B., H.W. Reese, and L.P. Lipsitt. 1980. Life-Span Developmental Psychology. *Annual Review of Psychology*, 31, pp. 65-100.

Baltes, P.B., H.W. Reese, and J.R. Nesselroade. 1977. *Life-Span Developmental Psychology: Introduction to Research Methods*. Monterey, CA: Brooks/Cole.

Baltes, P.B., and K.W. Schaie (Eds.). 1973. *Life-Span Developmental Psychology: Personality and Socialization*. New York: Academic Press.

Barrett, T.R., and M. Wright. 1981. "Age-related Facilitation in Recall Following Semantic Processing." *Journal of Gerontology*, 36, pp. 194-99.

Birren, J.E. 1959. "Principles of Research on Aging." In J.E. Birren (Ed.), *Handbook of Aging and the Individual*. Chicago: University of Chicago Press, pp. 3-42.

Birren, J.E., and W.R. Cunningham. 1985. Research on the Psychology of Aging: Principles, Concepts, and Theory. In J.E. Birren and K.W. Schaie (Eds.), *Handbook of the Psychology of Aging* (2nd ed.). New York: Van Nostrand Reinhold, pp. 3–34.

Birren, J.E., and B. Hedlund. 1986. "Contributions of Autobiography to Developmental Psychology." Unpublished manuscript, University of Southern California, Los Angeles.

Birren, J.E., and V.J. Renner. 1977. In J.E. Birren and K.W. Schaie (Eds.), *Handbook of the Psychology of Aging*. New York: Van Nostrand Reinhold.

Birren, J.E., and C.A. Stacey. 1984. Paradigms of Aging: Growth Versus Decline. Paper presented at the Symposium, *Ethics and Aging*, The University of British Columbia, Vancouver.

Blau, Z.S. 1956. Changes in Status and Age Identification. *American Sociological Review*, 21, pp. 198–203.
Blau, Z.S. 1961. Structural Constraints on Friendship in Old Age. *American Sociological Review*, 16, pp. 429-39.
Blau, Z.S. 1973. *Old Age in a Changing Society*. New York: New Viewpoints.
Boss, M. 1977. *Existential Foundations of Medicine and Psychology*. New York: Aronson.
Botwinick, J. 1967. *Cognitive Processes in Maturity and Old Age*. New York: Springer.
Botwinick, J. 1977. Intellectual Abilities. In J.E. Birren and K.W. Schaie (Eds.), *Handbook of the Psychology of Aging*. New York: Van Nostrand Reinhold, pp. 580-605.
Brim, O.G. 1976. Theories of the Male Mid-life Crisis. *The Counseling Psychologist*, 6, pp. 2-9.
Brim, O.G., and C.D. Ryaff. 1980. On the Properties of Life Events. In P.B. Baltes and O.G. Brim (Eds.), *Life-Span Development and Behavior*, Vol. 3. New York: Academic Press, pp. 367-88.
Brown, B.B. 1981. A Life-Span Approach to Friendship: Age-related Dimensions of an Ageless Relationship. In H.Z. Lopata and D.R. Maines (Eds.), *Research on the Interweave of Social Roles, Vol. 2: Friendship*. Greenwich, CT: J.A.I. Press, pp. 23-50.
Brown, R. 1977. *A Poetic for Sociology: Toward a Logic of Discovery for the Human Sciences*. Cambridge, MA: Cambridge University Press.
Buhler, C., and F. Massarik. 1968. *The Course of Human Life*. New York: Springer.
Bultena, G., and V. Wood. 1969. The American Retirement Community: Bane or Blessing? *Journal of Gerontology*, 24, pp. 209-18.
Butler, R.N. 1963. "The Life Review: An Interpretation of Reminiscence in the Aged." *Psychiatry*, 26, pp. 65-75.
Butler, R., and M. Lewis. 1977. *Aging and Mental Health*. Saint Louis, MO: Mosby.
Cameron, P. 1972. "The Generation Gap: Time Orientation." *The Gerontologist*, 1, pp. 117-19.
Cavanaugh, J.C., J.G. Grady, and M.P. Perlmutter. 1983. "Forgetting and Use of Memory Aids in 20- and 70-year Olds' Everyday Life." *International Journal of Aging and Human Development*.
Cohen, F., and R.C. Lazarus. 1980. Coping With the Stresses of Illness. In G.C. Stone, F. Cohen, N. Adler, and Associates, *Health Psychology: A Handbook*. San Francisco: Jossey-Bass, pp. 47-79.
Cohler, B.J. 1982. Personal Narrative and Life Course. In P.B. Baltes and O.G. Brim (Eds.), *Life-Span Development and Behavior*, Vol. 4. New York: Academic Press, pp. 205-41.
Comfort, A. 1956. *The Biology of Senescence*. London: Routledge & Kegan Paul.
Costa, P.T., and R.R. McCrae. 1980. Still Stable after All These Years: Personality as a Key to Some Issues in Adulthood and Old Age. In P.B. Baltes and O.G. Brim (Eds.), *Life-Span Development and Behavior*, Vol. 3. New York: Academic Press, pp. 65-102.
Danish, S.J., M.A. Smyer, and C.A. Nowak. 1980. "Developmental Intervention: Enhancing Life-Event Processes." In P.B. Baltes and O.G. Brim (Eds.), *Life-Span Development and Behavior*, Vol. 3. New York: Academic Press, pp. 339-67.
Deutscher, T. 1959. *Married Life in the Middle Years*. Kansas City: Community Studies.

Donelson, E., and J. Gullahorn. 1977. *Women: A Psychological Perspective*. New York: Wiley.
Dowd, J.J. 1980. *Stratification among the Aged*. Monterey: Brooks/Cole.
Ekerdt, D.J., R. Bosse, and J. Mogey. 1980) "Concurrent Change in Planned and Preferred Age for Retirement." *Journal of Gerontology*, 35, pp. 177-84.
Elder, G.H. 1979. "Historical Change in Life Patterns and Personality." In P.B. Baltes and O.G. Brim (Eds.), *Life-span Development and Behavior*, Vol. 2. New York: Academic Press, pp. 117-57.
Elkind, D. 1977. "Erik Erikson's Eight Stages of Man." In L.R. Allman and D.T. Jaffe (Eds.), *Readings in Adult Psychology: Contemporary Perspectives*. New York: Harper & Row, pp. 7-15.
Erikson, E. 1964. *Childhood and Society*. New York: Norton.
Erikson, E. 1968. *Identity: Youth and Crisis*. New York: Norton.
Festinger, L.A. 1954. "A Theory of Social Comparison Processes." *Human Relations*, pp. 117–40.
Friedman, E., and R. Havighurst. 1954. *The Meaning of Work and Retirement*. Chicago: University of Chicago Press.
Friedman, E., and H. Orbach. 1974. Adjustment to Retirement. In S. Arieti (Ed.), *American Handbook of Psychiatry*. New York: Basic Books, pp. 609-45.
Gardner, E.F., and R.H. Monge. 1977. "Adult Age Differences in Cognitive Abilities and Educational Background." *Experimental Aging Research*, pp. 337-83.
George, L. 1980. *Role Transitions in Later Life*. Monterey, CA: Brooks/Cole.
George, L., and G. Maddox. 1977. "Subjective Adaptation to Loss of the Worker Role: A Longitudinal Study." *Journal of Gerontology*, 32, pp. 456-62.
Gergen, K.J., and M.M. Gergen. 1983. "Narrative of the Self." In T.R. Sarbin and K.E. Scheibe (Eds.), *Studies in Social Identity*. New York: Praeger, pp. 254-73.
Gilligan, C. 1982. *In a Different Voice: Psychological Theory and Women's Development*. Cambridge, MA: Harvard University Press.
Glenn, N. 1980. Values, Attitudes, and Beliefs. In O.G. Brim and J. Kagan (Eds.), *Constancy and Change in Human Development*. Cambridge, MA: Harvard University Press, pp. 596-640.
Goffman, E. 1959. *The Presentation of Self in Everyday Life*. New York: Doubleday Anchor.
Goffman, E. 1961. *Encounters*. Indianapolis: Bobbs-Merrill.
Goffman, E. 1963. *Stigma: Notes on the Management of Spoiled Identity*. Englewood Cliffs, NJ: Prentice-Hall.
Goffman, E. 1967. *Interaction Rituals*. Garden City, NY: Anchor Books.
Gould, R.L. 1972. "The Phases of Adult Life: A Study in Developmental Psychology." *American Journal of Psychiatry*, 127, pp. 521-31.
Greenwald, A. 1980. "The Totalitarian Ego: Fabrication and Revision of Personal History." *American Psychologist*, 35, pp. 603-18.
Grossman, M., and P. Bart. 1980. "The Politics of Menopause." In A.J. Dan, E.A. Graham, and C.P. Beecher (Eds.), *The Menstrual Cycle: A Synthesis of Interdisciplinary Research*, Vol. 1. New York: Springer, pp. 179-89.
Gumbrium, J. 1975. "Being Single in Old Age." *Aging and Human Development*, 6, pp. 29-41.
Hall, G.S. 1922. *Senescence: The Last Half of Life*. New York: Appleton Press.
Handler, P. 1960. "Radiation and Aging." In N.W. Schock (Ed.), *Aging*. Washington, DC: American Association for the Advancement of Science, pp. 199-223.

Holt, R.R. 1962. Individuality and Generalization in the Psychology of Personality. *Journal of Personality*, 30, pp. 337-404.

Horn, J.L., and G. Donaldson. 1980. Cognitive Development in Adulthood. In O.G. Brim and J. Kagan (Eds.), *Constancy and Change in Human Development*. Cambridge, MA: Harvard University Press, pp. 445-529.

Howes, A.B. 1962. *An Outline of English Composition*. New York: Doubleday.

Hultsch, D.F., and F. Deutsch. 1981. *Adult Development and Aging: A Life-Span Perspective*. New York: McGraw-Hill.

Hultsch, D.F., and J.K. Plemons. 1979. "Life Events and Life-Span Development." In P.B. Baltes and O.G. Brim (Eds.), *Life-Span Development and Behavior*, Vol. 2. New York: Academic Press, pp. 1-36.

Jacques, E. 1977. "Death and the Mid-Life Crisis." In L.R. Allman and D.T. Jaffe (Eds.), *Readings in Adult Psychology: Contemporary Perspectives*. New York: Harper & Row, pp. 315-25.

Kagan, J. 1980. "Perspectives on Continuity." In O.G. Brim and J. Kagan (Eds.), *Constancy and Change in Human Development*. Cambridge, MA: Harvard University Press, pp. 26-74.

Kaplan, M. 1975. *Leisure: Theory and Policy*. New York: Wiley.

Kent, G. 1985. "Memory of Dental Pain." *Pain*, 21, pp. 187-94.

Kleemeier, R.W. 1962. "Intellectual Changes in the Senium." *Proceedings of the American Statistical Association*, 1, pp. 290-95.

Kon, I.S., and V.A. Losenkov. 1978. Friendship in Adolescence: Values and Behavior. *Journal of Marriage and the Family*, 40, pp. 143-55.

Labouvie-Vief, G. 1982. "Growth and Aging in a Life-Span Perspective." *Human Development*, 25, pp. 65-79.

Leech, S., and K.L. Witte. 1971. "Paired-Associate Learning in Elderly Adults as Related to Pacing and Incentive Conditions." *Developmental Psychology*, 5, p. 180.

Levinson, D.J., with C.N. Darrow, E.B. Klein, M.G. Levinson, and B. McKee. 1978. *The Seasons of a Man's Life*. New York: Knopf.

Levinson, D.J., C.N. Darrow, E.B. Klein, M.G. Levinson, and B. McKee. 1976. "Periods in the Adult Development of Men: Ages 18 to 45." *The Counseling Psychologist*, 6, pp. 16-20.

Lipman, A., and N. Osgood. 1982. "Retirement: The Emerging Social Institution." In N. Osgood (Ed.), *Life After Work: Retirement, Leisure, Recreation, and the Elderly*. New York: Praeger, pp. 29-64.

Loftus, E.F. 1974. Reconstructing Memory: The Incredible Eyewitness. *Psychology Today*, 8, pp. 116-19.

Lopata, H.Z. 1969. Loneliness: Forms and Components. *Social Problems*, 17, pp. 248-62.

Lopata, H.Z. 1971. *Occupation: Housewife*. New York: Oxford University Press.

Lopata, H.Z. 1972. *Widowhood in an American City*. Cambridge, MA: Schenkman Publishing.

Lopata, H.Z. 1973. "Self-Identity in Marriage and Widowhood." *The Sociological Quarterly*, 4, pp. 407-18.

Lowenthal, M.F., M. Thurnher, and D. Chiriboga. 1975. *Four Stages of Life*. San Francisco: Jossey-Bass.

Mancini, J.A. 1980. "Friend Interaction, Competence, and Morale in Old Age." *Research on Aging*, 2, pp. 416-31.

McCall, G., and J.L. Simmons. 1966. *Identities and Interactions*. New York: Free Press.

McCrae, R.R., and P.T. Costa. 1982. "Self-Concept and the Stability of Personality: Cross-sectional Comparisons of Self-reports and Ratings." *Journal of Personality and Social Psychology*, 43, pp. 1282-92.

Mead, G.H. 1934. *Mind, Self and Society*. Chicago: University of Chicago Press.

Miller, S.L. 1965. "The Social Dilemma of the Aging Leisure Participant." In A. Rose and W. Peterson (Eds.), *Older People and Their Social World*. Philadelphia: F.A. Davis, pp. 72-92.

Mortimer, J.T., M.D. Finch, and D. Kumka. 1982. "Persistence and Change in Development: The Multidimensional Self-concept." In P.B. Baltes and O.G. Brim (Eds.), *Life-Span Development and Behavior*, Vol. 4. New York: Academic Press, pp. 263-313.

Murray, H.A. 1938. *Explorations in Personality*. New York: Oxford University Press.

Mutran, E., and P.J. Burke. 1979. "Personalism as a Component of Young and Old Adult Identities." *Research on Aging*, 1, pp. 187-212.

Neugarten, B.L. 1970. "Dynamics of Transition to Old Age." *Journal of Geriatric Psychiatry*, 4, pp. 71-87.

Neugarten, B.L. 1974. "Age Groups in American Society and the Rise of the Young-Old." In F. Eisele (Ed.), *Political Consequences of Aging*. *Annals of the American Academy of Political and Social Science*, 415, pp. 187-98.

Neugarten, B.L. 1976. "Adaptation of the Life Cycle." *The Counseling Psychologist*, 6, pp. 16-20.

Neugarten, B.L. 1977. "A New Look at Menopause." In L.R. Allman and D.T. Jaffe (Eds.), *Readings in Adult Psychology: Contemporary Perspectives*. New York: Harper & Row, pp. 308-14.

Neugarten, B.L. (Ed.). 1968. *Middle Age and Aging: A Reader in Social Psychology*. Chicago: University of Chicago Press.

Neugarten, B.L., and N. Datan. 1973. "Sociological Perspectives on the Life-Cycle." In P. Baltes and K.W. Schaie (Eds.), *Life-Span Developmental Psychology: Personality and Socialization*. New York: Academic Press, pp. 53-69.

Neugarten, B.L., and G.O. Hagestad. 1976. "Age and the Life Course." In R.H. Binstock and E. Shanas (Eds.), *Handbook of Aging and the Social Sciences*. New York: Van Nostrand Reinhold.

Nunnally, J.C. 1978. *Psychometric Theory* (2nd ed.). New York: McGraw-Hill.

Okun, M.A. 1976. Adult Age and Cautiousness in Decision: A Review of the Literature. *Human Development*, 19, pp. 220-33.

Oresick, R., S. Broder, and C. Shapiro. 1986. *Autobiographical Reports of Stressful Life Change Events and Academic Performance*. Paper presented at the meeting of the American Psychological Association, Washington, DC.

Perlmutter, M., R. Metzger, K. Miller, and T. Nezworski. 1980. "Memory of Historical Events." *Experimental Aging Research*, 6, pp. 47-60.

Philbad, C.T., and D.L. Adams. 1972. "Widowhood, Social Participation, and Life Satisfaction." *Aging and Human Development*, 3, pp. 323-747.

Poon, L.W. 1985. "Differences in Human Memory with Aging: Nature, Causes, and Clinical Implications." In J.E. Birren and K.W. Schaie (Eds.), *Handbook of the Psychology of Aging* (2nd ed.). New York: Van Nostrand Reinhold, pp. 427-62.

Reese, H.W., and D. Rodeheaver. 1985. "Problem-Solving and Complex Decision-Making." In J.E. Birren and K.W. Schaie (Eds.), *Handbook of the Psychology of Aging* (2nd ed.). New York: Van Nostrand Reinhold, pp. 474-99.

Riegel, K.F., and R.M. Riegel. 1972. "Development, Drop, and Death." *Developmental Psychology*, 6, pp. 309-16.

Riley, M.W., and A. Foner. 1968. *Aging and Society: An Inventory of Research Findings*. New York: Russell Sage Foundation.

Rogers, C.R. 1961. *On Becoming a Person*. Boston: Houghton Mifflin.

Rosow, I. 1970. "Old People: Their Friends and Neighbors." *American Behavioral Scientist*, 14, pp. 59-69.

Runyan, W.M. 1984. *Life Histories and Psychobiography: Explorations in Theory and Method*. New York: Oxford University Press.

Salthouse, T.A., and B.L. Somberg. 1982. Time-Accuracy Relationships in Young and Old Adults. *Journal of Gerontology*, 37, pp. 349-53.

Schulz, R. 1986. The Effects of Control and Predictability on the Psychologial and Physical Well-Being of the Institutionalized Aged. *Journal of Personality and Social Psychology*, 33, pp. 563-73.

Sheehy, G. 1974. *Passages*. New York: Dutton.

Shulman, N. 1975. Life-Cycle Variations in Patterns of Close Relationships. *Journal of Marriage and the Family*, 37, pp. 813-21.

Siegler, I. 1975. The Terminal Drop Hypothesis: Fact or Artifact? *Experimental Aging Research*, 1, pp. 169-85.

Smith, A.D. 1980. "Age Differences in Encoding, Storage, and Retrieval." In L.W. Poon, J.L. Fozard, L.S. Cermak, D. Arenberg, and L.W. Thompson (Eds.), *New Directions in Memory and Aging: Proceedings of the George A. Tallard Memorial Conference*. Hillsdale, NJ: Lawrence Erlbaum.

Statistics Canada. 1979. *Canada's Elderly*. Ottawa: The Ministry of Industry, Trade, and Commerce.

Strauss, H., B. Aldrich, and A. Lipman. 1976. "Retirement and Perceived Status Loss: An Inquiry into some Objective and Subjective Problems Produced by Aging." In J.F. Gumbrium (Ed.), *Time, Roles, and Self in Old Age*. New York: Behavioral Publications, pp. 220-34.

Suedfeld, P., and L.E. Piedrahita. 1984. "Intimations of Mortality: Integrative Simplification as a Precursor of Death." *Journal of Personality and Social Psychology*, 47, pp. 848-52.

Suls, J., and B. Mullen. 1983. "From the Cradle to the Grave: Comparison and Self-Evaluation across the Life-Span." In J. Suls and A.G. Greenwald (Eds.), *Psychological Perspectives on the Self*, Vol. 1. Hillsdale, NJ: Erlbaum, pp. 97-125.

Svanborg, A., and J.E. Thornton. 1986. "Subjective Health in Relation to Aging and Disease in a Representative Sample at Age 70, 75, and 79." Unpublished paper available from the Department of Geriatric and Long-Term Care Medicine, University of Gothenburg, Sweden.

Thomae, H. 1970. "Theory of Aging and Cognitive Theory of Personality." *Human Development*, 13, pp. 1-16.

Thomae, H. 1979. "The Concept of Development and Life-Span Developmental Psychology." In P.B. Baltes and O.G. Brim (Eds.), *Life-Span Development and Behavior*, Vol. 2. New York: Academic Press, pp. 281-312.

Thompson, G. 1983. "Work vs. Leisure Roles: An Investigation of Morale among Employed and Retired Men." *Journal of Gerontology*, 28, pp. 339-44.

Treat, N.J., and H.W. Reese. 1976. "Age, Imagery, and Practice in Paired-Associate Learning." *Developmental Psychology*, 12, pp. 119-24.

Valle, R.S., and R. von Eskartsberg, (Eds.). 1981. *The Metaphors of Consciousness*. New York: Plenum Press.

Ward, R. 1982. Occupational Variation in the Life Course: Implications for Later Life. In N. Osgood (Ed.), *Life After Work: Retirement, Leisure, Recreation, and the Elderly*. New York: Praeger.

Winn, F.J., J.W. Elias, and P.H. Marshall. 1976. "Meaningfulness and Interference as Factors in Paired-Associate Learning." *Educational Gerontology*, 1, pp. 297-306.

Wrightsman, L.S. 1980. *Personal Documents as Data in Conceptualizing Adult Personality Development*. Presidential address presented to the Society of Personality and Social Psychology (Div. 8) at the Annual Meeting of the American Psychological Association, Montreal, PQ.

Wood, V., and J.F. Robertson. 1978. "Friendship and Kinship Interaction: Differential Effects on the Morale of the Elderly." *Journal of Marriage and the Family*, 40, pp. 367-75.

3

Other Writers on Elderly Drivers

Grow old along with me!
The best is yet to be,
The last of life, for which the first was made:
Our times are in this hand
Who saith "A whole I planned,
Youth shows but half; trust God: see all nor be afraid"

(Robert Browning's *Rabbi Ben Ezra*)

When we filter the models, theories, and social perspectives found in gerontology through the traffic-safety net, a thick residue of commonality forms. Many ideologies, perspectives, and metaphors prevalent in studies of aging are also evident in elderly driver research.

Invariably the elderly drivers are stigmatized as problems, and to solve problems a technical perspective is usually actualized. So, in the traffic safety literature, elderly drivers have been envisioned as an entity that can be dissected, quantified, particularized, causally identified, manipulated, and to some extent mystified. Observe the following examples of elderly driver typecasting:

1. A statistically significant accident-prone group (Jolles 1971).
2. People with behavioral deficits and medical disability (Planek and Overend 1973).
3. People with reduced physical or mental abilities (Robinson 1985).
4. People involved in stimulus overload (Petrocine 1979).
5. People less well equipped . . . (Panek et al. 1977).

Researchers dissect elderly drivers in order to diagnose deficiencies in their driving-related lives. Component parts such as vision, reaction time, concentration, or hand-to-eye coordination are isolated and treated accordingly. In sociolinguistics, Lakoff and Johnson (1980) would consider these to be "synecdoches"—parts standing for the whole.

In traffic safety literature, there are numerous examples of synecdoches, where elderly drivers are defined according to:

1. Muscular degeneration (Binion 1986).
2. Sensory decrements (Corso 1971).
3. Visual deficits (Petrocine 1979).
4. Perceptual style (Barrett et al. 1977).
5. Attention problems (Botwinik 1973).
6. Dichotic listening detriments (Craik 1965).
7. Reaction time (Birren 1965).
8. Sensory diminution deterioration (McFarland et al. 1964).
9. Psychomotor slowing (Panek et al. 1977).
10. Glare impairment (Pulling et al. 1980).

The list goes on. It represents, very briefly, a raison d'être of research interest in elderly drivers. For empirical purposes, the whole "elderly driver" is reduced to articulated elements. Once the latter have been thoroughly measured and defined, they are used to frame elderly drivers' thoughts, attitudes, and actions. These second-order descriptions become the objects of planning for future technical intervention strategies. Once implemented, so the reasoning goes, the original characteristics will be eliminated or reduced, creating a positive effect on the elderly drivers' overall traffic behavior.

Further evidence of a technical orientation dominating elderly driver research is the repeated use of such orientational metaphors as deficit, degeneration, deterioration, depreciation, diminishment, and decline. These signs refer to a determinism that aging is:

> a deterioration of a mature organism resulting from time-dependent essentially irreversible changes intrinsic to all members of a species, such that, with the passage of time, they become increasingly unable to cope with the stresses of the environment, thereby increasing the probability of death [Handler 1960:200].

To age is to decrease in the ability to function. Countering the decline in function requires intervention. How well the intervention relates to measurable ends, or the extent to which it compensates for natural aging deterioration becomes the indicator of success. This unidirectional means-ends perspective becomes a standard.

Age-Related Degeneration

A closer look at age and physical deterioration confirms that vision or matters related to sight are highly relevant. A synopsis of the literature shows visual deterioration begins to be significant in old age, compounding common hazards such as traffic patterns, road signs, and weather conditions.

Vision as Sensory Impairment

Recently the Motorists' Vision Committee of the American Optometric Association stated that 80 percent of drivers sixty years and over have visual problems which could make them a risk on the highway.

The basis for the committee's claim lay in data obtained from rigorous experimental studies. One of those projects was undertaken by Daniel (1978). Three groups of motorists (young drivers, elderly drivers, and control group drivers specially outfitted to simulate handicaps) drove a ten-mile test route in Ann Arbor, Michigan. Focus was on vision, hearing and touch. After observing the three groups, the investigator compiled a list of factors that produced unease in the drivers. First and foremost were complaints about vision. The elderly subjects and controlled drivers reported difficulty with depth perception, glare and reading traffic signs at a distance. More specifically, rectangular information signs with black letters on white backgrounds, and color contrasts on street signs and traffic lights were problematic. Daniel concluded that as people age, their eyes' focal lengths take longer to shift.

Evans and Ginsburg (1985) tested thirteen volunteers aged nineteen to thirty and seven more aged fifty-five to seventy-nine. Binocular contrast sensitivity measures were obtained using three microprocessor-controlled contrast sensitivity testers. "T" and crossroad sign configurations were used. The authors found that the younger group could discriminate road signs at significantly greater distances than could the older group.

When sign identification was related to nighttime driving, Sivak et al. (1981) established that older subjects (aged sixty-two to seventy-four) perform "substantially worse" than younger drivers (eighteen to twenty-four years of age) on a nighttime legibility task using a wide range of available sign materials.

Another vision focus featured by some researchers was voluntary visual occlusion. Mourant and Mourant (1979) engaged ten young and thirteen elderly subjects in a battery of visual search, embedded figures and motor tests. Three road tests were also included to establish mean time for open eyes, visual fixation, and velocity. Thc investigators noticed that:

1. Aged drivers had longer eye open times than young drivers for all driving tasks.
2. The aged driver group had larger standard deviations than the young driver group for the two nighttime driving tasks (Mourant and Mourant 1979:250).

Based on the conclusions, the authors advised that aged drivers require more time to acquire the minimum information needed for vehicle control.

Davison (1985) expanded on vision by linking it to accidents. In a British Columbia city, police officers randomly stopped 1,000 motorists and asked them to test for vision screening. The results were correlated with personal information and driving records over the last three years. Davison concluded that hyperphoria, or vertical balance, was associated with accidents in the fifty-five and older age group, but not in the under fifty-five group. Davison's Canadian study confirmed Hills and Burg's (1977) earlier work with American drivers.

Poor vision is often discussed alongside headlight glare. Pulling et al. (1980) proposed that glare impairment in aging results from gradual degeneration of the eye lens. Light is scattered over the retina, leading to degraded image contrast. The ability to see low-contrast objects at night is lowered. After developing tests to investigate physiological glare threshold, headlight glare resistance, and subjective glare resistance, the researchers proposed that headlight glare resistance decreases significantly at sixty years of age. Panek et al. (1977) found that it was not only glare that affected elderly drivers but also that recovery time from glare situations is slower for older age groups.

Other visual problems associated with aging include a diminished visual field, cataracts, glaucoma, senile macular degeneration, and diabetes (Allen 1985). A cataract is a detrimental change in lens transmission with age that scatters and absorbs light in proportion to its severity. It reduces contrast in the retinal image so that low contrast objects may not be seen. Ongoing headlights become excessively glaring, making night driving difficult or impossible. Although persons with cataracts may pass vision tests for licensure, they usually restrict themselves to daytime driving because of the difficulties nighttime travel poses. The treatment for cataracts is surgery and spectacles, or a lens implanted in the eye. The correction that one can get is excellent. Often the implanted lens can give visual performance equivalent to that of a much younger person. Once the eyes have been corrected, the elderly drivers should have generally unimpaired vision for driving. The only blemish may be the blind zone at the edge of the lenses.

Other eye conditions may not be so treatable as cataracts. For example, glaucoma is a gradual loss of visual functioning beginning at the periphery. It is attributed to increased interocular pressure. Standard prescribed drugs lower the pressure. If this fails, surgery is advised. A dangerous side effect is that some of the glaucoma treatment drugs cause cataracts and reduce the sensitivity of the retina. These drug effects are harmful to driving. Unfortunately, our standard driving tests consisting of acuity screening or peripheral vision do not detect such vision problems.

Due to neurological change, senile macular degeneration sets in the important central macular vision area. Vision may deteriorate to 20/400 or worse, while peripheral vision may remain normal. Fortunately, this damage can be discovered in a driving test. Finally, diabetes causes a complex of visual problems which are harmful to driving: early changes in refractive error, cataracts, and diabetic retinopathy.

Physical Frailty

Ailments of advancing years are generally considered in the evaluation of elderly drivers' risk potential (Baker 1965). For example, heart and artery conditions may suddenly incapacitate elderly drivers. Arthritis, considered by gerontologists to be, in part, a degenerative disease affecting the elderly, limits the facility with which a victim can control a vehicle.

The American Medical Association publicized a series of serious ailments that affect driving ability—diabetes, thyroid, and cardiovascular diseases (Kent and Novotny 1961). The renowned medical researcher Julian Waller (1967) argued, after extensive study, that "senile oldsters" and "oldsters with cardiovascular changes" had *greater accident and violation rates* than others. But, he noted, the differences were not statistically significant.

Without pinpointing any specific diseases, Partyka (1984) argued the case that the elderly have an increased chance of fatality stemming more from their decreased resistance to crash forces than any increase in crash force experienced.

Psycho-Physiological Characteristics

In 1984, Kobayashi concluded that reaction time, particularly selective reaction time, is prolonged for elderly people aged sixty and over. Individuals in this age bracket have problems in traffic situations where quick and appropriate judgment is required. More precisely, Kent and Novotny (1961:275) pointed out that:

> The average person in his eighth decade has a reaction time in response to light that is 7.6 percent slower than that of the average teen-ager. The response to sound is 9.2 percent slower for the aged and 11 percent for brake reaction time.

As early as 1954, a physician named McFarland conceptualized that with aging comes a gradual decline in physiological and mental abilities. A young driver can better meet an emergency because he can lift his foot from the accelerator and apply brake pressure a quarter- or a half-second faster than an older individual. This finding was later verified by Wellford (1977) and Barrett et al. (1977), among others. The latter group of researchers stressed that more intensive studies should be conducted to determine if the elderly drivers' information-processing capacities and reaction times differ from younger drivers.

A popular treatise is that because of age-related physical and psychomotor degeneration, elderly drivers should be retested at regular intervals before they are granted a driver's license. For example, Jolles (1971) argued that there should be agreed-upon, acknowledged physical standards upon which normative tests determine whether the elderly are fit to drive. He warned that the motorist's personal physician should not administer the test because of their difficulties explaining to patients that they can no longer drive. Rather, a doctor specialized in "motoring" should have testing responsibilities.

Testing and Licensing

In any discussion on testing we must remind ourselves of two propositions raised by Baker (1965). The first is that senior drivers cannot be given more stringent tests than other people. To do so would be to discriminate against older drivers. The second is that we must accept the idea that older drivers may be required to be reexamined at more frequent intervals than young ones, because after middle age, faculties and abilities are much more likely to fail. The problem facing administrators is whether to examine all drivers superficially, perhaps every three years, or fewer drivers more frequently.

According to Baker, reexamination should not be an option. It must occur. Factors such as driving record (accident and driving experiences) and age are absolutely relevant. He cautioned that it is difficult to determine a specific age or a period since last examination at which older drivers should receive special attention because the age at which people begin to fail varies as much as twenty-five years. He believed that a number of reports on an older driver with a previously unblemished record would be a better clue to the need for reappraisal than any age limit or time since last examination. He did argue, however, that we should consider establishment of an age limit beyond which there must be a reappraisal of the driver's risk. This should coincide with license renewal.

Orr et al. (1986) confirmed Baker's hesitation of using age as a retesting criterion. Although they argued for retesting and reeducation, they were uncertain as to the conceptual rationality for doing so. According to the authors, it is impossible to set an age at which a driver should be retested, because everybody is different. Many elderly people experience age-related perceptual problems behind the wheel. Their eyesight is weaker from age fifty on, their hearing is poorer, and there is slower reaction time. Many have trouble judging distance, driving at night, turning, passing, reversing, and stopping suddenly.

However, Orr et al. (1986) recognized that these shortcomings are not problematic for everyone. An argument for voluntary retesting could be reasonably made.

Hedin (1980) attempted to answer the age factor as it pertains to vision. He undertook a study designed to answer four major questions: At what age should retesting take place?, Which visual functions should be included in the retest?, Who should carry out the retest?, and, Which test procedures should be established?

Hedin found no data that clearly show the break point or age at which reduction of visual acuity accelerates. So no basis for age recommendations could be made. Hedin did, however, suggest that further research projects be designed to test contrast sensitivity in nighttime driving conditions.

For most researchers, reexamination specifically for the elderly is a scientific and legal question (Wiener 1973). But several authors raised social concerns. Borchardt (1965) interviewed elderly drivers and found near consensus among them that chronological age should not be the sole criterion for measuring driving ability. The older people know that the years count. Age brings certain physical and mental impairments. But they also believe in compensating factors such as better judgment and attitudes more oriented toward safety.

Borchardt further concluded that driving is especially important for older people who, because of failing energy and minor infirmities and handicaps, have to have a reliable means of getting around. The psychological effects of driving an automobile are potent and far-reaching. It is no wonder that older persons feel a real loss of independence and that their lives are over when their licenses are not renewed.

According to Borchardt, failure to pass the test for renewal of a driver's license is a traumatic experience. The injury to the ego is so deep that many seniors never recover. Physical and mental deterioration take place. Depression and pessimism set in, especially for men. Also, senior citizens dislike the loss of a driver's license because this license serves as a means of identification when writing checks for purchases.

Borchardt (1965) believed that senior citizens know that driving a car is a privilege. They appreciate it more at sixty-five than they did at twenty. Despite the belief that old people cannot change, that they are inflexible, there is no real scientific evidence to prove this.

Wiener (1973) presented a thorough reexamination process linked directly to licensing elderly drivers. His plan is based on five basic assumptions:

1. The accident record of those drivers over sixty-five, while not the worst of the population of licensees, is worthy of concern.
2. The absolute number and proportion of drivers over sixty-five will increase in the next few decades.
3. Older drivers may require special scrutiny by officers issuing driver permits.

4. The private automobile will remain the transportation choice of Americans and Canadians with no satisfactory substitute on the horizon.
5. If the special problems of the elderly driver are ignored, not only will that population be placed at risk, but also the public interest will suffer.

Considering licensing as a control mechanism, to ensure driver quality and injury reduction is to engage in failure. The tests have low predictive validity, a major weakness that could be challenged by the courts. Since chronological age cannot be constitutionally used as a basis for denying a license or requiring special examination, Wiener proposed a driver screening test composed of several stages.

In stage one, drivers of all ages submit to a rapid screening for vision, hearing, and gross measures of sensory motor functioning. Those passing legally accepted criteria, as set by the state medical advisory boards, branch to the driving skill stage of testing. Those with remedial defects are referred to the proper source of correction: physician, optometrist, prosthesis technician, etc., and would reenter for examination. Those with serious or possibly remediable problems are referred for more extensive examination and treatment and may or may not later reenter the licensing system.

The next stage consists of testing basic driving knowledge. People with high proficiency scores are issued unconditional licenses, individuals with low scores are failed but could reappear for testing later, and those with moderate scores or certain deficiencies have a number of alternatives such as a road test with an examiner, a restrictive license, or retraining and reexamination. A few tests that Wiener would include in a test battery are:

1. A fast adapting test of visual acuity
2. A fast adapting test of auditory threshold
3. A test of vigilance
4. Various biographical and health related experience data
5. A simulated driving test
6. A simulation of emergency conditions.

Elderly Driver Education

In 1981, Beno engaged in a thorough investigation of driver education and the elderly. He articulated the fact that there was little trace of research which determines driver education needs of people over the age of fifty-five. However several programs were available for review.

Beno first concentrated on a program that originated in Denver, Colorado, in the early 1960s. Its content was pedestrian safety, skills needed to operate a motor vehicle in various environmental settings such as winter and mountain driving, and an extensive review of state and local traffic laws. Beno then expanded the discussion by describing a series of programs found in New Jersey, New York, Wisconsin, Illinois, and Florida. Topics covered in these courses were motor vehicle performance capabilities, limitations of the roadway, driving strategies, procedures for identifying hazardous driving environments, review on driver behaviors that lead to accidents, descriptions of insurance laws and state laws, driver licensing examination procedures, and rules of the road reviews.

More recently the American Association of Retired Persons and the National Retired Teachers Association (1986) introduced the "55 Alive Mature Driving Course." It is a six-hour refresher course, designed for senior citizens. It links aging to vision, hearing, reaction time, and medication to the driving task. Stressed in the program are rules of driving pertinent to the aged driver, accident-prevention measures, adverse driving conditions, other road users, local driving problems, license renewal, and perpetual problems to be encountered in various driving environments. Most of these programs have one common element—all are refresher courses for the already licensed driver.

According to the OECD (1985) there are a number of major impediments to successful elderly driver education. Trying to change the behavior of the elderly is not only a problem of conveying information and training for defensive skills. Behavior is strongly influenced by stereotypes held by contemporary society, as well as the society from which the elderly (early in life) acquired some predominant views on aging. The elderly's attitudes may reflect:

1. Fatalism: their problems are accepted as the expected and inevitable effects of aging.
2. Pessimism: even when their situation could in principle be helped, they consider it to be a waste of time and effort as they have seen failure so often in their life.
3. Suspicion: offers of help and suggestions are seen as attacks on their integrity, symptomatic of a society that wishes to limit their independence.
4. Self-assertion: they do not see themselves as the ones who should change their behavior—people of their age deserve respect and it is up to other people to adapt their behavior.
5. Bias: feelings that they are now being discriminated against—suggestions that age obliges them to consider limiting or even abandoning driving without regard for individual differences in performance are considered proof of age discrimination.

In spite of the obvious importance of the attitude problem, there is practically no research on how the elderly view different situations in life and how this affects their behavior.

To overcome the five shortcomings, the OECD recommended a three-pronged strategy: the individual approach (e.g., primary health care team communicate information to the elderly), the group approach (e.g., giving lectures to clubs or senior citizen residences), and the mass media (nation- or region-wide appeals through campaigns). Here the message should be specific, comprehensive, and unambiguous.

Assumptions About Testing and Educating the Elderly

It might prove useful that, at this time, we stop for a brief moment and reflect on testing and educating elderly drivers. To help us, we could review Hollis' (1977:5, 74) model of "plastic" and "autonomous" people. Whereas the "plastic" person is "[a] programmed feedback system, whose inputs, outputs and inner workings can be given many interpretations," the "autonomous" elderly person has "some species of substantial self within. . . . He has a clear interest in a notion of role which is both a source of reasons for action and a vehicle giving him control of his own social life."

If researchers view the elderly as actors in life-encompassing plays, they assume those people to be autonomous. However, if researchers believe that the elderly identities are socially created and their behaviors are technically defined, they are considered plastic.

The typical recommendations researchers have made for testing and educating elderly drivers are built on the framework of "plastic." The elderly drivers' roles and positions are determined, and all matters of performance and individual embodiments are predefined. They are considered to be growing problems, more inclined to be involved in accidents per mile than . . . , road hazards, traffic safety risks, in part because they are physically and psychologically unfit to drive.

A consequence of this position is that researchers consider all elderly people within the expectations of the definition. This assumption paves the way for greater control of elderly people's actions. Legislation is introduced to control driving privileges; reeducation programs are designed to change elderly driver attitudes and behavior. Universally accepted behavioral norms which are beyond time, place, and criticism can now thrive in the refined actions of the elderly.

In a normative sense, the elderly drivers have internalized roles and functions related to their physical status, and their understanding of society's priorities. This realization helps certain traffic safety professionals control the elderly. If the elderly drivers are what they are defined to be because they lack the power to redefine themselves, they can be easily reprogrammed to meet certain ends.

Labonte and Penfold (1981) referred to this situation as "victim-blaming." The emphasis is on the weakness of the person as he or she represents all persons of a group. Social structures that may constrain individual behavior and life-style choices are obscured.

Traffic Factors

The social etiology of the elderly drivers marked in the biomedical writings is similar in descriptions of traffic factors. Here again they are considered to be victims of age.

Research on age and driving has found that significant age-related changes that affect driving start around age fifty-five. However, there is limited confidence in this claim. Some changes may start as early as fifty. In the United States, drivers fifty-five and over constitute 22 percent of the licensed drivers (i.e., there are about 25 million drivers). Those over sixty-five constitute about 10 percent of the drivers. By the year 2000 it is projected that 28 percent of drivers in the United States will be over the age of sixty-five.

Canadian census data also suggest that the percentage of licensed drivers fifty-five and over is increasing steadily. According to Statistics Canada (1986), drivers over the age of fifty-five comprised 19.6 percent of the total driver population. There are, however, dramatic differences among provinces. To illustrate, the proportion of licensed drivers aged fifty-five plus for the following Canadian provinces are: Saskatchewan, 23.3 percent; Manitoba, 22 percent; Ontario, 21.7 percent; British Columbia, 21.5 percent; Quebec, 16.8 percent and Alberta, 14.9 percent. For British Columbia the proportion of elderly drivers, by the year 2000, is expected to rise to over 30 percent. This is consistent with Devereaux's (1986) census highlight that the high growth rate of the Canadian population aged sixty-five and over will continue into the next century.

In an award-winning essay entitled, "Aging and Driving," Marsh (1960:14) maintained that twelve main factors dominate the increase in elderly licensed drivers. They are as relevant today as they were at the time the article was published. In abbreviated form they are:

1. The rapid increase in the number of motor vehicles and drivers since the mid-1920s.
2. The strong desire of numbers of people to continue to drive while past sixty-five.
3. The greatly increasing numbers living to old age.
4. The oncoming greatly increased number of women drivers reaching age fifty-five.
5. The increasing proportion of the population becoming drivers.
6. Improving health of those in their sixties and above.
7. Improving economic status of many who are and become sixty-five and over.
8. Much more leisure with the advent of a shorter work week for many still employed and, as the increase in retirement plans and other benefits result in more retirements at age sixty-five, one of the popular uses of driving will be leisure.

9. Good roads and increasing paved mileages make driving more attractive.
10. Easy availability of needed and desired services along the road.
11. Cars which are dependable, simple to operate, and which, with power steering and braking, require only light physical exertion to drive.
12. The growing dispersion of places of residence in suburban areas.

Despite mitigating factors such as health impairments, economic problems, diminishing driving competence, automobile insurance difficulties and potential for decrease in self-confidence, the outlook, according to Marsh, is that for years into the future there will be "very large" increases in the numbers of drivers aged sixty-five and over. Looking at Marsh's conclusion retrospectively, it is evident that the driving span of years has certainly increased in the 1980s and will continue to do so for the next thirty years.

Within the real and projected increase in the number of elderly drivers on the road lies the claim that, on the basis of statistical ratios, the number of accidents and motor vehicle fatalities will rise. What the research literature has to say on this assumption will be discussed next.

Accident Involvement

Accident statistics that publicly display elderly drivers and their accident involvement are usually illustrated in one of two ways. The first is accident index, frequently used by the National Safety Council and other safety oriented agencies. In short, it is the percent of accidents measured against the percent of drivers in any given category (Kent and Novotny 1961). The second frame within which statistics are organized is exposure. Rates are based on the annual distance travelled by a particular age group, or the number of accidents per mile driven.

The benchmark study on accident index is Finesilver's (1969) statistical evaluation of motor vehicle collisions. After the author analyzed accident data and driver populations from thirty-one jurisdictions in the United States, he concluded that "the older driver has less than his proportionate share of all accidents, fatal accidents and injury accidents." Although elderly drivers represented 7.4 percent of all drivers, they were involved in only 4.8 percent of all accidents. Similar findings were demonstrated by Freeman (1972) and Torpey (1986).

Data from the 1982 National Accident Sampling System showed that the incidence of moderate-through-fatal injury decreased with driver age. For example, drivers under the age of twenty-one sustained 28.4 moderate to fatal injuries for every 1,000 licensed drivers. The elderly, by comparison, only sustained 6.2 injuries per 1,000 motorists—a ratio just over a fifth of that for the young. However, once we document fatalities, the picture changes. While the under-twenty-one age group is overrepresented at 39.4 fatalities per 100,000 licensed drivers, the elderly, that is, people over sixty-five, have a ratio of 14.2 fatalities per 100,000 drivers. This is over a third of the young-driver ratio.

According to the OECD and WHO (1985), when the injuries for the group sixty-five and over in eighteen member countries was compared with the injuries for the twenty-five to sixty-four year old drivers, an index of .4 was established. This may be a high estimate of real accident involvement. Compared to the younger driver, there is an increased probability for the elderly accident victim to become injured. Also, the injuries were not accurately recorded in some less-advanced OECD countries. The ratio between relative fatality and relative casualty is a more valid estimate of elderly traffic casualties. The overall value of this estimate is 2.66. This indicates that the elderly traffic casualty dies from the injuries around two to three times more often than do traffic casualties in the twenty-five to sixty-four year old group.

After Winter (1984) reviewed a series of studies, she determined that older drivers (over sixty-five) have the lowest median accident involvement index of any age group. But because they are less likely to survive accidents, they are more likely to be involved in fatal accidents than drivers within the thirty-five to sixty-four year old range.

These data are a little blurry. They do not recognize the difference the annual number of miles driven makes. To compare accident indices between countries may prove deceptive because we do not know the relative distance different age groups in different countries travel or the state of the roadway environment.

Indeed, when exposure is considered—how many miles driven, where, when, and so forth—elderly drivers have higher rates of accidents than drivers in the middle years (Burg 1968; Planek and Overend 1973). It is this rate of accident involvement researchers today believe is the most accurate and penetrates most deeply into the problematic area of elderly drivers.

Marsh (1960) was one of the first researchers to maintain that the best measure of accident rates is accidents compared to miles driven. He based his decision, in part, on a classical study completed in 1948-49 by Dr. Lauer, who noted that accidents per 100,000 miles driven increase sharply for both men and women over the age of sixty. Marsh reinforced the notion that for the over-sixty-four age group, involvement in accidents is much more frequent at low speeds on main rural roads than at higher speeds. In summary, he stated that mileage driven should be ascertained and any comparison between age groups should account for accidents as a function of miles driven. Other exposure factors such as proportion of driving in daytime and proportion of driving in rural areas should also be ascertained for reliable accident statistics.

Allgaier (1965) made the salient point that there is very little information on the actual miles driven by persons in any age group. He did assume, however, that above a certain age, people do less driving and less walking. To test his hypothesis, Allgaier asked 5,451 motorists of various age ranges to estimate their annual driving mileage. Much to his surprise, people in the sixty- to seventy-five-year range judged their annual miles driven to be relatively high, with responses averaging 10,400 miles. Allgaier considered these numbers to be unreliable, "on the high side." Still he argued that it makes more sense to compare groups involved in accidents according to mileage data. The difficulty in the procedure is to arrive at reliable estimates.

Waller (1972) also assumed that the elderly drive fewer miles per year than do younger drivers. But she introduced a new twist. It was her belief that part of the reason for high crash rates among the elderly was simply the fact that they drive low mileages. She quoted studies that indicated low-mileage drivers of any age are worse drivers per mile than high-mileage drivers. Unfortunately, the data upon which these studies were based depended completely upon self-reported trips made by only a fragment of households in the United States. Therefore, they should be viewed with some caution. Waller concluded that according to the accident index, the elderly form a relatively safe group of drivers involved in fewer accidents than drivers of any other age group. But when measured by exposure, there is a possibility that they do have accidents out of proportion to the time they spend on the road.

According to Planek et al. (1968), many drivers start to exhibit a decline in the number of miles driven at the age of fifty-five. More recently the OECD and WHO (1985) reported that the annual distance travelled by the elderly is, on average, considerably lower than distance travelled by younger age groups. To illustrate:

United States	30% lower
Sweden	35%
United Kingdom	37%
Germany	40%
Netherlands	43%
Denmark	45%

Younger groups use the automobile for about 76 percent of the distance they travel each year (as driver and passenger) while the elderly travel only 55 percent of their annual distance in an automobile. The proportion of distance travelled by the elderly in autos is about evenly split between drivers (29 percent) and passengers (26 percent). By contrast, the younger age groups are almost three times more likely to travel as drivers than as passengers (56 percent vs. 20 percent).

Although older drivers do not drive as great a distance as younger drivers, the frequency with which they use their vehicles does not differ much from younger drivers. Data on distance travelled and frequency of use suggests that the travel pattern of the elderly driver involves reasonably frequent but short distance trips (OECD and WHO, 1985).

With a reduction in miles driven comes a decrease in exposure to what might be called difficult driving situations such as rush hour, daily driving, driving after dark, and winter travel (Planek 1973). When male drivers were asked how often they drive in rush hour, 46 to 50 percent of the twenty-five to sixty-four year old members answered about once a day. However, less than 30 percent of those aged sixty to sixty-nine and only 15 percent of those seventy to seventy-four said once a day. Past the age of seventy-five, the percent drops to about 10 percent. The numbers are similar for women.

High-risk exposure night driving is also believed to decline steadily with age, as does winter driving. For drivers past sixty-five, night driving comprises about 9 percent of total driving, while for drivers fifty-five to sixty-four it comprises 20 percent, and for the twenty-five to fifty-four year olds, 24 percent.

In summary, what is generally known and assumed in the traffic safety research world is that decrease in driving occurs with increase in age. So accident rates per miles driven increase. The decrease in mileage found among older drivers may reflect the more difficult miles—the high-risk exposure times.

Accident Types

Overall, accident data arising from studies done in the 1950s and 1960s indicate that the elderly have higher rates of accident involvement arising from actions such as failure to yield the right of way, turning improperly, ignoring stop signs and red lights, and starting up improperly into traffic. Recent data have not altered this picture. The elderly also tend to be overly involved in accidents resulting from changing lanes, merging, or leaving from a parked position, giving the appearance that the elderly have difficulty with complex driving situations. Brainin (1980) supported these conclusions. He cited left-hand turns at uncontrolled intersections as a particular problem for elderly drivers. He also confirmed that inattention to traffic, failure to yield the right-of-way or obey stop signs, and traffic lights are accident causation factors specifically identified with elderly motorists. The situation gets worse once the drivers reach the age of seventy-five. It must also be said that Brainin found no evidence that slow driving, backing-up, or changing lanes were substantial causes of accidents.

An Australian researcher, Henderson, generally agreed with previous research findings. He imputed personal factors to the causes. For Henderson (1971) the fact that elderly drivers' sensory and motor capacities, in many cases, fell behind the requirements of the increasingly complicated traffic situations meant that these individuals are more likely to be involved in accidents because of failure to yield or give the right of way, turning at inappropriate times, and ignoring advisory and mandatory road signs.

Partyka (1984) took issue with former researchers who attributed such a wide scope of blame to the elderly motorists. Her review of data related to surviving drivers in two-car fatal crashes showed that failure to yield was a contributing factor for drivers over sixty-five, far out of proportion to other drivers. But she also found that there was no difference between the elderly and other age groups in things like inattention or failure to observe traffic signs or control signals. But, Partyka's data did illustrate that turning incidents predominated in accidents involving elderly drivers. The researcher placed parentheses around the latter finding. She had some reservations about the data she analyzed, which did not specify types of turns and did not clarify whether the turns were generally a factor for all drivers over sixty-five or just a factor for a small group such as those over seventy-five.

"A Review of Traffic Collisions in Washington" (1986), prepared by the State of Washington Traffic Safety Commission, reported on contributing circumstances in collisions. The driver population was broken down into fifty-five to fifty-nine, sixty to sixty-four, sixty-five to sixty-nine, seventy to seventy-four, seventy-five and older groups. In all five age groups, the highest percentage of collisions involved failure to yield right-of-way. The number of collisions reflecting this cause increased with age. For example, for the fifty-five to fifty-nine group, it was 29.4 percent; for the sixty to sixty-four group, it was 35 percent; sixty-five to sixty-nine group, 37.7 percent; seventy to seventy-four, 42 percent; seventy-five and older, 49.1 percent. The second most frequent contributing factor for the fifty-five to fifty-nine age group and the sixty to sixty-four year-old group was driving too fast for conditions (fifty-five to fifty-nine was 12.6 percent, sixty to sixty-four was 11.8 percent). For the oldest three age groups; sixty-five to sixty-nine, seventy to seventy-four and seventy-five and older, however, the second most prevalent contributing circumstance was disregarding traffic signs (10.4 percent, 11.5 percent, 11.3 percent respectively). Other contributing circumstances were following too closely, driving while under the influence, operating defective equipment, crossing over the center line and exceeding the legal speed limit.

With cause comes blame. A California Department of Motor Vehicles report (1982) clearly demonstrated that "older drivers" in accidents were more often considered to be at fault by law enforcement agencies than members from other age groups. With respect to convictions, drivers seventy or older were more often convicted of violating laws pertaining to traffic signs and signals, right-of-way, and turning. This trend repeated itself in data presented by the California Department of Motor Vehicles (1982).

In South Australia, the demerit point records indicated that the frequency of various traffic offenses per thousand license holders increased after the age of eighty. Failure to give the right-of-way increased strongly with age. German traffic accident statistics on car-to-car collisions also show elderly drivers to have a higher responsibility ratio (OECD and WHO 1985). The ratio is based on the calculated share of responsibility. For example, a ratio of "greater than one" means that more than 50 percent of a group of drivers in accidents is responsible and, therefore, less than 50 percent is not responsible. If causation odds for car-to-car injury accidents (according to age) are considered, the ratios are determined to be: sixty-five to sixty-nine—1.62; seventy to seventy-four—2.28; seventy-five to seventy-nine—4.00; and eighty to eighty-four—3.67. This can be contrasted with an average causation ratio of 1.07 for twenty-five to sixty-four year olds.

Gender Differences

Based on the literature, the elderly driver on the road is more likely to be a man than a woman. Women drivers between the ages of twenty-five and fifty-four represent 45.3 percent of all American drivers in that age group. The proportion of female drivers drops to 40.9 percent in the sixty to sixty-four age bracket and to 33.1 percent among drivers aged seventy and over. This is surprising in light of the fact that, on average, women live seven years longer than men.

Men who drive an average of 19,000 miles a year when they are in their thirties and forties drive 16,000 miles annually at the age of fifty and fewer than 14,000 miles by the time they are sixty. This figure falls to 7,000 miles a year for men seventy-five and over. Women drive considerably less than men, but the dropoff is less dramatic. They drive about 8,000 miles annually in their thirties and forties. This number falls to 7,000 miles for women in their late fifties, is further reduced to 6,000 miles at age sixty-five, and to 4,000 miles by the time they are seventy-five years old.

A life-span rationale may prove fruitful at explaining the difference. Whereas the sudden decline in men's annual mileage is related to retirement from the work force, for elderly women there is a tendency to maintain a level of activity experienced in younger years (Planek et al. 1973).

A report on data collected by the Insurance Institute for Highway Safety (1982) indicates that among elderly drivers, women were more likely than men to be responsible for both one- and two-car crashes. Also, the number of female drivers is increasing at a rate faster than that for male drivers (Winter 1984). Between the ages of sixty-nine and seventy-eight, the number of licenses issued to women older than fifty-nine increased 10.8 percent. The estimated ratio of male to female drivers declined from 7.6 to 3.2 percent.

These changing trends could be a result of more women living longer than men. This brings on new problems. In a survey of widows, the following female-relevant problems were enumerated: women had only recently learned how to drive, they were afraid to drive on freeways and to drive at night, and they had visual problems which interfered with driving (Winter 1984). The problems outlined by Winter surely transcend gender. Nevertheless, they are relevant to women.

As older beginners, women's traffic risks increase sharply. In a 1982 article entitled, "Crashes that Kill: Who's Responsible and Why?" a *Journal of American Insurance* writer, unnamed, reviewed a study completed by the Insurance Institute for Highway Safety. The author (1982-83:26-27) concluded that:

> . . . responsibility for fatal crashes most likely rested with drivers in two extreme age groups: the very young and the very old . . . up to about the age 35 in the case of two vehicle crashes, and age 55 in both one and two vehicle crashes, men were more likely than women to be responsible for the fatal crash. Among elderly drivers, however, women were more likely than men to be responsible.

Drinking and Driving

Parker et al. (1983) introduced their study on elderly drinking-driving offenders with the claim that, according to the research, problem drinking in the population over age sixty is based primarily on low socioeconomic status and stressful life changes such as death of a spouse. Based on interviews with ninety-two DWI offenders in Mississippi, Parker et al. (1983:435) stated that:

1. The occurrence of a first-time DWI offense at an older age is related to the occurrence of potentially stressful events.
2. Drinking problems early in life might predispose individuals to experience some types of life stressors, possibly compounding the increased risk of social losses associated with growing older.

The State of Washington Traffic Safety Commission (1986) reported that for the fifty-five-and-older age group, the number of weekend accidents involving alcohol is fewer per driver population than for other groups. For example, of drivers involved in alcohol-related collisions, 6.2 percent were aged fifty-five and over. However, this age group made up 23.8 percent of licensed drivers. By comparison, drivers thirty to fifty-four made up 47.9 percent of licensed drivers, and 34.4 percent of those involved in alcohol-related collisions. On the other end of the scale, sixteen to twenty year-old drivers constituted 17.1 percent of those in alcohol-related crashes, but were only 7.7 percent of all licensed drivers.

The analysis of epidemiological data and other statistical artifacts has been the central thrust for researching elderly drivers and accident involvement. These means-ends data are the bench marks upon which much empirical research is done.

Nontechnical Perspectives on Elderly Drivers

Hermeneutics

There is evidence that several research projects began with a hermeneutic perspective—understanding life without prescribed lenses. Rather than ask, "What are the elderly drivers?", researchers asked, "Who are the elderly drivers?"

Within the "understanding framework," elderly drivers are considered to be autonomous individuals who can control their actions by means of adjustments, reasoning rituals, and negotiations. They do not only have identities defined and thrust upon them, but they also have a repertoire of behavior appropriate to a different set of contingencies (Goffman 1971).

Hollis (1977) quoted Sharif (1977:89):

> Self is a developmental formation in the psychological make-up of the individual, consisting of interrelated attitudes that the individual has acquired in relation to his own body and its parts, to his capacities and to objects, persons, family groups, social values, goals, and institutions, which define and regulate his relatedness to them in concrete situations and activities.

Binion provided excellent insight of the understanding perspective related to an elderly driver's self and life contingencies. Her text (1986:28) read:

> "I drive about the same as I did 25 years ago," explains Ethel, age 76, who drives mostly on Chicago's congested streets. "I still have good reflexes. And I check my mirrors constantly. When another driver cuts me off or does something stupid, I curse. I say the most awful things! My husband laughs, because he would never dream of using that kind of language."
>
> Ethel's husband, Al, only recently got his license back after an eight-month suspension. Al had failed his eye exam. His vision problem was diagnosed as macular degeneration. A specialist prescribed corrective lenses that allowed Al to pass the vision test, and Al now has a restricted license that permits driving in daylight hours only and requires frequent vision retesting. But Ethel says Al's restored driving privileges, even though limited, have given him a new lease on life, making him feel less dependent and powerless.

In 1960 Marsh presented the research world with a challenge to head toward an "understanding" perspective. Although Marsh's basic thrust in his article was technological, he felt that there was a need "for the development of a whole senior driver program, of many parts." Functional age should be stressed over biological age. This would include recognition of elderly drivers' corrections and compensations for potential detrimental effects due to the aging process.

Several elderly-driver projects addressed the individual as an autonomous person. A person-focus code was used. Henderson and Kole (1965) wrote about understanding the elderly drivers' need for independence and mobility—their frustration with society. Group discussion techniques were used. Practical experiences were considered to be primary data sources for research.

When an understanding perspective is employed by researchers, it signifies an interest in the life-world—sharing and creating reality. The driving world becomes an environment of multiple meanings and behaviors at the personal level.

Critical

A few sources in the elderly driver literature included a critical perspective. Authors who stressed this viewpoint examined or questioned the views and/or findings found in other research reports. These researchers promoted a theory of person and society that is rooted in self-determination; they shared an interest in liberating the elderly from bureaucratic and empirical control.

The critical papers that were reviewed were select. They did not compare in numbers to the abundant technologically oriented reports. But, the ones that were reviewed included strong statements reflecting the need for self-determination. Witness:

> With the senior citizens, the renewal of a driver's license is a very big issue. The entire business is fraught with and accompanied by mental anguish. From renewal to renewal, it occupies the mind consciously and unconsciously. The individual loses confidence with so much at stake, and with the departure of assurance often will not even try to take the test. This should not be! [Borchardt 1965:7]

> In dealing with this older age group we must be aware of their need for independence and mobility. As long as the senior citizen is frustrated in his attempt to be part of society, we are faced with manpower loss—a losing battle in which the skills and achievements of this individual are wasted [Henderson and Kole 1965:3].

In the technologically framed articles, elderly drivers were pulled out of the ongoing stream of life because they were different; namely, they were problems. Follow-up actions were designed to remove or solve problems. In the critically framed papers, the authors focused on equality. The elderly situation was reviewed within the overall confines of driving. Stereotypes or stigmas that were evident in so many articles were seriously questioned. Examine:

> The elderly driver has been accused of being a road hazard and of being responsible for more than his share of the ever-mounting number of automotive accidents. Examination of existing data and studies reveals insufficient evidence to warrant this conclusion. Periodic examinations and other measures designed to decrease accidents are appropriate for all age groups. To single out the aged is discriminatory.
>
> This search for causes has turned the spotlight upon elderly drivers, with many people accusing them of being road hazards. It is our contention that facts now available do not support this conclusion and that this view of older drivers stems from an unrealistic stereotype [Kent and Novotny 1961:271].
>
> Judge Finesilver expressed the opinion that "the senior driver has been made a scapegoat. The widespread beliefs that the older motorist is a 'nuisance' or a 'hazard' may not be justified [*Traffic Safety Editor* 1969:20]."
> Learning should be a requirement of citizenship in later life. As part of continuous learning, driver improvement courses should be included and be required of all age groups. Thus bad driving habits can be corrected and hostile and aggressive attitudes on the road changed [Borchardt 1965:7].

The above illustrations support the fundamental assumption of critical analysis, namely that there is a need to focus on rationalizations and typifications that serve as institutional barriers for alternative viewpoints. The critical writers outlined the social and existential weaknesses of the predominant elderly driver problem stance, or worse yet the perspective offered by Baker (1965) that older drivers, regardless of other age groups, have specific driving problems.

Conclusion

There is an overwhelming technological perspective underlying elderly-driver research. The elderly are either explicitly defined, or implicitly assumed, to have problems resulting from biological, cognitive, and social degeneration. There is little emphasis upon their everyday reality. There are but a few research studies that have moved beyond the technical design of aggregate data analysis and survey methodology to include interviews, content analysis, and observation.

In point form, the traditional context for elderly driver research is composed of the following established conclusions or major thoughts:

1. The percentage of people fifty-five and over who are licensed drivers has been increasing steadily since the 1960s and will continue to increase into the 2000s.
2. There are two major accident involvement propositions: the accident index and driving exposure. The first, a ratio of the percent of accidents to the percent of drivers, shows that the elderly drivers are underrepresented in accident statistics. On the basis of exposure, or annual miles driven, the elderly drivers are the second most problematic age group of all drivers.

3. In the majority of accidents in which elderly drivers were involved, the senior motorists were to blame for such actions as failure to yield the right of way, turning improperly, ignoring traffic signals, and starting up improperly into traffic.
4. With respect to drinking and driving, the elderly drivers, compared to other drivers, are considered to be underinvolved according to number of alcohol-related collisions per population of licensed drivers.
5. Aging means degeneration of physical and psychomotor abilities. More precisely, vision factors such as depth perception, glare, visual occlusion, and hyperphoria are problematic for elderly drivers, placing them in higher driving risk categories. Physical frailty makes elderly drivers more prone to become fatalities in collisions, and slower reaction time and coordination makes them less able to deal with emergency driving maneuvers.
6. Because age brings with it physical impairments that increase the risk of traffic accidents, elderly drivers should be retested, but not on the basis of chronological age.
7. Elderly driver education programs are usually refresher courses that do not focus on researched driving needs.

References

AAA Foundation For Traffic Safety. 1985. *Drivers 55 Plus: Needs and Problems of Older Drivers*. Proceedings Of The Older Driver Colloquium, Orlando, FL: February 4-7.

Allen, M.J. 1985. "Vision of the Older Driver: Implications for Vehicle and Highway Design for Driver Testing." In *Needs and Problems of Older Drivers: Survey Results and Recommendations*. Proceedings of the Older Driver Colloquium, Orlando, FL: February 4-7.

Allgaier, E. 1965. "Accident Involvement of Senior Drivers." *Traffic Digest and Review*, 3(3), pp. 17-19.

Aoki, T. (Ed.). 1978. *Curriculum Evaluation In A New Key*. Vancouver: Centre for the Study of Curriculum and Instruction, University of British Columbia.

Aristotle. 1968. *Poetics*. Englewood Cliffs, NJ: Prentice-Hall.

Aron, R. 1968. *Main Current In Sociological Thought I*. Garden City, NY: Anchor Books.

Baker, J.S. 1965. "Evaluating The Older Driver." *Traffic Digest and Review*, 13(3), pp. 23-30.

Barrett, G.V., W.L. Mihal, P.E. Panek, H.L. Sterns, and R.A. Alexander. 1977. "Information Processing Skills Predictive of Accident Involvement for Younger and Older Commercial Drivers." *Industrial Gerontology*, 4(3), pp. 173-82.

Belbin, E. 1956. "The Effects of Propaganda on Recall Recognition and Perception." *British Journal of Psychology*, 47, pp 259-70.

Beno, J.A. 1981. "Driving Education Programs For the Aged: The State of the Art." *Educational Gerontology*, 7, pp. 89-96.

Binion, J. 1986. "Key Advice for Older Drivers." *Family Safety and Health*, 45(4), pp. 28-30.

Birren, J.E. 1965. "Age Changes in Speed of Behavior: Its Central Nature and Physiological Correlates." In A.T. Welford and J.E. Birren (Eds.), *Behavior, Aging and the Nervous System*. Springfield, IL: Charles, C. Thomas.

Borchardt, B. 1965. "Licensing the Senior Driver." *Traffic Digest and Review*, 13(3), pp. 7-8.

Botwinik, J. 1973. *Aging and Behavior: A Comprehensive Integration of Research Findings*. New York: Springer Publishing Co., Inc.

Brainin, P. 1980. "Safety and Mobility Issues in Licensing and Education of Older Drivers." Washington, DC: U.S. Dept. of Transportation.

Briggs, R.P. 1987. "Is Selective Screening of Older Drivers for Vision Feasible?" Proceedings of Human Factors Society— 31st Annual Meeting.

Burg, A. 1968. "Vision and Driving." *Highway Research Record*, 216, pp. 1-12.

California Dept. of Motor Vehicles. 1982. *Senior Driver Facts: Report Number 82*.

Carp, F. 1971. "On Becoming an Ex-driver: Prospect and Retrospect." *Gerontologist*, 11(2), pp. 101-3.

Combs, A.W. 1979. *Myths In Education*. Boston: Allyn and Bacon, Inc.

Corso, J.F. 1971. "Sensory Processes and Age Effects in Normal Adults." *Journal of Gerontology*, 26, pp. 90-105.

Coser, L. 1971. *Masters of Sociological Thought*. New York: Harcourt Brace Jovanovich.

Craik, F.I.M. 1965. "The Nature of the Age Decrement in Performance on Dichotic Listening Tasks." *Quarterly Journal of Experimental Psychology*, 17, pp. 227-40.

Cresswell, W.L., and P. Froggatt. 1962. *Causation of Bus Driver Accidents: An Epidemiological Study*. London: Oxford University Press.

Daniel, G. 1978. "Older Drivers . . . More Courteous? More Careful? More Dangerous?" *Retirement Living*, pp. 20-22.

Davison, Peter A. 1985. Interrelationships between British Drivers' Visual Abilities, Age and Road Accident Histories. *Ophthalmology, Physiology and Optometry*, 5(2), pp. 195-204.

de Coppens, P. 1976. *Ideal Man in Classical Sociology*. University Park: Pennsylvania State University Press.

Destrem, H. 1964. "On Driving of Cars by Elderly Persons." Symposium, Gerontological Society of Bordeaux.

Devereaux, M.M. 1987. "Aging of the Canadian Population." *Canadian Social Trends*. Winter.

Drews, E.M., and L. Lipson. 1971. *Values and Humanity*. New York: St. Martin's Press.

Edie, J.M. 1965. *An Invitation to Phenomenology: Studies in the Philosophy of Experience*. Chicago: Quadrangle Books.

Egerbrink, H.O., P.F. Lourens, and H. van der Moler. 1986. "Driving Strategies Among Younger and Older Drivers When Encountering Children." *Accident Analysis and Prevention*, 18(4), pp. 315-24.

Evans, D.W., and A.P. Ginsburg. 1985. "Contrast Sensitivity Predicts Age-Related Differences in Highway-Sign Discriminability." *Human Factors*, 27(6), pp. 635-42.

Fales, Edward. 1981. "Are Automakers Listening to the Older Driver? *50 Plus*, pp. 13-17.

Finesilver, S.G. 1969. "How Safe are Senior Drivers?" *Traffic Safety*, 69(4), pp. 20–21.

______. 1985. "Let's Keep Older Drivers on the Road." *Traffic Digest and Review*, 13(3), pp. 4-6.

———. 1969. "The Older Driver—A Statistical Evaluation of Licensing and Accident Involvement in 30 States." Denver: University of Denver College of Law.

Finn, P., and B.W. Bragg. 1986. "Perception of the Risk of an Accident by Young and Older Drivers." *Accident Analysis and Prevention*, 18(4), pp. 289-96.

Ford, Larry. 1986. 55-Alive Mature Driving Program. *California Highway Patrolman*, 50(2), pp. 89-90.

Freeman, J.T. 1972. "Elderly Drivers: Growing Numbers and Growing Problems." *Geriatrics*, pp. 46-56.

Gilbert, N.G., and M. Mulkay. 1984. *Opening Pandora's Box: A Sociological Analysis of Scientists' Discourse*. Cambridge: Cambridge University Press.

Goffman, I. 1963. *Stigma*. Englewood Cliffs, NJ: Prentice-Hall.

Gordon D.A., Hugh W. McGee, and Kevin G. Hooper. 1984. Driver Characteristics Impacting Highway Design and Operations. *Public Roads*, 48(1), pp. 12-16.

Gouldner, A. 1971. *The Coming Crisis In Western Sociology*. New York: Avon Equinox.

Hames, L. 1974. "Driving Problems of the Elderly." *Traffic Safety*, 74(7), pp. 21; 37-38.

Handler, P. 1960. "Radiation And Aging." In N.W. Shock (Ed.), *Aging*. Washington, DC: American Association for the Advancement of Science.

Hedin, Anders. 1980. Retesting of Vehicle Driver's Visual Capacity. *Journal of Traffic Medicine*, 3(8), pp. 18-21.

Heinonen, M., and T. Makinnen. 1981. "Knowledge of an Opinion Concerning Road Safety of the Aged." Central Organisation for Traffic Safety in Finland.

Henderson, H.L., and T. Kole. 1965. "Senior Citizens Can Drive Safely." Supplement No. 5 to Bulletin, Adding Life To Years, Iowa City: University of Iowa.

Henderson, M.A. 1971. "Traffic Accidents and the Aged." Contribution to the *Journal of Geriatrics*. Traffic Accident Research Unit. Department of Motor Transport. New South Wales.

Hills, B.L., and A. Burg. 1977. A Reanalysis of California Driver Vision Data: General Findings. *Transport and Road Research Laboratory Suppl. Report.*

Hollis, M. 1977. *Models of Man: Philosophical Thoughts on Social Action*. Cambridge: Cambridge University Press.

Hopkin, J.M., P. Robson, and S.W. Town. 1978. "The Mobility of Old People: A Study in Guildford." *Transport and Road Research Laboratory*, Report LR 850. Crowthorne.

Hugunin, E. 1960. *What's Ahead for the Aging Driver*? Chicago: National Safety Council.

Insurance Institute for Highway Safety. 1982. *Status Report*, 17(13), pp. 1-2.

Jolles, K. 1971. "The Elderly Driver." *Autocar*, 135(3952).

Journal of American Insurance. 1982-83. "Crashes That Kill: Who's Responsible and Why?" pp. 26-28.

Kaneto, Y. 1980. "The Aged in a Society on Wheels." *IATSS Research Vol. 4*.

Karsten, A., J. Jeuk, V. Schmidt, and A. Trilling. 1977. "The Present Situation of Traffic Information and Education for Old People in the Federal Republic of Germany." In A.S. Hackert (Ed.), Proc. Int. Conf. Ped. Safety. Haifa.

Kent, D., and G. Novotny. 1961. "Age and Automotive Accidents." *Geriatrics*, pp. 271-77.

Kevelson, R. 1983. *The Inverted Pyramid: An Introduction to a Semiotics of Media Language*. Bloomington: Indiana University Press.

King, H.F. 1955. Age Analysis of some Agricultural Accidents. *Occupational Psychology*, 29, pp. 245-53.

Kobayashi, M. 1984. "Driver Behavior and Accident Characteristics of Elderly Drivers in Japan." *IATSS Research Vol. 8.*

Kuhn, T.S. 1966. *The Structure of Scientific Revolutions*. Chicago: University of Chicago.

Labonte, R., and S. Penfold. 1981. *Health Promotion Philosophy: From Victim-Blaming to Social Responsibility*. Vancouver: Western Region Office, Health and Welfare Canada.

Lakoff, G., and M. Johnson. 1980. *Metaphors We Live By*. Chicago: University of Chicago Press.

McFarland, R.A., G.S. Tune, and A.T. Welford. 1964. "On Driving of Automobiles by Older People." *Journal of Gerontology*, 19(2), pp. 190-97.

______. 1966. "The Older Driver and Accidents." *Police*.

______. 1954. "Problems of Older Drivers in Relation to Highway Safety." Massachusetts Governors Highway Safety Conference.

Malfetti, J.L., and D.J. Winter. 1978. "Development of a Traffic Safety and Alcohol Programme for Senior Adults." Safety Research and Education Project, Teachers College. New York: Columbia University.

Mann, W.A. 1960. "Problems of the Older Driver." *MSU Center Letter*, pp. 3-5.

Marsh, B.W. 1960. "Aging and Driving." *Traffic Engineering*, 31(2), pp. 11-29.

Marsh, B.W. 1985. The Driving Situation and Drivers 55+: Comments by a Long Interested Retired Traffic Engineer. In *Needs and Problems of Older Drivers: Survey Results and Recommendations*. Proceedings of the Older Driver Colloquium, Orlando, Florida. AAA Foundation for Traffic Safety, Oldschurch, VA: pp. 32-37.

Marshall, V. (Ed.). 1987. *Aging in Canada: Social Perspectives*. Markham, ON: Fitzhenry and Whiteside.

Moore, R.L., I.P. Sedgley, and B.E. Sabey. 1982. "Ages of Car Drivers Involved in Accidents, with Special Reference to Junctions." Transport and Road Research Laboratory, Supp. Rep. 718. Crowthorne: (OECD Report).

Mourant, R., and R. Mourant. 1979. "Driving Performance of the Elderly." *Accident Analysis and Prevention*, 11, pp. 247-53.

Natanson, M. (Ed.). 1966. *Philosophy of the Social Sciences*. New York: Random House.

OECD and WHO. 1985. *Traffic Safety of Elderly Road Users*. Paris: Organization for Economic Co-operation and Development.

Orr, Fay, and Brad Oswald. 1986. Cracking up—Should Old Drivers Be Retested? *Alberta Report*, p. 9.

Overend, Robert B. 1985. "Popular Perceptions of Safety are at Odds with Reality." *Traffic Safety*, 85(6), pp. 6-7; 25-28.

Panek, P.E., G.V. Barrett, H.L. Sterns, and R.A. Alexander. 1977. "A Review of Age Changes in Perceptual Information Processing Ability with Regard to Driving." *Experimental Aging Research*, 3(6), pp. 387-449.

Parker-Wells, E., S. Miles, and B. Spencer. 1983. "Stress Experiences and Drinking Histories of Elderly Drunken-Driving Offenders." *Journal of Studies on Alcohol*, 44(3).

Partyka, S.C. 1984. "Simple Models of Fatality Trends Using Employment and Population Data." *Accident Analysis and Prevention*, 16(3).

Petrocine, W.J. 1979. "Driving—Age 65 and Older." *American Correctional Therapy Journal*, pp. 16-33.

Planek, T.W., M.E. Condron, and R.C. Fowler. 1968. "An Investigation of the Problems and Opinions of the Aged Driver." National Safety Council.

Planek, T.W., and R.C. Fowler. 1971. "Traffic Accident Problems and Exposure Characteristics of the Aging Driver." *Journal of Gerontology*, 26, pp. 224-30.

Planek, T., W. Mann, and E. Wiener. 1972. *Aging and Highway Safety: The Elderly in a Mobile Society*. Chapel Hill, NC: University of North Carolina Highway Safety Research Center.

Planek, T.W., and R.R. Overend. 1973. "Profile of the Aging Driver." *Traffic Safety*, 73, pp. 9-10; 37-39.

Pulling, N.H., E. Wolf, S.P. Sturgis, D.R. Vaillancourt, J.J. Dolliver. 1980. "Headlight Glare Resistance and Driver Age." *Human Factors*, 22(1), pp. 103-12.

Rackoff, N.J., and R.R. Mourant. 1979. "Driving Performance of the Elderly." *Accident Analysis and Prevention*, 11, pp. 247-54.

Robinson, C.C. 1985. "Highway Mobility and the Safety of Older Drivers and Pedestrians." *ITE Journal*, pp. 34-36.

Rosenthal, P. 1984. *Words and Values*. Oxford: Oxford University Press.

Rothe, J.P. 1985. "Phenomenological Analysis of Distance Education Textual Materials." *Ziff Papier* 59, Hagen, Germany.

Rothe, J.P., and W. Werner. 1986. *Doing School Ethnography*. Edmonton, Alberta: Faculty of Education Publications, University of Alberta (second printing).

Sacks, S. (Ed.). 1978. *On Metaphor*. Chicago: University of Chicago Press.

Salvendi, G. 1974. "Discrimination in Performance Assessment Against the Aged." *Perceptual and Motor Skills*, 39(3), pp. 1078-99.

Schwartz, H., and J. Jacobs. 1979. *Qualitative Sociology*. New York: Free Press.

Selling, L.S. 1944. "Old Age from Standpoint Of Traffic Situation." *American Journal of Orthopsychiatry*, 14.

Shiner, D. 1978. "New Vision Testing for Driver Licensing." Unpublished manuscript, Indiana University.

Sivak, M., P.L. Olson, and L.A. Pastalan. 1981. "Effect of Driver's Age on Nighttime Legibility of Highway Signs." *Human Factors*, 23(1), pp. 59-64.

Sklair, L. 1973. *Organized Knowledge*. Suffolk: Paladin.

Stagner, R. 1971. "An Industrial Psychologist Looks at Industrial Gerontology." *Aging and Human Development*, 2(1), pp. 29-37.

Stahl, A. 1983. "Elderly People in the Traffic System." Lund Institute of Traffic Report. Lund.

State of Washington. 1986. *A Review of Traffic Collisions in Washington, 1986*. Washington Traffic Safety Commission, Olympia.

Statistics Canada. 1986. Population: Age, Sex and Marital Status, and 1986 Census of Canada. Ottawa, ON.

Timasheff, N. 1967. *Sociological Theory: Its Nature and Growth*. (3rd Edition), New York: Random House.

Torpey, S.E. 1986. *Licence and Retesting of Older Drivers*. Report 2, Road Traffic Authority, Australia.

Traffic Safety of Elderly Road Users. 1965. Report prepared by an OECD Scientific Expert Group in cooperation with WHO, Paris.

Turbayne, C.M. 1962. *The Myth of Metaphor*. London: Yale Press.

U.S. Department of Transportation. 1986. Fatal Injury and Accident Rates. U.S. Government Printing Office, Washington, DC.

Van Coevering, V.R. 1973. "An Exploratory Study of Middle-Aged and Older Widows to Investigate those Variables which Differentiate High and Low Life Satisfaction." Ph.D. thesis (unpublished), Wayne State University.

Waller, J.A. 1967. "Cardiovascular Disease, Aging and Traffic Accidents." *Journal of Chronic Diseases*, 20, pp. 615-20.

Waller, Patricia F. (Ed.). 1972. "Aging and Highway Safety: The Elderly in a Mobile Society." *Proceedings of the North Carolina Symposium on Highway Safety*, Vol. 7.

Wellford, A.T. 1977. "Motor Performance." In J.E. Birren and K.W. Schaie (Eds.), *Handbook of the Psychology of Aging*. New York: Van Nostrand.

Werner, W. 1978. "Evaluation: Sense-Making of School Programs." In T. Aoki (Ed.), *Curriculum Evaluation in a New Key*. Vancouver: Centre for the Study of Curriculum and Instruction, University of British Columbia.

Werner, W., B. Connors, T. Aoki, and J. Dahlie. 1983. *Whose Culture? Whose Heritage*? Vancouver, B.C.: Centre for the Study of Curriculum and Instruction, University of British Columbia.

Wiener, E.L. 1973. "Licensing the Elderly Driver—Legal and Scientific Problems." *Traffic Safety*, 73(5), pp. 8-11; 36-37.

Winter, D. 1984. "Needs and Problems of Older Drivers and Pedestrians: An Exploratory Study with Teaching/Learning Implications." *Educational Gerontology*, 10, pp. 135-46.

Yanik, Anthony J. 1985. "What Action and Data Reveal about Elderly Drivers." Presented at the Passenger Car Meeting, Dearborn, Michigan, September. Published as Essay E, Technical Paper Series 851688.

Ysander, L., and B. Herner. 1976. "Traffic Behaviour of Elderly Male Automobile Drivers In Gothenburg, Sweden." *Accident Analysis and Prevention*, Vol. 8, pp. 81-86.

Zaidel, D., and I. Hocherman. 1986. "License Renewal for Older Drivers: The Effects of Medical and Vision Tests." *Journal of Safety Research*, 17, pp. 111-16.

Yee, Darlene. 1985. A survey of the traffic safety needs and problems of drivers age 55 and over. In *Needs And Problems Of Older Drivers: Survey Results and Recommendations*. Proceedings of the Older Driver Colloquium, Orlando, Florida. Sponsored by AAA Foundation for Traffic Safety, pp. 96-125.

4

The Research Schemata

> Old age takes from the intellectual man no qualities save those which are useless to wisdom.
>
> (Joseph Joubert, *Pensées*)

To overcome the limitations of the traditional research context, we developed a conceptual plan that captures the strengths of the intellectual and empirical qualities found in research paradigms, while stepping over the weaknesses. The impetus for our conceptual mold came from the social sciences and philosophy. We attempted to harmonize preserves of data and methodologies such as gerontology, social psychology, sociology, and epidemiology into a unity to overcome the predominant technological thrust. This chapter, therefore, serves as the methodological center for the book. It intersects the dimensions into a system that can be demonstrated and described. But before the system is demonstrated, a few assumptions need to be clarified.

Our Assumptions

Behavior in one part of life cannot be divorced from influences in other parts of life. To remove, separate, and isolate life events from other relevant events amounts to Einstein's optical delusion.

With respect to elderly drivers, we consider their driving within their social and physical environments. Normative-span life events such as retirement, relocation of home, or death of a spouse impact social relationships and self-identities which, in turn, influence driving behavior. On a more positive note, an elderly person's feelings of competence behind the wheel may bolster his confidence, enhance his well-being and strengthen his self-concept.

Operating a vehicle is as much social and psychological as it is manipulative. Motorists negotiate the roadway in relation to self-esteem and other people, whether they be vehicle operators, bicyclists or pedestrians. The elderly, therefore, cannot be perceived as scrubbed automatons, programmed to ignore social influences while driving. They have expectations of other road users, assign personal meanings to their own and other people's conduct, reason through their behavior according to beliefs and norms, and they experience reactions according to other people's judgments or accusations. All of these influence the elderly driver's road performance.

Yet the traditional technological approach to elderly drivers dismisses social and personal characteristics and only notes isolated behaviors or factors of as large a number of instances as possible. The researchers then generalize about all instances of that phenomenon (Rex 1961). Weber, one of the most influential sociological thinkers ever, endorsed the statistical approach, except (1947:90–91):

> All interpretation of meaning, like all scientific observation, strives for clarity and verifiable accuracy of insight and comprehension (Evidenz). The basis for certainty in understanding can be either rational, which can be further subdivided into logical and mathematical, or it can be of an emotional empathic or artistically appreciative quality . . . . Empathic or appreciative accuracy is attained when, through sympathetic participation, we can adequately grasp the emotional context in which the action took place.

According to Weber, social meaning has both objective, rational and subjective, empathetic dimensions to it. This is not unlike Cooley (1930) who wrote that a description composed entirely of "statistics" is superficial unless it includes "empathetic" knowledge. The concept of different perspectives on the same phenomenon was also promoted by such notable intellectuals as Znaniecki (1934), Sorokin (1937), McIver (1942), and Bruyn (1966), among others.

On the basis of the great chain of being where behaviors are linked to other experiences, moods, and future projections, a research framework was developed entitled "complementarity." It was designed to assimilate or include the strengths of previous research endeavors and to transcend the shortcomings.

The definition of complementarity has undergone a facelift since the one used in *Rethinking Young Drivers* (1987). It has been discussed and debated lately in SWOV's (1988) conference in Holland, and at the Multi Perspective Conference on Traffic Safety in Vancouver (1988). It is the essential foundation upon which our elderly driver research platform is erected.

Complementarity: Development

There is a dearth of tradition and authority supporting descriptions of human behavior along with statistical analyses (Abel 1948). Strategic grounding for complementarity is founded in the physical sciences where Bohr, a

Danish physicist, recognized a basic epistemological problem while exploring the elementary properties of light and matter. According to Bohr (1958), physical phenomena, like individual atomic processes, were essentially determined by the interaction between the objects in question, and the measuring instruments necessary for definition of experimental arrangements. After further examining knowledge and physical objects, Bohr concluded that complementary descriptions may be used to explain the essential aspects of knowledge resulting from the two forms of interaction (1958:26):

> Information regarding the behavior of an atomic object obtained under the definite experimental conditions may, however, according to a terminology often used in atomic physics, be adequately characterized as "complementary" to any information about the same object obtained by some other experimental arrangement . . . . Although such kinds of information cannot be combined into a single picture by means of ordinary concepts, they represent indeed equally essential aspects of any knowledge of the object in questions which can be obtained in this domain [emphasis added].

Other physicists such as Born (1932), Compton (1935), and De Broglie (cited in Matson 1975) suggested that while physics is an objective science, it has a human referent. This substantiates a peculiar cognate relationship between scientific methodology and human interpretation. Human interpretation plays a key role in knowing the physical world.

Polyani (1966), Northrop (1947), Merton (1949), and Gurvitch (1942), among others, helped root complementarity in sociology by suggesting that people's actions and their expressions of convictions can be interpreted in terms of causes (normative ideals or facts) which determine them, or the reasons people have for them (actuality or values). If we concentrate only on responses to a given set of stimuli without recognizing interpretations of human affairs, we obliterate any grounds on which justifications for the action can be given or disputed.

In psychology, Maslow (1954), Giorgi (1971), and Van Kaam (1969) specified that to achieve an appropriate interpretation of behavior, the psychologist requires background understanding. To attain this understanding, qualitative data are needed which complement the traditional behavioral perspective composed of quantitative data (tests). The two perspectives are not discrete dichotomies, but they tend to coalesce into two unitary worldviews, making up a whole.

Insofar as behavior and experiences differ from each other, the manner in which these aspects become psychological data also differ. Generally, behavior becomes datum only when its "relevant" aspects are measured, and experience becomes datum only when people meaningfully describe the "relevant" aspects of a situation (Giorgi 1971).

Van Eckartsberg (1971) and Van Kaam (1969) recommended a description of human interaction and shared experiences, to provide an interpretive context for traditional behavioral research. As such, quantitative and qualitative research methodologies, although different in purpose and worldview, dialectically interrelate. This concept became the pivotal center for our development of complementarity.

A metaphoric representation of the interrelationship between the quantitative and qualitative research methodologies is "Bergson's Box." According to Bergson (1949), there are "two profoundly different ways of knowing a thing." The first implies moving around the object; the second, entry into it. The first kind of knowledge may be said to stop at the relative; the second, in those cases where it is possible, to attain the absolute. If a social phenomenon is envisioned as a box, the existence of an inside is seen. With this recognition an outside comes to mind. Although different, the inside and outside are mutually dependent, for the existence of the inside presupposes the existence of an outside, and vice versa. The inside of the box consists of an individual's "life-world" or "Lebenswelt" whereas the outside consists of generalized understanding of human actions, the "external world" or "Auswelt." According to Schutz (1971:62):

> If the social sciences' aim is to explain social reality, then the scientific constructs on the second level, too, must include a reference to the subjective meaning an action has for the act . . . . All scientific explanations of the social world can and for certain purposes, must refer to the subjective meaning of the actions of human beings from which social reality originates.

Schutz's recognition of scientific and second-level constructs refers to the existence of the "external world." Although they are envisioned as being "more scientific," still they originate from the "life-world." One world complements the other. According to Dilthey, categories researchers use to investigate the outside of the box are adequate for an objective explanation of a phenomenon such as elderly drivers. But they include "little possibility for understanding the inner life of those people." Inside the box the phenomenon can contain different systems of relationship. Qualitative research is then used to focus on the expressions of life or the existential-social relationships within the life-world (Palmer 1969). When the outside and inside are combined, a phenomenon such as elderly drivers is understood in terms of outside generalities and inside particularities.

The basic design of Bergson's metaphysical box was conceptually extended to that of a framework. This design, which originally appeared in *Rethinking Young Drivers* (1988), is as follows:

Complementarity Design of Elderly Drivers

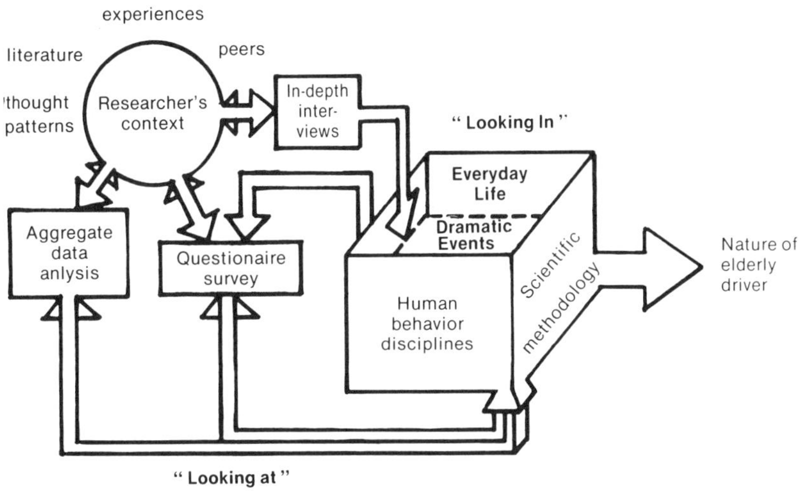

There are two distinct entities: The elderly driver and the researcher. The researcher's intent is to study elderly drivers and describe them as close to reality as possible. To do so attempts are made to gain insight into the elderly drivers' everyday reality or life-world. Researchers "look in" to find the information. However, researchers also attempt to analyze the complexity of elderly drivers by topographically charting the variables and uncovering empirical structures—forms, laws, patterns, or principles. The variables represent the rationality within a discipline. They "exist" somewhat independently of the individuals whom they are intended to define (Schwartz and Jacobs 1979). This component has been labelled "looking at."

But, as was described in Chapters Two and Three, researchers do not operate in isolation. Their perspectives reflect the research context. The conceptual environment helps the researcher to define the problem and to attempt to address it in normative, puzzle-solving fashion. For our elderly driver study, the researchers' context becomes problematic and deserves to be framed.

Complementarity Schemata

The complementarity schemata consists of cognitive schema, or patterns, each of which is significant in our research. The schema were abstracted from writings reflecting academic disciplines. Each schema described takes on a life of its own. But, cojoined with the other schemas to form a whole, tied together conceptually, they form a tightly knit family of outlooks.

Researcher-Oriented Schemata

The researcher-oriented schemata describe moves in thought which draw attention to the researchers' domain of operation. Their avoidance or exposure of objectification, hypostatization, reification, or stigmatization describes a kind of thinking to deal with complex processes as if they were static tangibles.

Schema 1. Affirmation of the Primacy of Perspective. In its primary form, research is basic to the nature of existence and knowledge shared by predecessors, present activists, and future researchers. The researchers' primary perspective on problem definition, epistemological primacy of aging and puzzle solution are the baggage of business-as-usual shared by traffic safety researchers (Kuhn 1962).

The attention to the research context and fundamental patterns within it create a background which other researchers use for direction. The context, composed of past and present colleagues, establishes a view on the nature of individual, society, and knowledge.

As researchers we cannot run before we learn to walk. Once we have learned to walk by being aware of the context and comprehending the traffic safety literature on elderly drivers, we are in a better position not only to walk a little faster but to walk in different directions. Elderly driver research can then evolve into something beyond the constraints of previous research perspectives.

The evolution does not mean we engage in processes removed from traditional empirical research. Rather, we take out of the context what is important and intellectually recognized and add constitutive elements that move beyond the history of research exhibits. To do this we need an overall display of what the elderly driver research context is. Chapters Two and Three present a series of viewpoints which were brought to bear in the development of this study.

Form-Oriented Schemata

Statistical reconstructions of a phenomenon form generalizable descriptions of structural properties that transpose to other people's experiences. They are, most often, elements within the whole, described in structural, functional, or equilibrational terms. Forms are outlined and relationships are asserted.

Schema 2. Description of Forms Based on Accident Data Base Analyses. At a furthest point of generalization is the development of forms and structures that are located within the larger whole of data bases. Within this schema, the other schemas can be extended to their fullest extreme. It is the structure that contextualizes, at a broad reconstructive element, all the other data.

From a "looking at" perspective, elderly drivers as a group are defined by specific external characteristics gathered from controlled statistical research. The boundaries of definition and the potential of the characteristics for explaining the nature of elderly drivers are predetermined according to a rationalization of society and behavior (Bruyn 1966). Statistical and mathematical techniques are used to express uniformities of the elderly driver phenomenon as they illustrate some consistency of character in the behavior of aggregates. Other things being equal, the consistency of character is refined into trends which provide us with some predictive insight into future course of events. Projection of elderly driver behavior is achieved according to a predetermined classification of analytic characters, as for example, in psychology (stimulus-response or aggression theory), sociology (alienation, socialization, institutionalization), education (cognition and pedagogical models), epidemiology (risk-taking,) and engineering (perspicuity).

Schema 3. Description of Forms Based on Surveys. After the accident data base analyses, surveys are next on the level of generalization. Forms recognize elements of behavior as they appear on questionnaire items. They define the elderly drivers' worlds in hypothetical terms. When they are analyzed it is assumed that both the meaning of the items and the differential responses to them are invariant to people's situational interpretations of reality. Also, the items relate to significant variables featured in the aggregate data base analysis.

Although questionnaire items are designed to reflect both the kinds of thoughts the elderly use to manage their lives and statistical findings arising from Schema 2, the "forced" character of responses restricts elderly drivers from interpreting the items in any other way than that intended by the researcher. Social behavior is reduced to hypothetical norms and attitudes. Surveys reflect a "looking at" perspective because the items seek to measure elderly drivers' values, attitudes, opinions, norms, and the like through fixed-choice structures, ignoring the emergent, innovational, and problematic character of everyday life.

The fixed-choice questionnaire features standardized propositions from the researchers' perspectives. It provides a determination of frequency and distribution of predefined elderly driver characteristics, and an outline of relationships between various elderly driver aspects (Sanders 1976).

Life-World-Oriented Schemata

Life is movement. The accumulation of movements gives us personal experiences which are of value in bringing things together at any behavioral moment. It is people's feelings about self, their reference to the process of being with other people, their reactions to life events, good or bad, and their everyday reasoning as guide to action. The life-world is the constitutive arrangement of the individual as person acting and reacting on the basis of situational variables and social possibilities.

Schema 4. Affirmation of General Life-Worlds. Within complementarity, the life-world is recognized as people's daily lives composed of behavioral events which follow rules of action. These rules are recurrent and identifiable. They govern the describable properties of people's actions.

Elderly drivers' life-worlds include their thoughts and actions within different situations (Dewey and Bentley 1949). What older people do, know, and believe is a function of the groups to which they belong, their background experiences, their thought models, their intents, and their particular interpretations of experiences (Geertz 1973; Lazlo 1973).

In the every-day world, elderly drivers' knowledge about driving is cyclical and cumulative. It is cyclical in that their thought processes advance from everyday experience to inquiry and reflection, to judgment. They then revert back to new experiences (Lonergan 1958). It is impossible for elderly drivers to define their driving behavior in terms of anything but their life-world as they experience it, and as they interpret it to be real (Combs and Snygg 1959). Research into the life-world is considered to be a "looking in" perspective. Researchers, therefore, should discover and verify the existence of elderly drivers' realities through their own meanings—to gather data "that which is given" as feelings, influences, fears, yearnings, disillusionments, relations, perspectives, and experiences (MacLeod 1964).

Schema 5. Recognition of Dramatic Events in Life-Worlds. As a construct, Schema 5 refers to a kind of everyday life wariness and to how elderly drivers regard unstable, unexpected, highly dramatic life episodes. Dramatic moments referred to in German philosophical literature as "Erlebnis" are non-routine experiences that, at the time of happening, bring together the elderly drivers' reasoning structures and perceptual apparatus of what is normal.

Dramatic experience lifted out of the elderly drivers' stream of life corresponds to Frankl's (1963) concept of "neo-dynamics," Michiavelli's (1963) "man-in-episodes," and Lofland and Lofland's (1980) "episodes."

As traffic safety researchers, we need to study the impact that injury-producing crashes have on older people. This allows us to formulate general sequences as to how elderly drivers reason through disparate traffic experiences.

To characterize a dramatic moment is to imply that it is an unforeseen, but recognizable, interval within ongoing normal lives. Dramatic events tend to have the following characteristics (Basseches 1984):

1. They tend to appeal to other events occurring over a time.
2. They often emphasize the uniqueness of the event being described.
3. They often appeal to events occurring after and before the event.
4. They often communicate the expectation of change by referring to the dramatic nature.

Dramatic encounters are usually reasoned through by elderly drivers and others in terms of unusual disruption of normal driving situations. This impingement of a cause gives the meaning of the self and the crash.

The schemata reflects complementarity, which is structured upon the principle of hermeneutics, or continuity of analysis—from aggregate data analysis, to survey finding, to focus group interviews, to crash victim interviews.

Complementarity and Methodology

Nothing occurs in isolation. Research projects are but formally organized activities which occur within a context of previously written works, strategies and perspectives. Our first concern, therefore, is to clarify as much as possible the context of elderly driver research.

Step One in the methodology consisted of an inquiry into the overall research intents and designs of elderly drivers to date. Traditional "review of the literature" structures were employed. Furthermore, a conceptual clarification of the overall elderly research world was provided. A critical analysis was completed to get a handle on what the latent and manifest meanings of the elderly as represented in relevant elderly driver text are.

The "looking at" component included in-depth data analysis of the British Columbia accident and driver record data bases. The methodology is more clearly defined in Chapter Five.

The link between the statistical or reconstructed views of elderly drivers and their everyday lives was made by a questionnaire survey of 904 elderly drivers aged fifty-five plus. To overcome the weakness of total reconstruction we engaged in a series of group interviews to establish how life features are defined by the elderly. Expansion of the methodology is found in Chapter Six.

The "routine lives" component of the elderly drivers' "life-world" was reached through small-group interviews with 325 elderly people. The small-group interviews were arranged to provide respondents the milieu of a comfortable group situation, yet have ample opportunity to voice individual opinions. Shared perspectives were more easily reached on the everyday life of elderly citizens. For a thorough description of the methodology, refer to Chapter Seven.

Imaginative participation in small interview groups composed of elderly drivers provides the interviewers with opportunities to gather group-relevant data (Schwartz and Jacobs 1979). Verification between and among group participants' statements provides a clearer picture as to what is considered a cohort's normative behavior. Interviewers negotiate the interviews to unearth maximum data about elderly drivers' everyday lives and the boundary conditions that influence them.

To arrive at the "dramatic episodes" of injury-producing car crashes, semistructured, intensive, face-to-face interviews were organized. A set of introductory questions was developed which allowed for further emerging questions and answers.

In social psychology, early theoretical work suggests that self-disclosures are positive. Jourard (1964) wrote that the opportunity for people to reveal personal information to interviewers is a sign of psychological health, a state which should be judged favorably. Further, Cazby (1972) believed that personal revelations often reduce uncertainty about disclosures and that uncertainty reduction is pleasurable.

To support the process of face-to-face interviews for understanding elderly drivers' dramatic life events, Worthy et al. (1969) concluded that persons respond favorably to disclosure about tense episodes.

Jourard and Friedman (1970) supported Worthy et al.'s views on disclosure by quoting from their empirical research. They suggested that personal disclosure about relevant life events is psychologically healthy and socially beneficial. Therefore, properly trained interviewers are able to extract personal accounts about injury-producing crashes in ways that are beneficial to the researchers and respondents alike.

The informal process of give-and-take was undertaken with 130 drivers fifty-five years of age and older who were involved in injury-producing crashes. The sixty-minute interviews provided ample opportunity for feedback and alteration of questions emerging from the definition of the situation (Lofland 1971). For a thorough description of the methodology, see Chapter Eight.

The complement of methodologies employed led to a multiperspective research report which should prove useful for future research and program development.

Conclusion

Often traffic safety researchers begin and conclude their studies from a social pathological perspective, whereby elderly drivers are considered to be problems. Data are ordered so as better to group the label, scope, and character of deviation from the original conceptions.

An alternative perspective on elderly drivers is that the humanly experienced and cognitively understood should be sought. As researchers, we should envision elderly drivers as individuals who do not behave idiosyncratically, but rather act according to the canons of the context. Since behavior is the result of meaningful experiences, interpretations of reality and understandings of conduct, it is necessary to establish the latter without preordained judgments. Rather than ask the question, "How are elderly drivers different from other groups?" the questions should be, "How do elderly drivers' common-sense actions and motives lead to a statistical, demographic trend? How do elderly drivers use common-sense reasoning similar to other people? How do they structure their reality, and how does this structuring lead to driving behaviors? What motivates elderly drivers to do what they believe is proper to do?"

References

Abel, T. 1984. "The Operation Called Verstehen." *The American Journal of Sociology*, 54, pp. 211-18.

Basseches, M. 1984. *Dialectical Thinking and Adult Development*. Norwood, NJ: Ablex Pub. Corp.

Belshaw, C. 1969. *The Conditions of Social Performance*. London: Routledge and Keegan Paul.

Berger, P., and T. Luckmann. 1966. *The Social Construction of Reality*. New York: Doubleday.

Bergson, H. 1949. *An introduction to Metaphysics*. Toronto: University of Toronto Press.

Bohr, N. 1958. *Atomic Physics and Human Knowledge*. New York: John Wiley and Sons.

Born, M. and G. Pollard. 1932. "The Significance of Complementarity for the Life Sciences." *American Journal of Physics*, XX, pp. 36-48.

Bourdieau, P. 1981. "Structures, Strategies and the Habitus." In C. Lemert (Ed.), *French Sociology: Rupture and Renewal Since 1968*. New York: Columbia University Press.

Bruyn, S. 1966. *The Human Perspective in Sociology*. Englewood Cliffs, NJ: Prentice Hall.

Cazby, P.C. 1972. "Self-Disclosure, Reciprocity and Liking." *Sociometry*, 35, pp. 151-60.

Cicourel, A.V. 1964. *Method and Measurement in Sociology*. New York: Free Press.

Clark, M. 1979. "The Dance Party as a Socialization Mechanism for Black Urban Preadolescents and Adolescents." In *Sociology: A Descriptive Approach*, edited by J. Nash and J. Spradley. Chicago: Rand McNally College Publishing Co.

Combs, A.W., and D. Snygg. 1959. *Individual Behavior: A Perceptual Approach to Behavior*. New York: Harper and Row.

Compton, A. 1935. *The Freedom of Man*. New Haven: Yale University Press.

Cooley, H.E. 1930. *Sociological Theory and Social Research*. New York: Scribners.

Dewey, J. and A. Bentley. 1949. *Knowing and the Known*. Boston: Beacon Press.

Dilthey, W. 1961. *Pattern and Meaning in History: Thoughts on History and Society*. New York: Harper and Row.

Durkheim, E. 1951. *Suicide*. New York: Free Glencoe Press.

Frankl, V. 1963. *Man's Search for Meaning*. New York: Pocket Books.

Geertz, C. 1973. *The Interpretation of Culture*. New York: Basic Books.

Giorgi, A. 1971. "Phenomenology and Experimental Psychology." In *Phenomenological Psychology I*, edited by A. Giorgi, W. Fisher and R. van Eckartsberg. Pittsburgh: Duquesne University Press.

Green, B.F. 1954. "Attitude Measurement." In *Handbook of Psychology*, edited by Ian G. Lindzey. Reading, MA: Addison Wesley.

Gurvitch, G. 1942. *Sociology of Law*. New York: Philosophical Library and Alliance Book Corp.

Jourard, S.M. 1964. *The Transparent Self*. New Jersey: Van Nostrand.

Jourard, S.M., and R. Friedman. 1970. "Experimenter Subject Distance and Self-Disclosure." *Journal of Personality and Social Psychology*, 19, pp. 59-63.

Kuhn, T.S. 1962. *The Structure of Scientific Revolutions*. Chicago: University of Chicago Press.

Lazlo, E. 1973. *The Systems View of the World*. New York: George Braziller.

Lofland, J. 1971. *Analyzing Social Settings*. Belmont, CA: Wadsworth.

Lofland, J. and L.H. Lofland. 1984. *Analyzing Social Settings*. Belmont, CA: Wadsworth Publishing Co.

Lonergan, B. 1958. *Insight: A Study of Human Understanding*. New York: Harper and Row.

Lundberg, T. 1939. *Foundations of Sociology*. New York: Macmillan Co.

MacLeod, R.B. 1964. "Phenomenology: A Challenge to Experimental Psychology." In *Behaviorism and Phenomenology*, edited by T.W. Wann. Chicago: University of Chicago Press.

Maslow, A. 1954. *Motivation and Personality*. New York: Harper and Row.

Matson, F. 1964. *The Broken Image*. New York: George Braziller.

McIver, R.M. 1942. *Social Causation*. Boston: Ginn and Company.

Merton, R.K. 1949. *Social Theory and Social Structure*. Glencoe, IL: The Free Press.

Michiavelli, N. 1963. *The Prince*. New York: Washington Square Press.

Northrop, F.S.C. 1947. *The Logic of the Sciences and the Humanities*. New York: Macmillan Co.

Palmer, E. 1969. *Hermeneutics*. Evanston, IL: Northwestern University Press.

Parsons, T., E. Shils, K. Naegele, and J. Pitts (Eds.). 1961. *Theories of Society: Foundations of Modern Sociological Theory*. New York: Free Press of Glencoe.

Platinga, T. 1980. *Historical Understanding in the Thought of William Dilthey*. Toronto: University of Toronto Press.

Polyani, M. 1966. *The Tacit Dimension*. Chicago: University of Chicago Press.

Rex, J. 1961. *Key Problems of Sociological Theory*. London: Routledge and Keegan Paul.

Rothe, J.P. (Ed.). 1987. *Rethinking Young Drivers*. North Vancouver: Insurance Corporation of B.C.

Rothe, J.P. 1985. "Linking Quantitative and Qualitative, Distance Education Research Through Complementarity." Hagen, W. Germany: Ziff Papier 56, Fern University.

Rothe, J.P. 1982. "Researching Native Education: An Ethnomethodological Perspective." *Canadian Journal of Native Education*, 9, no. 4.

Rothe, J.P., and S. Tod. 1980. "Social Studies Needs Assessment: An Alternative Approach." *The History and Social Science Teacher*, 16, no. 2.

Sanders, W.B. 1976. *The Sociologist as Detective*. New York: Praeger Publishers, Inc.

Schutz, A. 1971. *Collected Papers II: Studies in Social Theory*. The Hague: Martinus Nijhoff.

Schutz, A. 1970. *On Phenomenology and Social Relations*. Chicago: University of Chicago Press.

Schwartz, H., and J. Jacobs. 1979. *Qualitative Sociology*. New York: Free Press.

Sorokin, P. 1962. *Social and Cultural Dynamics*. Englewood Cliffs: Bedminster.

Truzzi, M. 1974. *Verstehen: Subjective Understanding in the Social Sciences*. London: Addison-Wesley Publishing Co.

Van Eckartsberg, R. 1971. "On Experiential Methodology." In *Phenomenological Psychology I*, edited by A. Giorgi, W. Fisher and R. van Eckartsberg. Pittsburgh: Duquesne University Press.

Van Kaam, A. 1969. *Existential Foundations of Psychology*. Garden City, NY: Image Books.

Weber, M. 1949. *The Methodology of the Social Sciences*. Glencoe, IL: The Free Press.

Weber, M. 1947. *The Theory of Social and Economic Organization*: Glencoe, IL: The Free Press.

Worthy, M., A.L. Gray, and G.M. Kahn. 1969. "Self-Disclosure as an Exchange Process." *Journal of Personality and Social Psychology*, 13, pp. 59-63.

Znaniecki, F. 1934. *The Method of Sociology*. New York: Farrar and Rinehart.

5

Different Ages, Different Risks: The Realm of Accident Statistics

P.J. Cooper

"You are old, Father William," the young man said,
"And your hair has become very white;
And yet you incessantly stand on your head—
Do you think, at your age, it is right?"

"In my youth," Father William replied to his son,
"I feared it might injure the brain;
But now that I'm perfectly sure I have none,
Why, I do it again and again."

"You are old," said the youth, "as I mentioned before,
And have grown most uncommonly fat;
Yet you turned a back somersault in at the door—
Pray, what is the reason of that?"

"In my youth," said the sage, as he shook his grey locks,
"I kept all my limbs very supple
By the use of this ointment—one shilling the box—
Allow me to sell you a couple."

"You are old," said the youth, "and your jaws are too weak
For anything tougher than suet;
Yet you finished the goose, with the bones and the beak
Pray, how did you manage to do it?"

"In my youth," said his father, "I took to the law,
And argued each case with my wife;
And the muscular strength, which it gave to my jaw,
Has lasted the rest of my life."

P.J. Cooper is Manager, Traffic Safety Planning and Research, Insurance Corporation of British Columbia.

"You are old," said the youth, "one would hardly suppose
That your eye was a steady as ever;
Yet you balanced an eel on the end of your nose—
What made you so awfully clever?"

"I have answered three questions, and that is enough,"
Said his father; "don't give yourself airs!
Do you think I can listen all day to such stuff?
Be off, or I'll kick you downstairs!'"

(Lewis Carroll, *Alice in Wonderland*)

We are now ready to initiate the research drama, by opening the curtain on statistics. We ask the question of why, on a broad scale, should the elderly driver be considered for empirical attention? What is the broad picture that requires more detailed examination? The answers to these questions provide a backdrop of relevance—one that urged us to continue further investigation. Let us begin.

As was already described, currently about 21 percent of British Columbia drivers are fifty-five years of age or older. By the year 2000 this proportion is expected to rise to 30 percent or more.

Not only is life expectancy increasing, but people are staying physically active longer. Mobility is an important aspect of North American society and it is not an advantage relinquished easily. The automobile has become firmly ensconced as an integral part of our social fabric.

In addition, the previously accepted standards of compulsory retirement at age sixty-five are being challenged. The area of human rights has now been taken up by the elderly to fight job discrimination based on age.

Some elderly people, especially women, who did not learn to drive as young people in the pre-World War II era are now finding, with spouses perhaps being incapacitated or passed away, that driving is a useful and even necessary ability.

All of these developments point in the same direction; toward an increasingly greater role being played by the elderly in vehicular travel and traffic accidents. In order to understand the nature of this role and how it may affect accident rates generally, we need to study the statistical evidence related to driving and vehicular crashes. This chapter is not concerned with accident consequences. The increased risk of injury for older persons is well known. Rather, the aim of the analyses reported here has been to investigate the "why," "how," "where," and "when" of collisions involving elderly drivers. We are interested in the factors leading up to accidents and also the characteristics of elderly drivers that may predispose them to have more or fewer crash involvements.

To this end, we created a data base consisting of 5,853 drivers fifty-five years of age or older who were involved in traffic accidents during 1986. The "control" group consisted of 8,210 middle-aged (thirty-six to fifty year old) drivers also involved in 1986 crashes. For each driver, we collected information on the events surrounding the accident, demographic data, past accident and conviction histories, and details concerning the vehicle driven. These data were obtained from police reports, driver records, and insurance files. No identifying information remained after matching of data was completed, and thus driver anonymity was ensured.

Our data base was restricted to accidents which the police actually attended. While it contained a good mix of casualty and property-damage-only (p.d.o.) accidents (about 60 percent), it is thus somewhat weighted in the direction of the former than would be a random sample of all crashes. It was found, however, that the proportion of accidents involving casualties was similar for elderly and middle-aged driver groupings. Conclusions can thus be drawn with respect to accident-involvement rates of elderly versus middle-aged drivers without the confounding effect of differential injury likelihood referred to above.

From time to time in this chapter, we will refer to the results of two interview surveys we conducted: one involving 904 elderly drivers randomly selected from the driving population, and the other involving 130 elderly drivers who had recently been involved in an injury-producing crash. Both of these surveys are reported in a limited way in this chapter for purposes of comparison with accident data. Later chapters will describe the interview process and results in more detail.

How Do Elderly Drivers Get into Accidents?

Are the factors that precipitate accidents for elderly drivers different within the over-fifty-five group, and are they different from drivers in the middle-aged group of thirty-six to fifty?

Using police-recorded precrash variables such as accident location, driving conditions, time of day, driver condition and precollision actions we performed a principal factor analysis. The data base consisted of 8,210 drivers aged thirty-six to fifty; 2,962 drivers aged fifty-five to sixty-four; 2,018 drivers aged sixty-five to seventy-four; and 873 drivers aged seventy-five and over. All drivers had been involved in a police-attended accident during 1986 in British Columbia. For the thirty-six to fifty age group, four very clear factors emerged: a driver action and fault factor, a road site geometry factor, a time of day factor, and a vehicle maneuver factor. The results for the fifty-five to sixty-four age group were identical to this, but the two groups representing over-sixty-five drivers showed some differences. For both sixty-five to seventy-four and seventy-five-plus age groups, the vehicle maneuver and road site geometry factors were combined into one. In addition, for the age seventy-five-plus drivers, there was an extra factor representing road class (number of lanes and whether divided or undivided facility).

Tables 1 through 4 present the factor analyses results. Since the variables which were not continuous were effect-coded, not all the categories are exhibited.

For drivers aged sixty-five and older especially, vehicle maneuvering prior to the accident was strongly tied to the location or precise road geometry. Upon further investigation, one possible problem was found to be left turns at uncontrolled or stop/yield sign-controlled intersections. Drivers aged fifty-five to sixty-four had 13 percent of their accidents while turning left at uncontrolled or sign-controlled intersections, as compared to only **10.9** percent for those aged thirty-six to fifty. This figure rose to **15.4** percent for the sixty-five to seventy-four age group, and again to **19.5** percent for the seventy-five-plus age group. Similarly, the importance of turning as a prelude to the accident, regardless of location, increased significantly with age. Drivers aged thirty-six to fifty had **19.3** percent of their accidents immediately after turning. This rose to 22.2 percent for fifty-five to sixty-four year old drivers, to **26.6** percent for sixty-five to seventy-four year old drivers, and to **32.9** percent for drivers seventy-five years of age or older. (All differences which were significant at the 95 percent level of confidence or better in a nonparametric chi-square test are shown to one decimal place and identified in bold type.)

Also, while road/weather conditions were not identified as part of a composite factor having a significantly independent presence, there was some evidence to suggest that, for older drivers, weather was more closely associated with time of day than was the case for drivers under sixty-five. For example, for drivers aged sixty-five and over who were involved in accidents during peak traffic periods (6:00-9:00 a.m. and 3:00-6:00 p.m.) there was a significantly smaller likelihood of poor road or weather conditions being present than was the case for drivers under sixty-five (**33.9** percent vs. **44.4** percent for poor road conditions and **19.9** percent vs. **25.8** percent for poor weather conditions, respectively). Possibly, since most drivers older than sixty-four are not involved in daily work trips, travel at this time may be largely a matter of choice and may be foregone if bad weather or road conditions prevail.

The relationship among driver age, accident time and weather/road condition is shown in Figure 1. For drivers aged thirty-six to sixty-four, the proportion of nighttime accidents on wet or icy road surfaces is slightly less than the proportion for daytime peak periods. For drivers over age sixty-four, the proportion of poor road condition accidents at night greatly exceeds those during day (both peak and off-peak periods). This suggests that a combined

TABLE 1
Principal Factor Analysis of Pre-crash Variables—Rotated Factor Pattern of Standard Regression Coefficients for Driver Age Group 36-50

	Factor 1	Factor 2	Factor 3	Factor 4	
Vehicle type	−.0344	.1501	−.0465	−.0725	Passenger car
Safety equipment used	−.0817	.0843	.0538	−.0362	Safety belt worn
Roadway alignment	−.0109	−.4328	−.0051	−.1380	Straight road
Day of week	−.0060	.0477	−.0492	−.0359	Weekday
Number of road lanes	.0068	.3590	−.0489	−.3984	
Divided/undivided road	−.0358	−.2041	.0361	.3750	Undivided road
Driver experience	−.0206	−.0943	.0176	.0493	
Number of passengers	−.0410	−.0318	−.0694	−.0129	
Main contrib. factor (1)	.8974	−.0036	.0058	−.0139	Human action
Main contrib. factor (2)	.6862	−.2072	.0293	.0163	Veh./environment
Acc. responsibility	.6814	.1405	−.0097	−.0421	Caused accident
Pre-collision action (1)	−.0710	.0430	−.0382	.4632	Driving straight
Pre-collision action (2)	.1237	.2378	−.0378	.4451	Turning
Time of day (1)	−.0061	−.0253	.7012	−.0194	Daytime peak
Time of day (2)	−.0038	−.0032	.6951	.0044	Daytime off-peak
Traffic control (1)	−.0266	.6589	.0427	.0235	Controlled intersection
Traffic control (2)	−.0115	.5227	.0532	.1293	Uncontrolled intersection
Land use	−.0158	.4211	.0109	.0088	Urban area
Weather/road conditions	−.0270	.1344	−.0618	−.0174	Good
	Driver Action & Fault Factor	Road Site Geometry Factor	Time of Day Factor	Vehicle Maneuver Factor	

Note: According to convention, only coefficients of 0.4 or greater (underlined above) are considered for factor identification.

TABLE 2
Principal Factor Analysis of Pre-crash Variables—Rotated Factor Pattern of Standard Regression Coefficients for Driver Age Group 55-64

	Factor 1	Factor 2	Factor 3	Factor 4	
Vehicle type	−.0196	.1396	−.0522	−.0329	Passenger car
Safety equipment used	−.0182	.0689	.0247	−.0433	Safety belt worn
Roadway alignment	−.0051	.4328	.0128	−.1408	Straight road
Day of week	−.0189	−.0051	−.0701	−.0005	Weekday
Number of road lanes	.0154	.3408	−.0260	−.3524	
Divided/undivided road	−.0373	−.1995	.0420	.3394	Undivided road
Driver experience	−.0347	−.0288	−.0046	.0128	
Number of passengers	−.0380	−.0591	−.1114	−.0423	
Main contrib. factor (1)	.8892	−.0057	.0079	−.0219	Human action
Main contrib. factor (2)	.6930	−.2269	.0154	−.0017	Veh./environment
Acc. responsibility	.6616	.1453	.0040	−.0135	Caused accident
Pre-collision action (1)	−.0975	.0026	−.0110	.5127	Driving straight
Pre-collision action (2)	.1268	.2109	−.0208	.4723	Turning
Time of day (1)	.0125	−.0287	.6813	−.0019	Daytime peak
Time of day (2)	−.0147	−.0024	.6711	.0028	Daytime off-peak
Traffic control (1)	.0042	.6622	.0549	.0163	Controlled intersection
Traffic control (2)	.0218	.5287	.0230	.1002	Uncontrolled intersection
Land use	−.0035	.4698	.0008	−.0309	Urban area
Weather/road conditions	−.0247	.1886	−.0490	−.0303	Good
	Driver Action & Fault Factor	Road Site Geometry Factor	Time of Day Factor	Vehicle Maneuver Factor	

Note: According to convention, only coefficients of 0.4 or greater (underlined above) are considered for factor identification.

TABLE 3
Principal Factor Analysis of Pre-crash Variables—Rotated Factor Pattern of Standard Regression Coefficients for Driver Age Group 65-74

	Factor 1	Factor 2	Factor 3	
Vehicle type	−.0255	.0774	−.0429	Passenger car
Safety equipment used	.0011	.0658	.0187	Safety belt worn
Roadway alignment	.0089	.3159	−.0057	Straight road
Day of week	.0133	.0645	−.0486	Weekday
Number of road lanes	−.0044	.1235	−.0590	
Divided/undivided road	.0054	−.0268	.0448	Undivided road
Driver experience	.0085	−.0472	.0197	
Number of passengers	−.0968	−.0711	−.0906	
Main contrib. factor (1)	.8765	.0082	.0056	Human action
Main contrib. factor (2)	.6941	−.1712	−.0039	Veh./environment
Acc. responsibility	.6405	.1020	.0210	Caused accident
Pre-collision action (1)	−.0825	.2546	−.0468	Driving straight
Pre-collision action (2)	.1643	.4314	−.0822	Turning
Time of day (1)	−.0024	−.0338	.6797	Daytime peak
Time of day (2)	.0277	−.0415	.6822	Daytime off-peak
Traffic control (1)	.0062	.6548	−.0059	Controlled intersection
Traffic control (2)	.0092	.5726	.0401	Uncontrolled intersection
Land use	−.0252	.4105	.0249	Urban area
Weather/road conditions	−.0271	.0943	−.0457	Good
	Driver Action & Fault Factor	Road Site Geometry & Vehicle Maneuver Factor	Time of Day Factor	

Note: According to convention, only coefficients of 0.4 or greater (underlined above) are considered for factor identification.

TABLE 4
Principal Factor Analysis of Pre-crash Variables—Rotated Factor Pattern of Standard Regression Coefficients for Driver Age Group 75+

	Factor 1	Factor 2	Factor 3	Factor 4	
Vehicle type	−.1023	.0924	.1004	.1434	Passenger car
Safety equipment used	−.0491	.0658	.0400	−.0062	Safety belt worn
Roadway alignment	−.0475	.3472	.0542	.2692	Straight road
Day of week	−.0098	.0106	−.0615	−.0793	Weekday
Number of road lanes	−.0153	.0409	−.0240	.4773	
Divided/undivided road	−.0706	.0918	.0226	−.4122	Undivided road
Driver experience	−.0380	.1061	.0172	−.0502	
Number of passengers	−.0626	−.0636	.0074	−.0255	
Main contrib. factor (1)	.8346	.0079	.0074	.0096	Human action
Main contrib. factor (2)	.5657	−.2089	.0005	.0685	Veh./environment
Acc. responsibility	.6013	.1507	.0070	−.0360	Caused accident
Pre-collision action (1)	−.0622	.2308	−.0181	−.2136	Driving straight
Pre-collision action (2)	.2146	.3970	−.0057	−.0513	Turning
Time of day (1)	.0244	−.0433	.6553	.0222	Daytime peak
Time of day (2)	−.0166	.0412	.6568	−.0195	Daytime off-peak
Traffic control (1)	.0272	.6235	−.0038	.0064	Controlled intersection
Traffic control (2)	.0557	.5367	−.0261	−.0488	Uncontrolled intersection
Land use	−.0817	.3942	−.0048	.0463	Urban area
Weather/road conditions	.0019	.0795	−.0126	−.0685	Good
	Driver Action & Fault Factor	Road Site Geometry & Vehicle Maneuver Factor	Time of Day Factor	Road Class Factor	

Note: According to convention, only coefficients of 0.4 or greater (underlined above) are considered for factor identification.

FIGURE 1
Proportion of Accidents on Non-Dry Road Surfaces by Time Period for Various Driver Age Groups

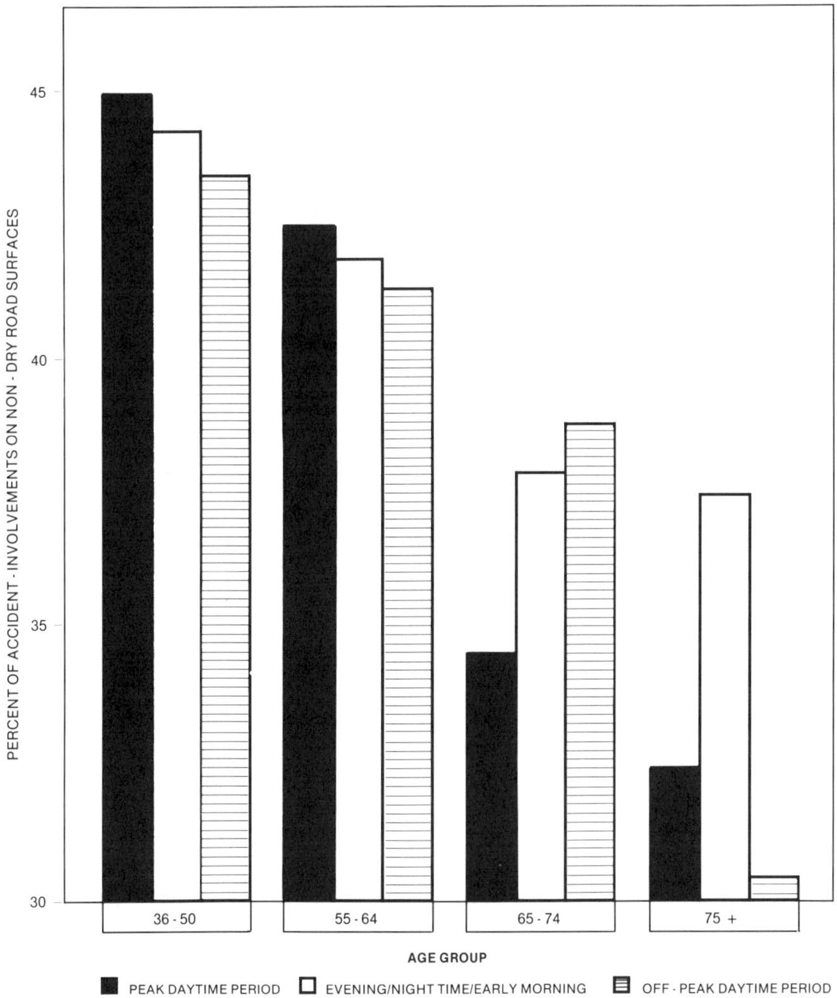

effect of low light levels and slippery roads may overtax the abilities of a number of older drivers to perform the driving task effectively.

Examination of the other variables involved in the principal factors leading to accidents showed that many of these also became more important as age increased. For example, intersection-related driver errors such as failure to yield the right-of-way and ignoring a traffic control device increased from **12.5** percent and **3.1** percent, respectively, of police-assigned contributing factors for thirty-six to fifty year old accident-involved drivers, to **17.3** percent and 3.8 percent for fifty-five to sixty-four year old drivers, to **24.0** percent and **4.9** percent for sixty-five to seventy-four year old drivers and to **32.6** percent and **6.4** percent for drivers aged seventy-five and older. On the other hand, the percentage of drivers not assigned any contributing factors and also the percent not committing any chargeable offense fell significantly as age increased. For age thirty-six to fifty drivers, **46.5** percent had no assigned contributors and **69.0** percent were not charged. These proportions fell to **42.8** percent and **66.5** percent respectively for fifty-five to sixty-four year old drivers, **33.1** percent and **57.4** percent for sixty-five to seventy-four year old drivers and 20.2 percent and 48.0 percent for those aged seventy-five and over.

The apparent importance of this driver action and fault factor makes it worthy of examination in more detail. We know (Flint et al. 1988) that while elderly drivers have fewer accidents per licensed operator than younger age groups, yet they seem to be less safe when amount of driving exposure is taken into account. Is such a differential characterization explained by accident responsibility? In other words, while elderly drivers are good insurance risks because they drive infrequently and therefore are involved in proportionally fewer crashes than younger drivers, are they as good drivers as younger operators when they *are* on the road? Are they more or less likely to be judged responsible for the accidents in which they are involved?

In order to answer this question, we created a relative responsibility index or ratio (Table 5) based on two years of accident data. This ratio consisted of the percent of all responsible drivers represented by each age group, divided by the percent of all not-responsible drivers represented by each age group. The definition of responsibility is illustrated schematically in Figure 2. Where there is no predisposition towards responsibility for accidents, age-group ratios should therefore be equal to one or less. Figure 3 illustrates the results graphically. Accident responsibility was assessed through examination of specific police and insurance adjuster statements and ratings. The smallest sample size representing a single data point was 118. Most data points had well over a thousand drivers. As expected, young drivers (under twenty-five years of age) had a ratio of over one and all other age groups up to age sixty-five were at less than one. But beyond age sixty-five the situation changed dra-

TABLE 5
Relative Probability of Accident Responsibility by Age Group

Age Group	Responsible Number	Responsible Percent (A)	Not Responsible Number	Not Responsible Percent (B)	Relative Probability (A/B)
16-20	11,688	18.38	2,937	12.03	1.53
21-25	11,805	18.56	4,013	16.44	1.13
26-30	8,619	13.55	3,602	14.76	0.92
31-35	6,661	10.47	3,072	12.59	0.83
36-40	5,638	8.86	2,828	11.59	0.76
41-45	4,108	6.46	2,089	8.56	0.75
46-50	3,086	4.85	1,515	6.21	0.78
51-55	2,658	4.18	1,230	5.04	0.83
56-60	2,508	3.94	1,046	4.29	0.92
61-65	2,084	3.28	899	3.68	0.89
66-70	1,816	2.86	584	2.39	1.20
71-75	1,476	2.32	363	1.49	1.56
76-80	923	1.45	165	0.68	2.13
81-85	404	0.64	58	0.24	2.64
86-90	110	0.17	8	0.03	5.67
91-95	14	0.02	0	0.00	—
96-100	1	0.00	0	0.00	—
Total	63,599	100.00	24,409	100.00	—

matically. There was an exponential-looking increase in accident responsibility from age sixty-five up. These results are very similar to those presented by McKelvey and Maleck (1988) and also Verhaegen et al. (1988). Since judgment of accident responsibility involves some subjective elements and preconceptions about elderly drivers, it may conceivably inject some bias into the process. Nevertheless, the judgments are usually the result of the opinions of a police officer and one or more insurance adjusters. There can thus be a reasonable level of confidence placed in these results.

One conclusion to this accident fault analysis could be that elderly drivers make more errors—in perception, in judgment, in decision-making, and in reaction.

Returning to our single-year accident sample of 5,853 elderly drivers, we examined responsibility assessment in terms of gender differences. Overall (aged fifty-five plus), female drivers had a slightly, but significantly, higher proportion of accidents than did males for which they were judged responsible (**65.9** percent vs. **63.1** percent for males). A higher proportion was found in each of the three age groups but was not significant at the age group level.

The time-of-day factor, important in all age groups, was again one which changed with age. Peak period and nighttime (including dawn/dusk) involvements decreased somewhat from **38.7** percent and **24.6** percent respectively

FIGURE 2
Fault Decision Flow Diagram

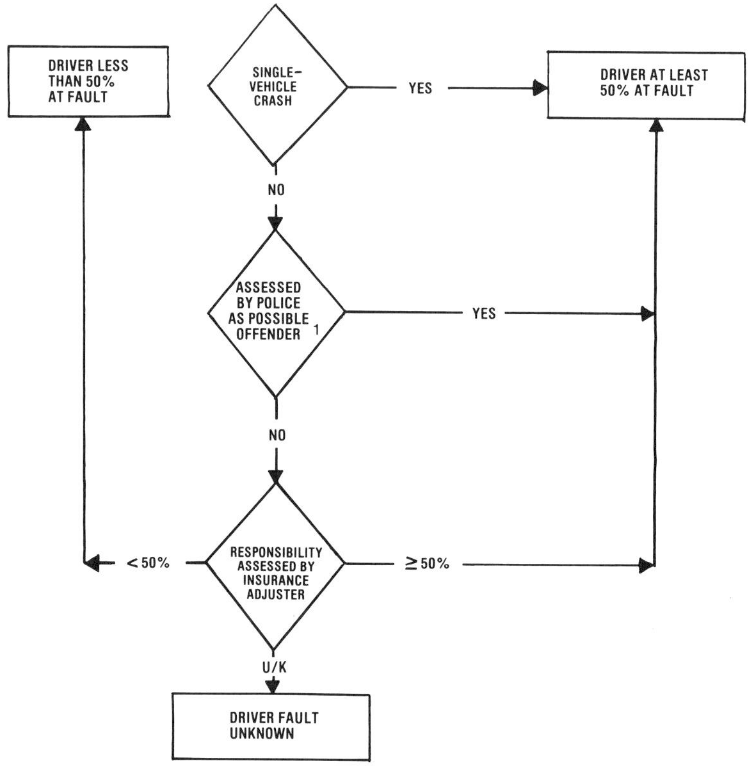

[1] There is a specific code on the police accident form for this purpose. Such an assessment is often, but not necessarily, supported by the laying of charges. The police only assign a possible offender designation to about 30% of drivers, which implies that the evidence must be reasonably strong.

FIGURE 3
Relative Probability of Accident Responsibility by Age
(88,000 Accident-Involved Drivers)

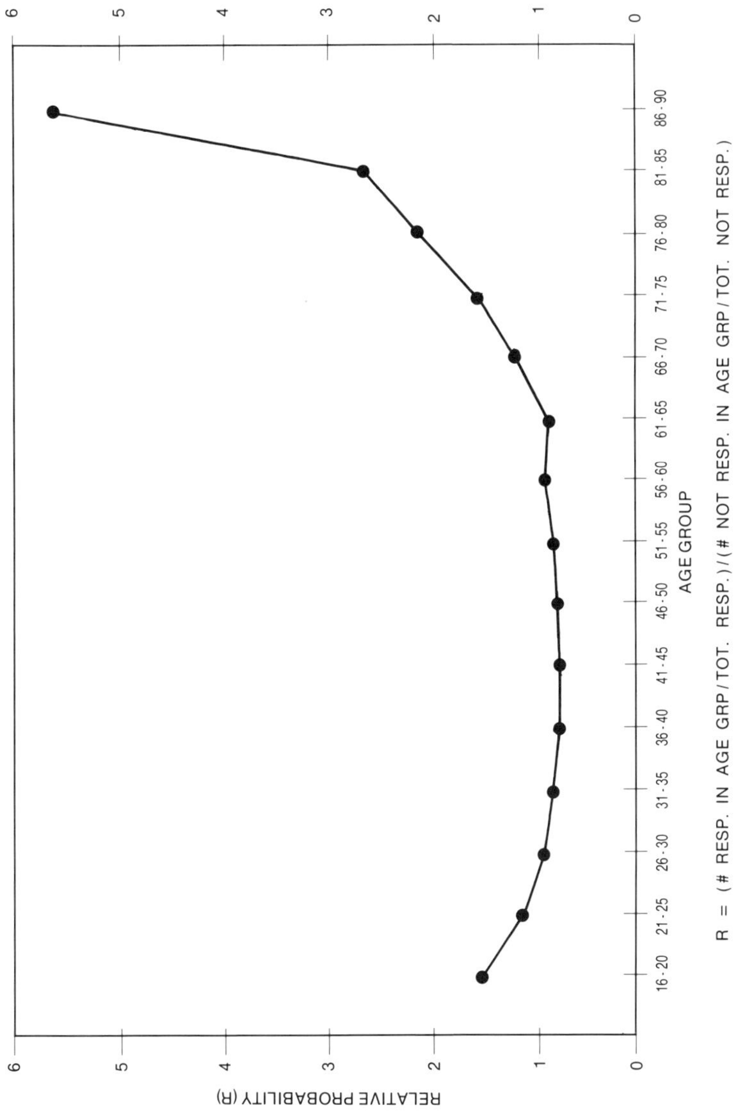

for drivers aged thirty-six to fifty to 36.8 percent and **18.5** percent for fifty-five to sixty-four year old drivers, and from there decreased more substantially to **31.5** percent and **15.9** percent for sixty-five to seventy four year old drivers, and 31.7 percent and **11.7** percent, respectively, for those seventy-five years and over. The greatest part of the difference in peak hour involvements seemed to occur between ages fifty-five to sixty-four and ages sixty-five to seventy-four. Figure 4 illustrates this. This would be an expected result of changing driving patterns following retirement. These time changes were also reflected in significant decreases in accidents occurring under dark or dawn/dusk conditions.

Roadsite geometry, as represented by intersections and type of traffic control, also exhibited a trend. For example, while **66.5** percent of thirty-six to fifty year old drivers' accidents took place at intersections (including exits from driveways and alleys), this level increased to **69.2** percent, **70.7** percent and **76.0** percent for ages fifty-five to sixty-four, sixty-five to seventy-four, and seventy-five plus, respectively. In terms of traffic control, while there were no significant differences between thirty-six to fifty year old and fifty-five to sixty-four year old drivers, the two oldest groups (sixty-five to seventy-four and seventy-five plus) were significantly more oriented towards stop/yield sign locations and less toward either uncontrolled or signalized locations. Stop/yield sign locations constituted **47.3** percent and **51.5** percent of sixty-five to seventy-four and seventy-five-plus driver age group accidents, respectively, while the proportions for the thirty-six to fifty and fifty-five to sixty-four age groups were **39.8** percent and **39.6** percent.

Finally, as alluded to earlier, weather or road condition were less-important factors with elderly drivers than with the middle-aged "control" group. This was more likely a result of less exposure during poor conditions than of increased ability to handle adverse situations. Following retirement, many vehicular trips become optional or at least capable of being rescheduled. While drivers aged thirty-six to fifty had **44.3** percent of their accidents on non-dry road surfaces, and **25.4** percent under actual precipitation conditions, this reduced to 41.9 percent and 23.5 percent, respectively, for fifty-five to sixty-four year old drivers, to **37.4** percent and **20.8** percent for sixty-five to seventy-four year old drivers, and to **31.9** percent and **19.6** percent for drivers aged seventy-five and older. Again, the major effect can be seen following age 64.

How Are Elderly Drivers Different From Middle-Aged Drivers?

We have previously seen how elderly drivers compare with their middle-aged counterparts (thirty-six to fifty years) in terms of general pre-crash factor combinations and with respect to accident responsibility. But which, if

FIGURE 4
Change in Peak Time Accident Involvement with Age

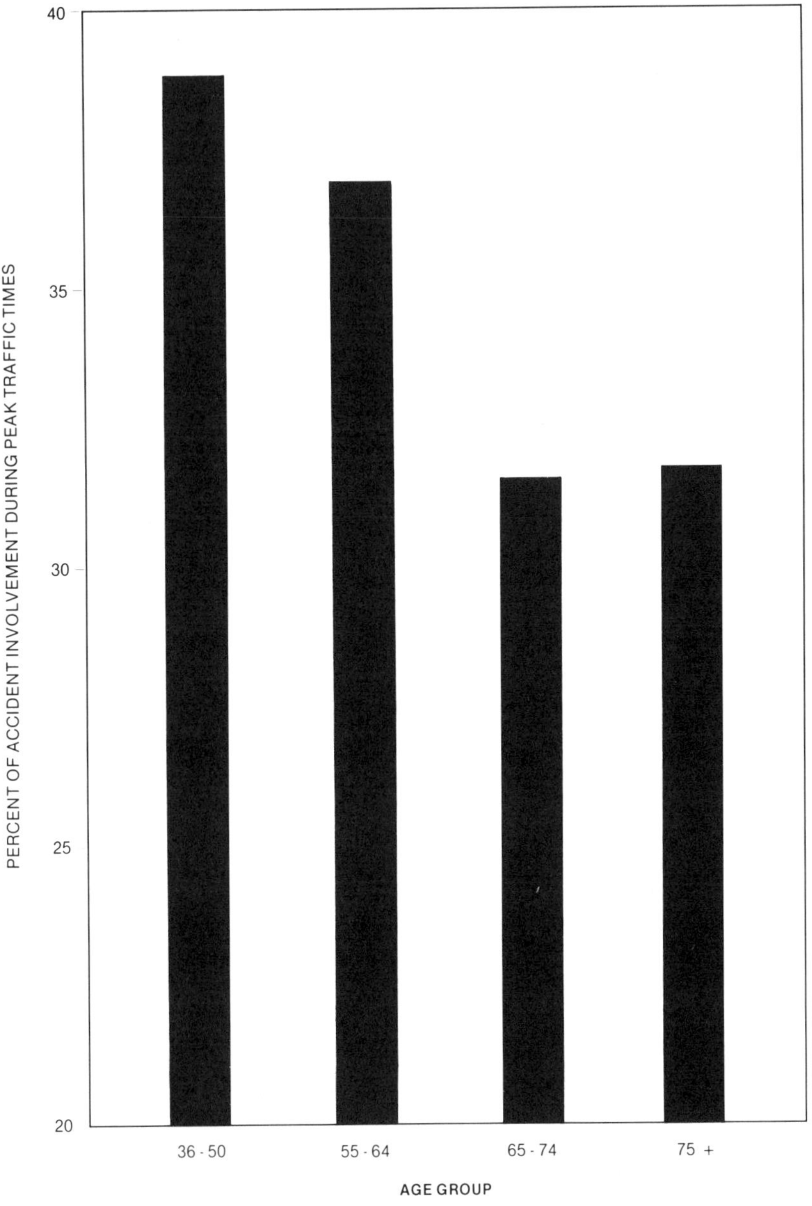

any, individual components of these factor categories, plus sociodemographic factors, can be shown to be significantly different?

In order to answer this question, we undertook a series of discriminant analyses: the thirty-six to fifty age group as compared to, successively, the fifty-five to sixty-four age group, the sixty-five to seventy-four age group, and the seventy-five-plus age group. A discriminant analysis tells us which of the tested driver characteristics are significantly different from one group to the next. Seven sociodemographic and pre-crash variables were significantly different (at the 99 percent confidence level) for all three elderly driver age groups when compared with those aged thirty-six to fifty.

Number of Convictions Accumulated in the Five Years Prior to the Accident

Only a few drivers had been driving for fewer than five years, and this length of time was also the greatest over which we could be reasonably sure that all records had been retained. For those drivers having an official experience of fewer than five years, an adjustment factor was applied to estimate a five-year total. It was based on the average rate of conviction accumulation in subsequent years of those with five years of experience and differing levels of initial conviction rates.

The average number of reported convictions was less for the elderly drivers than for the middle-aged group and the difference became more pronounced with the higher age categories (**2.39** vs. **1.58**, **1.13** and **0.81**). In terms of the proportion of drivers having one or more previous convictions, this went from **82.1** percent for the thirty-five to fifty age group to **74.3** percent, **61.6** percent and **50.1** percent for ages fifty-five to sixty-four, sixty-five to seventy-four and seventy-five plus, respectively.

Obviously, an important factor to be considered is driving exposure (both frequency and duration). This will be discussed in detail later, but for now it would simply be useful to know how many of the drivers' convictions did not likely arise from accidents. If older people drive less but are more likely to cause the accident in which they are involved, then we would expect a greater proportion of their recorded convictions to be associated with accidents than would be the case for younger (middle-aged) drivers. Comparing dates of past convictions with the dates of past accidents for each driver we arrived at the percentage of convictions associated with accidents for each age group. We then applied these percentages to the average yearly conviction rate per driver in each age group to arrive at the rate associated with "normal" (i.e., non-accident) driving. We ignored, for expediency, the fact that a few drivers would move up one elderly age category within the five-year period. When these accident-related convictions are subtracted from the average number of

TABLE 6
Data on Driver Conviction History by Age Group

	Age Group			
	36-50	55-64	65-74	75+
avg. no. of prior convictions related to accidents (per driver)	0.17	0.23	0.31	0.31
avg. no. of prior convictions in the course of "normal" driving	2.22	1.35	0.82	0.50
total no. of prior convictions (average per driver in 5 years)	2.39	1.58	1.13	0.81
proportion of prior convictions which resulted from accidents	7.2%	14.6%	27.1%	38.4%

total convictions, the range representing these "ordinary driving" violation convictions is wider than that for total convictions and especially wider than that for convictions related to accidents. Table 6 illustrates this.

From Table 6 it can be seen that for the age seventy-five-and-over drivers, for example, about 38 percent of their convictions resulted directly from accidents. This compares to the much smaller 7 percent applicable to thirty-six to fifty year old drivers. The increase in this percentage, especially beyond age sixty-four, undoubtedly reflects increasingly lower levels of driving exposure.

A further interesting result came from comparing age groups in terms of the proportion of charged drivers who were subsequently convicted. For the thirty-six to fifty year old drivers, **81.4** percent of those charged with an offense following their 1986 accident were subsequently convicted. For drivers aged fifty-five to sixty-four, this proportion rose to **86.1** percent, and for those aged sixty-five to seventy-four and seventy-five plus the proportions were **91.2** percent and **89.4** percent, respectively. This does not necessarily mean that older drivers are more often actually guilty, however. Charges against older drivers are less likely to be those of a criminal nature which are routinely contested owing to the potential serious consequences. Also, since not contesting the charge automatically produces a conviction, it is likely that respect for, or fear of, the court process deters more elderly drivers than young or middle-aged ones from fighting tickets. That "authoritarian submission" is more characteristic of the elderly than the young, or even middle-aged, is a notion well grounded in psychology. Older people tend to be more passive, conforming, and conservative in their attitudes toward social legislation and control (Kimmel 1974).

Time of the Accident

As we saw earlier, time of day is an important factor in describing accident occurrence. The time of the crash, whether in daytime peak travel hours (6:00-9:00 a.m. and 3:00-6:00 p.m.), daytime off-peak periods (9:00 a.m.-3:00 p.m.), or during mainly nighttime (6:00 p.m.-6:00 a.m.), was a significant discriminating variable between middle-aged drivers and all three elderly driver age groups. As age increased, the off-peak daytime travel period assumed more importance—largely at the expense of nighttime and evening trips. Off-peak accident association increased from **36.7** percent for the thirty-six to fifty age group; to **44.6** percent for those aged fifty-five to sixty-four; to **52.6** percent for sixty-five to seventy-four year olds and to **56.6** percent for drivers aged seventy-five and older. At the same time, nighttime (including dawn and dusk hours) involvements went from **24.6** percent to **18.5** percent, **15.9** percent and **11.7** percent, respectively.

Driver Gender

The proportion of male drivers increased between the thirty-six to fifty and fifty-five to sixty-four age groups (from **63.8** percent to **68.0** percent), and again between the sixty-five to seventy-four group and that of age seventy-five plus (**66.0** percent to **75.4** percent, respectively). The small drop between age group fifty-five to sixty-four and age group sixty-five to seventy-four was not significant.

While the proportion of males in the overall population decreases with older age groups due to greater longevity of women, most of the latter gender grew up in a society where driving was not a common activity for a woman. Even with the more rapid diminution of the number of males due to mortality, the proportion of drivers who are females still decreases with age. Such a gender shift is also seen in the proportion of licensed drivers.

Type of Vehicle Driven

As age increased, the proportion of drivers operating vehicles other than passenger cars decreased. This was especially so beyond the fifty-five to sixty-four age group. While **27.7** percent of thirty-six to fifty year old drivers and **23.2** percent of those fifty-five to sixty-four operated trucks, motorcycles, etc., the proportion for the sixty-five to seventy-four age group dropped to **15.5** percent. With the upper age range of seventy-five plus, only **8.4** percent were not driving passenger cars. To some extent, this phenomenon may be related to professional truck drivers who retire at age sixty-five, but even ordinary pickups are not generally favored by the elderly. Perhaps the image is wrong or else the need to haul the occasional load of lumber no longer exists.

Accident Contributing Factors Related to Driver Action

The proportion of accidents judged by the police to have resulted from driver action (error, misjudgment, or actual violation) increased with age grouping. For thirty-six to fifty year old drivers, only **36.7** percent were assigned such factors, while the proportion rose to **42.0** percent, **53.1** percent, and **66.3** percent for drivers in the fifty-five to sixty-four, sixty-five to seventy-four, and seventy-five-plus age groups, respectively. Conversely, the proportion of drivers not assigned any accident-contributing factor decreased from **46.5** percent to **42.8** percent, **33.1** percent and **20.2** percent respectively.

This result is similar to that reported by Verhaegen et al. (1988), who found accidents for which an elderly driver was responsible to be characterized by problems related to perception and decision-making. The investigators did not find that such problems were especially related to crashes for which younger drivers were responsible.

Pre-collision Driver Action

Pre-collision driver action relates to the driver action immediately prior to the final crash sequence (collision configuration). With pre-collision action, the increasing importance of turning movements associated with accident involvement by the elderly, and especially those over age sixty-four, was quite evident. While only 19.3 percent of pre-collision actions for thirty-six to fifty year olds involved turning, the proportion rose to 22.2 percent for fifty-five to sixty-four year olds, **26.6** percent for sixty-five to seventy-four year olds, and **32.9** percent for those seventy-five and over. The apparently increasing problem associated with turning maneuvers which is encountered by the elderly was mentioned in an earlier discussion.

Collision Configuration

For older age groups, the proportion of "right-angle" collision configurations increased from 30.1 percent of all crashes for thirty-six to fifty year old drivers to 32.7 percent, **36.9** percent and **38.7** percent for the three elderly driver age groups—fifty-five to sixty-four, sixty-five to seventy-four and seventy-five plus, respectively. Crash configurations involving vehicles in the act of turning also increased, especially for drivers seventy-five years of age and older (**13.3** percent for age thirty-six to fifty drivers vs. **20.8** percent for those aged seventy-five plus). At the same time, however, the proportion of rear-end configurations decreased.

In addition to the seven common factors described above, two other variables were significant in comparisons between the thirty-six to fifty age group and the two elderly driver groups beyond sixty-four years of age (sixty-five to seventy-four and seventy-five plus).

Road Surface Condition

Road condition was only significant as a factor differentiating the thirty-six to fifty age group from the last two elderly driver groups (age sixty-five and older). While **44.3** percent of middle-aged drivers' accidents were under wet or icy road conditions, only **37.4** percent and **31.9** percent respectively of sixty-five to seventy-four and seventy-five-plus year old drivers' accidents occurred in such environmental situations.

Either elderly drivers are better at driving on poor roadway surfaces than younger drivers, or else they tend to restrict their driving to occasions when road conditions are nonthreatening. The fact that the change was only significant beyond age sixty-five, when retirement for most makes driving a more flexible activity, supports the latter supposition.

Responsibility for the Accident

While this factor was not a significant discriminator between the thirty-six to fifty and fifty-five to sixty-four age groups (see also Figure 3), it was significant between the middle-aged drivers and both the sixty-five to seventy-four and seventy-five-plus age groups. While **51.8** percent of the thirty-six to fifty year old drivers were probably at least 50 percent responsible for the accident in which they were involved, fully **68.2** percent and **80.1** percent of the sixty-five to seventy-four and seventy-five-plus year olds respectively were so assessed. Again, this increased accident responsibility with age was discussed earlier.

Can We Distinguish Good From Bad Drivers among the Elderly?

The pre-crash factors from the accident data base discussed previously were combined with driver demographic information and past accident/conviction histories. The resulting data base contained 5,751 drivers aged fifty-five and older.

The question we wished to answer was: which, if any, of these driver-related factors, either exhibited during their last recorded accident or else representing general attributes, could be significantly related to the frequency of previous incidents—whether accidents or violation convictions—independent of other factor effects? Because of the mix of categorical and continuous variables in the data base, the best approach to the problem was to employ multivariate analysis of variance (MANOVA) techniques.

Since the maximum length of driving record available in our sample was just over five years, we created two new variables representing the total accumulated accidents and convictions in this period. For drivers having fewer than five years of experience, a correction factor was introduced. This was derived from the average rate of accumulation of accidents and violations by year for 441 drivers of differing initial conviction rates who had commenced driving five years prior to their 1986 accident. The details of such a process were described in Rothe and Cooper (1987). The past accident and conviction rates reflected driver histories prior to the 1986 accident of record. For purposes of multivariate analysis, these rates were normalized using a square-root transformation.

From the SAS.GLM procedure (with effect-coded variables) several significant main effects were identified.

Variables Related to Accident History

At the 99 percent level of confidence (the usual standard of significance required in a multivariate analysis) four variables were prominent: driver age, driver responsibility in the last accident, weather/road conditions prevalent during the last accident, and the driver conviction history.

This last factor, convictions, was by far the best indicator of past accidents. Drivers with higher yearly conviction totals were also more likely to have higher annual accident totals.

With the effect of conviction experience accounted for, however, age appeared to have an independent effect. Older drivers had more accidents. This was an interesting result, since the average number of accidents per driver accumulated over the five years previous to their 1986 crash was slightly (although not significantly) less for drivers older than fifty-four than for those in the middle-ages of thirty-six to fifty. The average numbers of accidents per driver for age groups thirty-six to fifty, fifty-five to sixty-four, sixty-five to seventy-four, and seventy-five plus were 0.515, 0.432, 0.402, and 0.434 respectively. For drivers aged fifty-five and up there was no clear trend and certainly no indication that older age groups were any less safe.

But we have already mentioned the lower amounts of driving undertaken by elderly drivers. If accumulation of convictions (at least those which are independent of accidents) is a surrogate for driving exposure, then when conviction history is held constant, older drivers may be seen to have a higher crash-involvement risk. If we use the estimated number of convictions in the course of "normal" driving (that is, not resulting from accidents) which appeared in Table 6, we can divide the above average accident totals by the conviction totals to produce a ratio of accidents per non-accident conviction. These are shown below in Table 7.

It is evident from Table 7 that the number of accidents was higher with increasing age, independent of the number of convictions accumulated during "normal" driving. Even using total convictions, the accident/conviction ratio still rises (from 0.22 to 0.54).

TABLE 7
Ratios of Accidents to Non-Accident Convictions by Age Group

Age Group	Accidents in Previous 5 Years (per driver)	Non-Accident Convictions in Previous 5 Years (per driver)	Accidents per Non-Accident Conviction
36-50	0.52	2.22	0.23
55-64	0.43	1.35	0.32
65-74	0.40	0.82	0.49
75+	0.43	0.50	0.86

The data base we used was one consisting of all police-attended accidents during 1986. Such accidents represent, in British Columbia, about two-thirds of all reported crashes, but include virtually all casualty producing incidents. Thus, the police-attended records, while having the advantage of being more reliable and having less missing data, are also biased in favor of casualty accidents. Since it has been well documented (Sammons 1987) that the elderly are more likely to be killed or injured than younger drivers in accidents of comparable severity, the question must be asked whether the increase in accidents with age beyond fifty-five years could simply result from this phenomenon.

In fact, the proportions of casualty producing accidents by age group in our data base showed no significant differences. For both thirty-six to fifty and fifty-five to sixty-four year old drivers, 41 percent of their accidents resulted in casualties, and the figures for the sixty-five to seventy-four and seventy-five-plus age group drivers were not significantly different at 40 percent and 41 percent, respectively. Given the acknowledged propensity for older drivers to be more easily injured, why was this not evident in the data? The answer most probably lies in the type of driving—most especially the speeds. While 19 percent of fifty-five to sixty-four year old drivers had their last accident in a seventy kilometer-per-hour or over speed zone, only 16 percent of sixty-five to seventy-four year old drivers and 15 percent of seventy-five-plus year olds were associated with such high-speed areas. While these differences were not statistically significant with the sample sizes available, nevertheless they do suggest a consistent downward trend in high-speed (and therefore high severity) exposure which could offset the otherwise expected greater likelihood of injury.

Another factor related to age and accident accumulation is collision fault assessment. As we might expect from previous findings, those drivers judged to have been 50 percent or more responsible for their last crash had significantly higher levels of past accidents than did those who were not.

Finally, the type of driving day on which the last accident occurred was found to be significantly related to past accident accumulation. Interestingly, those drivers whose last collision involvement had taken place under poor weather or road conditions were found, when other factors were accounted for, to have lower past accident totals than were those whose last crash had been in good conditions. We have already seen that drivers in the over-sixty-four age groups had a significantly smaller proportion of their crashes under poor environmental conditions than did middle-aged drivers. In fact, this lower proportion was significant in a univariate sense even against age fifty-five to sixty-four drivers.

Yet an examination of previous accident accumulation for those whose last crash occurred under good conditions as compared with those whose last crash was under poor conditions, showed consistently higher totals for the former in all three elderly driver age groups.

It is obvious from Figure 5 that the major part of the effect was manifested for drivers having three or more total convictions in the five-year period (about 15 percent of all the drivers). In addition, those whose last crash occurred under poor driving conditions had, overall, more past convictions than those whose last crash was in good conditions (1.38 vs. 1.26 respectively). If such a characteristic reflects greater driving exposure for the former, then the accident difference shown in Figure 5 might be related to the way in which these people drive. Perhaps relatively high-mileage elderly drivers are generally more competent than those who drive less. But poor weather is a great equalizer. Not driving under poor road surface or visibility conditions could be a means by which some elderly drivers either consciously or unconsciously compensate for deteriorating driving abilities.

If previous convictions are, in this case, primarily representative of driving exposure, then the poor-weather-accident drivers would certainly be defined as safer drivers having significantly fewer previous accidents per conviction than their good-weather-accident counterparts. These relatively safe drivers may have normally avoided venturing out in hazardous driving conditions owing to a general feeling of discomfort with such situations but yet being unaware of the full extent of their inability to cope with them. Perhaps much of their safe rating is due to avoidance of high-risk opportunities. Then when force of circumstance placed them on the road in bad weather they found themselves unable to cope with unforeseen events.

The correspondence of five-year conviction proportions with annual travel mileage from a 1979 Transport Canada survey (discussed in detail below in *The Travel Characteristics of the Elderly*) can be seen in Figure 6. It is evident that the conviction proportions are more closely related to the mileage proportions than to the percentage of drivers involved. Even though some differences in violation rates may occur between age groups and genders, generally speaking the more one drives the more convictions one will tend to accumulate. Thus, with large, relatively homogeneous groups, convictions may provide a

FIGURE 5
Relationship Between Past Accident/Conviction Experience and the Environmental Conditions of the Last Crash for Drivers Age 55 and Over

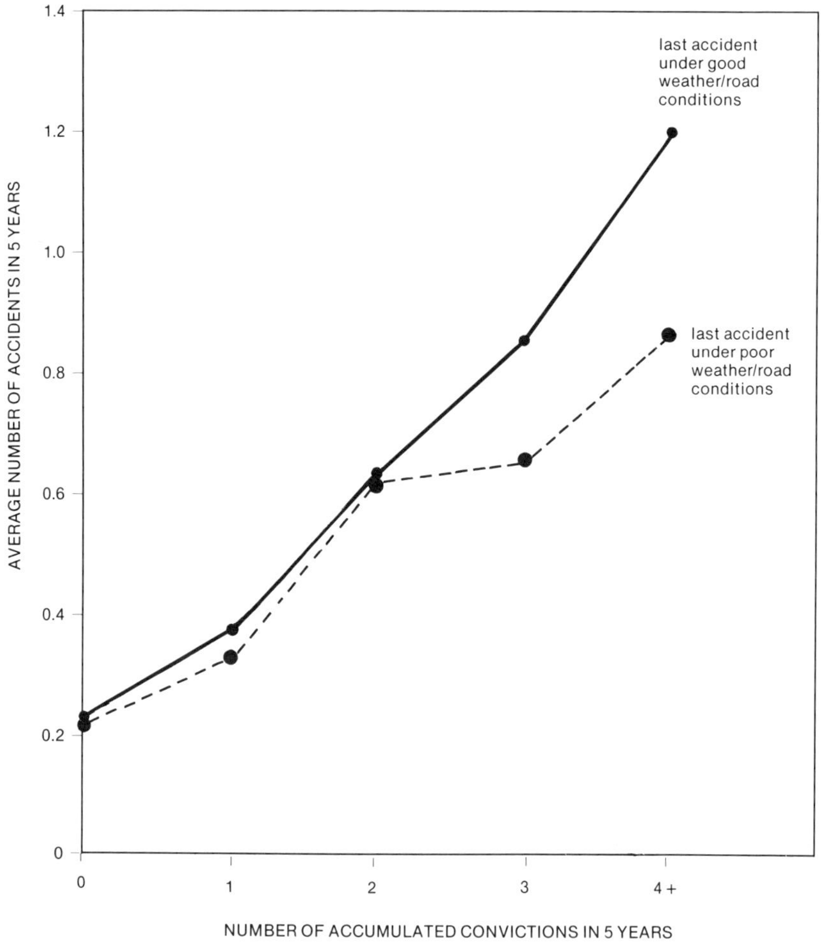

FIGURE 6
Applicability of Conviction Totals as a Surrogate for Amount of Travel

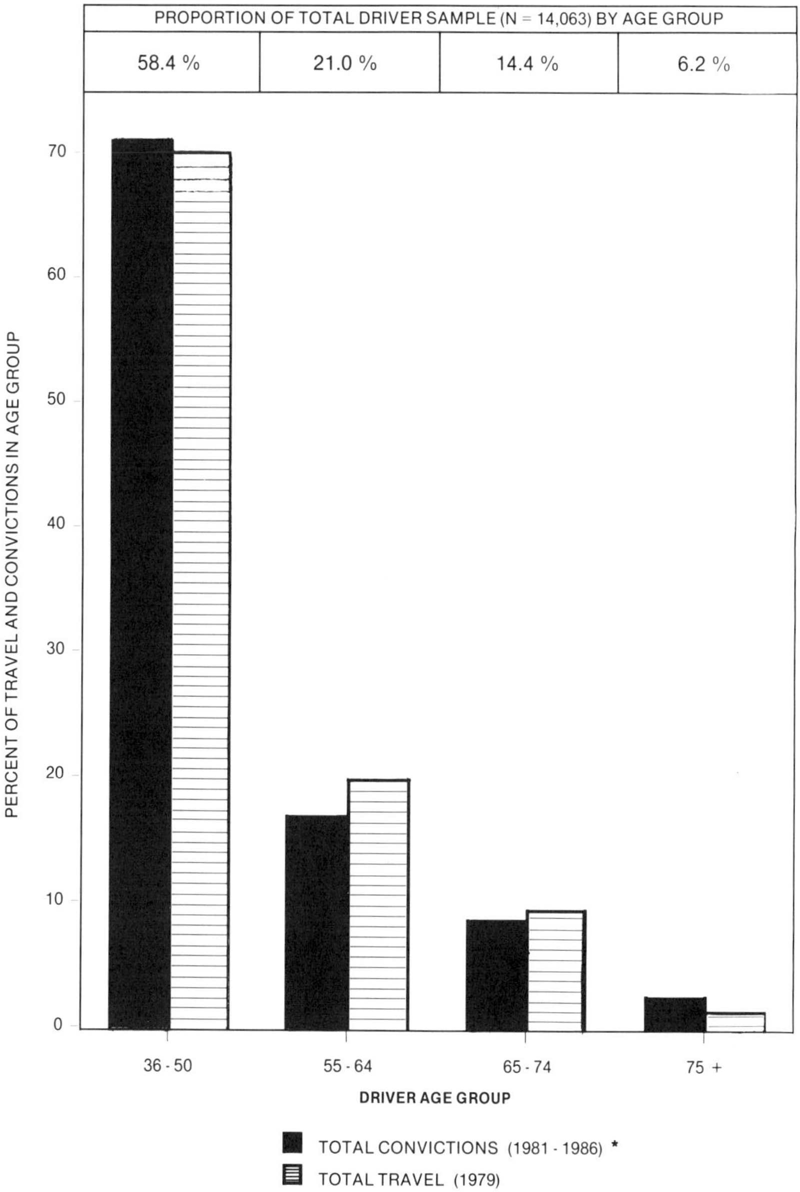

* Not associated with accidents.

useable surrogate for travel estimates. For example, five-year accident relative risks for elderly drivers calculated on the basis of estimated mileage and on the basis of convictions unrelated to accidents were reasonably similar. For ages thirty-six to fifty, fifty-five to sixty-four, sixty-five to seventy-four, and seventy-five plus, the relative risks based on population estimated mileage proportions were 0.90, 0.97, 1.46, and 3.29, respectively. Based on non-accident-related conviction proportions, they were 0.88, 1.11, 1.54, and 2.08, respectively.

Our 130 in-depth interviews reported in Chapter Eight provided us with a sample of elderly drivers who had all very recently been involved in injury-producing crashes. With a random survey sample of 904 elderly drivers, in Chapter Six on the other hand, only 3 percent had been involved in an injury-producing crash within the last five years. The sample of 130 drivers thus probably represents a historically higher-risk group than the larger population sample. Of our 904 interviewed elderly drivers from the general population, **74.8** percent said they avoided driving under one or more of the following conditions: rain, fog, snow, or ice. However, of the 130 elderly drivers recently involved in a serious accident, only **46.9** percent said that they avoided driving under any one or more of these conditions. It may thus be reasonable to suggest that low accident-risk drivers are typically those who avoid going out in bad weather or other uncomfortable circumstances, whereas the higher-risk drivers may be somewhat more competent under adverse conditions. Of the 130 accidents involving the in-depth interviewed drivers, only **21.5** percent occurred under poor road or weather conditions. This compares with **38.9** percent for our overall accident data base sample of elderly drivers.

Perhaps low-risk elderly drivers tend to get into trouble when they drive in unfamiliar or poor conditions, but higher-risk elderly drivers' problems stem from general driving habits, and not specifically from poor road or visibility conditions for which they make adjustments. This theme came out over and over again when we examined the 130 in-depth driver interviews. The majority of drivers were at least nonchalant, and many almost boasted, about their ability to handle any weather conditions. They were experienced and confident. They considered themselves able to make the correct adjustments. Possibly the same confidence which serves them well under adverse environmental conditions becomes overconfidence or lack of caution when "perfect" weather prevails.

In order to gain some further insight into the matter, we examined charges laid by police following the last accident. We looked at only those elderly with high previous conviction totals (three or more) and compared "good day" vs. "poor day" accident-involved drivers. We found that those who were involved under good conditions had a significantly higher proportion of their charges related to errors in attention and/or decision making than did those who crashed in poor conditions. For the former, **40.0** percent of charges were for disobeying traffic control devices, driving without due care, lane line and passing infractions, and improper turns. For the latter group, these violations made up only **22.8** percent of all convictions.

A slightly greater proportion of the high conviction record drivers involved on a "good day" were judged responsible (65 percent) than was the case for their "poor day" counterparts (62 percent); but a substantial number of the latter were judged responsible simply as a result of their failure to adjust to the poor driving conditions.

As Verhaegen et al. (1988) have suggested, it may be that accident responsibility among the elderly is related to problems of perception and decision making. Also, persons who exhibit such driving errors may be poor accident risks generally and thus have higher past levels of accident accumulation than those who do not. Later in this chapter we will discuss the relation between age and changes in recognition and response capabilities that lead to such driving errors, and which have been postulated to have a detrimental effect on safety.

In closing this discussion on the multivariate analysis of accident characteristics, it should be noted that all significant interactions (down to the 95 percent confidence level) between variables were investigated for disordinality or "crossing" effects. No such disordinalities were discovered, and thus the findings with respect to the main effects described above can be considered valid.

Variables Related to Conviction History

In terms of conviction history, the greatest independent determinants were age and gender. Older drivers had fewer convictions, a fact which has already been interpreted as likely an outcome of lower exposure. And male drivers had more convictions than females. This does not necessarily mean that males are more prone to committing violations than females. Again, it is most likely a reflection of the greater amount of driving done by males. From the 1979 Transport Canada driving survey results, we estimated that 74 percent of the annual mileage by drivers aged fifty-five and older was accumulated by males even though they formed only 63 percent of the licensed drivers at that time. In terms of accidents, the effects of increased exposure by males was evidently accounted for by the inclusion of convictions as an independent variable. No similar exposure surrogate was available when examining conviction accumulation itself.

Both age and gender effects on conviction frequency are thus most likely the result of driving exposure differences. Independent of age, however,

TABLE 8
Past Average Conviction Totals for Drivers by Age and Responsibility for Last Accident

Driver Age Group	Responsible in Last Accident	
	No	Yes
21-35	3.53	4.00
36-50	2.34	2.44
55-64	1.65	1.53
65-74	1.38	1.01
75+	1.21	0.71

driver experience was significantly (at the 99 percent confidence level) associated with convictions. Those with more driving experience, regardless of age, had fewer convictions. This agrees with the finding with respect to motorcyclists cited by Rothe and Cooper (1987) that more convictions are accumulated within the first few years of licensure than in later years.

Unlike the case with accident records, being judged not responsible in their last crash was a significant indicator of more convictions on drivers' records. This was a very surprising finding. In examining accident-involved motorcycle riders, virtually all of whom were under forty-four years of age, Rothe and Cooper (1987) found that those identified by police as possible causers had significantly higher levels of past convictions than those who did not. The suspicion that the different direction of these two reported effects is age related is substantiated by Table 8, which shows average past conviction rates for responsible vs. not responsible drivers in different age groups ranging from young to elderly.

Table 8 illustrates that for younger drivers, last-accident responsibility is clearly linked to worse conviction records but this effect reverses itself as age increases beyond fifty-five years, and becomes steadily more pronounced right through to the oldest driver grouping. A possible explanation may relate to greater respect or anxiety produced in elderly drivers by authority figures, such as police and judges, as was discussed earlier in this chapter. We have already seen that elderly drivers are probably more likely to plead guilty if charged. Since we are starting with a group of drivers involved in accidents during one particular year of record, the probability of such accident involvement is not relevant here. The only issue is "were they or were they not responsible?" Those elderly drivers who had previously (within the prior five years) received a conviction for a traffic offense could conceivably have been shaken enough by the experience to cause them to take care that it did not happen again. Thus, the accident in which they were subsequently involved was less likely to be their fault. Young drivers may have the confidence (albeit misplaced) to repeat their mistakes, whereas elderly drivers may not—at least when it comes to definable violations.

The use of safety belts was another item significantly associated with conviction history. Those drivers reported by the police not to have been wearing restraints during their last accident had worse conviction records than those who the police did not identify as nonwearers. This relationship is probably even more pronounced than it appears since we know that in British Columbia about 15 percent of nonwearers are probably shown on the accident report form as wearers (Cooper 1986).

Another variable whose direction was at odds with young driver research (Rothe 1986) was the carrying of passengers. Elderly drivers carrying a passenger or passengers at the time of their last accident involvement had lower conviction records than those driving alone. In examining the relationship among passenger carrying, age, and conviction record, it appeared that such a result applied to middle-aged as well as elderly drivers. Driving alone, for example, may be more associated with alcohol in the case of older drivers than the very young, whose drinking is almost invariably in groups. Twice as great a proportion of solitary elderly drivers in our accident sample were associated with drinking and driving than was the case for elderly drivers who carried a passenger. Also, the in-car social interactions which adversely affect young drivers' performance may, in older drivers, enhance alertness and produce more responsible actions. After all, in later life such passengers are most likely very close friends and loved ones as opposed to the more casual acquaintances who may ride with young drivers. Two-thirds of our 904 surveyed drivers in Chapter Six indicated that when they carried passengers these were most likely to be either immediate family or other relatives.

The time of the last accident was also found to be significantly associated with past convictions. Those elderly drivers whose 1986 crash had been during the evening or at night were more likely to have higher previous conviction counts. Likewise, drivers who were proceeding straight ahead immediately prior to the accident had more previous convictions than those performing other actions. Both nighttime and higher speed roadways with fewer intersections (i.e., more chance of straight-ahead travel) could relate to social activities, possibly involving drinking. Even at intersection locations, however, going straight could involve failure to yield right-of-way.

Again, as with accident history, no disordinal interactions, which could invalidate the main effects presented above, were found.

The Travel Characteristics of the Elderly

In 1979, Transport Canada conducted a major driving exposure survey using a "diary" format (Lawson and Stewart 1981). Drivers who agreed to participate were instructed to log all trips over a specified period. Over 22,000 trips were reported by those surveyed in British Columbia during the all-year period over which the survey was conducted. About 4,200 of these trips were by drivers fifty-five years of age or older.

While the survey was conducted almost ten years ago at time of writing, the levels of traffic accidents and driving activity (as measured by gasoline sales) were not very different from the current situation. This is because in British Columbia, the intervening years have seen an economic recession (1981) and subsequent recovery (1983 to present) which has left us today in much the same place as we were in 1979-80 (for a discussion of the economic effects on accidents in B.C. during this period, see Cooper 1986). The proportion of drivers in the fifty-five-and-older age bracket increased between 1979 and 1986, but only by 0.5 percent—not enough to warrant the introduction of correction factors for 1979 exposures.

Fortuitously, therefore, since there has been no subsequent investigation of such scope and comprehensiveness, the results of this survey are still probably valid at least insofar as relative proportions of travel by driver age category in British Columbia are concerned. Percentages of total travel by age group will thus be reported in the analyses which follow, rather than actual mileage or numbers of trips.

The Transport Canada "diary" survey approach is considered a more accurate method of gauging actual distance driven than is asking people (especially elderly people) to estimate how many kilometers or miles they drive in a year. Thus, we would not expect a very close agreement between the Transport Canada results and our elderly driver questionnaire survey reported in Chapter Six. Nevertheless, the findings of the two surveys are not greatly different in respect to the percent of total elderly driver mileage by age group. The Transport Canada results give 66 percent of the mileage accruing to drivers older than fifty-four as being associated with the fifty-five to sixty-four age group, 28 percent associated with drivers aged sixty-five to seventy-four and 6 percent associated with those aged seventy-five or over. Our questionnaire produced proportions of 56 percent, 32 percent, and 12 percent respectively.

While Canada-wide results of the Transport Canada survey have been reported in the literature (Lawson and Stewart 1981), the analysis which follows is based upon British Columbia data extracted from the national data base. Such an analysis had not been undertaken prior to this current study except in a less comprehensive manner as a basis for an earlier assessment of accident risk factors (Cooper 1985).

The 22,194 reported trips from the Transport Canada survey were broken down by age and gender as shown on page 115.

Average Length of Trip

Since the survey was not designed to produce accurate estimates of total miles

	16-19	20-24	25-44	45-54	55-64	65-74	75+
male	1,253	1,756	5,617	2,392	1,473	1,013	283
female	978	1,063	3,878	1,041	986	372	89
Total	2,231	2,819	9,495	3,433	2,459	1,385	372

Total	
13,787	(62.1%)
8,407	(37.9%)
22,194	(100.0%)

or kilometers travelled per year by different age groups, the approach we took in reporting these figures is a comparative format. In other words, we addressed the question, "how long is the average trip taken by fifty-five to sixty-four year old drivers relative to that taken by drivers in another age group?"

For male drivers, the longest trips (average miles per trip) were taken by those aged forty-five to fifty-four. With these expressed as units, the relative average trip lengths by age group for male drivers were as follows:

Age Group	Trip Length
16-19	0.64
20-24	0.66
25-44	0.78
45-54	1.00
55-64	0.88
65-74	0.59
75+	0.46

The low ratio for young drivers needs some clarification. For example, while sixteen to nineteen year old male drivers apparently take shorter trips, they take many of them. Thus, in terms of total distance travelled, they are overrepresented in comparison with their proportion of the driving population (**5.3** percent of licensed drivers but **8.2** percent of annual travel).

For female drivers, we found that those aged twenty-five to forty-four took the longest trips, although forty-five to fifty-four year olds were not far behind. Relatively speaking, female age groups compared as follows:

Age Group	Trip Length
16-19	0.73
20-24	0.72
25-44	1.00
45-54	0.98
55-64	0.90
65-74	0.77
75+	0.41

It can be seen from the above figures that females as compared to males had less variation in average trip length, at least between the ages of sixteen and seventy-five, suggesting a life continuum. For both male and female drivers, the average trip length seems to fall off substantially after age sixty-four. However, there is a continuous decline from age fifty-five on.

In order to compare males and females directly, we can calculate relative trip lengths for females by age group using male trip lengths as the baseline (i.e., males = 1.00) in each group.

Age Group	Trip Length
16-19	0.73
20-24	0.65
25-44	0.76
45-54	0.58
55-64	0.61
65-74	0.76
75 +	0.53

Evidently male drivers take longer trips than females in all age groups, but especially in the seventy-five-plus category.

Trip duration times were also recorded by Transport Canada researchers in their 1979 survey, and these were obtainable from our data base in terms of frequency distributions by age and gender. Table 9 gives results for all drivers surveyed in British Columbia.

Generally speaking, it can be seen that very short trips (ten minutes or less) are less popular with older drivers. On the other hand, long trips of an hour or more comprised a somewhat larger proportion of the travel of elderly drivers fifty-five to seventy-four years old than was the case with drivers in the sixteen to forty-four age categories. Drivers seventy-five years of age and older, however, had a smaller percentage of trips in the one-or-more hour category.

Comparing male and female drivers, it was evident that in all age groups below that of seventy-five plus, females had a higher proportion of very short (less than or equal to ten minutes) trips than did males. Males, on the other hand, had a greater percentage of their trips in the over-twenty-minute categories than did females.

Trip Purpose

The age categories reported in the foregoing discussion of trip length covered the full range of sixteen to seventy-five-plus years. This range was reported so as to put into perspective the amount of driving done by the elderly—especially in light of previous assessments of accident risk and col-

TABLE 9
Distribution of Trip Duration Time by Age Group

	Age Group						
Trip Duration	**16-19**	**20-24**	**25-44**	**45-54**	**55-64**	**65-74**	**75+**
≤10 minutes	49.3%	44.9%	45.6%	39.6%	40.2%	40.9%	36.0%
10-20 minutes	26.0%	29.1%	28.0%	31.4%	32.1%	27.4%	33.9%
20-30 minutes	11.6%	12.3%	13.9%	12.6%	13.1%	13.5%	15.1%
30-60 minutes	9.7%	9.9%	9.0%	12.3%	10.0%	12.7%	12.6%
1-2 hours	2.4%	3.1%	2.5%	2.9%	2.9%	4.1%	1.8%
2-3 hours	0.5%	0.4%	0.5%	0.6%	1.0%	1.0%	0.3%
3-4 hours	0.4%	0.2%	0.2%	0.2%	0.5%	0.2%	0.3%
4-6 hours	0.0%	0.1%	0.2%	0.2%	0.1%	0.1%	0.0%
>6 hours	0.1%	0.0%	0.1%	0.2%	0.1%	0.1%	0.0%
	(100.0%)	(100.0%)	(100.0%)	(100.0%)	(100.0%)	(100.0%)	(100.0%)

lision responsibility. With trip purpose and other factors which follow, however, we wish to make a comparison with our accident data and thus information presented will be restricted to the three elderly groups as compared to a middle-aged category of thirty-six to fifty. This age range represents the lowest portion of the culpable accident risk curve in Figure 3. Since thirty-six to fifty year olds were not one of the Transport Canada programmed survey groupings for extraction, data relative to this category have been computed as a weighted average of the twenty-five to forty-four and forty-five to fifty-four groups.

The accuracy of such a weighted averaging process was checked in the case of total estimated miles of travel, which had the most potential for variation. Aggregate totals for each individual age were available and the actual cumulative total for those aged thirty-six to fifty could be compared with the weighted average (by year-of-age frequency) of the twenty-five to forty-four and forty-five to fifty-four accumulations. The weighted average estimate was found to be higher than the summation by 9 percent (i.e., a factor of 1.09). Such a level of possible error was less than the coefficients of variation associated with the twenty-five to forty-four and forty-five to sixty-four age group mileage samples themselves.

Trip purpose was coded on the Transport Canada survey in five categories: commuting, business, shopping, personal/family, and social. Business driving is conceptually different from other forms of road travel in that it is not a negotiated event. Sales people, for example, have to be on the road to make a living. Also, it is typically without a principal origin and destination. To illustrate, a truck driver may make numerous pickups and deliveries over an eight-hour period. We wished to examine how elderly people exercise driving options, not how they are required to perform as part of employment. Thus commuting is a viable point of comparison between age groups, because it entails time, route, and modal options for most, whereas business- or work-related driving is not. Accordingly, business travel has been excluded from our analysis. Similarly, when we examined accident involvement, those taking extended vacations away from their city or community of residence were excluded from further consideration.

The 1979 survey produced the following estimates of trip purpose proportions by age group, as shown in Table 10. Male and female responses have been combined.

The largest change with advancing age is obviously in the proportion of commuting trips. These fall dramatically after age sixty-four as expected. Replacing commuting for drivers over sixty-four seem to be largely socially oriented trips and, to a slightly lesser extent, shopping. Trips related to personal or family matters (visiting a doctor or one's married children, for example) do not, interestingly, seem to become noticeably more pronounced.

TABLE 10
Proportion of Non-Business Trips by Trip Purpose and Age Group—Driving Exposure Survey

			Age Group		
Trip Purpose	**36-50**	**55-64**	**65-74**	**75+**	**55+**
Commuting	30.3%	28.0%	9.7%	4.0%	19.7%
Shopping	20.4%	24.1%	29.8%	36.4%	27.1%
Personal/family	23.6%	23.1%	29.0%	24.2%	25.2%
Social	25.7%	24.8%	31.5%	35.4%	28.0%
	(100.0%)	(100.0%)	(100.0%)	(100.0%)	(100.0%)

The proportion of commuting trips by age group in Table 10 is very similar to the percent of persons in our questionnaire survey (Chapter Six) who reported using their car for driving to and from work. In the fifty-five to sixty-four, sixty-five to seventy-four and seventy-five-plus age groups these were 23 percent, 6 percent, and 4 percent respectively.

In terms of gender, there were some notable differences in travel patterns. A much higher proportion of males than females in all age groups undertook commuting trips. Shopping was more heavily favored as a trip purpose by females than males in the under-sixty-five groups, but the proportions began to even out beyond this age, until by age seventy-five and over males reported a higher proportion of trips related to shopping than females. On the other hand, social trips were relatively more important to females than to males in all age groups.

Of those 130 drivers age fifty-five and older whom we interviewed in-depth following their involvement in a relatively serious crash, the breakdown of stated trip purposes at the time of the accidents was somewhat different from that shown on the right of Table 10. Only about 7 percent of our interviewees were engaged in commuting, and social activities also ranked low at 15 percent. Personal/family matters constituted the most common purpose at 40 percent, closely followed by shopping trips at 38 percent. One aspect of their trips which stood out, however, was that when either origin or destination was given as "home" it was more likely to be the latter. Sixty percent were heading home rather than leaving home, and home was the destination for 49 percent of all the drivers interviewed.

In order to see whether or not such an emphasis on home trips among accident-involved drivers was specifically a characteristic of the elderly or was true for younger drivers as well, we examined claim files for a random subset of 240 of our 14,063 accidents; 120 within the thirty-six to fifty age group and forty in each of the three elderly driver age categories. Twenty-nine percent of randomly selected accident involvements from the large data base were found to contain no trip purpose information when the files were examined in detail. A total of 337 files were thus examined in order to arrive at the final 240 utilized. The same trip circumstance exclusions (business and vacation) as described previously were made.

While of all drivers aged thirty-six to fifty, 36 percent were on their way home when the accident occurred, this proportion rose to 53 percent for fifty-five to sixty-four year old drivers, and was a very similar 58 percent and 50 percent for drivers aged sixty-five to seventy-four and seventy-five plus, respectively. The overall average for drivers aged fifty-five and over was 53 percent, a figure not unlike the 49 percent found with the in-depth interview sample. This proportion of **53.3** percent for all drivers aged fifty-five and over was significantly higher than the **35.9** percent found for the thirty-six to fifty age group. Where home was either the trip origin or destination, elderly drivers' accidents were found to happen on the way home 73 percent of the time, as compared to 55 percent of the time for middle-aged drivers.

Home featured more prominently as either the origin or destination of elderly drivers' trips than for those of middle-aged drivers. The latter were more likely to have both origin and destination of the same trip as locations other than home. For example, going back to work after lunch or leaving the hairdresser to go shopping. The elderly seemed more "home-based."

In terms of age and gender, the claim-file subset was distributed as follows:

	36-50	**55-64**	**65-74**	**75+**	**Total**	
male	70	22	26	29	147	(61.3%)
female	50	18	14	11	93	(38.7%)
Total	120	40	40	40	240	(100.0%)

The trip purpose breakdown for the accident-involved subset is as shown in Table 11. By far the greatest proportion of elderly driver accidents were on trips classified as personal or family-related.

Comparison of Tables 11 and 10 leads to estimation of relative accident risks for different trip purposes by age group, i.e., middle-aged (thirty-six to fifty) vs. elderly (fifty-five and over). These are shown in Table 12 where the relative risk of an accident is calculated as the ratio of the percent of all

TABLE 11
Proportion of Non-Business Trips by Trip Purpose and Age Group—Accident-Involved Drivers

	Age Group	
Trip Purpose	**36-50**	**55+**
Commuting	39.4%	11.3%
Shopping	15.9%	22.5%
Personal/family	21.3%	40.8%
Social	23.4%	25.4%
	(100.0%)	(100.0%)

TABLE 12
Relative Risk of Accident by Trip Purpose and Age Group

Trip Purpose	Age Group 36-50	55+
Commuting	1.23	0.62
Shopping	0.75	0.90
Personal/family	0.85	1.76
Social	0.86	0.97

accident-involved trips to the percent of all reported trips using the total sample of drivers (aged thirty-six to seventy-five plus) as the basis. A relative index of 1.0 represents a neutral risk, i.e., the percent of all accidents equals the percent of all trips. The reader must be cautioned against applying these, and subsequent, risk estimates within the total driving population. They are only applicable when considering the subset of drivers thirty-six years of age and older.

As with Table 11, Table 12 gives no breakdown of elderly driver age groups. All drivers aged fifty-five and older are considered as one group. This was done of necessity because of the small accident sample sizes in each age group. In order to have sufficient numbers for meaningful analysis in all cells of a full 4 x 4 matrix of trip purpose vs. age group, a sample size of many hundred elderly drivers would have been required. The necessity of hand-searching files for hard-copy trip information made this impractical.

Not unexpectedly, the highest relative accident risk for middle-aged drivers was found to be on commuting trips (to or from work). Presumably time pressures, stress, and preoccupation with work problems have an effect, and the presence of higher traffic volumes at such times of day make inattentive or aggressive driving even more dangerous.

As we will see later, high-traffic afternoon peak periods are also a problem for elderly drivers but not, apparently, when they are driving home from work. Commuting trips were associated with relatively low accident risk for elderly drivers. Perhaps those who still work have largely abandoned the "rat race" to their younger colleagues. Where elderly drivers do seem to run into problems, however, is on trips related to personal or family matters. For example, visiting their doctor, bank, hairdresser, or grown children, or having their car serviced. Such situations may well generate a greater-than-average level of anxiety or preoccupation which, in turn, leads to lack of attention to driving and lessened ability to react properly to unforeseen situations.

There is most probably a certain amount of overlap between shopping and personal trips, since both purposes may be accomplished on the same outing. Thus, the greater emphasis on shopping trips within the interview sample of 130 drivers in Chapter Eight may be partly because more detail concerning trips was given here than was available from claim files. On the other hand,

TABLE 13
Proportion of Trips by Start Time Period and Age Group—
Driving Exposure Survey

Driver Age Group	Trip Start Time (24 Hour Clock) 0-7	8-10	11-15	16-18	19-20	21-24	
36-50	10.7%	17.0%	32.4%	23.9%	8.5%	7.5%	(100.0%)
55-64	11.0%	16.0%	38.2%	22.1%	6.7%	6.0%	(100.0%)
65-74	4.7%	19.6%	47.2%	15.1%	7.5%	5.9%	(100.0%)
75+	3.6%	23.1%	43.6%	18.4%	5.8%	5.5%	(100.0%)

the interviewed drivers were obviously involved in a much higher proportion of injury crashes than those in the data base subset (100 percent vs. 41 percent). Perhaps the risk of serious accident by trip purpose differs somewhat from that of minor crashes.

Trip Time

Table 13 lists percentages of trips begun by time period for middle-aged and elderly drivers.

The most evident change with advancing age is probably the reduction in pre-7:00 a.m. starts beyond the age of sixty-four. This mirrors the drop in commuting trips noted in the previous section. At the same time the figures generally show more driving during off-peak periods for the elderly as the previous analysis of accident records seemed to indicate.

In terms of gender differences, males had a greater proportion of very early morning (before 7:00 a.m.) trips, but late afternoon peak trips were relatively evenly balanced except for the seventy-five-plus age group, where females predominated. Since females in all but the seventy-five-plus age group had a greater proportion of their trips between 8:00 a.m. and 3:00 p.m. than did males, we evidently have a situation where outgoing (from home) trip times vary by trip purpose but return trips tend to bunch together in the afternoon peak hours regardless of trip purpose. For example, commuters leave for work at 7:30 a.m. and return home between 4:00 and 6:00 p.m., and shoppers leave home between 8:00 a.m. and 3:00 p.m. and also may tend to return between 4:00 and 6:00 p.m. This produces a phenomenon well known to traffic engineers—the afternoon peak is usually heavier than the morning one. This period of time is especially associated with accidents in urban areas (Oppenlander 1976). For support, we searched through the information obtained from our 904 interviewed elderly drivers. We found that almost half (44 percent) of the respondents usually drove during both morning and afternoon periods.

Accident times were available for each of the 14,063 crashes on our 1986 data base. The distribution of accidents by age and gender was as follows:

	36-50	55-64	65-74	75+	TOTAL	
male	5,236	2,015	1,330	658	9,239	(65.7%)
female	2,974	947	688	215	4,824	(34.3%)
Total	8,210	2,962	2,018	873	14,063	(100.0%)

TABLE 14
Proportion of Accidents by Time Period and Age Group—
Accident-Involved Drivers

Driver Age	Accident Time (24 Hour Clock)						
Group	0-7	8-10	11-15	16-18	19-20	21-24	
36-50	6.5%	16.4%	33.5%	25.2%	9.4%	9.0%	(100.0%)
55-64	4.4%	16.4%	40.7%	24.0%	7.1%	7.4%	(100.0%)
65-74	1.5%	12.3%	48.8%	24.7%	6.9%	5.8%	(100.0%)
75+	1.2%	12.6%	52.1%	23.5%	6.6%	4.0%	(100.0%)

The accident data can also be sorted into time categories. Table 14 shows this.

As we did previously with trip purpose, we can use the proportions of all accidents and all trips represented by the main age groups (middle-aged and elderly) to estimate relative risks by trip time. Owing to relatively small survey sample cell sizes in the seventy-five-plus age group (as low as thirteen in one time category), ages sixty-five to seventy-four and seventy-five plus have been combined. The results are shown in Table 15.

Table 15 indicates clearly that the time period from 9:00 p.m. to midnight is most hazardous for drivers between the ages of thirty-six and sixty-four. The level of hazard during this nighttime period is similar for drivers aged sixty-five and older, but for this latter group the worst time of day appears to be 4:00-6:00 p.m.—the afternoon rush period or peak time and, in the fall and winter, dusk. Given the previously identified problems elderly drivers seem to have with intersections (turning, failing to yield, etc.), it is perhaps not surprising that the busiest traffic period, with the added potential of glare, is when they have the most difficulty.

TABLE 15
Relative Risk of Accident by Trip Time and Age Group
Accident-Involved Drivers

	Age Group		
Trip Time	36-50	55-64	65+
0-7	0.59	0.36	0.39
8-10	0.94	0.92	0.75
11-15	1.01	0.96	1.32
16-18	1.03	0.98	1.91
19-20	1.07	0.96	1.17
21-24	1.16	1.11	1.10

TABLE 16
Trip Day by Age Group—Driving Exposure Survey

Age Group	Day of Week of Trip Weekday	Weekend	
36-50	77.3%	22.6%	(100.0%)
55-64	77.7%	22.3%	(100.0%)
65-74	75.9%	24.1%	(100.0%)
75+	74.6%	25.4%	(100.0%)

Trip Day

The time of the week favored for trips is a factor which we might expect, like time of day, to change with driver age. Because most work-related commuting trips occur on weekdays, it would be logical to expect a substantial falling-off in the proportion of travel which occurs on weekdays as age increases—especially beyond sixty-four years. As Table 16 indicates, such a reduction does indeed seem to occur, but not nearly to the extent which we anticipated.

Obviously, while retirement eliminates the need for work trips, persons sixty-five and older still drive proportionately almost as much on weekdays as they did while they were working. As the figures in Table 13 suggest, they may simply leave home later in the morning.

There were no noticeable differences by gender for the elderly driver age groups in the proportions of driving associated with weekends or weekdays.

How does the trip distribution by weekday/weekend split compared with that of accidents? Table 17 shows the accident proportions and Table 18 provides estimates of relative accident risk by age and time period.

The above risk indices are interesting for two reasons. First, they confirm what has already been suggested in discussing factors related to past incident frequency. That is, while the fifty-five to sixty-four year old drivers are at no greater risk, and may even be at lower risk generally, than their thirty-six to fifty year old counterparts, the risk levels rise for drivers in the over-sixty-five groups. Secondly, while weekends appear to be higher-risk days for middle-aged drivers than weekdays, the reverse seems true for elderly drivers aged seventy-five and over. For drivers in the fifty-five to sixty-four and sixty-five to seventy-four age groups, the risks on weekdays and weekends are essentially the same.

As suggested in the previous section, this high weekday risk, like the high 4:00-6:00 p.m. risk, may well be related to heavy traffic and intersection locations.

Season of Trip

The influence of weather conditions has already been discussed in some

TABLE 17
Trip Day by Age Group—Accident-Involved Drivers

Age Group	Day of Week of Accident Weekday	Weekend	
36-50	74.8%	25.2%	(100.0%)
55-64	71.3%	28.7%	(100.0%)
65-74	75.1%	24.9%	(100.0%)
75+	77.8%	22.2%	(100.0%)

TABLE 18
Relative Risk of Accident by Day of Week and Age Group

Age Group	Day of Week Weekday	Weekend
36-50	0.94	1.08
55-64	0.90	0.90
65-74	1.08	1.13
75+	1.83	1.55

detail but the effect remains speculative. The results of our analyses were confusing at best.

On the one hand, elderly drivers (over sixty-four years) were found to have a smaller proportion of their last accidents under poor environmental conditions than were middle-aged drivers. On the other hand, those who did crash under adverse conditions were found to have fewer previous accident involvements than those whose last accident occurred in good conditions.

Are poor driving conditions hazardous for elderly drivers? The proportion of trips and accidents by season are shown in Tables 19 and 20. On the west

TABLE 19
Trip Season by Age Group—Driving Exposure Survey

Age Group	Trip Season Winter	Spring/Summer/Fall	
36-50	39.4%	60.6%	(100.0%)
55-64	35.6%	64.4%	(100.0%)
65+	30.1%	69.9%	(100.0%)

TABLE 20
Trip Season by Age Group—Accident-Involved Drivers

Age Group	Trip Season Winter	Spring/Summer/Fall	
36-50	45.6%	54.4%	(100.0%)
55-64	43.1%	56.9%	(100.0%)
65+	41.3%	58.7%	(100.0%)

coast, wet weather generally prevails from November to March. So we have divided the year in two: winter (November-March) and spring/summer/fall (April-October). Because of relatively high month-to-month variations in the number of trips reported for drivers seventy-five years of age and older, coupled with the much smaller sample size in this category, we combined the sixty-five to seventy-four and seventy-five-plus age groups.

It can be seen from the above figures that the proportion of trips taken during winter months goes down as age increases and so does the proportion of accident involvements during this period. It is evident, however, that the trip proportions reduce more than the accident percentages. When we calculated relative risk indices based on the full sample of drivers aged thirty-six plus, we arrived at the results shown in Table 21.

TABLE 21
Relative Risk of Accident by Season and Age Group

	Trip Season	
Age Group	**Winter**	**Spring/Summer/Fall**
36-50	1.12	0.87
55-64	1.10	0.80
65+	1.70	1.05

Evidently, winter trips (when poor weather is more likely) are relatively risky for all age groups, but especially for the elderly (over sixty-four years of age). Elderly drivers apparently strive to avoid these trip situations (Table 19) but when they cannot or, because of other priorities, choose not to, they are more likely to be involved in crashes (Table 21).

All this suggests that many elderly drivers may be, to a certain degree, aware of their reduced ability to cope with poor driving conditions. Drivers who thereby acknowledge limitations on their driving ability may be more cautious. To the extent that accumulated convictions are at least partially a function of driving exposure, they may thus have fewer accidents per conviction. When they do finally have to drive under adverse conditions, however, their inability to compensate adequately makes them more prone to accident involvement. That the distribution of convictions by age group is a reasonable representation of the amount of travel involved, was originally shown in Figure 6.

How Does the Aging Process Affect Driving Performance?

Visual distractions are increasingly a problem for elderly drivers as age increases (Sammons 1987). Sorting relevant information from a "sea" of competing stimuli becomes ever more difficult with advancing years. In driving situations of high complexity, recognition/response tasks become harder to complete successfully and elderly drivers' performance has been found to fall off sharply (Flint et al. 1988). This is especially true when subsidiary tasks, such as tuning a car radio or operating a cellular telephone, are added. Simulator studies (Billheimer et al. 1986) have clearly shown disproportionate safety-related driving performance detriments among those over fifty-five years of age when these additional tasks are added to the driver's work load. Wilson et al. (1987) found perception times to be significantly longer for older drivers than for younger ones.

Once the pertinent information has been extracted from the driving environment, however, there is still the decision as to what to do about it. Here again, elderly drivers are at a disadvantage. Not only do they require more information on which to base decisions (Yanik 1986), but they also take more time to choose a response (Sammons 1987). They tend to inspect cues longer before making a decision. Thus in driving simulator test situations where the appropriate response is to maintain the current vector, elderly drivers do well, but where decisive action is warranted they do not (Flint et al. 1988). They exhibit greater response delays and a higher level of inappropriate responses to driving "threats" or surprise events than do younger drivers. Again, this situation may be exacerbated by the presence of secondary in-car tasks.

Nowhere is the range of visual stimuli so great and the demands of task identification and performance so critical as at intersections. We found, as did McKelvey (1988), that elderly drivers were overrepresented in intersection crashes. Further, their past records clearly indicated an increasing preponderance of intersection-related convictions such as failure to yield, disobeying traffic controls or making improper turns, as age increased (Figure 8). At the same time, convictions for more typically non-intersection related violations such as speeding became less frequent with increasing age.

Yanik (1986) has suggested that the short-term memory and problem-solving difficulties experienced by the elderly become especially acute around age seventy. Our calculations of relative risks of crashes tended to confirm the sixty-five to seventy-four age group as a critical transition category. It is certainly evident from our results that elderly drivers (beyond fifty-four years old) do not constitute a homogeneous group.

Do elderly drivers effectively compensate for poor task recognition and response? Some studies (Flint et al. 1988) have found no evidence that elderly drivers who exhibit poor performance on driving simulators make any compensating adjustment in amount of driving exposure. The most obvious conclusion might be that they are unaware of their problems (Flint et al. 1988). However, it is still possible even if this is so that such drivers may avoid certain broad driving situations because they feel uncomfortable in them (Yanik 1988) without actually admitting lack of competence or significantly reducing overall exposure. Thus we found that elderly drivers drove propor-

FIGURE 7
Change with Age in the Proportion of Previous Convictions Related to Speeding and Drinking-Driving

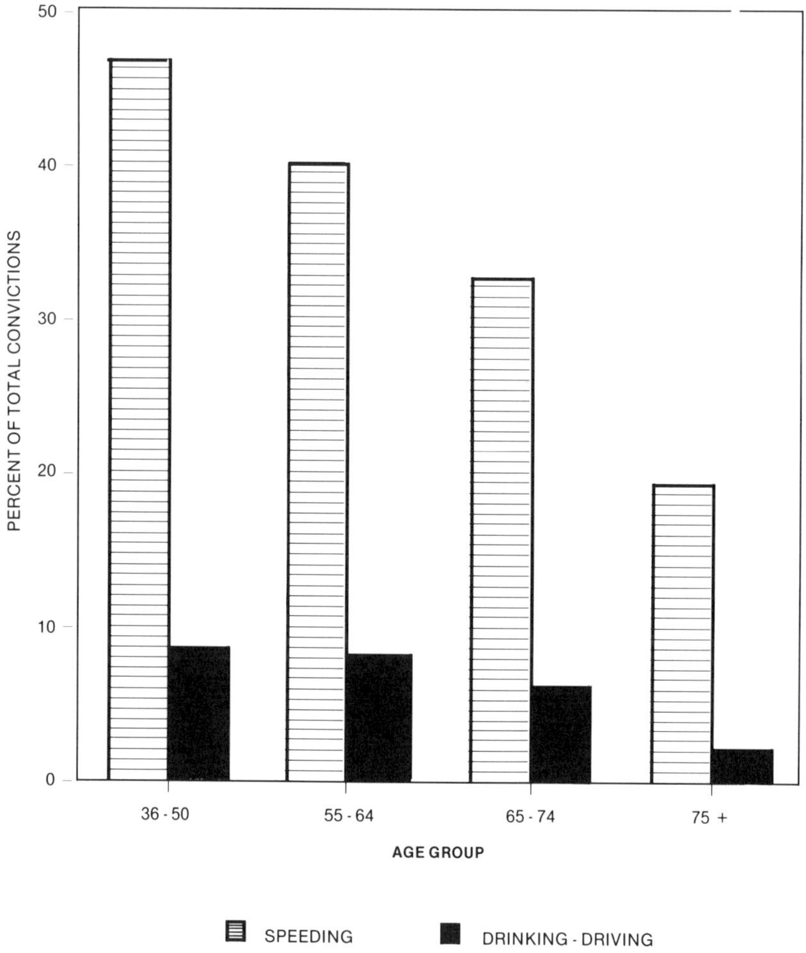

tionately less under poor visibility conditions than did their younger counterparts (see also Yanik 1986), and less when there was likely to be high traffic density. Similarly, the higher intra age-group relative accident risk for elderly drinking-drivers when compared with those for younger drivers (Cooper 1985) may have something to do with the lower incidence of drinking-driving convictions that we found, and which is illustrated in Figure 7. If they are justifiably uncomfortable in such situations perhaps they limit their exposure to them.

When considering such measurable physical detriments as visual acuity and so forth, one of the more interesting is depth perception. While the elderly may compensate for poor acuity by slowing their driving speed (Figure 7) and avoiding low-illumination conditions (Tables 13 and 19), problems involving depth perception will transcend all driving conditions. Many elderly, even at age fifty-five, have been found to have reduced depth perception (Yanik 1986). The inability to properly judge gaps in approaching traffic inevitably leads to poor gap acceptance decisions and thereby to accidents for which the elderly will often be charged with "failure to yield the right-of-way." As Figure 8 shows, the proportion of previous convictions represented by "failure to yield" increased dramatically with age group in our accident-involved driver sample.

Elderly drivers appear to be more at risk of accidents when on the road and especially more at risk of causing a crash than are middle-aged drivers who, according to studies reported by Yanik (1986), have the best readiness to respond quickly to unpredictable events of any age group. When controlled for estimated distance driven, the elderly (over sixty-four years of age) in our study were more at risk than were middle-aged drivers in virtually all categories of driving situation. This result agrees with those reported by Flint et al. (1988) and, in relating to a data base of accidents ranging from minor property-damage-only to fatal, it does not appear to reflect just the greater susceptibility of the elderly to injury.

That the elderly drive less than their younger counterparts, however, more than compensates for this increased accident risk. Our results showed that accumulated convictions were a reasonable surrogate for driving exposure by the elderly (Figure 6) and in this area we, like Flint (1988), found substantially lower involvements by seniors. Furthermore, this difference between elderly and middle-aged drivers was not found to be a function of experience. Even for drivers with less than two years' experience, the elderly (defined as fifty-five plus) in our study had significantly fewer convictions than those in the thirty-six to fifty age category (**0.22** per year vs. **0.66** per year).

Compensation for increased accident risk through lower levels of driving exposure thus does occur. The question remains, however, as to whether or not such compensation results from a clear understanding by the elderly of the

FIGURE 8
Change with Age in the Proportion of Previous Convictions
Related to Failure to Yield Right of Way

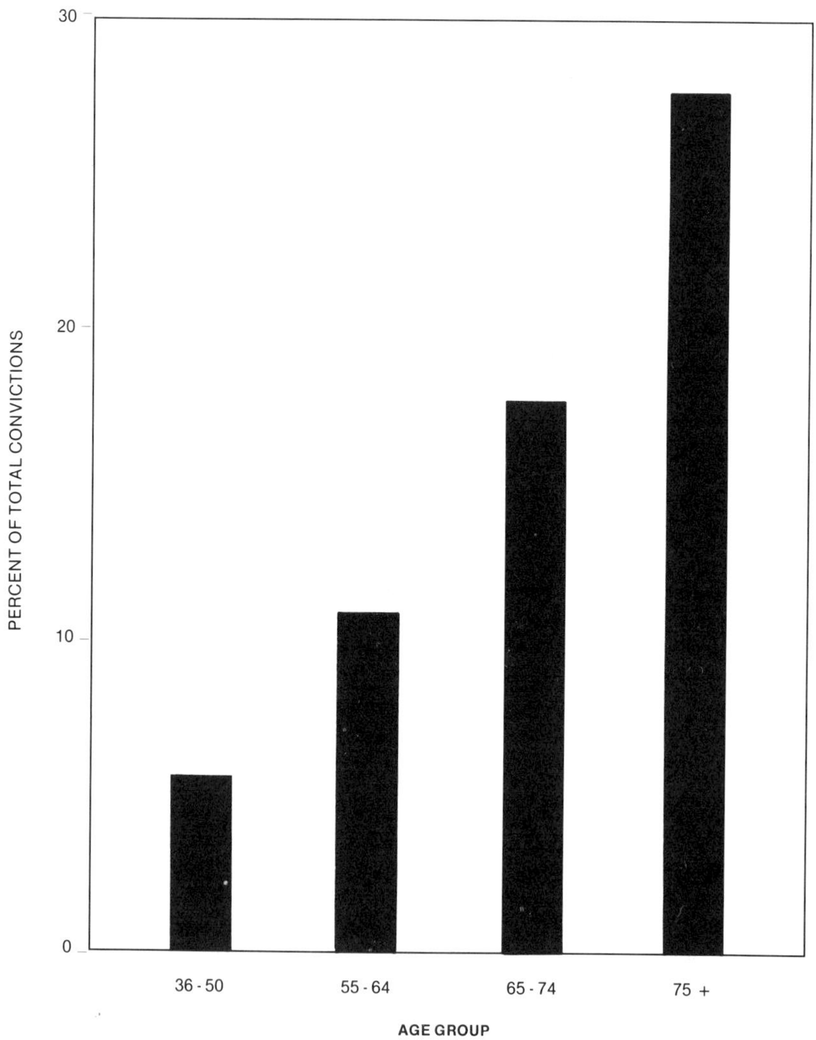

increased risk faced by many as a result of deteriorating performance. Perhaps it follows simply from a general discomfort with stressful driving situations coupled with reduced necessity for mobility which allows seniors to choose their times (Yanik 1988). The evidence, on balance, seems to favor the latter possibility, and this leaves room for the development of comprehensive educational programs for elderly drivers.

Concluding Remarks

The dichotomy with respect to the elderly in terms of motor vehicle operation is that they have always been represented as good automobile insurance risks but poor drivers. To what extent is this true?

Certainly, they have fewer accidents and traffic convictions. They drive less. These things make them good insurance risks. But while they are actually driving it appears that their risk of accident involvement is higher than is the case for their middle-aged counterparts. Moreover, this risk increases with age especially beyond the sixty-five to seventy-four year old grouping. Of interest, however, is the fact that those in the youngest group of elderly—the preretirement age bracket of fifty-five to sixty-four years—seem to be no more at risk while driving than are middle-aged persons.

In addition to being more at risk during driving, it seems that, beyond sixty-five years of age, there is a rapidly increasing probability for elderly drivers to be deemed largely responsible for the accidents in which they are involved. This increased accident responsibility seemed, if anything, more associated with women than men. Consistent with this finding was the fact that, on the basis of estimated miles travelled, elderly women drivers had a higher overall five-year accident relative risk then elderly males in the over-sixty-five age groups.

Even though drivers aged fifty-five to sixty-four did not appear to be more at risk than those aged thirty-six to fifty, there were numerous significant differences found in accident characteristics between the two groups. For example, pre-collision actions associated with turning, the assignment of contributing factors by police, and nighttime involvements to mention just a few. All of the differentiating accident factors exhibited consistent trends with advancing age, beginning at the fifty-five to sixty-four age group and with the most extreme variation from the middle-age characteristics always being associated with the oldest category (seventy-five-plus years). Concrete evidence of increased driving risk may not be manifest until later years (i.e., age sixty-five plus), but the onset of driving difficulties may occur earlier.

The most obvious conclusion is that there is no single homogeneous group that we can categorize and deal with collectively as "elderly drivers." Had we the sample size to break down our broad age groupings into further constituents, we undoubtedly would have been able to draw similar conclusions with respect to drivers in each of the fifty-five to sixty-four, sixty-five to seventy-four and seventy-five-plus age categories as well. The problems that elderly drivers as a group are confronted with, such as changes in information processing efficiency, depth judgment, decision-making ability, and reaction speed, are all subject to extreme individual variation. The onset of such difficulties may occur at different ages for different people and, furthermore, the exact relationships between such physical or mental changes and accident risk are not yet fully understood (Yanik 1986).

It seems possible, however, that many elderly drivers may have an incomplete understanding of their specific limitations with respect to driving. That they drive less during times and under conditions which make them uncomfortable seems evident, but do they completely comprehend the reasons for their discomfort and act accordingly? For example, older drivers seem to avoid driving in poor weather conditions where possible, and this is justified since their accident risk under such conditions is especially high. Yet those who were involved in accidents in poor conditions during 1986 had significantly fewer previous accidents than those whose crash occurred under good conditions. Possibly, these former persons were ordinarily safe drivers who were unaware of the full extent of their inability to cope with poor driving conditions, even though they may have normally avoided such situations owing to their general discomfort concerning them.

Obviously before we make further claims about the elderly drivers' understandings, perspectives, life-style influences, and medical conditions, we need to broaden our inquiry. Chapter Six begins to put meat on many of the statistical bones we have uncovered in the accident data.

References

Billheimer, J.W., R.E. Lave, A.C. Stein, Z. Parseghian, and R.W. Allen. 1986. *Mobile Telephone Safety Study—Final Report*, SYSTAN Inc. in association with Systems Technology Inc., Los Altos, CA.

Cooper, P.J. 1985. *The Relative Risk of Casualty Accident Involvement for Various Classes of Driver, Vehicle and Roadway in British Columbia*. Insurance Corporation of British Columbia, Vancouver.

Cooper, P.J. 1986. "The Effects of Economic Changes on Traffic Safety." Paper presented at the Highway Safety Outlooks Conference, Ontario Ministry of Transportation and Communications, Toronto.

Flint, S.J., K.W. Smith, and D.G. Rossi. 1988. "An Evaluation of Mature Driver Performance." Paper presented at the 14th International Forum on Traffic Records Systems, San Diego.

Kimmel, D.C. 1974. *Adulthood and Aging*. New York/Toronto: John Wiley and Sons.

Lawson, J.J., and D.E. Stewart. 1981. "National Driving Survey 1978-9." Paper presented at the Annual Conference of the Canadian Association of Applied Social Research, Halifax.

McKelvey, F.X., T.L. Maleck, N. Stamatiadis, and D.K. Hardy. 1988. "Highway Accidents and the Older Driver." Paper presented at the 67th Annual Meeting of the Transportation Research Board, Washington, DC.

Oppenlander, J.C. 1976. "General Traffic Characteristics." In *Transportation and Traffic Engineering Handbook*, John E. Baerwald (Ed.), Institute of Transportation Engineers, New Jersey: Prentice-Hall.

Rothe, J.P., and P.J. Cooper. 1987. *Motorcyclists: Image and Reality*. Insurance Corporation of British Columbia, Vancouver.

Sammons, J.H. 1987. "Aging Changes Discussion." In *The Aging Process and Driving Safety*, General Motors Corporation, Detroit.

Verhaegen, P.K., K.L. Toebat, and L.L. Delbeke. 1988. "Safety of Older Drivers: A Study of Their Over-Involvement Ratio." Proceedings of the Human Factors Society, 32nd Annual Meeting.

Wilson, F.R., J.A. Sinclair, and T. Akpata. 1987. "The Measurement of Collision Avoidance Times." Proceedings, Roads and Transportation Association of Canada, Annual Conference, Saskatoon.

Yanik, A.J. 1986. "Aging Factors That Affect the Driving Task." Presented at the Fourth International Conference on Mobility and Transport for Elderly and Disabled Persons, Vancouver.

Yanik, A.J. 1987. "Driving Safety Discussion." In *The Aging Process and Driving Safety*, General Motors Corporation, Detroit.

6

Trends, Factors and Patterns

Send me a postcard drop me a line, stating point of view
Indicate precisely what you mean to say, yours sincerely wasting away
Give me your answer fill in a form, mine for evermore
Will you still need me, will you still feed me, when I'm sixty-four.

(John Lennon and Paul McCartney, "When I'm Sixty-Four")*

To discover something about the limits and potentialities of elderly drivers and to see how they are molded by various factors is essential to gathering requisite knowledge of this group. The purpose of this chapter is to gain some orderly and systematic insight into the world of elderly drivers—one which moves beyond the aggregate data analysis outlined in Chapter Five.

In a fundamental sense, an information gathering approach is based on logic, tempered by experience. The idea is to create a band, a line moving from the statistical to the personal. This chapter portrays, in statistical fashion, how elderly drivers view and interpret their driving practices, attitudes, and related behaviors. This fertile area of data was harvested by a 61 multiple item questionnaire. The instrument, comprised of particularized factors of experience, was completed by 904 elderly drivers through person-to-person interviews. For consistency, an in-depth description of the methodology that was employed to arrive at the information demonstrated in the following pages is found in the appendixes.

For the convenience of the reader, the text is structured around the following major themes: characteristics of elderly driver participants, driving history, characteristics of vehicle drivers, driving patterns, personal views on driving, driving difficulties, opinions on licensure, driver education, driving changes over time, and driving competence.

The write-up is stylized for easy comprehension and thought-provoking discussion. For those who demand statistical verification of claims, refer to the back of the book where a series of tables are exhibited. Perhaps occasions will arise whereby the inquisitive reader may discover relevant tabulations that were not expanded in the text. If this is the case, we are delighted to serve interests that go beyond the confines of pages allotted for interpretation and description.

Characteristics of Elderly Driver Participants

For a tabulated illustration of the sociodemographic characteristics of the survey participants, see Table B-1. In abbreviated form, the mean age in this study was sixty-nine. Not only was there an almost even split between men and women overall, but also within each age group—fifty-five to sixty-four, sixty-five to seventy-four, seventy-five and older. To reach proper conclusions, an attempt was made to obtain an equal percentage of male and female motorists. Of the 247 respondents in the fifty-five to sixty-four year old category, the split, rounded off, was 45 percent male, 55 percent female, while the gender breakdown for the 490 sixty-five to seventy-four year old participants was 49 percent male and 51 percent female, and for the 167 seventy-five-years-and-older people the percentages were 56 percent male and 44 percent female. Precisely two-thirds of all the elderly drivers were married. This broke down to 61 percent in the older group (seventy-five and older), 65 percent for the sixty-five to seventy-four year olds, and a high of 72 percent in the youngest sector (fifty-five to sixty-four). As might be expected, the major reason for the unmarried motorists was the death of their spouses.

There were few in the older two groups who were employed while 34 percent in the fifty-five to sixty-four age group were employed either full- or part-time. Practically everyone in the study sixty-five years of age and over was receiving the Old Age Security Pension, but few people were receiving any Guaranteed Income Supplement (GIS) or the Guaranteed Annual Income for Need. The income information, combined with the education and occupation data, indicate a sample biased toward the upper end of the socioeconomic scale. Close to 40 percent completed some college or university courses and an additional one-quarter were secondary-school graduates. Slightly more than a third (38 percent) described their primary life occupation as professional or managerial. This upward bias in socioeconomic status is not confined to any age group but appears across the entire sample. To place these characteristics of our sample in perspective, Canadian or national figures for the over-sixty-five population show about half receiving full or partial GIS and only 19 percent either holding a college degree or having had some post-secondary education (Statistics Canada 1984).

In terms of total family annual income, elderly driver plus spouse or elderly driver if single, 57 percent reported that they earned within the $10,000 to $30,000 range. The median reported family income was between $20,000 and $30,000 per year. This compares to Statistics Canada's 1985 overall average family income in British Columbia at $37,655. The numbers clearly show an economic discrepancy between the elderly and other Canadian families, a fact well recognized by elderly lobby groups and social service agencies.

General State of Health

When the elderly motorists were asked to rate their health on a continuum ranging from excellent to poor, their responses were quite equivocal. For example, 89 percent in the fifty-five to sixty-four age group, 91 percent in the sixty-five to seventy-four group, and 88 percent in the seventy-five-and-over group considered their health to be either "good" or "excellent" (see Table B-2). Paralleling the high rating for health was the participants' evaluation of vision. Overall, 97 percent believed that their vision was either "good" or "excellent." Specifically, about 40 percent of the fifty-five to sixty-four and sixty-five to seventy-four year old groups rated their eyesight as excellent and more than half rated their eyesight as good. For the seventy-five and older group, only 31 percent rated their vision as excellent. A footnote needs to be added. Assessments of vision excluded possible situational weaknesses such as nighttime headlight glare. They only featured general, or overall, judgments.

Age differences were similarly apparent with responses to questions concerning hearing. The proportion of respondents reporting excellent hearing decreased as their ages increased. Thirty-nine percent of the fifty-five to sixty-four year old respondents reported having excellent hearing, whereas only 32 percent of those aged sixty-five to seventy-four reported such a level of hearing efficiency, and the percentage for those aged seventy-five and over reduced to 26 percent. Nevertheless, fully 87 percent of all the elderly drivers (aged fifty-five and over) reported having good or excellent hearing.

On Driving History

Driving-Related Learning

Learning in general is a lifelong process. But learning specific ends within structured time schedules is acknowledged as a defined process. Learning to drive falls within the latter definition.

As we might reasonably assume, the elderly driver population has accumulated a considerable number of years' driving experience. Overall, 44 percent of the motorists learned to drive fifty or more years ago (see Tables B-3 and B-4). Historically, this would place the time of instruction somewhere around the post-World War I, depression years.

A closer look at possible differences between male and female elderly drivers shows that the proportion of men to women who learned to drive forty or more years ago was almost two to one. Ninety-one percent of elderly males reported learning to drive forty or more years ago as compared to only 54 percent of elderly women.

Over the last thirty to fifty years, automotive and traffic engineering technology has changed considerably, as did the volumes of traffic, laws, and some moral attitudes of society. This finding begs the question of whether elderly drivers keep up-to-date, and if so how they keep current about changes in traffic, regulations, and road markings. The answer is that they do; at least 91 percent do (see Table B-5). Male and female drivers alike stated that they keep abreast with traffic related changes and there were no noticeable differences between age groups.

A more intensive look at the statistics showed that "keeping current" was more media updating than it was technical upgrading. For example, when the elderly drivers described how they kept abreast with current changes, the majority of individuals stated that they read newspapers (59 percent) and/or they were attentive to the radio or television (36 percent). Because those surveyed were invited to discuss as many sources of updating as they considered personally relevant, a sum percentage of 100 percent was not appropriate. Consequently, some elderly may engage in more than one source of awareness (see Table B-6).

"Word of mouth" was given as a primary source of awareness by 25 percent of the elderly drivers. Of these, 39 percent were male and 61 percent were female. Of the three major sources the elderly used to stay in touch with changes, word of mouth was the only one that produced a significant difference between males and females. Other sources of upgrading pale in comparison to the ones already described. For example, only 17 percent of those surveyed read Department of Motor Vehicle mailings and 14 percent reviewed insurance material.

When the elderly drivers learned to drive, they did so primarily within the social circle—a friend (38 percent) or parent (19 percent). (For clarification see Table B-7.) But, we also established that 25 percent of the motorists were self-taught. No instruction from any outside source was provided. Being taught by a driver training establishment received only 19 percent agreement. This is understandable, since driver training courses during the early 1900s were not as prominent as they were in the 1960s, 1970s or 1980s. The remainder learned through a number of miscellaneous sources such as the military or workplace. These findings closely resembled the American scene where Yee (1984) reported that 58 percent of the elderly drivers were never taught by formal training. Yet the incentive to upgrade was visible. During a lifetime, 41 percent of our elderly drivers completed driver education, training or retraining programs.

The proportion of drivers who reported being self-taught increased with age (18 percent, 25 percent and 33 percent for drivers aged fifty-five to sixty-four, sixty-five to seventy-four, and over seventy-four respectively). This could also reflect a lack of available "instructors" half a century ago. Also, far more females than males availed themselves of professional instruction (school or driving course)—28 percent vs. 10 percent (see Table B-8).

The traffic/educational concerns with learning to drive and keeping abreast of traffic safety changes reflect historical embeddedness. Most of the licensure occurred forty or more years ago, with instruction afforded by friends, parents, or selves. Popular communication strategies are the prominent vehicles the elderly use to keep abreast with the times. Keeping on top of changes is typically accomplished through the mass media and by word of mouth. Some elderly motorists did engage in driver upgrading, but it was usually many years ago.

Accidents and Violations

After careful scrutiny of the data, it was determined that 29 percent of all the sampled elderly drivers had, in the last five years, either a collision with another vehicle (21 percent), a single car crash (7 percent) and/or an accident involving a pedestrian (1 percent). (For further illustration see Tables B-10 and B-11.) Proportionately more men than women were involved in the crashes, but the difference was very slight. In our elderly driver sample, both genders were more or less equally represented in accident involvements. Males made up 49 percent of the interviewed drivers and 52 percent of those reporting accidents were male. This equal representation was a far cry from the experience of the overall driving population in British Columbia. In 1986, males constituted 56 percent of licensed drivers, but accounted for 71 percent of those involved in crashes. Of the sum of all three accident types, 11 percent were injury producing. This finding repeated itself when the elderly were interviewed in focus groups and when they discussed, in single person, their involvement in injury-producing crashes.

When respondents were asked about moving violations they had encountered during the last five years, no more than 3 percent in any of the three age groups reported violations for such infractions as failure to yield, going too slowly, not heeding traffic signals or signs, improper turning and tailgating. But, there was an exception—speeding. The self-reported incident of speeding was 23 percent for the fifty-five to sixty-four year old members, 12 percent for those aged sixty-five to seventy-four, and 12 percent for the seventy-five-and-older group (see Table B-12). This directly countered the universal stereotype of the "pokey old driver." While it is difficult to relate self reporting of violations during the last five years with published annual rates for all age groups, it is interesting that speeding had the highest reported incidence rate for all elderly drivers regardless of violation category.

Driving Patterns

Driving pattern is a major factor for exposure, which in turn gives us a clearer indication of risk. The issue is covered by four key concerns: when, how often, and why do elderly people drive, and with whom do they drive.

Frequency of Driving and Schedule of Trips

The mean or average number of days driven per week decreases significantly with age (see Table B-14). People aged seventy-five and older drive significantly less (mean number of days = 4.8) than drivers aged sixty-five to seventy-four (mean number of days = 5.2), and those aged fifty-five to sixty-four (mean number of days = 5.6). Also, males drove significantly more days per week than females (see Table B-15). If we further analyze days driven by two major difficult driving times—rush-hour traffic and travel during darkness—different significant findings are evident. For example, drivers in the younger old-age brackets (especially the fifty-five to sixty-four age group) drive significantly more during rush hour and after dark. The fifty-five to sixty-four year olds drove during rush hour on an average of 1.9 days per week and at night on an average 2.1 days per week. For those aged sixty-five to seventy-four, the averages were 1.3 and 1.7 respectively, and for drivers seventy-five and older these reduced to 1.2 and 1.3. In terms of gender difference, males drove significantly more at night than females. This is no earth shattering discovery, since we know that the majority of people aged fifty-five to sixty-four, and especially males, are gainfully employed and must travel during these times to and from work. Rush hour is usually negotiated and darkness is prevalent during work-related trips to and from work in the winter. The two older groups, as a rule of thumb, do not have to worry about these hazardous driving times.

A further understanding of driving pattern becomes evident when we capture the times of day that most of the driving occurs, and when we compare weekday and weekend travel. For time of day driven, the majority of trips elderly people take are either in the morning, the afternoon or a combination of the two (76 percent). There were no major differences between the age groups (see Table B-16). When considering the weekday-weekend pattern, there appeared to be a difference between the oldest members and the other two groups (see Table B-17). Only 7 percent of the fifty-five to sixty-four year olds usually drive only on weekdays. This rises to 17 percent for drivers older than seventy-five. A slight difference between age groups was also detected when senior citizens were asked "do you usually drive as frequently in the winter months as in other months?" Seventy-seven percent of the fifty-five to sixty-four year olds answered yes, as did 72 percent of the sixty-five to seventy-four year olds, but significantly fewer of those age seventy-five and over (67 percent) responded in the affirmative.

Finally, there is a linear relationship between age and annual number of miles driven (see Table B-19). Whereas 63 percent of the seventy-five-and-older drivers reported that they drive less than 5,000 miles per year, 67 percent of the fifty-five to sixty-four year olds and 62 percent of the sixty-five to seventy-four year olds estimated that they drive *more* than 5,000 miles per year. This difference is likely a function of the activities in which different age groups are involved and of the range of tasks or events for which the different groups use their car. Male elderly drivers, for example, used their cars more than females, with 78 percent driving over 5000 miles per year as compared to 41 percent for the latter (see Table B-20). Descriptions on purposes for which elderly drivers use their cars is described further on the next page and in Chapters Seven and Eight.

Carrying Passengers

The vast majority of elderly drivers, regardless of age and sex, feel comfortable about having passengers when they drive (96 percent). The only noteworthy distinction was between the male and female groups on the degree of comfort (see Table B-22). To clarify, 50 percent of the men compared to 39 percent of the women responded that they feel "very comfortable" having other people in the car.

The next question of note is, "who are the other people that often ride with elderly drivers?" A straight and direct answer is "no one." Although the motorists feel comfortable carrying passengers, this does not mean that they do so. Seventy percent of the 900 survey respondents answered that they usually drive alone (see Table B-23). If they do carry passengers, they are most likely to be a mate/spouse or a friend. The age group most likely to travel with passengers is seventy-five and older. The number of drivers in this group that reported they usually drive alone was 65 percent. Yet for the sixty-five to seventy-four year olds, the percentage increased to 70 percent only to rise again to 74 percent for the fifty-five to sixty-four year olds. When we relate this finding with those of driving exposure a more focused picture emerges. The younger old people drive more for a greater diversity of reasons that do not involve passengers than do the older old. The latter group drives less but the trips are more likely to involve passengers. This takes us to the point of clarifying in greater detail for what purposes elderly drivers go on trips.

Trip Purposes

Overall, the automobile is used as much for shopping (96 percent) as it is for visiting family and friends (96 percent) as shown in Table B-24. But almost as important are automobile trips for attending social, cultural entertainment, or recreational events (90 percent); for pleasure per se (85 percent); and health care services (78 percent). In further descending order are, trips for attending meetings (70 percent); vacation travel (69 percent); attending spectator sports events (52 percent); participating in volunteer activity (51 percent); and going to church services (42 percent). Going to and from work was not an overall predominant use of the car (11 percent).

Proportionately to other groups, drivers seventy-five and older appeared to take fewer journeys than the others. The only purpose for which the seventy-five-and-over age group had an equal or higher proportion of trips was going to church. In terms of gender differences, females were more likely than males to take trips to church and engage in volunteer activity, whereas males were more likely to take vacation, work, and sport-related trips. Interestingly, an equal proportion of males to that of females reported going shopping (see Table B-25).

When the automobile is not taken for the trips the most significantly used alternate mode of transportation is walking (62 percent) as shown in Tables B-26 and B-27. Less often used but still noteworthy are alternatives such as receiving rides from other people (34 percent) and taking the bus (26 percent). The fact that the numbers do not add up to 100 percent should not be interpreted as an error. Respondents were asked to give more than one response (if they so deemed appropriate) to the question, "In a typical week, other than driving there yourself, how do you get places?" These factors are again expanded in the next two chapters.

An interesting aside occurs in terms of friends or relations providing transportation for the elderly. Thirty-four percent of the respondents answered "yes" they receive rides. Of this group, 31 percent were men and 69 were women. It appears that some of the traditional roles of women as passengers and men as drivers may still be in play for the elderly driver group. In fact, adherence to historical roles is key. This causes some difficulties when the male spouse dies. Women, who previously did not have the opportunity, motivation, or socially approved right to drive, now have to learn at a late stage in life. Not surprisingly, most enjoy driving and participate without hesitation to fulfill obligations.

Loss of Driving Privileges

We know that the vehicle is used frequently during the year for a spectrum of reasons, all of which are vital for a quality of life. When the senior citizens were asked how their life would change if they could no longer drive, their focus was on becoming less mobile (84 percent), becoming less independent (82 percent) and having to change their life-style (65 percent). These thoughts were usually volunteered in the in-depth discussions to follow in the next chapters.

A strong reply to the obvious! That they would rely on other forms of transportation was noted at 96 percent yet in spite of this, 57 percent also said they would not venture far from home. Our findings confirm the widely held view that seniors see the automobile as a very strategic factor for independence and mobility. But the data also show that the elderly are adaptive. They would depend more on other forms of transportation, such as walking, public transit, and bicycles, to continue as much as possible their way of life. Of course, they realize that this would be difficult. They would likely stay closer to home and become less social. Staying close to home was an option favored more by the seventy-five-and-over age group than the younger elderly. Also, males expressed a greater tendency to stay close to home than females (65 and 50 percent respectively). Perhaps this relates to the previous finding of higher community involvement for women (i.e., church and volunteer activity trips). (For further clarification see Tables B-28 and B-29.)

Self as Driver

It is recognized that elderly drivers use their vehicles with regularity. How they drive is a matter of interpretation. Of special value to us is how the elderly drivers assess themselves as individuals and group members.

When the elderly drivers were asked whether their driving abilities are above average, average, or below average, 99 percent of the total sample judged themselves to be average or better. The two younger groups (fifty- five to sixty-four and sixty-five to seventy-four) rated themselves as "better than average drivers" a somewhat higher percentage of the time than did the members of the seventy-five and older group. In the fifty-five to sixty-four year old group, 43 percent thought they were better-than-average drivers, as did 42 percent in the sixty-five to seventy-four group, and 35 percent in the seventy-five and older group. But 62 percent of the older group judged their driving to be as good as the average driver (see Table B-30).

With respect to the male/female points of view, more men (47 percent) than women (36 percent) judged themselves to be more able than the average driver. But, 63 percent of the women believed that they drove as well as the average driver (see Table B-31).

By combining self-evaluation with perceptions of how others evaluate self, we arrive at a more comprehensive description of how elderly drivers perceive themselves. When they were asked about their opinions on how their family thinks about them as drivers 81 percent answered that they would likely be judged as "good" or "excellent." As in the self-evaluation findings, more men (23 percent) than women (16 percent) thought that family members considered them to be "excellent" drivers (see Table B-32).

Overall, how do elderly drivers feel about driving? Seventy-five percent said they liked it and 98 percent stated that they felt confident or comfortable being behind the wheel. Very few motorists reported that they feel anxious or distressed, or that they do not like driving. While a slightly higher proportion of drivers aged seventy-five and older than younger age group drivers said that they like driving, a lower proportion of this upper age group stated that they felt confident (see Table B-33). Females also felt somewhat less confident than males, (see Table B-34).

Dealing With Emotional Upsets

To depict how elderly drivers deal with emotional upsets when they are behind the wheel, we included three questions: "How do you usually feel when other drivers are discourteous or drive carelessly?", "When the driving behavior of other drivers annoys you, how are you most likely to respond?", and "When you are personally upset about something unrelated to driving, do you usually . . . ."

When other motorists are discourteous or drive carelessly, the majority of elderly drivers feel annoyed (62 percent). For 21 percent of the elderly, other road-user behavior does not bother them. The range of feeling was fairly uniform for all elderly drivers, regardless of age, although there was a slightly greater tendency for the younger ones to express anger (see Table B-35).

It is clear that annoyance is the reaction most elderly drivers have when meeting other discourteous or careless drivers. Their reaction is usually to "move out of the way" (45 percent) or "do nothing" (33 percent). To take specific actions like driving more aggressively or slowing down and blocking other drivers were not featured reactions (3 percent). The passive driving strategies were expressed more or less equally by seniors of all age groups and both sexes (see Tables B-36 and B-37).

Along with heightened emotions caused by others, being upset over personal matters while driving is an important factor for establishing a meaning of risk. From the survey we learned that when elderly drivers are upset they "drive as usual" (52 percent). Whereas most seniors did not consider mood to be a factor that requires preventative strategies, still, 29 percent stated that they do take extra care, and 16 percent responded that they avoid driving whenever they are upset or in an emotional or unsettled state.

The reaction to being upset is significantly different between men and women. Whereas only 9 percent of males would avoid driving, this action would be followed by 24 percent of the females. From a different perspective, 63 percent of the men would drive as usual compared to 41 percent of the women (see Table B-38).

Changes over Time

It was already established that an overwhelming majority of elderly drivers feel comfortable and confident driving and that they consider themselves to be as good or better than the average driver. Have there been any changes over time that have led to the elderly drivers' positive self evaluations?

Respondents were read twelve driving conditions. For each condition they were asked to rate whether they now drive better, the same, or worse than they did at age thirty-five to forty-five—an age grouping considered to be the least at risk.

The main driving conditions with which elderly drivers believe they cope worse than they did at age thirty-five to forty-five were nighttime driving (47 percent said worse) and coping with headlight glare (37 percent said worse). About 21 percent felt that they do not now drive as well as formerly in bad weather and about 11 percent believed their abilities in freeway or city driving had deteriorated. In terms of their own condition, the greatest problem appeared to be driving when tired or upset, with 27 percent reporting that they do not cope as well under these conditions as they did when they were younger. In this problem category the older driver groups expressed greater concern. Driving after drinking and driving after taking medication were only referred to by about 8 percent of the drivers as being more of a problem now than formerly.

The extent to which the elderly drive the same now, compared to their younger years, reflected a male bias. In short, men more often felt that they drive the same or even better today than they did when they were thirty-five to forty-five years old. This was especially true for driving in winter weather.

Do elderly motorists drive differently now than they did before? Yes, they drive more defensively (87 percent) and more cautiously (79 percent) (see Table B-39). But they do not necessarily drive more slowly (34 percent). Fifty-one percent of the age fifty-five to sixty-four drivers felt that they now get less upset than they used to, but only 39 percent of the drivers aged seventy-five or older felt this way. The seventy-five-and-older drivers were a little more inclined to drive slower while, quite surprisingly, more men (84 percent) than women (71 percent) said they now drive more cautiously. It appears that from all the data analyzed so far, women considered themselves to have always been cautious drivers. For them caution was not necessarily an age-related factor.

Concerns About Driving

By now the impression left from the elderly peoples' responses is that they are confident, good drivers who are generally accustomed to driving in a variety of traffic conditions, assumptions confirmed later in the book. The majority of senior motorists are not concerned about losing attention or concentration (80 percent), losing their license (72 percent) or losing their driving abilities (63 percent). Yet, when they were given the freedom to discuss their views, some of the concerns were shown to be more entrenched than questionnaire responses allowed.

Based on the information given, there are some concerns elderly drivers concede they have about driving. For example, 55 percent are concerned that they may injure a pedestrian and 43 percent fear the possibility of getting hit.

Although 72 percent of the respondents do not fear losing their license, still 28 percent do. Proportionately more drivers seventy-five years old and older are afraid than are the other two groups. With respect to gender, for all possible driving concerns, there was no significant difference between the opinions given by men or women.

Drinking and Driving

Two questions about drinking and driving were asked: "Do you drink and drive?" and "If no, why not?" Only 21 percent of the youngest, 14 percent of the middle and 8 percent of the oldest group responded "yes." A significantly higher proportion of males (22 percent) admitted to drinking and driving than females (8 percent). See Table B-40 for further clarification. Only thirteen of the 904 respondents did not answer this question, but when asked to give a reason for not drinking and driving, fully 147 failed to respond. The predominant reasons for not drinking and driving were, it is unsafe (53 percent), and that the elderly drivers do not drink alcohol anyway (40 percent). This latter factor may help to explain the lower level of drinking-driving among females. Forty-three percent of females said they didn't drink as opposed to only 37 percent of males.

Driving Difficulties

In the literature much is written about physical driving difficulties experienced by elderly drivers. In Chapter Five we discussed vision, hearing, and reaction time related to accident causation. It is now time to delve deeper into the assumed driving difficulties and explore how elderly drivers answered pinpoint questions on their abilities in terms of certain health conditions.

Traffic Signs

A difficulty many elderly drivers have is the placement of signs (43 percent). It is difficult for elderly drivers to see signs where they are placed, whether it be overhead, or on the side of the roads. Some signs are too near to the location where action needs to be taken, as, for example, a left turn sign.

Of the elderly drivers that do have problems with the placement of signs, the age most often answering yes was sixty-five to seventy-four years old (45 percent) followed by the fifty-five to sixty-four year olds (42 percent). The least problem with sign placement was registered by the drivers seventy-five and older (39 percent) (see Table B-41).

No major problems were reported to exist for shape of sign (no, 98 percent), sign colors (no, 93 percent), or lettering clarity (no, 90 percent) and the meaning of the message (88 percent). There was a slight indication of increasing age-related difficulties with size of sign and size of lettering and about 20 percent reported problems with these two factors.

When respondents reported difficulty with signs or signals they felt it was more likely to be the result of the physical design or placement of the sign than it was a problem of aging. Eighty-four percent of the elderly drivers who felt able to make this distinction said so, and the drivers within the fifty-five to sixty-four and sixty-five to seventy-four year old age groups were more likely to believe it than were those in the seventy-five and older category. Four percent of the respondents said it was either vision alone or a combination of vision and reaction time.

The last piece of information obtained relating to signage was the type of roads where difficulty with signs occurred. City streets appeared to be places where the greatest difficulty occurs, as 62 percent of those responding reported. Less than 20 percent reported difficulty on other types of roadways. Difficulty with traffic signs on city streets was reported to increase with age from 56 percent of the fifty-five to sixty-four year olds and 63 percent of the sixty-five to seventy-four year olds, to 70 percent of the seventy-five and older group.

On Dangerous Traffic Conditions

A smaller percentage of elderly drivers than we expected reported difficulty with night vision, night headlight glare and daytime glare (24 percent, 40 percent, and 26 percent). The oldest age group (seventy-five years plus) indicated the highest proportion of difficulty with all three kinds of visual conditions. The oldest group of drivers (seventy-five years plus) reported the most difficulty with night headlight glare (46 percent), compared to 34 percent of the fifty-five to sixty-four age group, and with night vision (32 percent) compared to 21 percent of the fifty-five to sixty-four age group. Difficulty with daytime glare showed little difference between the three age groups (see Table B-42).

A series of questions were asked as to the weather, road, or traffic conditions in which the respondents do not drive, or which they try to avoid. The conditions included night, rain, fog, snow, sleet, slush, freeways, rush hour, heavy traffic areas, and heavy holiday traffic. (See Table B-43 for a detailed illustration.)

Of all these factors, fog was considered to be the single most negative feature elderly drivers would try to avoid (66 percent), followed by heavy holiday traffic (58 percent), and other weather conditions such as snow, sleet or slush (57 percent). The feeling is generally consistent for all elderly drivers, but the older elderly drivers appeared more inclined to avoid nighttime and rain. The women appear to be more concerned about many of these driving hazards than do men. For example, 74 percent of them would either try to avoid or would definitely not drive in snow, sleet or slush, and 46 percent would do the same for dark (nighttime) conditions. The proportions were significantly lower for men where the percentages were 58 percent for the former and 33 percent for the latter situation.

Quite surprisingly, heavy holiday travel was a condition 67 percent of the elderly drivers would try to avoid or in which they would not drive. We should say that the emphasis is on "heavy" traffic. Driving on the freeways is not considered to be a threat (89 percent drive on them without any concern), and driving on holidays was earlier mentioned as a trip purpose reported by 69 percent of the drivers interviewed (see also Table B-24).

As we reported earlier, automobile trips are most often planned for the morning and/or afternoon. That is because 40 percent of the elderly drivers try to avoid nighttime trips or else they just do not drive at night. Similarly, 55 percent try to avoid or don't drive in rush-hour traffic. The most represented group here is those drivers seventy-five years or older (61 percent). The group fifty-five to sixty-four years old, if still working, may find it difficult to avoid these times. Almost 50 percent of them reported that they would drive during rush hours.

The final driving condition responsible for many accidents is rain. Surprisingly, only 19 percent of the elderly drivers would try to avoid or would not drive under this condition. Perhaps the West Coast has such a high annual rainfall, a motorist may have difficulty completely avoiding it.

Personal Impairment

When the elderly drivers were asked about personal factors, characteristics, or impairments that make driving difficult 63 percent reported they had none. The remaining 37 percent had a variety of one or more difficulties.

Of those who mentioned one or more specific impairments or difficulties, the following categories were prominent: glare, 15 percent; poor night vision,

10 percent; fatigue, 8 percent; inability to turn head, 5 percent; poor vision, 4 percent; and poor hearing, 2 percent. Because the interviewees could cite as many difficulties as they wished, the total of all difficulties exceeded 100 percent. With the exception of night vision and rain, the impairments were experienced relatively equally by all elderly drivers. In the case of the foregoing two categories, however, older elderly drivers reported more difficulty than their younger counterparts.

As one ages musculoskeletal problems are more common, therefore, drivers were asked how difficult it was for them to look over their shoulder when driving or backing up. As expected, there were age group differences with 15 percent of the youngest, 19 percent of the middle and 25 percent of the oldest group reporting either some or a great deal of difficulty.

Driving Faults

The following driving faults were read to the survey participants: driving too fast for conditions, speeding, failing to yield right-of-way, failure to come to complete stop at a stop sign, running a red light, running a yellow light, driving left of center, improper passing, improper turning, following too closely, driving too slow for traffic flow, and failure to signal. The elderly drivers were asked to list the driving faults they make most often. The driving faults elderly drivers said they make most often are running a yellow light (41 percent), failing to come to a complete stop at a stop sign (20 percent), and speeding/driving too fast for conditions (17 percent). More specifically, 51 percent of the drivers aged seventy-five and over indicated running yellow lights as their most common fault. The percentage dropped to 40 percent for the sixty-five to seventy-four year olds and 39 percent for the fifty-five to sixty-four year olds. (For further clarification see Table B-44.)

How fast elderly drivers usually drive was further investigated when respondents were asked to compare their speed to the general traffic flow. Keeping up with the traffic was the predominant answer. For example, 84 percent of the fifty-five to sixty-four year old group, 85 percent of the middle-aged group and 77 percent of the seventy-five-plus year old members reported driving the same speed as the general traffic flow. Only 11 percent of the youngest, 11 percent of the middle and 20 percent of the oldest group reported that they drive slower. The increased caution associated with the oldest group is notable. There were no obvious gender effects.

Difficult Driving Maneuvers

A topic in the elderly driver literature that has received a large amount of attention is the subject of difficult driving maneuvers. The data from this study is consistent with the literature in identifying those maneuvers that seniors considered to be hard. Motorists were read a list of driving maneuvers and asked to indicate how troublesome they found them by responding to the categories "frequently," "sometimes," "seldom," or "never" troublesome. Changing lanes (with 24 percent indicating sometimes or frequently troublesome) and making a left turn at an uncontrolled intersection (24 percent) appear to be the most problematic driving behaviors (see Table B-45). Entering an uncontrolled intersection, entering city traffic, backing up, entering the freeway, reading traffic signs, and parking the car also cause difficulties, but to a lesser degree (between 17 percent and 13 percent). Whereas there do not appear to be any differences between the three groups for most maneuvers, there is evidence of difference for backing up and parking, making uncontrolled left turns, and entering a stream of city traffic. Of these maneuvers, the oldest group has the most difficulty. All of these maneuvers involve some degree of head turning and multiple information processing. Thus the difficulties encountered by the very elderly may represent a combination of physical and perceptual processing problems.

However, certain maneuvers were found to be more difficult by women than by men. For example, 30 percent of the women reported they have trouble with changing lanes compared to 18 percent of the men (see Table B-46). Also, 28 percent have difficulty making a left turn at an uncontrolled intersection compared to 19 percent of men. Seventeen percent have difficulty backing up a car compared to 11 percent of the men; and 19 percent have trouble entering a freeway, compared to 10 percent of the men. In addition, of the 9 percent who indicated having trouble judging distance, 76 percent were women and 24 percent were men.

Licensure

Licensure is a topic on which drivers of all ages have definite opinions. But, no viewpoints are more relevant than those of the elderly drivers concerning the issues of cessation of driving and retesting.

Cessation of Driving

When or for what reasons should a driver stop operating a vehicle? According to the elderly drivers, the most likely reason is poor vision (94 percent). Other reasons which may warrant cessation of driving are poor health (86 percent), knowing that one's driving skills are slipping (80 percent) and physical impairment (71 percent). This latter factor was cited by a higher proportion of the seventy-five and older age group than by the younger two groups of drivers. Having caused a bad accident or having narrowly escaped one was considered by 57 percent of the respondents to be a legitimate cause for quitting. More women (67 percent) than men (48 percent) considered causing a bad accident as a reason to cease driving. Only 30 percent prescribed to the concept, "if you can't afford it, don't drive."

Respondents were also read a list of specific factors they would consider in determining whether they should give up driving. Two factors appeared on this list which also appeared in the previous consideration of reasons for stopping to drive. These were health (98 percent) and accident record (87 percent). We note that the number of drivers responding "yes" to health and accidents is higher on this question than on the previous question. This discrepancy suggests that while some older drivers would consider health and/or accident record to be important factors in assessing driving continuation, being responsible for an accident or suffering a health impairment alone would not necessarily cause them to stop. It should also be noted that while 83 percent of the drivers would consider road test results in formulating a decision to quit, mention of a road test decreased with increasing age (see Table B-47).

When the survey respondents were asked about the individual they feel should be responsible to recommend that it is time to give up driving, we see a fairly similar response rate among all drivers. The medical doctor's input was more important (90 percent); the drivers themselves (79 percent) and Motor Vehicle Department came next (74 percent). Again, more than one option was possible. While the overall response rates were similar, the two oldest groups (aged sixty-five plus) had more faith in the driver's opinion than did the youngest elderly group. While 82 percent of the sixty-five to seventy-four year olds and 84 percent of the drivers aged seventy-five and over favored reliance on self-assessment, only 69 percent of the fifty-five to sixty-four year olds thought the driver should make the decision.

Based on the statistics, it appears that elderly drivers consider the final decision on stopping to drive to be a joint decision between doctor, the Motor Vehicle Department, and the elderly driver. Sixty-two percent of the elderly motorists would even want family members to have input into the decision.

Retesting

Recently retesting drivers on the basis of age has become an issue hotly debated in the halls of legislatures. Perspectives from the drivers who will definitely be affected is, therefore, valuable. Senior drivers were asked three questions regarding reexamination. First, they were asked "Do you think reexamination should be required before a person's license is renewed?" If they answered yes, they were then asked to indicate the age at which it should be required.

Twenty-eight percent of the motorists were definite. They said no, reexamination should not be required before a person's license is renewed. Thirty-five percent were egalitarian about it. It should be mandatory for all ages. Thirty-seven percent of the elderly drivers had specific ages in mind—of these seventy years of age was mentioned by 35 percent, and this was followed by age sixty-five (22 percent), age seventy-five (16 percent), and age eighty (13 percent). More drivers (36 percent) in the fifty-five to sixty-four year old and sixty-five to seventy-four year old groups (37 percent) than in the seventy-five and over group (30 percent) wanted all drivers to be tested. However, a greater percentage of age seventy-five and over drivers (35 percent) than those sixty-five to seventy-four years old (24 percent), and those fifty-five to sixty-four year old drivers (31 percent), answered that they wanted no retesting at any age (see Table B-48). Men and women were more or less equally represented in their opinions.

If a reexamination is needed, 95 percent believed it should include an eye test, 87 percent felt it should include a road test, 57 percent a physical examination and 48 percent a written test.

When we questioned their own personal reaction, 34 percent of the respondents marked "yes" to the second question, "Would periodic reexamination make you feel nervous or threatened?" One might reasonably suspect that a high percentage of those who believe retesting should not be required are those who are threatened by reexamination. Given that the older drivers are more likely to have deteriorating physical and perceptual skills, they might feel more threatened by reexamination. Thus it is interesting to note that the older the drivers, the less threatened they felt by reexamination (40 percent of the youngest, 33 percent of the middle, and 29 percent of the oldest groups).

Discussion

As a group, the elderly are not a single entity, a monolith rigidly defined. It is made up, rather, of individuals or clusters of individuals, some of whom are like and some unlike themselves. To draw, therefore, a profile of the elderly and driving based on a statistical survey, we must consider both the similarities and range of differentiations between age groups and sexes.

Aging is a brutal fact of life. Hanging on to the back of aging are social, existential, physical, economic, and psychological factors. These factors contribute to becoming older as a motorist. They have manifold consequences, some of which were explored in the previous pages.

We could argue, with little exaggeration, that aging means biological deterioration. Vision, hearing, reflexes, and so on are not as sharp and distinct in one's seventies as they were in one's twenties. Yet elderly drivers rated their vision and hearing as being good or better. In fact, they considered their overall health to be good or excellent. When asked about specific factors that they believed affected their driving ability, only 10 percent reported poor night vision, 15 percent had problems with glare, 4 percent had generally poor vision, 5 percent had trouble turning their heads, 8 percent were often fatigued, and 2 percent had poor hearing. However, the drivers' responses to other questions indicated that these identified problem areas were present to a higher degree than our respondents were prepared to associate with their own driving ability.

Based on our findings, the majority of elderly drivers learned to drive forty or more years ago, with the largest numbers having learned fifty or more years ago. In historiographical terms, this places learning within the Depression and World War II years. Their learning opportunities were mostly provided by friends or parents. But, a quarter of the seniors taught themselves to drive. So we have a situation in which over the last fifty years tremendous technological, legal, and social changes have taken place in the traffic world, yet we have a sizeable group of people who have learned to drive on a tractor, in a 1943 Chevy, or even a Model T on a country road.

To improve their driving skills, 41 percent of the elderly drivers—the majority women—had completed a driver education, training, or retraining program. But over half of these had taken training over twenty years ago. To "keep current" with traffic-related change, the majority of elderly people rely on such communication strategies as newspapers (59 percent), radio/television (36 percent) and/or word of mouth (25 percent). Face-to-face talk is a source used more often by women (30 percent) than men (20 percent). Little reading of pamphlets or official literature containing laws and regulations, insurance policies, or driver rights is undertaken by this group of people.

Anyone who believes that the elderly drivers are so safe as not to become involved in problematic situations is sadly mistaken. Over the last five years 29 percent had an accident and about one-quarter of the drivers had been cited for violations of which speeding (at 15 percent) was the most frequent.

Exposure and Driving Difficulties

Overall, elderly drivers are quite active drivers. In a week the mean number of days driven per week by the three age groups, fifty-five to sixty-four, sixty-five to seventy-four, and seventy-five and over were, in order: 5.6, 5.2, and 4.8. Rush-hour traffic and night driving, traditionally hazardous driving situations for senior citizens, were undertaken more often by the fifty-five to sixty-four year olds than other groups. Roughly two days in an average week include rush-hour and/or nighttime driving. The two older groups do less.

Sixty-three percent of the seventy-five and older age group of motorists travel, on the average, less than 5,000 miles a year, whereas 62 percent of the sixty-five to seventy-four year olds and 67 percent of those aged fifty-five to sixty-four travel more than 5,000 miles per year.

The trips are usually taken alone. Although 96 percent of the motorists feel comfortable taking passengers, 70 percent said they usually drive by themselves. The most often taken trips are for shopping (96 percent), visiting friends (96 percent), pleasure (85 percent), entertainment (90 percent) and/or health care (78 percent).

When trips are taken, changing lanes (24 percent) and making left turns at uncontrolled intersections (24 percent) offer the most difficulty driving for elderly motorists. Changing lanes is particularly hard for elderly women.

On their trips, the mistakes most often made by elderly drivers are running a yellow light (37 percent), failing to come to a complete stop at a stop sign (18 percent), and exceeding the speed limit or driving too fast for conditions (17 percent). They try to avoid, if they can, foggy conditions (66 percent), snow, sleet, or slush (57 percent), and rush-hour traffic (55 percent). For the latter, those motorists aged seventy-five or over are more inclined to do so.

Reading traffic signs causes little difficulty if they can be seen. But seeing them may be a problem. The physical placement of traffic signs presents a problem to 43 percent of the senior drivers. For another 20 percent the limited size of signs or size of print presents problems.

Self As Driver

Everyone judges himself or herself in all features of life. These interpretations reflect judgments we have of ourselves in relation to others. With respect to the elderly drivers, 99 percent rated themselves as average or better than average drivers. The men were more positive in their judgments than were women. When they were asked how family members would rate them as drivers, 81 percent of the elderly stated "good" or "excellent." As before, men were more inclined to be "excellent" than were women.

Driving makes the elderly feel confident and comfortable (98 percent). They like it (75 percent). When careless drivers confront them on the road the elderly feel annoyed (62 percent). They would move out of the way (45 percent), or just leave the other driver to his or her exploits and "do nothing" (33 percent).

So often we hear the slogan, "we drive how we feel." When elderly drivers are upset about personal matters, 52 percent drive as usual. But among other options 29 percent recognize their mood and "take extra care," while a further 16 percent try to avoid driving while being upset. Taking extra precautions when being upset was more often done by women than men.

In a given series of driving situations, the elderly drivers believe they drive the same as they did when they were thirty-five to forty-five years of age.

These situations are driving in winter, snow, sleet or slush, rain or fog, driving on the freeway or in the city, driving during rush hour or on holidays. Nighttime driving was considered to be worse now than before. Men, more often than women, thought that they now drive the same or even better than when they were younger.

Elderly drivers believe that in their later years they drive more defensively (87 percent) and cautiously (79 percent), but not necessarily more slowly (34 percent). Looking at the number of senior drivers (15 percent) who received speeding related tickets within the last five years, slow driving can certainly not be considered as a pillar of meaning for elderly driving.

Licensure

Cessation of driving and retesting are high interest issues in the traffic world. The motor vehicle, a vital element in quality of life, is routinely used for shopping, visiting, recreation, pleasure, and holidays. If driving were no longer possible, over 80 percent of the elderly would be less mobile and independent. Sixty-five percent would have to change their life-style. They would use alternative transportation modes such as walking, buses, or asking friends for rides whenever possible, but the outcome would likely be that they stay closer to home and become less social.

If drivers' licenses were to be revoked, it would be most appropriate if for reasons of poor health (86 percent) and/or poor vision (94 percent). A poor accident record could also be an item that determines whether driving should be given up.

Related to reasons for stopping to drive are the elderly drivers' viewpoints on who should have the final decision. The action should involve three parties: the doctor (90 percent), the driver (79 percent), and the Motor Vehicle Department (74 percent). For the elderly (older than seventy-four), the emphasis for the decision to stop driving should be on the driver. For the other senior drivers, stress should be placed on the other two parties.

With respect to compulsory reexamination, 28 percent said no. Thirty-five percent suggested it should be mandatory for all ages. The others had specific ages in mind, varying from fifty to eighty-eight. Of all the age groups, more participants aged seventy-five or older did not want any form of compulsory reexamination.

Mandatory retesting would make 34 percent of the senior drivers nervous or feel threatened. It is interesting to note that the older the drivers, the less they seemed threatened by reexamination (fifty-five to sixty-four years old, 40 percent; sixty-five to seventy-four years old, 33 percent; and seventy-five and older, 29 percent).

The elderly drivers are diverse, but in their diversity they have similarities. Both the differences and similarities are important, especially when they provide us with greater insight on the broad and narrow spectrum of elderly driver characteristics.

References

Millstein, S., and G. Guttman. 1988. "Seniors' Attitudes Toward Driving Practices: Focus Group and Survey Data from the Lower Mainland, Vancouver Island and the Okanagan." Gerontology Research Centre, Simon Fraser University, Burnaby, BC, (unpublished).

Planek, T.W., M.E. Condon, and T.C. Fowler. 1968. *An Investigation of the Problems and Opinions of Aged Drivers*. Report No. 5/68. National Safety Council.

Statistics Canada. 1984. *The Elderly in Canada*. Catalogue 99-932.

Yee, D. 1984. "A Survey of the Traffic Safety Needs and Problems of Drivers Age 55 and Over." In *Needs and Problems of Older Drivers: Survey Results and Recommendations. Proceedings of the Older Driver Colloquium*. AAA Foundation for Traffic Safety, Falls Church, VA.

7

Face-to-Face

I have seen an old face much lined with nothing, and a smooth face in which all things were graven.

I know faces, because I look through the fabric my own eye weaves, and behold the reality beneath.

(Kahlil Gibran, *Faces*)

Up to this point a significant amount of information has been shared about the driving attitudes and practices of the elderly. However, in most cases the materials were based on accident statistics, opinions of experts and on highly structured questionnaires rather than on relevant and personal information provided freely by older persons themselves.

This chapter follows a different script. It further refines the nature of the elderly drivers' world through free and open discussion. In small focus groups the elderly were able to think, talk, support, debate, and imagine driving. The benefits from these discussions were announced. Everyone had something to say. Few had to search long and hard for relevant experiences or points of view.

To arrive at a description of everyday life, group participants were requested to address such issues as driving patterns, views of self and stereotyping, driving difficulties, perspectives on cars, licensure, and driver reeducation.

The bulk of the chapter includes factual descriptions of elderly people's attitudes and perspectives. The Appendixes at the back of the book include statistical tables to which occasional reference is made. All the numbers quoted in the text are based on statistical analyses that exclude missing data.

Participants

Socio-demographic

In the three age groups of interest, the male perspective predominated. The proportion of males in each age group ranged from 52.7 percent among those aged fifty-five to sixty-four, 67.8 percent for those sixty-five to seventy-four, to 69.0 percent among those seventy-five and over. Correspondingly, the proportions for licensed drivers within these age groups in British Columbia (1984-85) were 57.8 percent, 61.5 percent, and 72.3 percent. Approximately 69 to 81 percent in each age group were married (fifty-five to sixty-four: 75.7 percent; sixty-five to seventy-four: 81.4 percent, and seventy-five plus: 69 percent). Only 17 percent were employed full- or part-time. Almost all of these people were within the fifty-five to sixty-four age group. Virtually all of the elderly drivers older than sixty-five received federal Old Age Security Pensions.

When the three socioeconomic status indicators were examined, namely receipt of Guaranteed Income Supplement, education, and occupation, we found that our sample of discussants was biased toward the upper end of the scale. Only five of the 162 participants received a full or partial Guaranteed Income Supplement. Approximately half (53 percent) earned a university degree or had at least had some college or university training. Similarly, just over half of the respondents (52 percent) described their primary life occupation as professional, semi-professional, or managerial. This upward bias in socioeconomic status was particularly apparent in the oldest group, where nearly 62 percent reported at least some college, technical school, or university training, and 75 percent of the interviewees were in one of the top four occupational categories. In the general Canadian population aged sixty-five and over, half receive a full or partial GIS and only 18.5 percent hold a college degree or have had some post-secondary education (Statistics Canada 1984). When we re-align our age groupings to match Statistics Canada we find that 53 percent of the focus group participants aged sixty-five and over had some post-secondary education.

Self-reported Health Status and Use of Medications

By their own admission, the elderly spokespeople were a healthy group. When they were asked to rate their health on a continuum ranging from excellent to poor, 58 percent in the fifty-five to sixty-four age group, 36 percent in the sixty-five to seventy-four group, and 41 percent in the seventy-five-plus group rated their health as "excellent." Most of the remainder of elderly rated their health as "good" (overall average of 48 percent). Some use prescription medications on a regular basis. For example, 37 percent in the fifty-five to sixty-four age group, 44 percent in the sixty-five to seventy-four age group, and 48 percent in the seventy-five and older group reported using one or more prescriptions. Corresponding percentages for regular elderly use of one or more over-the-counter medications such as aspirin were 39 percent, 49 percent, and 41 percent. These data indicate that, based on self-reporting, our sample of elderly drivers was healthier than the average senior citizen. To illustrate, in other Canadian studies of persons sixty-five and older who live outside of institutions, health ratings of excellent ranged from 13-23 percent (Gutman 1980). According to Krupka and Vener (1979), 67 percent of the noninstitutionalized aged use at least one prescription drug on a daily basis; 65 percent use over-the-counter drugs regularly.

Alcohol Consumption

About a quarter of elderly drivers in each age group responded that they abstain from use of alcohol (fifty-five to sixty-four: 27 percent; sixty-five to seventy-four: 22 percent; seventy-five plus: 31 percent). The majority (60 percent) said they used it occasionally, several times a week, weekly, or monthly. Almost a sixth reported consuming alcohol on a daily basis, taking a drink to relax, fight boredom, or to soothe aches and pains.

Vision and Hearing Ratings

When elderly drivers were asked to rate their vision, some differences per age group were noted. For example, approximately one-quarter in the fifty-five to sixty-four and seventy-five plus rated their vision as excellent, compared to 41 percent in the sixty-five to seventy-four age group. Most of the remaining participants rated it as "good."

While the proportion reporting excellent hearing decreased with increasing age, overall less than 20 percent answered that they experience serious hearing problems.

Notes on the Everyday Behavior of Elderly Drivers

When presenting elderly driving routines and following their course of events, we study the rules of conduct in diffuse realms of public situations. Their conduct or behavior reflects social or group norms and standards.

Group norms are like punctuation marks that emphasize generally accepted behavior. Also they accent schemas of interpretation, or rules of conduct, that govern certain participations. In accordance with this line of reasoning, we have ordered the data and described them to reflect behavior and social meaning.

Using the Vehicle

It comes as no surprise that in western society the automobile is king. It provides mobility, sociality, economic gain, existential meaning, and social status. We have already received clues in previous chapters that, for the elderly, the vehicle is the enhancer of life-style. However, the extent to which personal meaning is attached to the automobile has yet to be uncovered. So we asked elderly drivers to describe their relationships with the car.

In order of frequency of mention, the five most common uses of the automobile in all three age groups were for shopping, for pleasure, to visit family or friends, for vacation travel, and to get to and from social or cultural events or entertainment.

Although there are strong indications that life-style is engrained in the vehicle, the more common rule of behavior seems to be that the car "fits" into life-style patterns. The automobile is used for customary everyday affairs like shopping or "bringing home the groceries." Driving to visit family and friends are daily, or at least regular occasions whereby elderly drivers "fit in" the car. As one woman suggested:

> Everything. I have to use it all the time, it's like two legs I use it all the time . . . shopping, library, movies if I go, visiting friends.

Driving for pleasure has a variety of meanings. It may be the main involvement, basically during the weekend, where some elderly drivers are "out on the road for fun." Or it can be a side event. That is, the vehicle is used to help senior citizens become involved in other events. They drive to their favorite place, whether it be a park, the woods, or shopping areas and go for walks. Driving fits into walking, and walking becomes an extension of driving.

Pleasure driving may be the response to a mundane or boring life at home. An elderly couple is retired. The husband and wife are removed from the challenges, needs, desires, and stresses of the employed. So, they get into a routine or "rut," feeling the need to initiate new experiences. Witness the following comments:

> We are a little bit bored at home. My wife is retired and I'm now retired and we just got to get out . . . My wife and I just hit the car. Our interests rest with what we're surrounded by, by mountains, rivers, seas, whatever.

> We often say let's just go for a drive. We still do that. No specific reason, but out, after we've been around the suite for a few hours and we've got nothing else . . . Any time at all.

Pleasure driving may also entail extended journeys. Part of our yearly plan is to go on holidays. It is considered to be a regular or central feature of life. Typically, major holiday travel occurs once a year—in the summertime. Not necessarily so for the elderly! It is common for them to travel several times a year to locations in Canada or the United States. When they do so, often trailers are pulled. Routinely, drivers considered pleasure driving synonymous with holiday travel. For many it is a tradition, one which has evolved over the life span. For others it is a continuation of their perceptions that they are cautious, competent drivers. So taking long distance journeys was considered to be a natural, safe form of pleasure driving.

Those who reported using their cars for business or to commute to and from work were almost exclusively in the fifty-five to sixty-four age group. Also, as one would expect, the proportion of elderly using their cars to get to health care increased (at age seventy-five) and the proportion using it to get to sporting activities or sporting events drastically decreased after age seventy-five. The most notable difference between age groups, however, was in the much higher proportion in the oldest group who reported using their car to visit family and/or friends (69 percent compared with 51 percent in the fifty-five to sixty-four age group, and 29 percent in the sixty-five to seventy-four age group). This appears to be a reflection of the greater importance that the older-old place on visiting, or it is a result of a decline in other activities. With more time on their hands, the seventy-five-plus seniors increase their interaction with family and friends.

Life Changes without the Car

A quick review of the role the vehicle plays in the lives of the elderly shows how it fits into the entire life-style. As we already established, the automobile is used nearly every day for purposes of shopping, visiting family and friends, driving for pleasure, holidaying, going to work, escaping boredom, participating in recreational activities such as golf, attending church, doing favors, or observing entertainment. Furthermore, it is an efficient system for fulfilling needs. One elderly woman revealed that the real benefit of the car is its time saving:

> . . . the time involved. I would resent it if I had to take three buses to get somewhere and think I could have driven there in such and such a time. That would irk me.

Obviously the loss of driving opportunities would be a major occurrence. This proved to be the case.

When asked how their lives would change if they could no longer drive, over one-third (35 percent) reported that it would have a negative emotional effect, one-quarter said they would become public transit users, and one-fifth answered that they would relocate nearer to public transit and certain facilities and services such as hospitals, churches, and stores. The emotional impact of losing the car would appear to be greatest for those in the sixty-five to seventy-four age group. For years they had to rely on themselves for mobility.

Without a support group, the sudden change would be unnerving, "mind wracking." Also, more discussants in this group than in the other groups felt they would need to relocate their home. It was in the oldest group (seventy-five plus), that the greatest proportion of members explicitly predicted a drastic change of life-style. They would stay closer to home. This results in new social challenges such as increased isolation and possible acceleration of health deterioration.

In terms of impact on the person, losing the car was described metaphorically as devastation, frustration, trauma, and heartbreaking. We must realize the tenor of the feelings because, for all practical purposes, once the elderly lose the privilege to drive, they will not regain it. Driving is forever terminated.

So the elderly person's life would be altered for all time. As one gentleman explained:

> My life would change absolutely and completely. I'm 2 1/2 miles from a shopping area and live a mile and a half from the bus. My life, my whole life would be completely upside down. It's a horrible thought when you come down to it.

To compensate for the loss, or at least to bring their lives into some form of equilibrium, the elderly drivers would consider becoming public transit users. For some this creates another problem—proximity to the bus line. At least one-fifth of the discussants would consider moving nearer to a bus line and/or shopping facilities. But, what about the seniors in rural districts, or suburban communities? If they moved, it would be a drastic cultural challenge, one which some elderly consider to be "frightening."

One thing remains clear. The possibility of losing the driver's license is entrenched in the elderly people's minds. See chapter 8 for a more thorough description. It is an ongoing concern that motivates them to think about alternatives and plausible venues. But, no matter how much thinking and planning has occurred, several facts remain. According to the focus group participants, holiday journeys by car will cease, staying closer to home will be a certainty, personal mobility will decrease, and social interaction will decline. In short, the loss of the driver's license would mean an altered life. Sociality in particular would decline. For some the change would be emphatic, while for others it would be more moderate. The major factor that influences the impact of losing the car is the distance the elderly live from children, extended family, and lifelong friends.

Meaning of the Automobile

The automobile is synonymous with mobility. And up to 24 percent of the elderly defined it as such. But, it means so much more:

> Mobility all right. But it also means enjoyment of culture, the arts, everything, church and . . . It's the avenue of your life.

For up to 59 percent of the respondents the car represents independence and freedom. It is an existential meaning that moves beyond a purely utilitarian concept of mobility or transportation. It helps the elderly drivers do what they wish, when they so desire, and without apology. The elderly people cling to a free life-style and the automobile is like the "dear friend" that enables them to become full participants in a free way of life. Without the car, life would be more enchained. The elderly would be more dependent on the whims of other people.

The strength of meaning the vehicle holds for senior citizens has evolved over the life span. As they have grown older they have begun to appreciate the automobile more and more. They have increasingly recognized their dependence on the vehicle to help them sustain the prized luxuries of freedom and independence. Furthermore, some elderly drivers believe that they have pioneered the fight for such freedom. They should now be entitled to enjoy the fruits of their labors.

Avoiding Driving Circumstances

Use of the vehicle is closely associated with nonuse. Approximately one-quarter in the fifty-five to sixty-four group, and 19 percent in the sixty-five to seventy-four and the seventy-five-plus age groups said that there were no driving conditions that they try to avoid. In other words, they would take trips whenever the need or desire arose. They would not "back up from anything."

However, the predominant theme was that certain driving conditions demanded careful scrutiny and wise decision making. As in the survey data, the most commonly mentioned driving features the elderly may avoid were bad weather, night driving, and rush-hour traffic.

But the questionnaire data failed to establish the social rule that avoidance does not necessarily equate with inability or weakness of will. It may be a fortuitous decision elderly drivers make for the sake of convenience. As one woman described, "It is a reality, not a fear." Routinely, elderly drivers schedule their driving times to arm themselves against consequential driving results—accidents, or to maintain a worry-free life-style.

However, when the purpose of travel is considered to be vital or important, some elderly drivers are prepared to forego their own evaluations of risk and drive in conditions such as rainy nights. For, as one woman said, she "avoids bad weather unless it's absolutely necessary." The consequences of poor driving conditions are risked for reasons such as doing favors (e.g., giving a friend or family member a ride to the hospital), picking up parcels, partaking in scheduled volunteer activities, or honoring promises to do things at other persons' residences. Avoiding to drive, therefore, may be interpreted as staying off the roads in certain conditions if, or when, no other influential social factors determine alternate actions.

The major difference between age groups was in the proportion of people who try to avoid night driving. The number increased from 28 percent in the fifty-five to sixty-four age group, to 49 percent for those aged sixty-five to seventy-four, to 56 percent among those seventy-five plus. Glare was the major reason for limited night driving. It became obvious that as the elderly age, they become more sensitive to headlight glare, thus limiting travel during such times. This proved to be especially true for glare on rainy nights.

As was already indicated, avoidance of rush-hour traffic does not automatically equate with avoidance of dangerous driving circumstances. Rather, it may connote the avoidance of experiencing unnecessary discomfort, or frustration resulting from "sitting in a lane and waiting for one and a half hours." Trip routes and travel schedules are planned so that elderly drivers do not get caught in long delays. They try to miss them "like the plague." Because they can "come and go as they feel like," elderly drivers can and do skirt afternoon rush-hour environments such as certain bridges, tunnels, intersections, or one-way streets.

In all three age groups, three-quarters or more of the focus group participants reported that they use their car daily (fifty-five to sixty-four: 82 percent; sixty-five to seventy-four: 75 percent; seventy-five plus: 86 percent); of the remainder, most use their car several times a week. Frequency of use of the automobile appears to decrease from the young to the middle old, only to increase to the old old. However, it is clear from estimates given on the Participant Information Form regarding the number of kilometers driven in a year, that overall, participants who are older than seventy-five do not drive as far as their younger counterparts. This has been verified in all stages of the research so far.

The amount of driving may take on a male-female difference. Whereas for many women, their husbands used to drive them, for reasons of their husbands' death or incapacitation the women must now drive and drive more often. They have become rather new players in the game of driving a car regularly.

In some instances, the occasion of driving reflects a senior citizen's inability to choose other forms of transportation. For example, the car is used on a regular basis, rather than other modes of transportation because of physical ailments such as amputated limbs, hip disorders and the like. Such conditions summon the comfort and convenience of the car. Psychologically, the fear of personal harm is less, or at least is seen to be less, in an automobile than, say, on a bus. Elderly persons reported that whenever they ride on a bus they often feel vulnerable to abuse or physical harm. The automobile, as a rule, is perceived to reduce those risks. For some, it is considered even less risky than walking. As one elderly woman suggested, "I'd rather bend a fender than break a leg on the ice."

Distance Travelled per Year

The estimated average distance elderly drivers travel per year is 13,800 kilometers or 7,375 miles. If we carefully review the purposes for trips and frequency of driving per day, it is not difficult to arrive at a significant distance travelled per year.

Another perspective on the amount of travel per year is the age of the automobiles the focus group members drive. We established that the mean age of vehicles driven by age groups were as follows: fifty-five to sixty-four: 8.03; sixty-five to seventy-four: 5.7; seventy-five plus: 7.5. In comparison, the mean vehicle age in British Columbia for 1987 was 8.26. It appears that the elderly do not differ, overtly, from the rest of the car owners. They may, however, have different perspectives on vehicles and age.

The relationship between the age of the car and distance driven was not discussed in any of the focus groups. It would have been interesting to know, for example, if elderly drivers refrain from driving long distances because they lacked confidence in their vehicles or alternatively, the number of seniors who retain an older vehicle because they don't drive long distances.

Financial status would, of course, also play a role in the decision to keep an older car as would a desire to conserve finances for transfer to their heirs. The latter is a rule that is directly relevant to elderly people's hierarchy of priorities. Rather than an "I want mine right now" orientation, a predominant concern is "What can I leave to the children?"

Perceptions on Driving

When we scrutinize the elderly's feelings about driving, we must remember that the seniors do not come to the operation of a motor vehicle fresh. Each elderly driver arrives with a long history characterized by major changes in traffic related technology and socially approved behavior.

To place feelings about driving into context, we have reworked the health slogan "you are what you eat" to "you are the kind of driver you feel you are." Generally speaking, elderly drivers feel positive about driving. Time and time again they reiterated that they feel comfortable, confident, and relaxed behind the wheel. They like and enjoy driving. These feelings are the products of years of successful and competent motoring.

Our analysis of conversational data on personal feelings toward driving produced an unanticipated caveat. A group of participants for reasons of health, employment, convenience, and foreign travel abstained from driving for an extended period of time. This reality produced different views. These individuals felt less confident and relaxed than did the other members. The following two examples should suffice:

> I used to be relaxed. But when I got away from it for a while and started driving again I lost my confidence you know. After my husband passed away everything was pushed on me.
>
> I have seen that for some older people who have not driven for a while they find it much more difficult.

The total number of interviewees who felt negative or tentative about driving was only about 20 percent. Mention of a critical point inevitably sparked spontaneous conversations among members in the different discussion groups. Often, an opening claim in a discussion was that elderly drivers were nervous about driving. The reasons given for their nervousness could be summarized in the statement that seniors were "not fully aware of what they were doing." This characterization received further clarification. For some participants, not knowing what elderly drivers are doing is the result of having lost that "certain something" over the years. Others rationalized that not knowing what a person is doing is not age related. Chances are seniors never had the proper skills or they lacked the motivation to upgrade their abilities.

An impression was left that group members did not sanction feelings of nervousness. Whenever someone spoke about being nervous, hesitant, or tentative while driving, other members were quick to rationalize the feeling. For example, to be nervous after an elderly driver has been ill is understandable. But, just to be nervous is indefensible.

Yet, when discussants proposed that although overall they are confident drivers, but nervous or anxious about certain driving conditions such as rain, ice, or snow, reinforcement from others was quickly forthcoming. One elderly woman reported that although she is a relaxed driver, travel on rainy nights makes her a little anxious. She received support from all group members suggesting that such feelings are "not unusual" and not restricted to any particular age group. Another elderly motorist expressed apprehension on approaching intersections. The supporting response was, "I think that's typical as we get a little older." The following excerpt portrays nicely the reinforcement that came into play when an elderly man explained his reason for being nervous:

> R1: I feel good about driving. There is nothing I particularly watch out for. Aah but I believe that I'm sometimes just a slight bit nervous on the blind side on my right when I'm in the left hand lane. And I'm very cautious about that. I suppose it's not recommended I turn my head and take a look and that's the only way I can see.

R2: Well it is recommended you do that in the law, I think.

R3: That's not so different. Blind side, everybody has that problem.

Characteristics of Elderly Drivers as Imputed by Others and Selves

A driver's self-concept is shaped in part by how he or she is evaluated by others. So it is with the elderly drivers. To a large degree a person's self is a "looking-glass self." Cooley, a pioneer American sociologist, first described this concept (1902). Krech et al. (1962:82-83), withdrew the most strategic elements and wrote thus:

> In a very large and interesting class of cases the social reference takes the form of a somewhat definite imagination of how one's self . . . appears in a particular mind, and the kind of self-feeling one has is determined by the attitude toward this attributed to that other mind. A social self of this sort might be called the reflected or looking glass self.
>
> "Each to each a looking glass
> Reflects the other that doth pass"
>
> The self that is most important is a reflection, largely, from the minds of others . . . We live on, cheerful, self confident . . . until in some rude hour we learn that we do not stand as well as we thought we did, that the image of us is tarnished. Perhaps we do something, quite naturally, that we find the social order is set against, or perhaps it is the ordinary course of our life that is not so well regarded as we supposed. At any rate, we find with a chill of terror that the world is cold and strange, and our self-esteem, self-confidence, and hope, being chiefly founded upon the opinions attributed to others, go down in a crash . . .

While involved in the life-as-usual, elderly drivers are not immune to the images other people assign to them. They help define the moral character of the elderly driver on the road, one which the senior motorists either sustain or oppose. For, as Byrne and Maziarz (1969) wrote, an individual finds in and through others, support for what he or she is or can be.

When the seniors were asked to extend their bounds of reality and reveal how they thought other people characterize them, "slow" was the common answer. Discussants, especially in the two older-age brackets, generally agreed that older drivers are resented. People criticize them, and have little patience for them. The elderly discussants, aged seventy-five plus, were not hesitant to express their feelings of insecurity. One-third of them believed that others "think older drivers are worse than other drivers" and one-fifth support the perception that others "feel older people should stop driving."

The features of other people's views contain two noteworthy elements. First, the other people's judgments were personally experienced by elderly drivers. Second, there was significant agreement with other drivers' negative perceptions.

Many times elderly drivers discussed personal experiences in degrading driving circumstances. Witness:

> Well, I have been told in no uncertain terms by young people and ladies. One of 'em said to me in the fruit market parking lot one time she said "You've got all day but I haven't." She was impatient and I was taking my time parking. I guess what she thinks is that we're just a bunch of old fogies.

With regular frequency, elderly drivers were the designates of rude comments, the proverbial fingers, critical commentary, and threats. Respondents have cataloged the experiences, ones in which they are pictured as slowpokes, menaces, and the like.

Although some elderly drivers refuted the claims and challenged their integrity, the general rule of interpretation concerning other people's perspectives on elderly drivers was agreement. In all three age groups, the terms "cautious" and "slow" were routinely used for characterizing other older drivers. Some members in the fifty-five to sixty-four age group described older drivers as "worse than younger drivers" (16 percent) or "not aware of other drivers, unpredictable and they don't signal" (21 percent). In the youngest group, respondents tended to qualify their answer by pointing to the heterogeneity of the older population. This was reflected in such statements as "they are all different" or "*some* are terrible/should be off the road." Two sample accounts are presented which make more intelligible the coded interpretations:

> It's a natural thing that the younger people look at the older ones as a little bit slow. Because they're so much faster and so much more confident. They're computing distances and travelling lanes and what not. They consider us slow and inefficient. And I think they're quite right. As we get older we get to be less efficient drivers. When we were their age we were doing the same thing what they were doing . . . we are older and wiser but not more competent.
>
> I think they think we're for the birds. Most people think oh look at that fool. You know they really do. And mind you, I agree with some of them. There are some people, maybe I'm one of 'em, I don't know, there are some people who should not be driving. In other words they're driving cars that are too big for them. Have you ever seen the old people, they're peering through the steering wheel.
>
> I think there's rhyme and reason to all things and that's what most of the young people think. And most times I don't blame them.

Closely related to group stereotyping is the concept of generation. The elderly drivers as a generation are judged by the standards and interests of young drivers—another generation. This is a natural process, an objective property of change in which the elderly drivers themselves actively participated. To illustrate:

> I used to be prejudiced of older drivers. They poked along and sort of drove slow and everything. I don't think that way now. That's really quite funny.

> When I was a working man using my car I used to boil over the old fogies on the road . . . People looking in stores and poking along.

Police Views of the Elderly Drivers. Group participants generally agreed that police officers demonstrate fairness in their treatment of elderly drivers. They were repeatedly described as treating older people "with respect," "as family," or "the same as others."

With ease, discussants characterized the police as being responsive to emergency or troublesome events. A commonly held belief was that if elderly drivers behave lawfully and act civilly towards police officers, then the police reciprocate. If not, then the elderly, or any other person, will "get what's coming to him." The kind of treatment people receive from law officers reflects the quality of interaction between driver and police after an event. It has nothing to do with age. According to the respondents, this is the way it should be. No special treatment, no far reaching stigmas or predetermined judgments!

Family Members' Views of the Elderly Drivers. Family perceptions of the elderly drivers were commonly understood in terms of concerted actions. Sixty-six percent of the discussants indicated that their family members consider their driving to be okay, good, safe, or superior. The background evidence for such statements were descriptions on how "comfortable kids are driving with them," how "the wife wants [the husband] to drive all the time," and that our participants were "never told differently." The implication was that noncriticism translates into compliment.

Although few respondents ever heard family members explicitly compliment them for their good driving, the elderly drivers based their perceptions on everyday driving events from which they inferred favorable judgments. It was an implicit assumption shared by many. To verify their perceptions the senior citizen may ask, "If I were not a good driver, would my grandchildren and children still want to drive with me?" To them the answer would be, "no, they would not." Since family members are ready and willing to drive with the elderly driver, surely he or she must be a good driver—so the reasoning goes. It was not believed to be otherwise.

When the three age groups were compared, it became apparent that there were differences in the proportions considered to be poor drivers by their families. For the fifty-five to sixty-four year old drivers, up to 51 percent of the respondents revealed that their families were critical of their driving behavior. Spouses and/or children felt that the interviewees drive too fast, that they are "bad" drivers, are nervous or critical, or the family members overall never liked how the elderly drive. Almost a quarter of the oldest group gave no indication of how their immediate family felt.

Whenever the elderly reported on family members' criticism, there was a tinge of disbelief, at times followed by rationalizations such as, "my son speeds" or "my wife is always critical."

There was a shared understanding that other people stress the slow-driving aspect whenever they criticize elderly drivers. To a large extent the seniors agreed with the routinely given assessment. In fact many, in their younger years, themselves had critical views of the elderly, and many today share these views about other elderly drivers. Although slowness may be a hindrance for young people, to the interviewees it usually reflects caution. Therefore, to drive slowly may be an accurate depiction of elderly-driver reality, but it is not necessarily a negative one. If slowness suggests caution, it is a positive feature, one younger people are not inclined to follow. This was a common group theme.

So, are the elderly good drivers? They think so. And they also tend to believe that their family members think so. After all, they are prepared to be passengers in cars driven by the elderly. They do not have much trouble with the police. So all in all their positive views of selves are considered to be legitimated by significant others, and often misunderstood by younger drivers.

Characteristics of a Good Driver and the Self

The good driver is recognized as a fact in driving. He or she is "out there" for people to see and define, with characteristics or properties that can be idealized and discussed. To the average driver these properties can be envisioned as (for all practical purposes) standards for judging what is real and preferred. Indeed, the driving world is not perceived by elderly drivers as a set of random, unpredictable, unique events and appearances. Quite the contrary; it is perceived as being orderly, meaningful and factual.

The good driver is therefore definable. An examination of the many extended discussions with elderly drivers revealed a list of essential characteristics and supporting narratives that identify the domain of good driver.

1. *Courteousness*. Courteous drivers respect other people's right on the road. They do not follow too closely, do not turn where they are not supposed to, and are willing to yield once in a while, especially to an older driver. The courteous drivers give the other drivers a break, such as allowing them to enter the roadway in front of them.
2. *Considerateness*. Considerate drivers are extensions of courteous drivers. They are attentive to the feelings of others, and they conduct their driving in a way as not to upset or hurt fellow motorists.
3. *Defensive Driving*. The defensive driving part of being a good driver means being alert at all times, anticipating possible problems, and being aware of other people, especially pedestrians.

4. *Patience*. Patience is a virtue for good driving. Patience means to double check before you leave a stop sign or enter an intersection. The patient drivers do not drive according to the clock. They wait and see; then they enter traffic.
5. *Alertness*. Alertness includes being aware of all that is going on around you. It entails keeping your mind on driving and not on other things like passengers.
6. *Lawfulness*. Obeying the rules of the road and driving according to the traffic signs is estimated to be another key characteristic good drivers possess. The emphasis is on speed signs and roadway markings that restrict passing.
7. *Automobile Sense*. Good drivers keep their vehicle in good shape at all times. They prepare cars for winter driving. Also, they do not overdrive the capabilities of their vehicles.

"Courteous" and "considerate" were the two most frequently mentioned attributes of a good driver. "Patience" was viewed as a key characteristic by increasing proportions as one moved across the age groups from youngest to oldest. A trend in the opposite direction was evident for defensive driving. It was mentioned most frequently by the youngest group.

It is interesting to note that the discussants' emphasis on good drivers is defined according to the quality of relationships drivers have with other road users. Good drivers show deference, respect, and civility. This becomes a prevailing moral code structured on social tact on the roadway. If all the qualities interviewees considered to be vital are combined to arrive at the ideal good driver, he or she would be courteous, considerate, defensive, patient, alert, lawful, and possess automobile smarts.

After having spoken of the elderly drivers' construct of a good driver, we may wish to overlap this construct on the elderly drivers themselves. The majority believe that their family considers them to be good or pretty good drivers. Their judgments are based on children or spouses willing to be passengers in cars operated by elderly drivers. Most participants drive differently now than when they were younger. How? They drive more cautiously, defensively, more slowly, and/or less stressfully. It appears that these properties are given as indicators of good drivers having evolved over the years. It would be safe to say that the majority of elderly drivers consider themselves to be good drivers—not especially skillful and physically reflexive, but wise, patient, cautious, and slow.

Traffic Violations

The ideal good driver is the kind of motorist elderly drivers think they are; the real driver is the operator they actually are. The ideal-real discrepancy is not uncommon among individuals, groups, and societies (Bierstedt 1974).

At the explicit level, elderly drivers consider themselves to be good drivers—ones who drive slowly or at least much more slowly than in previous years, and ones who are more patient and cautious. Yet at the implicit level the same motorists declared that they do commit traffic violations, the most-often cited in the last five years were exceeding the speed limit (65 percent), running a traffic light (17 percent), and coming to a rolling stop (10 percent).

Seniors are inclined to travel according to the traffic flow. They do so because it is faster and it reduces the likelihood of being caught by the police. When it comes to city driving they feel more inclined to follow the speed limits. However they may break other traffic laws at intersections.

Driving Difficulties

Even good drivers experience some maneuvers as difficult. Parking, or more precisely parallel parking, was described by 48 percent of the respondents as a complicated task. One elderly motorist explains:

> I find parking between two cars along the side of the road. I usually like vertical parking I can do that all right. But when you have to go this way, horizontal, it's so difficult for me, and I've been trying all my life to do it the first time.

Another concurs, placing the emphasis on the car design, not driving behavior:

> The curb disappears from your rear view mirror before you're really close. This leaves you kinda guessing as to how close you're getting to the curb. I find that with the car I'm driving now it's too much bulk on the side that where the mirrors are set. That disappears before I'm a foot off the curb. So from there on I'm guessing where the curb is.

Further to parallel parking is the less than easy process of backing the car out of a parallel parking situation. Judgment is the key factor, especially when the activity demands turning the head. Seventeen percent of the discussants indicated some inability to turn their heads. Arthritis and stiff necks were noted impairments.

Of utmost importance is that 43 percent of elderly drivers experienced no real or imagined difficult driving maneuvers. They left a tacit understanding that the competency rule was patented at an earlier age. Over the years, decline in ability was not suggested. There had not been problems with difficult driving maneuvers before and there are none now.

The kind of roads that senior motorists consider to be problematic are icy, snowy, or rainy (29 percent), gravel (25 percent), and narrow roads with ditches on both sides (15 percent). These road types worry some elderly drivers because they make vehicle control difficult. To maintain their image of competence, the discussants generalized that the above road conditions are troublesome for all drivers, not only the elderly.

At times, poor road conditions caused by inclement weather were considered to be just another extension of expressions about highway travel. Multilane highways or freeways, whether they are slippery or not, were considered to be difficult for driving—requiring patience and attentiveness. Most elderly drivers learned to drive many years ago on two-lane roads, in which speed and lane position were not featured concerns. Today, however, they are involved in multilane highways with cars "coming and going on either side" and travelling at great speeds. It makes some elderly drivers feel limited—based on lack of training and experience. But their ability to compensate helps erase the limitation.

A further observation about highway driving was that it has the potential to "put drivers to sleep." Because they "just go on for miles and miles," some senior motorists prefer to drive on secondary roads, where there is greater stimulation to the senses.

To induce greater emphasis on the highway situation, we need to refer to the elderly drivers who considered fatigue to be a personal impairment for driving. Over 13 percent said this was the case. And, not unexpectedly, fatigue was most often experienced during extended driving hours on the highways.

Within the formulation of personal impairments, vision was repeatedly introduced. Wearing glasses was considered by some as a nuisance, especially during night driving. So some elderly people take off their glasses to reduce headlight glare. While lessening the intensity of glare they also reduce vision. Whereas it is undeniable that over 95 percent of the respondents rated their vision as excellent or good, it is questionable in fact whether this is generalizable to nighttime or sunlight, where about one-quarter of the elderly stated they had an impairment.

Road and Traffic-Signal Design

In this section of the focus group discussions, respondents were asked what changes in road traffic signs or signals would make driving easier for them. They were also asked about pedestrian signals, crossings, and rules.

More than one-third of the respondents in each age group felt driving would be easier if signs were larger and/or had bigger letters, were dissimilar in shape, and if there were more left-turn lanes. For the seventy-five-plus age group, 44 percent supported changes in these matters. Furthermore, 18 percent of the respondents in the fifty-five to sixty-four year old group, 37 percent of the sixty-five to seventy-four year olds, and 35 percent in the seventy-five-plus group recommended standardized placement and structure of traffic signs and signals. In the fifty-five to sixty-four year old group, up to 43 percent felt driving would be easier if there were more lines, "cats eyes," and reflectors, and if larger signs and signals were unobstructed and placed in the center of the intersection. The support for the alternatives was shared by members of the seventy-five-plus group.

Nearly all the interactants agreed that avoiding pedestrians would be easier if pedestrians obeyed the rules and were more responsible and cautious. Recommendations were made that pedestrian crossings should be better lit and marked. The pedestrian-related concern should not be underscored. Intermittently, elderly drivers shared their concern about hitting and maiming a pedestrian. The scary part of the possibility is that pedestrians cross streets in an ad hoc manner, giving little warning of intent or disobeying crossing signals with impunity.

We noted that in response both to the question of whether road design and pedestrian crossings could be improved, a higher proportion of discussants in the oldest groups than in the other two groups recommended more advanced warning (i.e., of approaching exits and pedestrian crosswalks). This is consistent with the previously mentioned findings that close to 60 percent in this age group felt that slower reactions were a major cause of accidents involving older drivers.

Greatest Fears about Own Driving

Some psychologists maintain that a healthy dose of fear, or as Janis and Feshbach (1953) called it, mild fear appeal, is useful for inducing behavioral or attitudinal change. The recognition of one's own fear can produce strengthened determination to counter it or to live with it comfortably.

Once the focus group information was disassembled, three fear domains were rationalized as being manifestly important. They were loss of personal attributes, loss of driving privileges, and involvement in crashes.

Loss of Personal Attributes. Elderly drivers are not removed from the possibility that as they age their ability to be fully attentive to the roadway may deteriorate. Their reaction time becomes slower, and their concentration span is reduced.

Furthermore, they also fear losing some physical capabilities needed to drive. Examples given were arthritis, loss of vision, and a variety of disabling diseases or injuries.

The fear of experiencing health problems that would interfere with driving is difficult to counter. Hope and faith are the key ingredients for maintaining a proper attitude. As one woman said:

> I'm concerned about health problems that can force me to stop driving. I just hope my health stays well enough so I can drive for a long time.

Loss of Driving Privileges. The fear of losing a driver's license or being told by the doctor or some other authority that one can no longer drive is a major concern in its own right, and it is closely aligned with the fear of deteriorating health. Once one loses the ability to drive, one becomes a candidate to lose the formal right to drive. The result is the loss of a quality of life to which the elderly have become accustomed after years of toil.

Involvement in Crashes. The fear of an accident has a pluralistic affect to it. Forty-four percent of the elderly drivers are afraid that while on the road they may either get hit by another driver who is disobeying the law, that they may hit another car because they have not concentrated properly, or (as previously mentioned) they may injure a pedestrian because the latter is unpredictable.

The fear of an accident is real. To compensate for this fear, elderly drivers deliberately drive more slowly at strategic traffic situations such as intersections. They wait more patiently before leaving a stop sign, and they anticipate what the other driver may do. The monitoring strategies are based on a mistrust of other drivers—a fear that they speed, will not stop, are drunk, or are not paying sufficient attention. Examine the following quotes:

> I worry about getting hit, someone going through a stop light and aah I'm very careful going through a stop light. My eyes go that way and that way to make sure there's nobody coming. Especially late at night with drunks.
>
> Fear of being struck by someone else. So, I'll take enough care, I have the right of way. It happened to me a couple of years ago.
>
> I worry about what the other fellow can do to me. I see a car coming to a stop. I know he should stop. He's coming too fast I wait to see if he is going to stop. I may wait until he stops or until he is slowing down.

The rule of behavior, taking greater precautions on city streets because the other drivers or pedestrians are unpredictable and untrustworthy, became a norm accepted by the majority of elderly respondents. The "thinking about" and the "action on" were supported, reinforced, and approved by group members.

For some, the rule of fear characterizes, in part, aging. To grow older is to become more fearful. And as fear takes a greater foothold, taking greater precautions against those fears becomes the norm. One elderly gentleman demonstrated this prevalent theme when he said:

> You don't take chances, because there's one peculiar thing about growing old as you grow old you get frightened and it's absurd to think you you're gonna take a number of chances, the fact remains that fear enters our life at a certain stage. From this point of view you don't take the chances you did sixty years ago.

It appears that the overall assessment the elderly have of themselves as being good, cautious, and slow drivers may be as much an expression of fear as a judgment of competence. This is especially true for city streets. The fear of getting into an accident, of being the victim of another driver's dangerous acts, or of losing their power of attention and concentration is so real that compensatory strategies are in place. These actions are envisioned to be examples of good driving.

Annoyances

Being on the roads means being with other people. Like everyone, elderly drivers have little voice as to whom they would like to meet. The roadway is a sociometric reality, one in which elderly drivers make judgments about others, and others make judgments about them. We have already detailed how others define elderly drivers; it would now be informative to establish what kind of other drivers annoy the elderly.

Our analysis confirms that the driving behavior that is least accepted and most annoying to the elderly is lack of signalling. This is especially relevant to motorists older than seventy-five years of age (43 percent). They become aroused when motorists fail to signal, or when they signal too late. It is equally frustrating when drivers pass another vehicle without showing their intent to pull out of the lane or to reenter it.

One senior citizen defended his difficulties with lane changing. Before his revelation is inserted we must add a footnote that the statement received complete agreement from other members. The account:

> It's taken me a long time to learn to keep in that lane, to signal, to look before I get into that other lane. It's something I still have to contend with. It remains a problem for me and I still have to be very very careful.

Often the annoyance is tailgating, as reported by 29 percent of the interviewees. The anxiety level rises dramatically. Whereas signalling is an annoyance, or a frustration, tailgating is an anxiety producer—a threat to one's self-esteem and security. It is considered to be an infringement on the driver's comfort zone.

When motorists pass elderly drivers then cut them off, cut in and slow down or cut in to immediately make a turn are ongoing behaviors judged to be frustrating and aggressive by 20 percent of the respondents. They are considered to be selfish acts, ones which exceed the bounds of considerateness and safety. Elderly drivers resent people who engage in such actions.

Appropriate driving behavior, according to the structure and intent of lanes, also received impassioned discourse. By lane behavior we include lane hopping and driving at a speed inappropriate for the "fast" lane. The latter frustration concerned the elderly drivers the most. Several focus groups discussed why the elderly do not drive according to the speed registered for the fast lanes. In point form it went accordingly:

1. Elderly drivers misinterpret the concepts of slow and slower.
2. They are driving the speed limit but the flow of traffic exceeds the speed limit.
3. They do not drive in the right-hand lane because, to them, they are not driving slowly. They are driving fast, according to the speed limit.
4. They have become more conservative over the years and they believe it is their right to drive in the left hand or fast lane regardless of the other vehicles on the road.

On a lower level of annoyance-producing behavior are lack of courtesy, disobeying the rules of the road, driving aggressively, and honking horns.

Reactions to Annoyances. Krech et al. (1962) reviewed nine basic reactions to major frustrations. They are aggression, regression, withdrawal, repression, reaction formation, rationalization, projection, autism, and identification.

The style of reaction to roadway annoyances used most frequently and routinely by elderly drivers are withdrawal, autism, and aggression. Aggression appeared, but less frequently than the others. To illustrate, withdrawal means to walk away from the annoyance and allow it to proceed without taking a competitive or combative stance. Up to 60 percent of the elderly drivers reported that they slow down or let the annoying drivers have their way, ignore the frustrating motorist, accept the fact the driver is a certain kind of individual and not do anything about it.

Autism is a mechanism whereby people do not act against others, but they keep thinking about the events, talking to themselves about what they could have or should have done. Elderly drivers have a few choice words for their ears only, or they shake their heads in annoyance, frustration, or disbelief. The rationalization underlying autistic responses is that there is little time in which to take counteraction, and to respond more aggressively would not change what has already occurred. Often the result of such a response is repressed anger, tension, or stress. Autistic elderly drivers may end up becoming angry drivers.

Up to 25 percent of the elderly drivers stated that they may become aggressive. The major acts of aggression are swearing or shouting at annoying drivers and honking the horn. Although it may change little, it helps allay, at least temporarily, frustration and anger. After all, little can be done to meaningfully alter the situation or to change other people's behaviors.

Licensure

The topic of licensure is delicate. To remind the reader, elderly drivers considered it to be the second greatest fear of driving. To illustrate how this topic was handled we began by asking focus group participants if they thought people should be required to give up their driver's license at a certain age and if so, at what age. They were then asked what factors should be considered in deciding if someone should be relicensed. This was followed by two specific questions relating to relicensure: "If older drivers were required to be retested before their license was renewed, at what age should this happen?", and "Should a medical checkup, fitness test, eyesight test, road test or written test be conditions of license renewal?"

These questions were followed by three further queries concerning cessation of driving. The first asked what factors might stop the elderly discussants from driving. The second queried respondents on who should have the responsibility to decide when a person stops driving. The third question explored interviewees' feelings about the Motor Vehicle Act stipulation that physicians notify the licensing bureau about drivers who had an impairment that might affect their driving ability.

Reasons for Retesting

The predominant thought shared by respondents was that people should not be required to *give up* their driver's license because they reached a certain age. However, approximately one-third of the respondents considered age to be a reason for a person to be *retested*. The ages for reexamination varied from as low as fifty to as high as eighty. Other factors respondents felt should be considered for possible retesting, according to frequency of mention, were general good health (mentioned by 50 percent); driving record—in particular, evidence of traffic violations (37 percent); evidence of involvement in accidents—in particular, those in which elderly motorists were at fault (24 percent); visual problems (21 percent); specific illnesses such as stroke, epilepsy, or heart problems (21 percent); hearing problems (11 percent); and poor psychological test scores (9 percent).

Whenever general health was mentioned as a possible factor for retesting, it was usually articulated according to particular medical problems such as deteriorating vision, loss of hearing, or severe arthritis. Accumulated driving citations and accident experiences in recent years were also considered to be suitable factors for retesting. However, to have but a few penalty points "like everybody else," and to have been involved in accidents in which elderly drivers were not at fault were conceived as legitimate reasons for exemption. Psychological factors such as limited attentiveness and declining ability to think rationally were furthermore suggested as viable reasons for retesting. An examination of psychological factors was considered to be relevant to lessen the chance of "senile" people, especially those in the old old age bracket (eighty years and older), driving an automobile.

Participants older than seventy-five were more vocal than members of other age groups about their displeasure at retesting on the basis of age and/or specific medical problems. This reluctance was reflected in response to the question, "If older drivers were required to be retested before their license was renewed, at what age should this happen?" Forty-three percent in the seventy-five-plus group, compared with 21 to 33 percent respectively in the other age groups, stated that they were outrightly opposed to retesting on the basis of age unless there was some other specific reason to do so. For those who did specify an age for retesting, the preference was seventy. The next most popular age for commencement of retesting, given by approximately a third of the interviewees, was sixty-five.

Criteria for License Renewal

Close to 60 percent of the focus group participants felt that drivers should have to pass an eyesight test before their license was renewed. This could help in two ways. First it would remove a high risk driver from the road, but more importantly, it would help senior citizens become aware of their condition if they had not been tested before. Eyeglasses may help them.

Similar numbers of respondents would require an applicant to pass a medical test and a road test. An objective medical doctor should do these tests, not one appointed by the government. Forty-four percent felt applicants should have to pass a fitness test. Passing a written test was considered a criterion by 39 percent.

The main reason for an examination would be to establish how up-to-date elderly drivers were concerning the latest rules of the road. Clearly, imposition of these criteria was more strongly endorsed by the two younger groups than by the participants older than seventy-five. The oldest group was most vocal in stating that persons of all ages should have to pass such tests before their license was renewed. They considered the imposition of an age as reflecting bias, a stereotype position. They did not wish to be singled out. They also thought that by selecting a specific age, predetermined judgments have been made. The test would only serve to validate preconceived assessments.

Stopping to Drive

When asked to speculate about things in the future that might cause them, personally, to stop driving, the dominant response, given by almost two-thirds of the elderly in each age group, was "poor health." Significantly lower in emphasis were replies such as: poor vision; having a bad accident, a narrow escape or making mistakes; developing a physical impairment or handicap; becoming a hazard to oneself or feelings of "losing it"; being unable, financially, to keep driving; being a hazard to others; and developing a mental impairment such as senility. Support for any of the above weaknesses ranged from 10 to 17 percent.

In response to the question: "Who decides when you should stop driving?", the most frequent response, given by 47 percent of focus group participants, was "the doctor." Other answers, in order of their frequency of mention were these: "the person him/herself" (38 percent), someone on the "basis of scores on an unbiased test" (34 percent), "the licensing department" (23 percent), "the person's family" (16 percent), and "a panel of experts" (8 percent). Fifteen percent of respondents added that an appeal process should be available for dissenting views.

The most noticeable age difference was the heavier weight which respondents in the oldest group assigned to the individual personally making the decision. For these participants, self-determination was outweighed or of equal importance to the authority of the doctor. Members of this group believed they are the best judges. They can and do compensate for certain defects by, for example, driving more slowly, or staying away from troublesome circumstances like night travel. According to the respondents, another person cannot judge these endeavors objectively. The decision will be cut and dried, according to predefined specific criteria. The older people feel that an outside group would not be attentive to or pay sufficient attention to the elderly drivers' own initiatives to be good drivers.

The second reason that drivers aged seventy-five and older desired the opportunity to decide on whether to quit driving is the belief that it is their right. That right is based on the dignity of each person and on the freedom of the individual believed to be granted to all Canadians.

The British Columbia Motor Vehicle Act states that physicians must notify the Motor Vehicle Branch about persons who have impairments that could affect driving. A strong majority of discussants (91 percent) agreed with this policy. However, there was some residue of suspicion. Nineteen percent of the respondents added that they should be able to appeal or to get a second opinion before their license was revoked. Although the percentage is relatively small, the support given by others whenever these suggestions were offered was generous. An appeal board similar to the one employed by the Workers' Compensation Board was one suggestion openly endorsed. The second opinion should be given by an individual trusted by all parties as to his or her objectivity and expertise.

Whenever a decision is made to revoke a license, government officials should help build a network of volunteers that could help transport the elderly. This way the pain of not driving would be lessened and life-style would not be challenged as severely!

On the less personal topic of vehicle testing, 87 percent of all the focus group members agreed that such a procedure is appropriate for safety. The respondents were confident that it would eliminate a major accident hazard, and it would encourage all drivers to properly maintain their automobiles.

Driver Education and Experience

Throughout the interviews it became clear that all of the respondents learned to drive at a time when the roads were two lanes, the traffic was light, and the speed was moderate. Many learned to drive on country roads in cars that one elderly woman remembered:

> . . . had inner tubes. I could see it right through the tires. I could change a tire in eight minutes flat.

Over their driving lives a large percentage of elderly drivers, now residing on the West Coast, accumulated years of driving experience elsewhere in North America. Indeed they spoke eloquently of having braved the snow belt of the East, the snow and wind storms of the Prairies, or the Mid-West and the ice of the North. To them West Coast driving conditions, particularly in the Lower Mainland of British Columbia, are easier to negotiate than those with which they had been acquainted.

Yet much of the problem in driving lies in old patterns and attitudes, at least that is what some elderly drivers revealed. Because of their outdated driving education, usually provided by family and friends, and their original driving experiences in light traffic at comfortable speeds on two-lane roads, elderly drivers cannot or will not "learn to change lanes properly," "increase their speed on the on-ramp of a freeway," or "become aware of their role in heavily used four lane highways." There was no need to do this in the past and elderly drivers will, therefore, hesitate doing it in the present. One senior deliberated on the matter:

> They're not familiar exactly where they want to go. I used to drive out in the country a lot and I think they get into the habit of that country where they don't expect that much traffic. So when you do get into heavier traffic they do have problems on a two way road because they've got lots of time and they're impeding traffic.

The lack of original training, experience with modern driving, and technical ability, and the limited amount of upgrading were primary reasons given for the need of driver education, preferably a defensive driver course. According to our spokespeople, motorists should be learning all the time to keep up with changing driving conditions.

Course Content

The driver education course should allow the driver to "get the big picture." More specifically, about 40 percent of the volunteers in each age group felt that a driver education course for older people should focus on defensive driving techniques. This course should include information on current laws and regulations related to driving.

A similar concept that may be included in such a program is to show the benefits of daytime running lights. Although the following senior recognized the importance of this activity for educational purposes, he failed to become involved for other reasons:

> You know how that originated [keeping headlights on]. This is a true story. There was a retired Greyhound bus driver. He's driven 42 years without an accident. And they asked him now what'd you do different than anyone else. He said nuthin. He said as soon as I get in the bus he said I check it over and he said I put my lights on. No one ever thought of that. And they figured that's what contributed to his safe driving record. Now I don't put mine on because I'm afraid I'll forget to put 'em off.

No members of the focus group in which the story was offered knew about the automatic light switches that can easily be placed in vehicles for a very nominal cost.

Defensive driver courses should be publicized and widely advertised among the elderly. They should be made readily available. And, according to many respondents, the elderly drivers would take such courses and benefit from them. The reason for the optimism is that a number of respondents participated in the British Columbia Safety Council Defensive Driver Course. Although the course was attended years ago, the drivers still remembered parts of the program that, they believe, still help them today.

Conclusion

"A man's social self" wrote William James (1967), "is the recognition which he gets from his mates." This conception could well be the tenet of the chapter. It is in the context of social acts that the self arises. It is built up and reinforced in anticipation of the response to significant others (Coser 1972).

In this chapter we tried to take some of the mystery out of how the elderly drivers interpret themselves and others. In discussing the motorists' reasoning structures, we had occasion to elaborate a variety of perspectives that en masse form the social construction of the elderly drivers. We learned that elderly driving behavior is both proscriptive and postscriptive. They require certain kinds of conduct on the one hand and prohibit certain kinds on the other. Both the prescriptive and proscriptive sectors conformed to a variety of social and existential principles which reflect elderly driver life-styles. By emphasizing these we hoped to discover the locus of everydayness and how it guides driving behavior.

References

Bierstedt, R. 1974. *The Social Order*. New York: McGraw-Hill.

Byrne, E.F., and E.A. Maziarz. 1969. *Human Being and Being Human*. New York: Appleton-Century-Crofts, 1969.

Cooley, C.H. 1902. *Human Nature and the Social Order*. New York: Scribners.

Coser, L. (Ed.). 1972. *Sociology through Literature*. Englewood Cliffs, NJ: Prentice Hall, 1972.

Fozard, E., B. Wolf, A. Bell, A. McFarland, and S. Podolsky. 1977. "Visual Perception and Communication." In J.E. Birren and K.W. Schaie (Eds.), *Handbook of the Psychology of Aging*. New York: Van Nostrand Reinhold, pp. 497-534 (chapter 7).

Goffman, E. 1963. *Behavior in Public Places*. New York: Free Press.

______. 1974. *Frame Analysis*. New York: Harper and Row.

______. 1959. *The Presentation of Self in Everyday Life*. Garden City, NY: Doubleday Anchor Books.

Gutman, G.M. 1980. The Elderly at Home and in Retirement Housing: A Comparative Study of Health Problems, Functional Difficulties and Support Service Needs. In V.W. Marshall (Ed.), *Aging in Canada: Social Perspectives*. Don Mills, ON: Fitzhenry and Whiteside Ltd., pp. 189-200.

Gutman, G.M. 1986. *Focus Group Findings and Their Implications for Health Promotion with Seniors*. Report submitted to the Health Promotions Directorate, Health and Welfare Canada, Ottawa, March.

Gutman, G.M. 1988. *Focus Group Study of Seniors' Reactions to New Vista's Community Concept*. Report submitted to the New Vista Society, Burnaby, BC, April.

Gutman, G.M., S.L. Milstein, and V. Doyle. 1987. *Attitudes of Seniors to Special Retirement Housing, Life Tenancy Arrangements and Other Housing Options*. Ottawa: Canada Mortgage and Housing Corporation.

James, W. 1967. *The Writings of William James*. Chicago: University of Chicago Press.

Janis, I.L., and S. Feshbach. 1953. *Effects of Fear Arousing Communications. Journal of Abnormal Psychology*, 48, pp. 78-92.

Krech, D., R. Crutchfield, and E. Ballachey. 1962. *Individual in Society*. Tokyo: McGraw-Hill Koga Kusha Ltd.

Krippendorff, K. 1980. *Content Analysis: An Introduction to its Methodology*. Beverly Hills, CA: Sage Publications.

Krupka, L., and A.M. Vener. 1979. "Hazards of Drug Use among the Elderly." *The Gerontologist*, 19(1), pp. 90-95.

Leiter, K. 1980. *A Primer on Ethnomethodology*. Oxford: Oxford University Press.

Milstein, S., and G. Gutman. 1988. "Seniors' Attitudes toward Driving Practices: Focus Group and Survey Data from the Lower Mainland, Vancouver Island and the Okanagan." Gerontology Research Centre, Simon Fraser University, Burnaby, BC, (unpublished).

Motor Vehicle Department. 1986. *Transportation and Highways Report, 1984/85*. pp. 317-18.

Pineo, P.C., and J. Porter. 1967. "Occupational Prestige in Canada." *Canadian Review of Sociology and Anthropology*, 4, pp. 24-40.

Rothe, J.P. 1986. *British Columbia Secondary Students: Lifestyle and Driving Survey*. North Vancouver, BC: Insurance Corporation of British Columbia.

Rothe, J.P., and P. Cooper. 1986. "Young People and Drinking/Driving: A Complementary Approach." Paper presented at the International Symposium on Young Drivers, Alcohol and Drug Impairment, Amsterdam, Holland.

Statistics Canada. 1984. *Historical Tables for Census Education Data 1971, 1976 and 1981*. Catalogue 13-579, June.

8

Victims of Serious Crashes

He with body wage a fight,
But body won; it walks upright.

Then he struggled with the heart;
Innocence and peace depart.

Then he struggled with the mind;
His proud heart he left behind.

Now his wars on God begin;
At stroke of midnight God shall win.

(William Butler Yeats, "The Four Images of Man")

The elderly constitute a significant portion of the driving population. Members orchestrate their driving behavior in accustomed ways. Yet, as we learned in Chapter Seven, the elderly driving routines, although being well regulated, are wrapped around three prevalent fears: loss of attention, loss of license and, foremost, involvement in a car crash caused by another driver.

In effect, these three fears may be considered the seed bed of elderly driving. Within the elderly drivers' minds is the most disconcerting thought that they could, at any time, experience an accident. So they try to escape the possibilities by driving more slowly, patiently, and cautiously. But, as we found out in Chapter Five, the chances of the elderly becoming involved in serious crashes are not insignificant. We are left, therefore, with an information void. How do the unfortunate elderly who do crash particularize their involvement?

When experiencing traumatic events such as serious-injury-producing crashes, the elderly, as all drivers, spend a great amount of psychological, social, physical, and economic resources. In the following pages we will reassemble the lives of 130 accident victims and trace their attitudes, feelings, motives, physical involvements, social interpretations of events, and moral displays. In Chapter Five we already determined the presence of elderly-motorist-involved accidents. We shall now explore the nature of the accidents.

To succeed in the venture, we transcended the narrow position of causality. We reconstructed the circumstances that contributed to the stream of events resulting in crashes. Our first step was to explore pre-accident routines, circumstances, social behavior, moods, and thoughts that may have contributed to the crash. Next, we re-created the experiential reality of the accident by describing the psychological and social sensations lived through by the drivers. Then we attended to the elderly victims' interpretations of their misfortunes as they pertain to selves, other drivers, the roadway, the environment, and life-style. Finally we reviewed the dramatic events to see how they have been reintegrated into the elderly drivers' lives.

Pre-Crash

At first blush, logic tells us that crashes do not just happen. There is a seriality to them, a sequence of events that terminates in accidents. This sequence is like a path, a wholeness. For us the chain of events is strategic. It moves from the last activity in which the elderly driver was engaged before entering the automobile, to in-car behavior just prior to the crash, to the impact of the crash. Such a view serves two vital purposes: it provides a "big picture" of the crash, and it gives a portrayal of elderly driver life events.

Last Activity Before Driving to the Crash

Prior to the beginning of the fateful trip, normality and ordinariness prevailed. In short, elderly drivers routinely provided accounts or descriptions that personified normality or typicality. The responses reflected a matter-of-factness, a normative behavior pattern whose meaning gave a glimpse of life-style. Some common expressions follow:

1. Nothing unusual. Oh, I was at home here, probably washing dishes you know. It was seven o'clock at night. [Female, fifty-five to sixty-four]
2. Just shopping, just in the store getting some groceries and just got in the car and came home. [Female, fifty-five to sixty-four]
3. Well I had breakfast and we always have breakfast and something in the morning. [Male, fifty-five to sixty-four]
4. Well I think I was walking my dog Shirley, usually walk her every morning. [Male, sixty-five to seventy-four]
5. It was morning and the bank doesn't open before ten o'clock and I probably had breakfast about nine o'clock, it might have been a little bit earlier, so it was, you know, I'd probably have been, if anything, reading, or just talking to my wife. [Male, sixty-five to seventy-four]

The "living life as perfectly normal" theme was a common recollection. More specifically, the fifty-five to sixty-four year old group of elderly drivers characterized normality as daily work routines. Frequently, early morning rituals such as eating breakfast, drinking coffee, or engaging in personal hygiene were performed before the members entered their car to go to work. A slight variation of the theme happened for trips in the late afternoon, during which a group of fifty-five to sixty-four year olds had just completed normal employment duties in the real estate office, shop, bank, store, or restaurant before heading home. Then the accident happened.

The motif of normality included such activities as doing household chores, personal grooming, engaging in such routine activities as volunteer work and shopping. However, the routines were relived as featured events, something beyond everyday expectations. For example, the unusualness of shopping was not the event per se, rather it was the circumstances impacting on shopping that provided its significance. Witness the following discussion with a man, in the sixty-five to seventy-four year old group, who had to buy a few items for his truck. He was in a hurry:

I: Where were you going or coming from when the accident happened?

R: Well, I was just coming from downtown, going here, and ah . . .

I: Just coming home.

R: Just coming back home, yup.

I: What was the last thing you did in—before you got into your car to drive home?

R: Well on the highway down here, you just turn the corner from—on the highway. I went down to pick up some antifreeze, you know, windshield washer antifreeze stuff. I had been working on the truck, and I had it all fixed up and everything, and everything was fine but that. And my wife wasn't home yet, it was just before suppertime, well you know about 4:00 in the afternoon I imagine. I thought, "Well I'll whip right down there, and get windshield washer to put in." I had serviced it and everything else was fine, you know. So I did that, so I was in a bit of a hurry down there, and hurried to pick it up to get home before mom got home, you know. Then you know . . .

Another taken-for-granted guideline by which a group of elderly drivers directed their activities prior to their accident-bound trip was health care. Medically related functions are familiar to the elderly. For many they are commonplace.

Health-relevant functions can vary from being a patient, chauffeuring a friend or relative to a health professional, to visiting an infirm acquaintance. The following segments of conversation illustrate the range of medically related pre-trip activities:

1. R: We were coming from the specialist, a doctor, an eye specialist. Ah, there is a medical building over there—ah, it's just beyond the 94 Avenue. It's

just short of Surrey Place, on the right side. But entered that building not from King George we go to right side then around some buildings. From there we were coming straight to this house on King George Highway. We had to turn right on the 64th but it happened on 88th Street.

I: So the last activity that you engaged in before getting into the car was seeing the doctor?

R: Yes, yes. [Male, fifty-five to sixty-four]

2. I: What was the last activity that you did before you got in your car to make that trip?

R: Last activity? Uh, I took Clare to the doctor down at the medical . . .

I: Hmm. So you just waited for her and then you both came . . .

R: Waited until we got the medicine we supposed to get and then headed for home. [Male, seventy-five plus]

3. I: The last activity that you were engaged in.

R: Oh, the last accident?

I: No, the last activity.

R: Oh, the last activity? I just visited my nurse, or my aunt at the hospital.

I: Oh, I see.

R: No, I was just up there visiting her, and feeding her, yes. No, no, I wasn't worked up or excited about anything, I was coming along minding my own business. [Female, sixty-five to seventy-four]

4. R: Had breakfast, took a pill. Actually I felt good but I really think it affects you that pill, my husband said are you sure you feel o.k. and once I hit the road, I didn't feel . . . if I had felt sick I'd have stayed home. I'm not one to fool around, if I had felt sick or if it had any other effect on me, but I thought once the fresh air hit me I'd feel better, but actually it was the other way around. [Female, sixty-five to seventy- four]

5. I was going to the dentist, yeah. I was here at the house and I, ah, knew I had an appointment with the dentist so I got in the car and started right off. [Male, fifty-five to sixty-four]

6. I was going to the dentist to have a tooth pulled. [Male, seventy-five plus]

7. Well, I was coming from my brother-in-law's place, and I was going to the hospital for the therapy. [Male, seventy-five plus]

When we turned to the respondents' accounts we found a considerable array of actions that hinged on personal health. They were considered important. Common in discussants' accounts of involvement in health-related activities prior to the problematic journeys were characterizations such as need, and immediacy.

Reasons for Being on the Road

Serious car crashes can be viewed from different perspectives. The most usual is the view of the generalized other. That is, accidents happen with frightful regularity. But they always happen to other people. The second perspective pertains to the self: direct involvement. The accident typically denied at the general level becomes pointedly real and meaningful at the personal level.

Much of the meaning people attach to a crash in which they are involved pertains to the circumstances causing it, or phenomenal aspects or constitutive characteristics of it. Victims ask themselves, "What happened?" To answer this question it would be worthwhile to trace the events leading up to the accident. Our first query should be, "Why was the elderly driver on the road at the time of the crash?"

In Chapter Five we standardized trip purpose according to commuting, shopping, personal/family, and social. Social reasons were highest (28 percent), followed closely by shopping (27.1 percent) and personal/ family (25.2 percent). The statistical backdrop was further explored in Chapters Six and Seven, where the elderly reported that overall the automobile is used most often for shopping (96 percent), visiting family and friends (96 percent), social, cultural, entertainment or recreational events (90 percent), pleasure per se (85 percent), health care (78 percent), meetings (70 percent), and vacation travel (69 percent).

The descriptions so far are an inducement to search deeper. So, personal elements of trip purpose were documented, based on accident victims' verbalized accounts. A pattern of thought and action arose from the in-depth discussions.

It goes without saying that all the drivers had reasons for taking the trips. Most of the time the journeys were characterized in functionally specific terms. The reasons for driving the cars at the time of the mishaps were fundamental; in order to. . . . There was little improvisation in the driving patterns.

In Order to Shop. Elderly accident victims commonly reported that they drove their cars to complete practical projects such as shopping for groceries, clothes, household goods, gifts or other items, banking, or purchasing personal care services from such people as hairdressers or barbers. Such "everyday stuff" comprises the paramount reality, the world governed by immediate life-sustaining needs and interests (Schutz 1970).

Shopping for groceries is a familiar mundane event. It is done too often to mention. It is not special and is designated so by the motorist:

> . . . yeah, but I don't remember my shopping in detail. Lots of times I go shopping and do things but I can't remember.

Other elderly drivers confirmed the routine characteristics of their trips:

> Just shopping.

> Going to Place for some shopping.
>
> I was just going over to the shopping center.
>
> We were going to do a little shopping.
>
> Yeah it was just before holidays. I was going shopping you know, going to the store to buy something.

Nearly half of all the elderly accident victims were on the road for shopping-related matters. Once the purchases were made at the shopping centers (a popular shopping environment for the elderly), it was time to return home. This leg of the shopping journey proved to be troublesome. Over half of our shoppers crashed at this time. In fact the general concept of going home was so typical that it deserves a separate description.

In Order to Go Home. To "go home" is an expression of the highest degree of familiarity and intimacy. For the most part, people do not fully judge the worth of an event or the success of their involvements until they get home. Home turf becomes the base upon which events are judged, interpreted, or replayed. Here individuals find their identity pegs not evident elsewhere. Projects begin and end at home, in familiar surroundings. As one elderly woman portrayed, "Home is where my stove is."

Going home carries strong connotations of anticipation for the return to the familiar. Individuals have encountered varied experiences and now come home to engage in customary activities. The reasons for returning home could therefore lead to behaviors that account for accidents. "Making supper," "getting out of the drizzle," "getting sleep," and other expected "returning-home activities" give those trips a sense of urgency, a longing different from that of drivers leaving home. Behavior follows thoughts and desires, as revealed in the following excerpts:

1. I just picked up some groceries from the store and I was going home because I had to hurry to baby-sit my two grandchildren. [Female, sixty-five to seventy-four]
2. I was coming from a baby shower in the afternoon. But I know one thing, I didn't really want to go. I woke up that morning and wished that I didn't have to go. I guess I should've stayed home. [Female, sixty-five to seventy-four]
3. Oh well, I had just been visiting my sister-in-law, we had just had coffee, and just watched t.v., and that's all, and then I just drove home . . . I have a sister-in-law that lives on Street and we always, when we get home, we always phone one another. [Female, fifty-five to sixty-four]
4. Ya, it was actually, it was actually to go to my nephew's wedding in the afternoon. Well it was a morning wedding and I was coming home. And see there was no sun in my, if there was sun in my eyes, I would have said, "Well that might have something to do with it." But the sun was behind me,

> it was 4:30 in the afternoon . . . You've got to be very patient, I know. Sometimes it's ah I use to find it much easier when I commuted back and forth to Vancouver. I found it much easier going in than it is coming home. [Male, seventy-five plus]

As was already stated in Chapter Five, 53.3 percent of elderly drivers in a randomly selected sample of accident involvements were returning home. The prominence of this trip phase was also evident with our accident victims. Perhaps the anticipation to get home, combined with some fatigue from the visits or shopping duties placed the elderly drivers in a higher risk position than would otherwise be the case. The important point, however, is that to leave home means to return home, and the last segment of the trip appears to carry greater risk than the first one.

In Order to Visit. As citizens age, they live a happier and healthier life if they maintain a satisfying level of social involvement. Elderly people are pleased to engage others, particularly family and friends.

In their search and achievement of sociality, the elderly place a great deal of faith in the automobile. This is particularly true on the West Coast where many elderly live at distances twenty or more miles from family and old friends. It is not unexpected that because of poor mass transit opportunities, the elderly must drive in order to visit. Several illustrations follow:

1. I was going over to my son's place. He's got a new house and I was going to look at the basement. See what we could do to fix it up. Make a room or two. [Male, sixty-five to seventy-four]
2. I was going to Cloverdale. No, it wasn't White Rock it was Cloverdale. We have friends right through Cloverdale and up the hill that has cattle like myself. I was going to see them. [Female, fifty-five to sixty-four]
3. Nothing, we were just going to take a meal down to our son and daughter-in-law, because they had no food, and that's all, just put the stuff in the car, and went. [Female, sixty-five to seventy-four]
4. I was going to my daughter's house for lunch. [Male, seventy-five plus]
5. It happened on Christmas day, I had deliberately chosen that day, rather than go on Christmas Eve, to avoid getting into a situation where there would be a lot of people who had been drinking, ah, on Christmas Eve, and it was raining that night anyway, and so late in the day, I was going to take the presents to my granddaughter. Bearing this in mind, knowing that the risk of getting into an accident was that more involved, I thought that I would leave it until Christmas Day, knowing that they would be back from lunch, around about 1:00, so at that time of day, it's usually a little more quiet, even on a holiday. [Female, fifty-five to sixty-four]
6. We go visiting North Vancouver quite frequently, my daughter lives there and, ah, she had wanted a little bit of work done in her basement ah and being retired and nothing to do, I went over and I was doing it. I was travelling back and forth there for about a week. This was towards the end,

> I was just about finished there when this happened. [Male, sixty-five to seventy-four]

The responses give substance to gerontological research findings that the maximum distance for visits between adult children and elderly parents is about fifty miles (Marshall 1987). Parents whose children live closer tend to visit for face-to-face interaction or family assistance. The trips are usually taken within a given day. Elderly parents who live over 50 miles from their children are more likely to communicate by telephone or letter. The visits tend to be more extended and occur less frequently (Stone and Fletcher 1987).

In Order to Give Rides and Do Favors. A rival to shopping, pleasure driving, and visiting was the intent to do favors for others (e.g., giving them rides). For some, the motive for being on the road was to offer assistance. Consider the following explanation:

> I had been to get my daughter's contact lenses. This doctor on the road I got on to get on to Georgia. That's where his surgery is. I had to go to Willow and I'm really not used to driving in Vancouver and particularly it was quite late. It was heavy traffic. [Male, sixty-four to seventy-five]

A common theme found in accounts in which elderly drivers openly expressed their desire to help family members was the acceptance of risk and consequences. In their judgment, doing favors, and "lending a helping hand" are more important than trying to avoid "scary driving conditions." One elderly driver mentioned that although he dislikes rush-hour traffic, he is prepared to steer his way through it to give a family member a ride:

> Rush hour, well rush all the time eh? Taking my wife's cousin I guess it is down to the airport through the Deas Island Tunnel eh? And you know when you leave two spaces like you're supposed to you know what happens in rush-hour traffic somebody somebody's in there. [Male, fifty-five to sixty-four]

Poor weather and slippery roads were also formulated as negotiable if family or friends needed assistance. As one man suggested:

> Well I came from home and was going down to the ah to New Westminster or Burnaby to um with my wife to a doctor or chiropractor. . . . It was the first rain after the summer. . . .
>
> The road was slippery. If the road wasn't slippery I would have easy come to the stop. [Male, fifty-five to sixty-four]

Just doing a favor without considering risky traffic situations was also a common reason for taking the ill-fated trips. Through such deliberations as these:

1. We were going to Canadian Tire to get a dimmer switch for my sister's dining room. They had them on sale for a pretty good price. There were a couple of other things too. [Male, sixty-five to seventy-four]

2. I took my wife to an eye specialist over there just near 97 in area . . . We were coming from the specialist, a doctor an eye specialist. [Male, seventy-five plus]
3. It was a little bit before eight o'clock. My granddaughter from Montreal was staying here and she had a job. I was taking her to work . . . [Female, sixty-five to seventy-four]

elderly drivers revealed that doing favors with cars is a common occurrence.

Much of the elderly drivers' direction is toward maintaining some characterological fitness. They want to help, and to do that they are willing to drive, whether it be taking a "brother-in-law to therapy after a minor stroke," "picking up a package" or giving a neighbor a "ride to church."

Based on the data we could say that at the furthest point, consideration for people overrides consideration of personal risk. At the nearest level, ownership or access to an automobile signifies opportunities to grant favors. Access translates into action. For example, when an elderly woman was asked about her fateful trip she responded:

> It wasn't a unique event, it was just helping somebody out, you know? I mean we do that all the time, or what I've seen anyway.

Routineness of the Fateful Trip

As was already stated above, normality and routineness were watermark descriptions elderly drivers assigned to their activities *before* the trip. These descriptions were extended to the actual trips. With little equivocation, travel to or from shopping, family visits, medical facilities, or errands were considered to be routine automobile use. There was little deviation from this conception.

Some elderly people formulated routineness as driving a known route or using the vehicle for regular purposes; "another local trip" or "shopping." Others categorized it as regularity, in terms of visiting family members or engaging in activities they undertook "regularly," "all the time," "once or twice a week," or "often." At times the trip was considered to be an extension of a normal day.

Characteristics of the Accident Day

The general tenor of the accident day, as defined by some accident victims, could be distinguished as "like any other day." There were no highlights or lowlights; nothing unusual or out of the ordinary. This feeling of typicality can be sensed in the following remarks drawn from the corpus of accounts:

1. It was early in the morning. The day was just starting . . . Just an ordinary day. [Male, fifty-five to sixty-four]

2. Just an ordinary day. Nothing special. [Female, fifty-five to sixty-four]
3. An ordinary day like the rest. [Female, fifty-five to sixty-four]
4. It was an ordinary day you know. Well like ah no, it was just an ordinary day. It wasn't good or bad, you know. I was feeling fine. [Female, sixty-five to seventy-four]
5. I was having an average day. Neither good nor bad I live alone but I keep myself busy I don't sit around and mope and feel sorry for myself or anything like that. No it was an average day, probably a little above average I'd just managed to ah get some shopping done and I hate shopping. [Female, fifty-five to sixty-four]
6. I can't really say. It was a working day. Good to be going home. Just an ordinary day. [Male, sixty-five to seventy-four]
7. Not good, not bad. Just ordinary. [Male, seventy-five plus]
8. Normal day, I didn't have anything unusual you know. [Male, seventy-five plus]

The range of depictions of the accident day did not stop with normalcy. Good days were equally occurring descriptors. The following portrayals emphasize the point:

1. It was a good day. I looked a bit forward to go out and have my work done. It was a busy day because it was around what . . . it was in the afternoon. [Male, fifty-five to sixty-four]
2. A good day. I had breakfast before I left and, ah, there was no pressures or anything. I had nothing in mind or wasn't bothered or anything. [Male, seventy-five plus]
3. Well I have a good day every morning because I praise the Lord and I'm a Christian and that's how I feel. [Female, sixty-five to seventy-four]
4. I think it was a good day. I wasn't having any problems on the work I was doing. There was nothing to, ah, sort of get me mad or anything. [Male, fifty-five to sixty-four]
5. I was having a good day. It was Christmas Day, ah, being a religious person, it made me a very happy person to be alive on Christmas Day. Yeah, I was in a good frame of mind. [Female, fifty-five to sixty-four]
6. A good day. It was early in the morning and I was feeling good—ha, ha. Not that I don't feel good all day because I do. [Male, fifty-five to sixty-four]
7. Good day, oh my days are always good. Yeah I got the best wife in the world treats me like a. . . . I got a good woman all these years I been drinking all she'd ever say is, "Do you have to drink that much?" I said, "No but I like drinking." Never obnoxious or anything or mean to her that I know of because of my drinking. The only thing I'd come home from work and I'd eat supper and I'd go to watch the six o'clock news well you know what happens two hours later I wake up I miss the news then I'd have to catch it at 11:00. [Male, sixty-five to seventy-four]

A close look at the data shows that the "good days" were consciously felt reflections of good lives. If the elderly drivers judged their lives as good, or successful, chances are that the day of the accident was also good. This tacit understanding was especially noticeable for accident victims aged fifty-five to sixty-four.

Whereas, for some, the accident day was considered according to general life-style, for others, the kind of day reflected improvised living. The characteristic of the day reflected events that showed promise:

1. It was a beautiful day. It was a family day and they purposefully had a small wedding and they had it down at Stanley Park and the lovely clubhouse that's there for lawn bowling. And it was very lovely. [Female, fifty-five to sixty-four]
2. I was off. I was headed over to my kid's place. It was going to be a good day. I say going to be until this thing we're talking about. [Male, sixty-five to seventy-four]
3. In fact before I went to the cleaners, I was up with my daughter's and she had set my hair and I was going to a ladies' meeting that night so I had, ah, good outlook and a good attitude and all that, so. [Female, sixty-five to seventy-four]

At times, the affective responses given by the discussants showed an energy, a passion that went beyond the descriptions offered by the "normal day" victims. Pleasant, exciting ventures or upcoming special events marked the day as being a recognizably good day.

Of course life is not idyllic for everyone. A group of accident victims described the accident day according to health frustrations, general lethargy, upsetting circumstances with other people, or hectic occurrences. These days were problematic:

1. R: It was right early in the morning and I figured it was I might have been a little frustrated, ah, with the lad that was here I had to tell him to get out. Yeah, he was staying here and I kinda have a soft heart in a lot of ways and, ah, he was broke and he come to me for help so I said well what's the matter with your father? That father he had was a step-father and his mother was a nurse and, ah, she was giving him a little money now and again and of course he was a lazy young bugger he didn't want to work too long he was a good worker while he was at it. But, ah, I discovered he was more of a cheat than anything else. So I told him you got to go.

   I: That was the morning?

   R: No no I didn't tell him that morning I just got a little disgusted with him; the way he was eating, huh huh. And you don't like to say nothing so you bury your problems.

   I: This was something that was on your mind?

R: Yeah it sure was yeah. [Male, seventy-five plus]

2. R: I just didn't feel like going out. I think that might have been it. I wasn't feeling quite up to par that day. My sinuses were bothering me. [Male, sixty-five to seventy-four]

3. R: Well, I had some personal problems.

   I: On the day of the accident specifically?

   R: Um, no. Not really, I ah . . .

   I: So you weren't feeling too good that day, or how would you describe that day before the accident? I know you weren't feeling too good afterwards, but prior to it?

   R: Well I had things on my mind. I guess maybe it could have distracted me some. [Female, fifty-five to sixty-four]

4. R: I must confess a very bad day. Yes, having a disagreement with somebody, with the people I was dealing with, and informing him that I was going to start litigation against him, which I've done, but, ah, I can't really blame that on the accident, because I would have conducted myself exactly the same way as I looked at it. Even today, I would have done the exactly the same thing, outside of how to use my emergency brake, my hand brake. [Female, seventy-five plus]

The three basic characteristics of the accident day offered by accident victims signified attitudes of everyday life. A good life suggests good days, one of which was the accident day. But what of the trouble that life circumstances bring with them? Events or happenings such as arguments with other people, bothersome medical matters such as sinuses, or headaches, or personal problems contaminated the day, producing the descriptor, "bad day."

Finally, descriptions of the accident days as normal or ordinary were living documentaries on life-style. The accident day was like so many other days. Going shopping, running errands, or providing assistance were considered to be stable activities that were done routinely and unreflectively. There was constant feedback on the processing of life—regular events at defined times to meet prescribed needs.

Driving Conditions

Ordinarily, people involved in serious mishaps determine what driving conditions had the greatest impact on the event. It could be the weather, road conditions and/or time of day. Based on the conversations with our accident victims, a common prelude to the crashes was that it was getting dark and it was raining.

In Chapters Six and Seven we learned that the average elderly driver prefers to avoid driving on rainy nights or periods of dusk because of glare. Yet, many of the victims that were interviewed travelled the roads during such driving conditions.

Some elderly drivers left in the evening. It was raining. The roads were slippery. Cars had their headlights on, creating glare and making visibility "very poor." When asked what happened, answers such as "I'm not really sure," "I misinterpreted what was going on" and "it was pretty hard to tell" represented a general stream of thought. The responses were usually displayed in conjunction with extended descriptions on the hazardous driving conditions evident during the crashes.

At this point in time we should reflect on what the data tell us. Accident analysis findings showed that as drivers age, they are less likely to crash under conditions of wet or icy roads. Furthermore, the elderly drivers who did experience accidents under hazardous driving conditions have a better five year driver record than those who crashed during trouble-free driving times. Random samples of survey respondents and focus group participants clarified that nighttime driving and rain were uncomfortable driving conditions. The majority of elderly try to avoid them whenever possible. In our accident victim sample we found that although the majority of elderly drivers dislike rainy nighttime conditions, if the need arose they would not hesitate to drive their cars during this time. They may feel uncomfortable, but still competent enough to carry on. The acknowledgement of risk and danger was superseded by the felt need to help or desire to drive. And, as we have already noted, many of the elderly drivers became accident victims during nonpreferred driving times. Perhaps their perceptions of competency, combined with their willingness to overlook uncomfortable driving scenarios for the sake of sociality or preservation of self-image, are constructs of reality that give meaning to the statistics.

The prevalence of inclement weather and nighttime driving conditions during the time of the accidents should not be ignored. It helps us better understand the nature of accident-involved elderly drivers—in the way they think about their lives and driving; how they perceive risk. Yet dangerous driving conditions such as snow, fog, and black ice were seldom highlighted as determining conditions during the crashes.

For a minority of elderly motorists, the driving conditions were described as nice, ideal, or beautiful. From their perspectives, the accidents were not causally related to the conditions. Driver performance was to blame.

Goings-On Immediately Before the Crash

An automobile is many things. It carries numerous meanings, any one of which can predominate. Obviously the primary purpose for the car is to be an efficient mode of transportation. However, the act of going and arriving is juxtaposed with other meanings.

A 1949 Ford brochure declared: "The '49 Ford is a living-room on wheels!" A caption read:

> These pictures show, as well as pictures can, the space, comfort and smartness of the '49 Ford! There's room to spare for three people on each of these "sofa seats," trimly upholstered in new, modern fabrics. And there's "picture window" visibility . . . Yes, it's a living-room on wheels, this '49 Ford! (Marsh and Collett 1986:11)

Throughout the years the car has become a continuity of domestic or social themes. Radios and cassette players turn the automobile into a motorized entertainment center. A cigarette lighter and ashtray provide occupants the opportunity to satisfy oral fixation. There is room to spare for passengers. Much like a living room, passengers and drivers visit. Conversation arises, and it is structurally supported in the secure inviolable confines of the motor vehicle.

A car trip with passengers becomes a social occasion. And as with so many other social gatherings, the drivers employ certain interactive strategies which provide them with acceptable impressions of themselves. That is, the drivers cannot be solitary entities in a social environment. They have involvement obligations.

In 1967 Goffman wrote that, theoretically, individuals can excusably withdraw themselves from conversation, but practically few do so. The rule of sociability is too embracing. This has ramifications for drivers. Although they have a prescribed focus on operating the vehicle and to be wary of traffic conditions, they may respectfully interact with their passengers, in effect reducing their roadway wariness. Some elderly drivers recognized the clash of responsibilities.

One seventy-five year old female driver tried to resist the temptation to speak, and lost. Immediately before the crash:

> My friend was talking. She's a talkative person. There's not much question that she was talking, but I tried not to talk because when, as I said I like to concentrate on my driving . . . It could have distracted me . . . She hasn't driven with me too much in the car.

Two sixty-four year old female drivers also recognized the danger posed by driver and passenger interaction. According to them:

1. R: I was talking to my brother-in-law. It was at night, it was dark.

   I: Do you think that might have distracted you, and had to do anything with the accident?

   R: I'd like to say "No," but I couldn't be sure on that. Because, usually I can talk without, I don't as a rule talk when I'm driving because that does distract me. But, most times I don't talk. But, I can't say that I actually was not talking to him, I don't know.

2. R: The others was talking, and I was listening, you know, but I was trying to keep my mind on the road.

I: So you don't feel that what you were doing could have contributed to the accident at all.

R: Ah, I don't think so cause, ah, you know, I was trying to be very careful, because I had a couple of old ladies in the car and, ah, you know, I take my responsibilities serious.

A woman within the fifty-five to sixty-four year old category became involved in a conversation with an acquaintance. Just before the crash the woman was:

R: Trying to cheer her [colleague] up to be nice, and this is what I got for my toils.

I: Do you think it might have distracted you and contributed to . . . ?

R: Oh undoubtedly, undoubtedly it did because I'm under strain with this woman. I don't like her.

Two individual seventy-four year old men replied:

1. R: Well there were two women in the car so you can be sure there would be some talking. Sure it was distraction.
2. R: I guess we were chatting. We were talking about ah getting to this place before it would be closed or something.

   I: Do you think that might have distracted you and contributed in some way to your accident?

   R: Oh possibly, oh yes the fact that we hadn't planned our time too well. I'm one of the persons that say "Well we go out and we can do this as well." I tend to not keep it simple you know. My wife gets after me for that sometimes.

Less emphatic, yet present, were accounts of casual in-car interactions immediately before the crash. The conversations between drivers and passengers were not considered to have been disconcerting. According to the following drivers, talk arose, but it did not contribute to the crash:

1. R: I was talking to my wife at the time . . . I mean I was talking to my wife and I came off the intersection there and uh, I don't think it distracted me. I was watching the traffic and I noticed the traffic coming down the road and I made the judgment to cross in time, so the conversation I was having didn't distract me. [Male, sixty-five to seventy-four]
2. R: I talked but I never look over to the person I never do it and I don't have the radio on and I don't smoke so I mean . . .

   I: So you probably just talking but looking.

   R: Just talking I usually I don't look side to side cause that can distract you too much. [Male, sixty-five to seventy-four]

3. R: Well we could have been talking about going to our daughter's that's about all I can think of at the present at that time.

   I: Do you think that what you were doing might have distracted you in some way.

   R: I don't think so . . . I don't believe I was distracted. [Female, fifty-five to sixty-four]

Based on these elderly drivers' recollections, social interaction was incidental to other happenings on the road. It did not influence the pattern of events leading up to the crashes. Factors such as poor visibility or other drivers' unexpected actions were reasoned through as the "real" causes.

References that accident victims made to the social character of the automobile also included entertainment. A few senior citizens had the radio playing at the time of the accident. Based on the interviews, we established that music was not a big factor in the elderly drivers' travelling environment. Most preferred quiet and solitude. But there were a few exceptions. For example:

1. Oh yeah I always have the radio on. [Female, fifty-five to sixty-four]
2. I had the radio on and a cup of coffee in one of those holders you get from the gas station. [Male, sixty-five to seventy-four]
3. I usually have the radio on in the car and the truck. [Male, seventy-five plus]
4. Well, I had my radio on yes. And, I was humming along with it ya, um hum. But, as I said I wasn't distracted. [Male, fifty-five to sixty-four]
5. I have the radio on all the time, to this station. Just as background more than anything else. [Female, sixty-five to seventy-four]

Evident in the accounts on radio-playing was an accompanying normalization factor. Although some elderly drivers had the radio playing prior to the crash, they did not consider it to have been a distraction. Even when combined with other transient activities, such as drinking coffee or humming along, listening to the radio was not displayed as a relevant factor. A dramatic representation was provided by one elderly motorist who "always had music playing," as he rolled a cigarette with one hand while steering with the other. But according to him, these events did not cause the accident. Instead, fault lay with his mind being elsewhere "thinking of something else." He was daydreaming on the highway.

Attention directed toward projects other than driving was expressed by a group of discussants. Thought transfer, daydreaming and so forth figured in the following examples:

1. R: I didn't have the radio on, I don't smoke, um, I think the only thing I might have been thinking about was, ah, I wondered if my granddaughter would like her present. But that wasn't foremost in my mind, ah, I mean I'm watching the road. [Male, sixty-five to seventy-four]

2. R: No not really, probably thinking dreaming. The radio wasn't on I don't smoke there was no passenger in the car so I probably just had the mind off the matter for a moment.

   I: So do you think that you may have been distracted at all and that might have contributed to the accident?

   R: Distracted by what?

   I: Well you said you may be dreaming, do you think?

   R: Well I don't think driving occupies your mind fully at times. I think you think of other things and perhaps if you did, if that's what you mean by distraction perhaps I was distracted. I don't smoke in the car, my wife can't stand it. Ah, let's see. Now, the last thing I remember doing in the car there, there was, ah, I was thinking about that crossing there. Coming over it, I'm thinking about getting us to Tsawwassen, and getting back home again on Christmas Eve cause we had to put the tree up and everything, ha ha. [Male, fifty-five to sixty-four]

To be here in body but elsewhere in mind frequently happens to drivers. They may rehearse upcoming speeches, replay past arguments, review itineraries, miss loved ones or fret over problems. Yet most of them, most of the time, still maintain adequate control of their vehicles. According to our informants this appears to be their view as well.

More dramatic and pronounced are the cases in which elderly drivers were specifically attentive to matters aside from traffic or physical handling of the car. Relatively common in motorists' accounts was the theme that the accident victims were searching for certain streets, roadway signs, house numbers, or business establishments. Being in strange neighborhoods, rushing to find shortcuts or searching for anticipated but unknown freeways or side streets were major distraction factors that led to crashes. Witness:

1. R: I was looking for the freeway. Just for a second.

   I: Do you think that what you were doing might have distracted you and contributed to the accident?

   R: Well, I guess it did because he was stopped.

   I: When you looked up?

   R: Yes. [Male, fifty-five to sixty-four]

2. R: Ya, we were driving to, ah, along Lington and we were looking for the house of ah relatives of my son's wife, you know because they just moved the day before, they moved and, ah, my wife remembered they probably don't have the facilities for lunch, you know. So, she made up some food for them and we were taking it down to them in Deep Cove. They were not home, and they didn't have the phone connected, so we thought maybe they went to relatives, it's actually the sister of you know, so we remembered that the relatives lived on Lington.

I: Wellington. There's a Wellington in Burnaby.

R: Wellington.

I: Wellington ya, North Van.

R: Ya, and so we were going along Wellington, and we found the house, and we didn't see the car of our son there, so we were continuing from Wellington, and we were going on the next intersection, we were going to turn back, and go home. Then I remembered this Princess Park you know, on top of hill [?]. And it was on the afternoon, so I said to my wife, "Maybe we can go to Princess Park for a while." You know, for a walk and so it was just before that intersection Wellington and [?] and somehow I had missed the stop sign there.

I: There was a stop sign there and you didn't realize it?

R: I didn't see it, and my wife on Wellington didn't see it too, you know. So we went through the intersection and, ah, there was a car. Yes, looking for someone where I've never been before. [Male, sixty-five to seventy-four]

We do not wish to mislead the reader by suggesting that the majority of elderly driver accident victims were engaged in distractive behavior immediately prior to the crashes. Still, it recurred sufficiently often to qualify as prominent conduct.

The central explanation offered by respondents was that they were driving normally, partaking in prudent driver actions. This thought usually eventuated the characterization that the other drivers were to blame. Witness the following accounts:

1. Nothing, just driving and keeping my eyes on the road.
2. Just waiting for the traffic, for a break in the traffic for us to get through. We neither talking nor we, we don't play the radio unless we're on long trips, you know of an hour or so. We don't have the radio on, but then we were just sitting waiting for a break in the traffic. [Male, sixty-five to seventy-four]
3. No, I was looking to the left and this is why I think I have such stress on my right side. I was looking to see if the traffic was clear enough to go. [Female, sixty-five to seventy-four]
4. I was driving my car looking for a street and I was heading towards Kingsway, I looked to the right and I got to this corner. I saw this fellow way down the street but I thought I had ample time to cross the intersection. I went across the intersection and I hit his car. [Male, seventy-five plus]
5. No because I was alone and only thing what I tell you before that I watch this woman turning left she was really slow there was lots of cars behind me and this guy well I don't know if there's right of way to pass from right side but there was some cars parked on the right side you know so he was waiting to get through you know so that's why I I I was looking around you know what is happening that's the only thing. [Male, sixty-five to seventy-four]

Could See the Accident Coming

Can drivers foresee accidents? This is a difficult question because accidents are considered to be unforeseen or unplanned outcomes of a sequence of events which result in unintended injury, death and/or property damage. A sense of legitimacy is evident when certain events are labelled accidents. Because they could not be helped, or they were unanticipated, responsibility for them is negated.

For some elderly drivers, the unforeseen or unexpected nature of the accident was not evident. They anticipated the crash. But because of limited reaction time, slippery roadway, or heavy traffic, evasive action was judged to be impossible. Rather than take preventative measures, the elderly awaited the anticipated outcomes. A review of the following discussions demonstrates more clearly the anticipation-prevention theme:

1. R: No, I when I when I saw him first, ah, I guess it was just reaction that this fellow is going terribly fast and I can't get through here and I didn't know what was going to happen but I knew I couldn't get through the intersection. And, ah, so I decided to stay there and there was more than a length of a vehicle to go by. But the road turns off at the highway and he was coming off like this. He wasn't turning off at ninety degrees so he could come off there quite fast but it was raining and I figured about thirty kilometers would be the normal speed and the rest of the traffic was travelling and, ah, so, ah, there was nothing at that stage I would do at that stage to avoid the accident I could only stay there and, um, I guess that was the looking back at, ah, that was the best thing to do because I was only turned at a slight angle so he hit me in the right front side and broke, ah.

   I: Which is certainly better than broad sided.

   R: Yeah. [Female, fifty-five to sixty-four]

2. R: I took my wife to an eye specialist over there just near 97 in George area. In fact in George Highway and we were coming back. We were coming to the south on King George Highway, ah, just when we were approaching the 88th Avenue intersection there was one car ahead of me so I applied my, ah, I yield because there were red lights all ready red when I saw so I knew I had to stop and, ah, the car ahead of me it was a lady driving stopped, I applied my brakes it didn't stop. So then I got off from in this, ah, the left lane but there was another car coming who were going to turn left. And there was a car on my right side but nothing was left so the only thing I forgot which I couldn't do was I couldn't apply my hand brake because there was no time. This is what I thought when I thought back and then my car was, the car in front of me stopped and I was going at about forty kms, or something like this and bumped into that car. So because, ah, I had a sense that it was going to happen so I just braced myself. My wife didn't. I didn't tell her anything, she got a good jerk so the lady appeared out our window and asked me to turn right on the 88th

Avenue so I told her to just talk. She went there I started my car, because there was some [sliding slope ?] on that she stopped her car when I tried to stop behind her because my car won't stop. I didn't know what had happened. [Male, seventy-five plus]

3. R: Ah, when I applied the brakes I and the brakes wouldn't work so and the car ahead was about, ah, ten or fifteen yards away I knew the accident was going to happen. Because I saw this way and that way and there was no room for me to go this way and that way. I knew I should stop because there were red lights. [Female, sixty-five to seventy-four]

4. R: Yes I saw it coming, he'd be back about, oh, maybe thirty feet, forty feet and coming fast. Because he was getting into the into the line of traffic that he wanted to get into and in order to do it why he was in a hurry. [Female, fifty-five to sixty-four]

5. R: Oh I knew it was coming seemed a long while since I knew. We couldn't miss before it come but I knew it was going to hit. Although I I think maybe I would stop because it going so slow I know I slammed on the brake.

   I: Hmm.

   R: But I, I guess I slammed it on the inside of the pedal I wouldn't have the time to get across. [Male, sixty-five to seventy-four]

6. R: No I seen it coming it was far enough back that I had enough time . . . and she was swerving from one lane to the other. And I don't don't know whether it confused me but I didn't do something to get out of the road. But she was speeding. No doubt about it. [Male, fifty-five to sixty-four]

7. R: I, ah, I seen him come. I seen this farmer coming, and I thought gee what a funny looking outfit that is. Because it wasn't an ordinary truck, and it wasn't a camper, I found out later it was a home-made box with a kind of a door on the front part of the box, and then he had some vegetable boxes on it, and he had this thing flapping, and that's all I remember, and I thought that crazy fool, he's not even stopping, he's coming right out. So I jammed on the brakes, and hit black ice. [Male, sixty-five to seventy-four]

The elderly drivers who foresaw the misadventures, assessed that the roadway and/or traffic conditions were such that they could not, avoid the oncoming collision. They were disarmed. They did not, or could not, react quickly enough to the threatening lead-up events.

For the most part, the accident victims did not foresee or anticipate their accidents. There were no forewarnings, only shattered expectations:

1. I didn't see the taxi.
2. I was coming from a stop sign . . . I was in the right.
3. It was an empty street.
4. I just couldn't believe it.

5. I was waiting for a break in traffic, not looking in my mirror.
6. I figured when he seen that I was that far he would have slowed down.
7. I was right there and she should have been able to see it coming . . .
8. I never seen him until after I hit him.
9. I could see the lane and there was nothing in the lane.
10. You don't expect people to go through stop signs.

The accident happened. There was a great sense of disbelief. Because of the suddenness of the tragedy, responsibility for the cause was deflected away from the elderly drivers themselves. To compensate for the suddenness, the majority of automobilists implicated the environment and/or other drivers as the blame agents for the crashes.

The Accidents

In over 80 percent of motor vehicle crashes, responsibility is assigned by police to driver behavior. Injury producing and fatal crashes tend to be the consequences of certain driver activity. Such actions serve as reportable facts as seen by the people involved, ones which represent the flow of events leading up to the accidents.

The elderly drivers were asked the following three questions about their crashes:

1. In as much detail as possible, please tell me how the accident happened.
2. Could you see the accident coming, or was it a complete surprise?
3. Some accidents just happen. Was yours one of these or was there something that you or the other driver could have done to prevent it? What could have been done?

Through these questions the interviewees provided themes, behavioral patterns, or social rules which were discerned to represent some order to the corpus of data. The following descriptions are based on attributes accident victims assigned to their crashes.

Attribution of Accident Features to the Environment

Interestingly, approximately one-third of the elderly drivers claimed unequivocally that the cause of their accidents was the roadway environment. Most often the hazard was an object that obstructed the driver's vision. For example, for a seventy-five plus year old motorist the presence of a telephone truck created the setting for the accident:

> Yes, ah, I was going over to the Safeway store here in the middle of the morning and came to the corner, stopped at the stop sign, as I always do. There was traffic coming in on my right, coming west and that traffic went through but on the corner where I was making a left turn there was a big B.C. Tel white truck parked right on the corner and the B.C. Tel Company at that time were running some extra wire and on the other side of 130th and the new developments are going in there. And they also built a little something I don't know if you call it a relay station or what on the on the street just off the corner. And the big truck that was parked right at the intersection, there was another truck parked along side of it. So my view coming in off on my left was, ah, blocked completely. I stood there sat there for a while and I moved ahead a little bit to see if I could get a picture of through between these things and I waited and waited and I couldn't see or hear anything and finally thought it was clear and I went ahead just in time to be caught on the rear of my car. If I had been a split second ahead I probably would have been in the clear, a split second behind you wouldn't be interviewing me. It just caught just back of the my door on my side and it just swung me around in all directions and landed me on the other side of the street.

In ordinary driving circumstances, elderly drivers expect to have clear vision. A woman in the sixty-five to seventy-four year old age group excused her involvement in the crash because of an incline that she believed created a hazardous situation. To assure herself that her blocked vision was real and not just an imaginary excuse she returned to the accident site to examine it more closely. She explained:

> R: Well, it was, I suppose, very simple in a sense. I came up to a stop sign. I stopped. Ah, there was a large gravel truck facing me across the, ah, intersection. And I was watching him to see what he was going to do. If he had to turn the corner, I was going to let him go because they take a lot of room.
>
> I: Uh hum.
>
> R: And he showed no signals for turning. So, I presumed he was going straight through. And, he saw me look both ways. And, I literally, it's this, ah, what I call a semi-blind corner. And this is one point I feel strongly about. In this particular area there's an awful lot of blind, semi-blind corners. And to me, I had to go back and drive over that corner over where my daughter took me, because I said, "I can't believe me not seeing that car. Not you know, until it was too late." And, when my daughter took me, and I said, "You look down there, you can't see more than half a dozen car lengths, because of a slight incline."

Streets are lined by a variety of objects like trees, shrubs, buildings, light poles, traffic signs, and so forth. They can and do influence driving. For some senior motorists they were considered hazardous. According to one elderly man (sixty-five to seventy-four years old), his accident was directly related to reduced vision created by trees. He clarified:

> R: They come up from ah Number 10 Highway from there, so on that Sunday

morning there seemed to be not as much traffic, and I thought I'll just go. Now previous to this, I had called the municipality to cut some trees off on our left, um, coming because they were a hazard.

I: They were blocking your vision.

R: Ya, affecting the view coming from the west. The municipality did send somebody and cut some of those down, but they left a big branch that was right over across the highway, and that was a blind spot for me. So, when I stopped, I looked for clearance, and there was clearance, as far as I could see, and I crossed. The, um, car that hit me was coming from the west, and it couldn't of been coming terribly fast because it gentle, gently shoved me across the street.

Whenever reduced vision because of roadway obstacles was given as the cause, the interviewees were quick to offer follow-up commentary suggesting that they were not visually impaired. The implication was left that the obstacles would block any driver's vision, regardless of age. Also, self-competence did not become a focus of reflection. It was nearly always assumed.

Why did the accident happen? "Because of the poor road design, or bad corner" was a dominant response provided by some motorists. The roadway was described as being unsafe. At times there was a fatalistic tinge to the accounts. The street environment invites mishaps, proven by the fact that other people had accidents at the location. The accident-involved driver was one of many helpless victims. Witness:

1. R: Well I was driving coming east east to west on [thirty-two] you know there's no stop sign before that and then there's the Johnston Road. And a man came down west and with a stop sign that he went right through. So I mean . . .

   I: And hit you?

   R: And it's a very very bad corner I mean I've known three that have had accidents there.

   I: There's a bit of a hill there isn't there?

   R: I don't know what it is. The policeman even said visibility is not good and, ah, I have no idea what it is. Whether it's, ah, going along and just just think they shouldn't be maybe people think they shouldn't be but it is fairly busy. [Female, sixty-five to seventy-four]

2. I: Some people never feel really comfortable driving; are you one of those people?

   R: Particularly at this intersection at the end of the street. There have been some pretty close numbers there, but there wasn't much design when the engineering was done on that intersection I'll tell you. [Male, fifty-five to sixty-four]

3. R: There is so many accidents at that corner that the Chevron Station has a button that automatically presses for the RCMP, huh huh huh huh. So it's a popular spot I'm sure. [Male, seventy-five plus]

4. R: Well in the evening well the day this happened I had a phone call from Staff Sergeant I think his name was. I don't know him I never met him and as far as I know I have never seen him. He said "I just been looking over the reports for the day." And he said "I see you got caught on that awful corner," he said "I live not far from you," but he said "I've got into the habit of driving around two or three blocks if necessary instead of going through that corner." And he said "You have a chance to appear in court on this if you wish to, to dispute it." He says "If you will do that I will appear with you," and he said "We'll kill that charge." And when the time came I was to appear in court, the officer who appeared at the time of the accident, ah, phoned me he says "Well look if you want to appear all right but if you don't want to bother don't go," he says "I'm going in and I'm gonna kill the charge anyway." So I thought it was very very nice. You hear all sorts of remarks about the cruelty of the police but, ah, I thought that was . . . [Female, seventy-five plus]

These were judgments made about the roads. They neutralized the elderly drivers' self-evaluations of blame and responsibility.

Further negations of blame were evident whenever elderly drivers reasoned through their accidents as a consequence of poor weather conditions, whether as a single factor or as the cause of hazardous road conditions. This further proves that attempts to avoid bad weather driving situations are more on the basis of discomfort than on perceptions of incompetence or physical shortcomings. Several elderly discussants thus described:

1. Nothing distracted me, but it was dark. But I've driven a lot, like to Edmonton and Winnipeg. But the weather conditions were bad—it had just started to snow and his view may have been obstructed and maybe he couldn't stop. There was no yellow line and the road is wide in some places and narrow in another. [Male, fifty-five to sixty-four]
2. Yeah, you turn the first exit not the Colony Farm exit towards Essondale. The first exit you just sort of go around old Cape Horn Avenue and ah it has a tip and there's a road comes in with a stop sign and right after the tip this is where I went sideways and right into the ditch. But, ah, there is water always running across there, before that intersection part. But at that time there was no water it was frozen enough but the road surface itself later when I looked at it you know after the accident was just like you had, in in it they looked like stars in a way. It's not a frozen solid surface it's it's like in. . . . This is what I looked at. I hit one of those patches and I was going sideways and I couldn't go no place else. [Male, sixty-five to seventy-four]
3. We were coming from Lillooet to Lytton on Highway 12. Where we were staying was about five or six miles this side of Lillooet. The night before the day of the accident it started snowing. So, I thought we'd better get the heck out of there. We got up the next morning and it was snowing a bit. We watched the traffic going by, and none seemed to be having any problems. At about 5 to 11:00 we took off. We got out on the road and in several places I tried out the brakes to see what would happen—everything was fine—a

> little bit slippery but you just have to go with the road. We got down to this place and there was a sign at the top with an 'S curve.' We went around the first corner and we had just cleared the second one and the car just reversed on its own—it just went clean around. It went backwards. [Male, seventy-five plus]

Slippery roads can also mean black ice, a thin invisible layer often found on highways in shady areas during the winter months. The hazard is almost impossible to see:

1. I: Okay, in as much detail as possible could you tell me how your accident happened?

   R: Okay. Now it was December of last year. And it was on a Saturday morning, ten o'clock, I remember and it was cool, cold so I said "Well I'm going shopping." So I didn't have that car I have out there, I had my Pontiac and, um, just got over the tracks and I hit black ice and spinning around. Lucky no cars were coming. I spun around twice, went right in the pole and the car was buckled in half. Luck I wasn't killed, oh boy. Anyway, um, there were two gentlemen standing there and they came over and then the one fellow and then, uh, the police came and anyway the car was totally demolished, glass everywhere. Lucky I wasn't cut. I had a cracked rib and a bruised hip. So anyway, that was ten in the morning and the road was slippery and everybody else just crawled around after that. Anyway, this big truck came later after my accident with the sand. Now that's just in that gully in there and no sun gets there. Anyway, that's about it. I went to the hospital. [Female, sixty-five to seventy-four]

2. R: Do you think that the accident could have been prevented if you or the other driver had been more skilled at driving?

   R: When you hit black ice it is, ah, you have absolutely no control . . . because, um, I was so close to the farmer's bridge, and I tried, you know, the farmer's bridge was right here, and I landed right there. Like I landed right on the corner of his bridge and, ah, if I had any control, I would of had aimed over his bridge. Maybe about three feet, I would have, if I was three feet, you know, hit closer I could of zoomed over his bridge. But when you hit black ice you just, there's nothing there, you just, ya

   I: So you put on your brakes and you hit the ice and of course you can't see it until you're on it.

   R: And I wasn't going fast. But after I hit that, when I was going over that bridge, it seemed like I was just zooming. [Male, sixty-five to seventy-four]

An incident recalled by a senior man (aged sixty-five to seventy-four) gives some indication of how fog was held directly responsible for creating a serious crash. Fog is not unusual for the West Coast of North America. A person can cruise along a major highway in clear sunlight, only to be suddenly engulfed by dense, low-level fog. As the driver discussed:

> R: Returning from North Vancouver at approximately 9:15 or 9:20 in the evening I was coming south on Johnston Road and had just met the Nicomekl Bridge and where it narrows down to a single lane and I would guess I was about a hundred feet or so off the bridge and, ah, just prior to that I noticed the, ah, flashing red lights it was a car in this single lane which also had a double line and it had nothing over here on the bank so there was no way of getting around. And as I got off the Bridge my windshield seemed to fog all of a sudden I presume that that was caused by the, ah, different temperatures over the river and on the land sort of a thing. And, ah, it caused me to make a error in judgment in the distance between me and this vehicle with the flashing lights. So, ah, and I was approaching I would guess it's somewhere between twenty and thirty miles an hour and, ah, I misjudged the distance and hit this truck which was stopped there I, ah, giving another truck in front of it a battery boost you know what do you call and, ah, I hit this truck with my left fender left front. And, ah . . .

It goes without saying that rain also hinders vision. Some motorists reported instances where this environmental condition was considered to be the legitimate reason for the crash. The following example portrays the thinking:

> Well, I really didn't see him from the because it was drizzling like I said, so I could see headlights from the back because there was a long line of cars, and there was a big truck at my left, because I was on this side. So I really had didn't know that, ah, he was coming too fast. [Female, fifty-five to sixty-four]

More importantly, rain makes the roads slippery. To be safe, certain driving allowances have to be made. Normal driving behavior may have to be altered. Greater space for stopping may be required:

1. I went back again; it was drizzly weather, not raining; the road was slippery, that was one contributing thing to the accident. I was travelling normal speed just going along, nothing alarming, and a truck was in front of me, I couldn't see, you know it was quite a light-weight car and the truck was large. There were no crossroads. There were no traffic signs so the truck stopped abruptly, very abruptly. I saw his lights coming on and so I was approaching him quite quickly and so I had to jam my brakes on and so I went flying into the rear of his truck. Wheels lock, it happened with another light car of mine but the wheels are supposed to find friction on the road, the dirt and the lubrication, they can't find friction, you know, it's a mechanical sort of thing, once they can't find that friction, they come to a complete standstill the wheels, the brakes lock the wheels, they don't spin anymore. Once you're in that situation, then I, don't know if I did that or not, but normally you pump the brakes. But you don't have time to remember, all I did was I hung on to my steering wheel, you see, waiting for the impact. [Male, seventy-five plus]
2. Well, I came up to the intersection, ah, it just turned yellow. It was raining, and when I tried to stop, I couldn't, so I went through the intersection, and the car coming from my right, ah, that's when I hit. There was a three way, um, three lanes. I was in the center lane, there was a right hand lane and left hand lane. The lights, like I say, was going yellow. It was green when I was just almost up there. [Female, sixty-five to seventy-four]

3. [The driver in front of him] just slammed on the brakes, didn't slow down, didn't give any signals, nothing. I tried to respond as quickly as I could, but as I say, it was really pouring with rain, the roads were terribly slippery and, ah, I really do believe that I was a good distance away from her, but it just didn't stop, I couldn't control the car, it just kept on sliding. [Female, fifty-five to sixty-four]

Potential problems with depth perception outlined by previous researchers as age-related difficulties never surfaced in the interviews. Environmental factors were always proffered without reference to vision, reaction time or mental processing abilities.

Even though inclement weather can be hazardous, clear weather can also be disconcerting for some drivers. Bright sun can mean poor vision. Looking directly into the sun without proper eye protection can cause glare or momentary lapses in vision. For one senior the sun was problematic. He hit a child on a bicycle:

> Well it was early in the morning and the sun was shining from this direction and I had made my turn around the corner and I come to the King George Highway and I make my turn and I guess he come through on the, the boy was deaf and dumb and had no way no way of, ah, talking, ah, I I didn't really see him right away. Cause the light sunlight was shining and, ah, I guess he hit he hit the front of my car like we both hit at the same time. There was no injury to him, so the only thing that got hurt was his bike. So we bought him a new bike. And that was it.

Others said:

1. R: Well it's not much to say really, ah, I stopped at the stop sign I glanced, I always look to the first lane of traffic first before, ah, I venture out and I look to the close lane. I think basically it was just a matter of the way the sun was up and, ah, at least that was it. It was bright. The accident was my fault I can't, ah, give no hassle to anybody on that one.

   I: I see. So the accident was a surprise to you? A complete surprise?

   R: That's for sure. I had bounced off the windshield and I thought to myself "Eh what the heck is going on here?" I didn't have a clue that that car was coming and as I was easing out into the it's four lanes where I had the accident, as I was easing out I was primarily concerned with to what lane the cars coming up were in so that I would have the inside lane free to left turn and continue on. And then when I looked to the right I don't know whether it would be my eyes or the sun, or what but I thought both lanes were clear and the worst, she came from I'll be damned if I know. But obviously she came down the road so, ah, that's the whole story there. [Male, sixty-five to seventy-four]

2. R: In the morning, yeah. So it was probably twenty minutes to 8:00 or something like that. And just here on the corner. I think the sun just hit me in the eyes. The sun was just over the roof of the Pancake House. I'm sure I was doing something and I dropped my glasses and the whole thing happened in less than five seconds. Or I could have had a small blackout—I don't think so. But I think one of those two. I almost was up on the . . . near the intersection when the sun hit me. The light had been changing just at that moment. [Male, fifty-five to sixty-four]

Routinely, the roadway and natural environment were claimed to be major components of the accidents, whether singular or in conjunction with other factors. Obstacles like trees, embankments, overpass supports, large signs and buildings, poorly designed roads, bad weather, terrible terrain, and/or slippery road surfaces were some features elderly drivers blamed for production of the accidents.

The Other Driver as Cause

The degree to which elderly drivers attributed blame to the other driver portrayed definite regularities. Most often, in fact, over half of the interviewees considered the other driver to have deviated from expected driving behavior. The negative sanctions of other drivers were either in conjunction with some environmental feature such as driving too fast for rainy conditions, in relation to defending their own behavior, or as a straightforward accusation—it was the other driver's fault.

The Other Driver in Bad Driving Conditions. When it rains or snows, visibility is a problem. However if, according to some elderly drivers, the other drivers do not compensate for the conditions, the driving circumstances can easily lead to crashes. Witness one senior aged sixty-five to seventy-four:

R: Yup. Well when I left here in the evening, it was about 6:00 or 6:30, and it was raining really heavy, visibility was very poor, and I'm not really sure what happened.

I: Is that right?

R: I sort of think that the person I rear ended didn't have their lights on.

I: You didn't see any?

R: That's right, all of a sudden, you know my wife and I are driving along and all of a sudden there's lights, and there's the red light, you know. And I saw, you know I saw the traffic lights, but I didn't see any other lights. All of a sudden there's brake lights.

I: So did you rear end him?

R: Yes.

I: O.k., I thought you were, o.k.

R: Nope, I rear ended.

I: You didn't see the driver at all, and poor visibility?

R: Oh, the visibility was really bad.

To prove he was right, this senior citizen returned to the accident site in order to establish the probability that the other vehicle was driven without lights. As he explained:

R: A friend of mine that I met in the mall, a couple of days later, said, "You know so many people go out of this mall, and forget to put their lights on because it is so well lit."

I: Ya, that could have been the case.

R: So, I just went down a couple of nights and stood and watched, and there were all kinds of people running out without lights.

I: So you think that's probably what happened?

R: It's a possibility. You know I've been driving for a lot of years, and I'm a very careful driver, and I think as you get older you're probably a little more careful, a little more cautious.

In defense of self-image, some participants went to great lengths to explain that although the weather was poor, and technically they (the elderly drivers) were at fault, the other drivers were "really at fault." Witness this sixty year old man going out at Christmas time in rainy weather:

I: In as much detail as you can.

R: It happened on Christmas day, I had deliberately chosen that day, rather than go on Christmas Eve, to avoid getting into a situation where there would be a lot of people who had been drinking, ah, on Christmas Eve, and it was raining that night anyway, and so late in the day, I was going to take the presents to my granddaughter. Bearing this in mind, knowing that the risk of getting into an accident was that more involved, I thought that I would leave it until Christmas Day, knowing that they would be back from lunch, around about 1:00, so at that time of day, it's usually a little more quiet, even on a holiday, so I proceeded down the freeway to, um, the freeway, to um New Westminster and, ah, I got to the intersection, ah what's the name of the intersection? I can't remember the name of the intersection, can you stop it for a second?

I: Brunette and ?

R: I got to the Brunette intersection, and around the cloverleaf, and I was following a car across the bridge, the overpass, and as the two cars, neither of which were speeding, she wasn't speeding, neither was I, I thought that I was far enough away from her, and just as we were going over the overpass, coming from Burnaby, was an ambulance, with all its signals and sirens going. Emergency trip. And, we are in two lanes of traffic as we go over the overpass, anybody coming up from the freeway from Burnaby up the ramp, runs into a third lane. I knew this, and certainly didn't anticipate anybody coming to a dead stop, but the woman panicked and I have proof of this, because by strange coincidence, my boss and the other representative I work with, called at an office where she works as a receptionist in a doctor's office, and she admitted to them that she panicked, and she thought that the ambulance was going to come up, and that it was going to run into her. So she was driving, she had a male companion, and she just slammed her foot on the brakes, didn't slow down, didn't give any signals, nothing. I tried to respond as quickly as I could, but as I say, it was really pouring with rain, the roads were terribly slippery, and ah I really do believe that I was a good distance away from her, but it just didn't stop, I couldn't control the car, it just kept on sliding.

I: And you ran into her?

R: I tried to avoid it to somewhat, my left front hit her right rear, but badly enough you know to cause a fair amount of damage.

I: Some accidents just happen, was yours one of those, or is there anything that you could have done or the other driver could have done to prevent it?

R: Ya, the other driver without any doubt should not have panicked, she could have touched the signal brakes, or brake signals and flashed them, to have let me see, to let me that the, and it was a new car, so she had the extra brake light up in the rear view, um, in the rear mirror, ah, in the rear window, um, but, um, rather than just slow down and give me time to respond she just slammed on down, down bang, and that was it.

Snow is another dangerous environmental driving condition. According to one male fifty-five to sixty-four year old driver, two people were injured because the other driver:

R: Well she had to be travelling fast. I swear that she was coming forty miles an hour sideways. Cause it was just like it was just like moving I mean she wasn't driving she was just sliding.

I: Yeah out of control?

R: Oh yeah she, ah, there is something that a lot of people can avoid, ah, I hate to see that, ah, just slow down. Ah, you see ahead of yourself like when there is a little bit of snow, ah, coming to the stop sign I mean before you get into the stop sign, they should realize that you can only stop but they don't, they feel just like when you step on the brakes it's gonna stop. It doesn't happen that way because the car goes all over the road.

I: So you figure she she could have done a lot to avoid the accident?

R: Oh yeah, definitely. She was just travelling a way too fast. She had to because I mean when that poor kid passenger and she must have knocked the window out because there was two people in that in the car. But, ah, so many things happened there that somebody grabbed her and took her in.

In less-than-ideal roadway environments, the other driver was at times criticized for not driving according to the conditions:

R: It was in a shopping center. There was no yellow lines, there's no stop signs. You're supposed to use your imagination. Apparently the other fellow had the right of way because he was on the wide through lane and I was coming in, also on a wide through lane. While I was looking in the other direction, I hit him.

I: Could you see the accident coming or was it a complete surprise?

R: It was a complete surprise, I never even saw him until after I hit him.

I: Was there something that you or the other driver could have done to prevent it?

R: No.

I: Do you think that the accident could have been prevented if you or the other driver had been more skilled?

R: The other driver was driving too fast. [Male, seventy-five plus]

In several circumstances the road was wet. The elderly driver stopped in time but not the driver behind. So, according to one senior woman: "He might've been too close behind me. . . . It wasn't my fault."

Whenever poor driving conditions were evident, most often the accidents were interpreted as fatalistic, deferring blame to environmental factors or to the other driver's presence and behavior. Emphasis was placed on the untoward crash itself, as an uncontrollable event, an act of fate based on weather, or misfortune based on the other drivers who "didn't know what they were doing" in inclement weather conditions.

The Other Driver as Cover for Self. With regularity, senior drivers clarified the accident event in terms of self and the other. During the interviews, the elderly persons outlined their roles in the crashes, but just as quickly they deferred blame. A seventy-nine year old female said:

> In my opinion the other driver was speeding and if as he told the policeman he saw me come through the stop sign why didn't he stop? Because in the pictures that my son took the marks on the road were slightly over the length of his car to where he hit me. That's all I can tell you. He just came out from behind the other two cars I think he was frustrated having been held up on Johnston Road and up there you see? And then he saw there was nobody else in the inner lane and he came out and just put his foot on the gas pedal and came right through.

Intersections were the single most often mentioned situations in which the elderly drivers' behaviors contributed to the crashes, yet other drivers were blamed. The following quotes are offered for a contextual flavor of the reasoning process used by the victims:

1. R: Good, you know one thing, of course naturally and one of the things I know, and I never will do again is to pay attention to somebody honking behind me. But even at that, I looked, I had been there about three

minutes, and you know that intersection, well it's a one way intersection I guess, coming out there on King George, you know the little lead on comes here and then lead into that Johnston Road comes this way, then it's like an island here, and then King George is here. Now down here is 64th now I came out here right, and I stopped and I waited and the traffic was coming and coming and then finally I saw there was nothing coming this way and I looked down here and this little red car is coming out from the stop light and I said to myself, "Why heavens, that's such a difference there." From where I was here and there was nothing wrong with the way I stopped, cause I knew it was a small red car and I saw it, and I said, "The distance that I have to go over to get into that middle safe part, it's stupid of me to wait any longer." Now I thought I had been over careful and besides there was three cars behind me and I thought, "Those men are going to think that woman, why doesn't she move?" So this little car is way down here, now since then I have just for my own satisfaction and instruction I have watched cars and I have seen where they were as I was crossing roads as a pedestrian. And I thought, "My heavens." So anyway I said to the officer, "That car must have been really travelling." So he said, "Well sister it doesn't matter how fast she was going, she was on a privileged highway." Is that how you say it? [Female, sixty-five to seventy-four]

2. R: I was, ah, I don't know if it was 54th or 58th I'd have to look at my records I forgot the I guess it was 58th. I came out of 58th wanted to turn on Highway number 10, left turn. And across from us 58th across Highway number 10 was a very empty road there was no traffic at you know, but anyway in front of me was a red car in front of my friend there to show us the way. He made a left turn and I was going to make my left turn and he come, no lights nothing, and then while I was starting to do my left turn we saw two lights coming the two of us. My friend who was with me she only saw the lights when they came [two of us ?] she hasn't seen any lights either. So and, ah, then my first question was where did you come from?, where did you come from? And I then the police had quite a long time talking to those drivers before they came to me and people screamed "Don't say that you are at fault don't say that you are at fault." But because I wasn't feeling well shall I say that? I wasn't feeling very well that day I was very very upset, somebody upset me very much and I wasn't going to go any didn't want to go but I did and because I wasn't feeling so good I didn't argue about it but the friend from Cloverdale she went across the street to phone her son to help us to figure a way and he said "Tell her there were witnesses don't let her don't let her." Anyway, ah, so the police make me signing you know it that moment I knew a little bit upset I wasn't hurt not at all nothing not a scratch nothing and my mind was still very clear and the first thing was now I can't drive anymore the car was gone the car wasn't insured it's collision I couldn't drive anymore this is the end and I thank the Lord nothing happened further except a little bump on my friend's head and I had nothing. So and then, ah, those kids. What I think is he must have come somewhere out of the blue.

I: Side street?

R: You know from a side street there on that street.

I: Yeah.

R: And saw the green light and said "Oh I'll make it" and went through like an idiot you know. That's the only thing that I he came at the last minute which I didn't expect that's all I could see because there was no light coming to us and the other car didn't see any light. [Female, sixty-five to seventy-four]

3. R: And, ah, I was coming down Russel from the hospital, and there's a stop on Georgia, and I stopped to let a pedestrian cross. And I waited for them to cross, until he got his feet on the sidewalk, he's going south. I proceeded across the street I looked left, I looked right, I looked back left again, and I looked back right, and as I started to look this way, I was moving slowly. When I looked right, it was the second time, and I was moving slowly and I didn't see this truck coming. He saw me, he saw me wait for that pedestrian, he saw me start up, but he didn't come to a stop. Even though he had the right of way, and I had the, it wasn't, I didn't have the right of way. He, I thought he should have stopped, but he didn't, he kept coming, and I thought my God.

I: So he hit you on the side?

R: On the side. In front.

I: Could you see it coming at all, or was it a complete surprise?

R: Not until it was right there. [Male, seventy-five plus]

4. R: O.k. This one is, um, in a Honda, and I was going North on Johnson Road 152nd, and it was a Chinese restaurant, not a restaurant, but a store, um, you know, a grocery store. Now people zip in there and zip out of there. Now I probably wouldn't of hit if I hadn't of realized that, but I always watch that store because kids will zip in and zip out, so, now there is a house north of the store, and there was a car stopped, and those kids said they gave a lot, a lot of warning, but the car between me and the, her, didn't give me one, cause this is what happened, and as I looked in there and stopped, then she was right up behind then, and I put my brakes on and nearly got around her, but I didn't. If I would have had another foot and a half, I would have been around her.

I: So the front car was making a left-hand turn?

R: She was making a left-hand turn across Johnson Road, now that's, ah, quite legal. I don't know if they got a double line there now or not, but that was quite legal at that time. But, they said we, because they know how dangerous it is, and I know how dangerous it is, and that's why I was watching that store, eh, because my cousin used to live in that house, and I know that area, you know but, ah, so I applied my brakes, and I swung around, and I just didn't quite make it.

I: Could you see the accident coming, or was it a complete surprise?

R: No, no. It was a complete surprise, it really was because from the time, and I'm not one to stare and daydream, I look and I look back to the road, but if I had of seen those kids there, I would have been slowing down and

> signaling to the point that somebody behind me would know that there was a car there. But, that lady in the middle was in a real hurry, because she was checking her watch all the time that we were being interviewed by the policeman, and everything else. So she, I don't know, cause I was not in any rush, I had all, you know, I had lots of time to get where I was going. Um, yes, I would say that when she saw that car stopped, that she should have signaled. [Female, fifty-five to sixty-four]

Turning situations were evident for a significant number of the crashes. A unique logic was offered for defense of being assigned responsibility. When elderly drivers were making left-hand turns they expected other drivers to acknowledge the turns in progress and thereby compensate. Whenever the other drivers were judged not to have followed this rule they were accused of causing the crashes. Through such reasoning strategies the elderly drivers again denied blame. Their disclaimers of responsibility were convincing:

1. R: I was going, ah, west on 16th Avenue and, ah, sailing along perhaps a little dozily and a car, ah, stopped ahead of me to make a left hand turn and I plowed into it to it but braked just before plowing into it and, ah, damaged it. It was a minor crash but it turned out to be not so minor.

   I: Could you see it coming or was it a complete surprise to you?

   R: Not in time to really avoid it.

   I: Was yours one of the accidents that you or the other driver could have done something to prevent it or did it just one of those things that happen, do you think?

   R: Just one of those things that happen, looking back now I don't remember whether her directional signal was on but that I can't prove. It possibly was possibly wasn't I tried to look at the photograph you have in your mind. You wonder well now was that, ah, signal light on or not? I can't remember but who knows? No one could prove that. [Female, fifty-five to sixty-four]

2. R: So then the same thing is this guy here you see? Second accident, it was ten o'clock in the morning and there's no traffic hardly at all no place. I'm at the stop sign here and I want to make a turn here you see? Now this guy is coming and he's coming up he was really speeding.

   I: You're going to make a left turn from this?

   R: Yeah I'm gonna come in here. I don't even see this guy because when when I took off he was a long ways away but I tell you he was travelling at least a hundred miles an hour. So I floored it a little bit you know to get the hell out of his way to make that he wasn't going to smash into me. Now I get I'm just about straightened up on this lane here, this guy comes from behind here and he slams into my door. Just makes a little dent oh about this much and he's got a big truck bumper bent right into the wheel, the headlights smashed. Now tell me another thing, what would you think eh? How can he bump that just by making a little ting? I've got a little Chevette.

I: Huh huh huh. The damage was done previously.

R: Yeah and again you can't argue. The cop give me a gave me a ticket and then after he give me a ticket the other guy took off he says "He's 50 percent in the wrong." I said "Why didn't you give him a ticket?" I says "You let him go scot-free he hit me from behind I was straightened up here." If he can't see a car what would he do with a kid?

I: What was the ticket for?

R: For leaving the stop sign you see? There's only three cars on the bloody road, me and two other guys and this guy here he caused it all. [Male, sixty-five to seventy-four]

3. R: I got hit making a left turn. The other guy didn't see me.

I: Could you see the accident coming or was it a complete surprise?

R: Well, I could see him coming and I thought he saw me but I guess he was going faster than I thought.

I: Was there something that you or the other driver could have done to prevent it?

R: He could have stopped.

I: Or you couldn't have turned. Did you think you were all right to turn?

R: I thought I had plenty of time.

I: Do you think that the accident could have been prevented if either you or the other driver had been more skilled?

R: Skill? No. The kid that hit me was about twenty, not all that experienced. He should've known I was turning. [Female, sixty-five to seventy-four]

The illustrations suggest a sense of broken trust. According to many elderly drivers, other drivers should see what seniors are doing and compensate accordingly. Whenever other drivers were judged as not conforming to the senior people's interpretation of events, they were questioned or accused—as "being impatient," "jumping the gun," "going too fast," "not paying attention," "racing," or "cutting someone off."

Questions of fault or blame concerning other drivers tended to arise when the discussions featured leaving the stop sign. It seems that the elderly drivers who were involved in stop-sign-related crashes believed they were leaving them safely. The extent to which it was safe is a judgment call. Witness:

R: Well there is a little stop a little side street just comes from one side eh?

I: Yeah.

R: The other side of the King George. And I sat there and I 'til the light changed and all the traffic had gone on 72nd. All clear I looked up the other way and saw no cars coming and I start across and this guy hit me. Came out on one of these what you call 'em? Choppers? Big low slung, he hit me right on the

> side of the door I don't know where the hell he come from. No brakes didn't have his lights on. I thought "Sure this had to happen to me." I quit drinking a year ago because I had a bad liver and, ah, six months before that I sure look at now I quit drinking I drank all my life and never had a nothing happened. Okay. [Male, sixty-five to seventy-four]

To add legitimacy to the disclaimer of blame, many senior drivers spoke about their previous safe driving achievements. Since they had not experienced an accident for thirty years, then surely they were not responsible for the one in question. So the reasoning goes! As one seventy-eight year old man professed, "My record speaks for itself."

After fifty years of driving, senior drivers believe that they have learned all there is to learn. The proof of successful learning is that they have never had an accident in which they were assigned fault. This historical appeal to defensibility was commonly noted. That is to say, it reappeared with regularity in the data. So, quite naturally, the other drivers must be entirely or in part to blame.

The Other Driver as Blame Agent. Intersections are situations where most accidents occur for any age group of drivers. The elderly drivers are no exceptions. A common type of vehicle accident is the rear-end collision. The analytic convenience of such crashes is that the drivers behind are inevitably to blame. They failed to leave a safe distance between the vehicles according to the conditions of traffic, road conditions, or weather.

Of all the crashes relevant to this part of the study, a tenth were rear enders. That is, the elderly drivers either struck the car in front, or more often they were hit from behind, whether going straight ahead or in the process of turning:

1. I stopped at the bottom of a hill and I was getting ready to turn right. I took my foot off the brake and I slowly crept forward. There was a fellow behind me and I guess that he wasn't paying attention. I guess when he saw my car start to move he figured I was gone. I couldn't believe I'd been hit because I think I knew he was there. I knew there was a car stopped behind me and I couldn't believe that he was dumb enough to drive into me. [Female, sixty-five to seventy-four]

2: About 5:00 in the evening in December, it was fairly, ah, getting dark and we were stopped on [Dewdney Trunk Road], to make a left hand turn onto Norman, and traffic was whizzing by, like crazy, so I was stopped waiting for a break in the traffic. And all of a sudden, wham, I thought the rear of the car, I thought the gas tank exploded. Ah, you know we got hit so hard, and it was a heavier car, I think it was a Ford, that hit us. Anyway, ah, he would have pushed me into oncoming traffic, but somehow my wheels weren't turned enough and he pushed me right over into the bus, the bus stop. Ah, I had no idea, until the bang, we didn't have any idea that he was coming up behind us. There was quite a bit of damage to the car and, um, my wife, she was, ah, had injuries to her neck and her back, her knee, of

> which she is still going to the doctor but, ah, it was fortunate, as far as, you know, it could have been fatal but, ah . . . [Male, seventy-five plus]

In the process of stopping:

1. The Port Mann Bridge, I'm sorry, ya, and, ah, I was in the inside lane, the fast lane, and, ah, of course they were both the same, the traffic is very heavy at that time of day, and I was looking for a smart, you know for a great track, and cut over in the other lane, I like driving in that lane better, but, ah, I, ah, happened to look up and I saw the old stop lights going on and I hit my brake, and fortunately I managed to stop in time. I like to keep back a little ways so when this happens I don't hit the car ahead of me, so that's what happened in that case, but I was hit from behind. [Female, fifty-five to sixty-four]
2. Yes, I had come up the North Road, I had been in New Westminster on business, and I had come up the North Road or Columbia Street rather, to the Currey Street which is one street before the Columbian Hospital and, ah, apparently somebody was crossing the street there, and the traffic was stopped. I stopped in line of traffic and, ah, I no sooner stopped and wham right in that big back end I got a real dandy and, ah, it shook me for a minute or two . . . [Female, sixty-five to seventy-four]

While being stopped waiting for the next maneuver:

> The other driver hit the back of our car. My car was stopped. It was his fault, I was waiting at the intersection to make a left turn. The other driver was going too fast and wasn't paying attention. He admitted to that. We were pushed across the street by another car. [Male, fifty-five to sixty-four]

Hitting the vehicle directly in front is an "obvious" error made by the driver behind. Rear enders leave themselves wide open for blame and criticism. The elderly drivers engaged in this without hesitation. When they were rear ended they inferred that the other driver was "going too fast and wasn't paying attention," "must have been momentarily forgetful," "was sneaking the traffic light," or "was speeding and not driving with much care and attention." The blameworthy accounts are not unexpected for rear-end collisions. Such critical reflections illustrate that the other drivers' behaviors are features for scrutiny, judgment, evaluation, and criticism.

To place elderly driver perspectives within the statistical context provided by Chapter Five proves interesting. The elderly are most likely to crash at intersections making a left-hand turn or leaving a stop sign unsafely. They are most likely to be assigned responsibility for the crashes by either the police and/or the insurance adjusters. About 25 percent of their convictions result directly from accidents compared to 5 percent for the thirty-six to fifty year old group. Also, they are most likely to be convicted. Yet their views of self and the accidents avoid even the remotest mention of increased risk and responsibility for crashes.

Self as Cause

Whereas the bulk of elderly drivers involved in injury producing crashes justified their behavior in accordance with other drivers' behaviors, only 15 percent offered explanations in terms of self. They gave tacit accounts on how they were to blame. Their reasoning focused on mental, vision, or health faults.

Mental Faults. The mental factors that called attention to self-responsibilities ranged from "being mixed up in thinking," "being distracted," to "being inattentive." Individual differences in sensory capacity and mental abilities were evident in the accounts of vehicle crashes.

Many things happen on the roadway at any given time. It is up to the individual driver to process the various stimuli and come up with the appropriate decision and behavior. If the situational factors appearing at, for example, intersections are not properly perceived and organized, mixed up thinking can occur. This can be dangerous, as expressed by one elderly driver over the age of seventy-five:

> R: Well I was travelling from I went west and I came to 264 and there was stop sign there and the other guy was just coming ahead on me and he blinked to go to the left. Well of course we went east you know so and he turned right and that got me confused I thought it was clear and now I go ahead because there was another car behind him you know. So that's why I got mixed up on my thinking right there I thought the coast was clear for me to go and then when he turned to the right. . .
>
> I: It kind of confused you!
>
> R: Because he had the blinker on I'm sure about that to go to left.
>
> I: Hmm I see. And then the accident happened?
>
> R: Yeah I went ahead. Meantime a car came from south and went up north and I hit him right smack in the middle. [Female, seventy-five plus]

Action and reaction are basic rules of driving. In potentially dangerous situations drivers must process the information, decide on an action, and act swiftly. However, the behavior must also be appropriate. A driver needs to be sure that the brake is applied when the situation warrants it. Mixing up foot pedals in tight spots can happen. For several elderly drivers it did. One senior citizen stated freely:

> Yes. I had a sense, ah, in that moment of anxiety perhaps I may not have been pressing the brake, I might have pressed the [accelerator], I might have pressed the clutch, it was a standard. But when I tried to stop behind her on the 88th Avenue the car wouldn't stop. [Male, seventy-five plus]

Drivers do not just think about driving while they operate their vehicles. Their minds are always working. This view was explored previously in this chapter. Drivers' attention may change from, say, passengers to the radio to yesterday's lunch to the upcoming traffic lights. This is not unreasonable. For, according to Krech et al. (1962), any kind of cognition does not exist in isolation, but in larger cognitive systems.

It is commonplace that drivers think about something other than driving, but as the driving circumstances alter they quickly address the task at hand. If this cannot be accommodated, serious repercussions could easily be the final result. For example, if drivers pay more attention to passengers than they do to the multistimuli intersections, accidents may happen more easily. It matters little why a driver thinks more about the passenger than, say, a red light. The end result is an accident. Review the following account:

> R: Well I was approaching the intersection of Martin Drive and Sixteenth Avenue and apparently there was a red light and I didn't see it and I went right through it it was as simple as that first accident I've ever had.
>
> I: And you hit someone?
>
> R: No he hit me he was coming from the opposite direction from Martin Drive and, ah, he hit just about on my front right hand.
>
> I: Did you see him coming or was it a complete surprise?
>
> R: I didn't see him coming.
>
> I: Do you think there was something that you or the other driver could have done to prevent your accident? Some things just happen but . . .
>
> R: Yes I should have been watching. It was my fault entirely no two ways about it. I had a woman in the car with me a neighbor whom I don't particularly like, ah, for one reason or another but she'd just lost her husband or had at that time and I was taking her out to lunch I was trying to be nice but not particularly enjoying it and I was I'm not accustomed to having anyone in the car with me I usually drive alone and my mind was not on the road for a couple of seconds and that's all it took. [Female, sixty-five to seventy-four]

Sometimes drivers just have their minds on matters removed from the driving activity. The object of attention may be too vague to be specifically noted or identified. It is a distraction, recognized as such, imprinted as "mind wandering." For one elderly male driver between the ages fifty-five to sixty-four it was but a momentary distraction that led to the fateful crash:

> R: My attention was momentarily distracted and as I was distracted the light changed to red. I continued along the intersection and I collided with another car.
>
> I: Could you see the accident coming or was it a complete surprise?
>
> R: It was a complete surprise. I guess you could call it momentary distraction.
>
> I: Was there something that you or the other driver could have done to prevent it?

R: No, the only thing that could have been done, the other driver could not have done anything. The only think I could've done was to have anticipated by not having my attention distracted. Having that happen, there was nothing I could do.

I: Do you think that the accident could've been prevented if either you or the other driver had been more skilled?

R: No, it wasn't a question of skill. It was the distraction. Once I was there, there was nothing to do.

There is a fine line between distraction and lack of attention on one's activities. Often we do not pay attention to the activity at hand because we are distracted. And in traffic many things can distract us, whether they be objects, other drivers, or other things. Lack of attention to the immediate issue is hazardous. The distraction or attention to some other traffic event although relevant to the drive becomes, nevertheless, a costly maneuver:

> Ah well. How it happened? I was following a car it was a little slow on the lane he was driving so she was turning left close to that store what do you call that store in Langley? And somehow one car was passing on the right side so I was just watching these two cars and suddenly I forgot all about what is in front of me. And I looked up it was a red light and then I realized I was driving without any problems you know for a long time and suddenly here I am in front of a red light so I hit the brakes and it was too late. It was not a big bump you know but well that car was damaged.

Like some drivers who have driven for years, inattention may be considered safe because of a general feeling that traffic will continue as usual. It has been uneventful before, therefore there is no reason to believe things will change. If things do change there is little reason to panic, to think it cannot be handled in the usual way. For the seventy-five year old driver watching the cars to his right rather than in front of him, confidence was reevaluated as overconfidence:

> It was a surprise. Because you see I'm too confident I guess so I figured nothing is going to happen to me you know never because I'm watching you know every car around me.

In the interviews, several elderly drivers indicated that they specifically looked *for* something rather than looking *at* something. This is not unusual, for many motorists scan the sides of streets for direction signs, parking lots, certain stores, house addresses, and so forth. That the feature of looking for something contributes to accidents, can be displayed by the following illustration:

> He and I went to visit our cousin and we took a different street to the freeway, not the one we took before when we were coming in. It was freshly paved and

> looked like a four lane road. It looked like a thoroughfare. We were looking for Clearbrook Road exit and we didn't see the stop sign. The minute I realized, that I didn't see her coming at least thirty-five to forty mph. She didn't need to stop and I was half way in the middle of the road, I put my brakes on too late. I hit her; I had slowed down to look at the street sign and it was not visible; it was on the wrong side of the street. There should have been a light there because all of a sudden, it gets wider and right there the name changes, but not at the accident scene. It gave a feeling of being a thoroughfare street. I had to make a left hand turn. The streets weren't marked. Boy, was I shocked. All of a sudden I knew I was going to hit her. She was in shock something terrible. [Male, sixty-five to seventy-four]

While looking for certain markers, they expect all else to be continuing normally. Unforeseen circumstances are not expected. In fact, at times the responsibility is placed on other drivers to accommodate the searching motorist. It happens with regularity whenever tourists navigate through a maze of strange streets. Like a tourist, the elderly driver looks for a street exit not "expecting to see a stop sign" coming up. Perhaps vision problems which the elderly mentioned in Chapters Six and Seven may compromise roadway attention. By missing visual roadside clues, they slow down and concentrate on where they are, irrespective of traffic. They become tourists in their own town.

Vision Faults. Obviously, looking and not seeing is a problem experienced by everyone. It just appears to be more announced for the elderly. A review of police reports shows that many drivers who were involved in crashes reasoned through their circumstances as "I didn't see the stop sign, other car, pedestrian" and so on. To not see something although a driver may be looking directly at it is not unusual. At times some object does not register in the mental process. The popular saying that we can look but not see applies especially to some elderly drivers because they have a further possible stigma, vision problems. Consider the following examples:

1. Yes, well, I had about three lately. Was it the one where I was hit, they were all at intersections. Question? It was where the light had turned red. Oh yes, well, I was turning on the turn signal at green and a truck was coming and by the time the truck had gone through, the light had changed to red and along came another driver who I didn't see and he just kept coming and so I hit him. I talked to the former chief of police about this and he said that if the light had changed to red then I should have just stopped, but I didn't you see, I just kept going to get out of the intersection. It was a complete surprise. . . . I didn't see him coming. [Male, seventy-five plus]
2. I: How did it happen?

   R: Just that I was turning to come home, turning left and the other car was coming straight down the road and I didn't see the car coming.

   I: You didn't see it coming, eh?

> R: Even the policeman said he couldn't of seen it.
>
> I: So it was a complete surprise, you couldn't see what was going to happen?
>
> R: Yeah. [Female, fifty-five to sixty-four]

Health-Related Faults. A fault mentioned by several elderly drivers and worthy of discussion is that medical ailments or health-related events led to prominent crashes. For example, the consequences of a blackout while operating a vehicle produces visions of danger. An elderly accident victim over the age of seventy-five noted:

> R: Well it's nothing much to tell I, uh, I turned off of Sixteenth Avenue and had a blackout.
>
> I: You had a blackout?
>
> R: I had a blackout because my stomach was bothering me that day and, uh, I went straight into the path of another vehicle.

Another man within the fifty-five to sixty-four year old range stated:

> R: It's like I told the police. I don't know how it happened. I blacked out and woke up in a ditch or in the hospital. No explanation.
>
> I: You blacked out and went off the road?
>
> R: I hit a fence.
>
> I: Were you on any medication or anything?
>
> R: No, nothing. I'm in good health. There's no explanation for it.

A woman within the age range of fifty-five to sixty-four shifted the emphasis on health. Her quote was:

> You know how things are at Christmas time. Anyway, I had to go to work—we had company all day and I'm telling you things went to another end—do you think I could, I'm telling you; I didn't know if I was coming or going. One o'clock and I still hadn't fallen asleep so I woke my husband and said I have to get up at six o'clock in the morning and go to work. And I'd had so many late nights and I'm tired. And so my husband said—"Why don't you take one of my sleeping pills—and I'd taken one of his sleeping pills before, a half of one, I've taken before, but just that day (he has to have sleeping pills all the time)—he can't work you know, so that's why he takes them—it got so that he was taking three or four of them at a time. Just that day they gave a different strength—he didn't tell me this but triple strength sleeping pills, you see. They gave him. And I said these look different and he said "just take one." He said they won't hurt you. He was used to them but he'd only taken them for two days. You see it was a new prescription but I didn't know the strength of them. Well, I got up in the morning and I'm fine, I'm normal, no problem getting up and I get up and

> I think, gee, I'm a little dizzy. And I said to my husband "Gee, I feel a little dizzy" and he said, "well, you didn't get that much sleep. Are you feeling all right?" Well, when I got up I felt fine and I thought well once I get some fresh air, I thought well, I'll wake up. I remember leaving the driveway and I remember seeing a white line at Austin and do you know I don't remember anything else— I don't remember—I remember thinking, gee, there's not much traffic this morning. I don't remember going through—I must have gone through a red light someplace or, I felt good and then the next thing I know was I hit that post, you know and I'm thinking to myself, I've got to get to work. I'm still not with it, so I'm thinking I got to get to work and I'm trying to put the car in gear. The whole thing's all smashed, there's nothing there, nothing. Well, I got to get to work and then I had a broken nose so a fellow gave me some Kleenex and then I kind of looked and thought, gee, then I kind of realized.

Although emphasis on the elderly drivers' accident characteristics varied, a major trend predominated. Their perceptual palette contained blacks and whites. Simplified, environmental conditions and other drivers were to blame, either directly or indirectly. There was little room for ambiguity. Whenever some elderly drivers did propose driving behavior weaknesses, they quickly modified their perceptions by signifying other influencing factors over which they had little or no control. The impression they left was that, in the final analysis, the elderly did their best in bad circumstances caused by uncontrollable factors.

First Thoughts after the Accident

The accident happened. Most often it was unanticipated—the fault being assigned to the roadway environment, weather, and/or other drivers. Immediately after the collision, many elderly drivers focused on the safety of others. They "hoped no one was hurt," particularly their spouses.

Some offered assistance. They took the other party to the hospital:

1. I: Yeah. Do you remember your first thoughts after the accident?

   R: Oh I was worried about him.

   I: About his, ah, whether he was injured or not?

   R: Yeah because I took him to the hospital and I waited around. I figured it's the only Christian thing to do so because I'm a Christian myself. [Female, seventy-five plus]

2. I: What were your first thoughts after the accident?

   R: I didn't know what happened. The wife, how was she?

   I: How was she?

   R: Just a bit shaken up. I took her into Langley Memorial. [Male, fifty-five to sixty-four]

Others were worried about their own possibilities of injury:

1. To get up and get help—because I had gotten my head cut and my sternum broken. So I figured there's no question of time, I've got to get up on the highway and get help. So I went straight up, I couldn't make it all of the way—I fell at one point. It was just too steep. Finally some hunters came by and they saw the skid marks going over, so they threw me a rope and then they sent two fellas down to help the women down the rest of the mountain because it was just too steep to climb. [Male, sixty-five to seventy-four]
2. I couldn't breathe. My first thoughts were well what I thought was that I didn't want to get a whiplash that was when I saw this thing coming but the seat belt hurt me which you don't even think about like we got thrown into it twice because we hit him and then we went down into the deep ditch. [Female, fifty-five to sixty-four]
3. Um, my leg. My left leg that I had a lot of surgery done on it, I had a hip replacement, and then I'd had fractured tumor and, ah, it wouldn't heal, so they had to bone graft it, and that was the only thing that worried me, but it was all right. Um. [Male, fifty-five to sixty-four]

But concern about the other person, whether it was the spouse or other driver, predominated:

1. I was surprised and I wondered about the other fellow, whether he was hurt or not. [Male, sixty-five to seventy-four]
2. My prime concern was for him [husband] because he'd only been out of the hospital for a week. Aah . . . and the people in the other car, because I broadsided them and I thought, Oh boy that driver is going to be dead. [Female, fifty-five to sixty-four]
3. Well I looked over to see if this woman was hurt. [Male, fifty-five to sixty-four]

Besides worry or concern about the physical conditions of the accident victims, there were several other categorical reactions. The first could be termed emotional. Elderly drivers were shocked, horrified, stunned, bewildered, rattled and/or confused because of the "suddenness of the accident," "disbelief at what happened," or "unexpectedness of getting hit."

The second form of reaction prevalent in the data was more pragmatic. The victims' immediate thoughts were about the car, insurance or legal wranglings to follow. Witness:

1. Ah, I thought, "Oh dear this poor car is totaled." I looked out around the corner and I said to the policeman, I said, "It's totaled isn't it?" And he said, "You're right." Well the engine was just a mess. [Male, sixty-five to seventy-four]
2. I could see the dollar sign. I got a new car. [Male, fifty-five to sixty-four]

3. My new car, my car. I'd only had it for a month. [Female, fifty-five to sixty-four]
4. I had just had some work done on the truck not too long before that, and my, ah, my, ah, my reaction was, "Jesus Christ the truck is going to be out of commission, and I'm going to be afoot." But as it was, I took it to the to, ah, I took it to the body shop right down here, near the place where I was reporting, and they loaned me a car while they fixed mine. So I was all right. [Male, sixty-five to seventy-four]
5. All I know that I was driving sensibly and I was as careful as I could be and, ah, my thought was "You damn fools know my insurance will go up and all this" you know that's all I'm thinking about old age pension, living on a pension and these things happen to you you think "Well gee whiz." It makes you mad. I do a lot of driving eh? [Male, seventy-five plus]
6. I suppose the first thing was, "Holy smokes, what part did I play in this." You know? I, ah, years ago I was in a similar five-car rear ender type of accident, and I guess you say, "Oh here we are again." To a certain extent, and from a Leo point of view, I have to learn from the other one they were both quite the matching type of thing but they're one of those difficult things or impossible things, well the legal side of things, to ascertain blame. The person on the far end usually almost automatically gets blamed for everything having presumably pushed everybody ahead and whether that's true or not. So anyway I had a background there, so I guess my mind immediately said, "Holy, here we are again." [Female, seventy-five plus]

The third pattern of reaction could be classified as blame. The driver's first thoughts pertained to the other drivers. For example:

1. My first thought was "Where the hell is his brakes?" that's the only thing or his signal light. That's the only thing I said "What the hell goes on here?" you know? [Male, sixty-five to seventy-four]
2. Well I wondered how come he rammed into me, that's about the size of it. [Female, sixty-five to seventy-four]

Of course, first reactions following a dramatic accident cannot be categorized as a certain type. Reactions covered a variety of moods and intense feeling. Within the explanations of those emotions some distinct themes could be identified. They were concerns about the victims, emotional upset, pragmatics, and blame. Some elderly drivers could not respond to the question of reaction because they "blacked out" and woke up later in the hospital.

Accident Prevention?

Any discussion on the possible prevention of an accident carries suggestions of blame and fault. Whoever is perceived to be the cause of the accident whether directly (other driver) or indirectly (roadway engineer) is the person who could have taken preventative action.

Accordingly, to the elderly drivers, the preventability of their accidents was real: indeed the other drivers could have or should have taken precautionary initiatives. After all, they were to blame. Witness the following accounts arising from the question, "Could you or the other driver have done something to prevent the accident?":

1. Oh, the other driver obviously could. He told the police that, ah, his attention was, ah, temporarily, that he was temporarily distracted. He never explained why, and I thought possibly charges would be laid as driving with undue care or attention, but nothing happened, except the insurance company had, ah . . . [Male, seventy-five plus]
2. Well I think if they'd a been watching they could have dodged me they could have went round behind me. But he didn't have his foot on the brake pedals and even if there wasn't even a brake mark. [Female, fifty-five to sixty-four]
3. Nothing on my part. She could have prevented it by watching more carefully. [Female, sixty-five to seventy-four]
4. Well, I don't know what I could have done to prevent it. I was driving slowly because of the road conditions and the weather conditions, ah, if the other person didn't have their lights on and I couldn't say whether they did or not, but if they didn't they could have put their lights on. That would be a preventive measure. [Female, sixty-five to seventy-four]
5. I don't think I could have, well maybe if I would have looked, I'd have stepped on it. Maybe, you know, stepped on the gas. I might have. I don't know but, ah, the other fella, well he may have speeded. He had two lanes, and it was clear. He could have, I think avoided it. [Male, fifty-five to sixty-four]
6. We could have looked in the rearview mirror. The other driver should have left at least two car lengths between us. [Male, seventy-five plus]

For the majority of elderly drivers who were interviewed, the connection between prevention and blame was clear and precise. So often the suggestions were pinpoint. The other driver should have "slowed down," "stopped," "not changed lanes," "paid attention," "waited until it was safe or clear," "looked ahead." These were semiautomatic responses.

An important footnote must be introduced at this point. In most instances the accidents were preventable. Even in those accidents where the elderly drivers defined themselves as victims of circumstances, they could think of some action which could have been taken to prevent the misfortune. "Put in lights," "cut the trees," "put in a stop sign" were some suggestions offered to highway engineers. If the roadway environment had been properly designed and/or maintained, the following elderly driver would have seen the stop sign:

> Well there was something done maybe two to three weeks after the accident. I went, we were just getting ready at the time it was a holiday and my wife, so

> we went after the accident and, ah, when I come back in the middle of December that accident was 18th of November, I forget just what day I come back from from ah . . . so they put in the other stop made a four way stop instead of a two and ah that's what I think there should I think there should be more four way stops if they don't want to go for lights lights are expensive. I feel four way stops [?].

Again, the elderly victims employed as a guiding principle the assumption that other persons were responsible because of their courses of action. Occasionally the crash was the elderly drivers' fault. They could have prevented it, sometimes singularly, or more often in conjunction with the proper behavior of the other driver:

1. Well, if she'd gone slower I'd have made it. But I wasn't supposed to turn up on that street. So it was my fault just the same. But it was both our faults. I think the policeman gave me two, three points for it, but it doesn't matter much. But then we were standing there and people were coming up the road like me and I don't know why the police didn't give them any points. So it was a freak accident. I don't drink or anything like that. [Female, sixty-five to seventy-four]
2. No, I don't think we could've prevented it because I was so far out and that guy thought I was lucky. [Male, fifty-five to sixty-four]
3. The only way it could have been prevented is if I'd waited longer for the car to go by. [Male, sixty-five to seventy-four]

It is quite natural that when drivers anticipate a crash they make special efforts to escape it. Sometimes the alternative may prove more severe than the probable. For example, by trying to prevent a collision with another road user, drivers may risk hitting a power pole. This is not unusual. As with several elderly drivers, they attempted to avoid a "possible head-on collision" only to collide with a car in the other lane or to hit the ditch. One man's response was:

> When you say "could I see it coming," I didn't plan on it. No, I wanted to pull into the other lane, so I looked in the mirror to see what was coming and there was a car coming. I tried to miss it by putting on the brakes but because of the gravel and the snow, I couldn't stop. All I could do was try to miss it; which I didn't. [Male, sixty-five to seventy-four]

Post-Accident

Treatment by Officials

When officials such as police officers meet drivers immediately after injury producing crashes, the latter undergo a feeling of unsureness or insecurity.

How will they be received? Will they be accused?, rejected?, officiously handled?, helped?, or sympathetically understood? Such doubt is especially relevant for elderly drivers. On a societal basis they are generalized as a problem group. Witness the literature reported in Chapter Three. Researchers demonstratively portray them as problem drivers who require special licensing procedure. Their right to drive, their physical and mental capabilities and their commitment to follow the traffic flow are questioned.

Undoubtedly, the elderly drivers are aware of their stigma. They may, therefore, be reluctant to engage in official contact. Connidis' (1987) research on the likes and dislikes of the elderly showed that the treatment the elderly received from officials is suspect. Yet in the focus group interviews reported in Chapter Seven, the majority of elderly drivers were complimentary of officials like the police. They were confident that the police would treat them fairly if they were ever involved in trouble.

But, not surprisingly, there were some elderly people who support the assumption that blame or fault in an accident is unreflectively attributed to age. A mature but younger driver who is involved in the same difficulty as an older person may be excused, whereas the elderly person is judged according to the stigma of age. The following expanded conversation reflects this point of view:

I: How do you feel you were treated by the officials following the accident?

R: Well, not to my liking.

I: Can you elaborate on that a bit?

R: I was very upset and, ah, the girl that hit me I call her a girl because she was very young. She had her two children with her. I was terribly upset and I wasn't talking she kept trying to act like an authority like you know this poor old lady you know she doesn't know what she is doing. You know I didn't like her attitude so I didn't talk.

I: Hmm and you were kind of, um, shocked I guess?

R: Well I was.

I: By the accident?

R: I was terribly upset and for a minute after I don't know how I was after the accident before I got out of the car because I think I blacked out. And the people that were in the bus depot were all hovering around her and her mother arrived and hovered all over everything and they all talked and whispered among themselves and treated me as if I was you know a criminal. Then the police came and he was handed all the data that the other fellow had taken down and completely ignored me, he talked to her and took her outside and talked to her and my son arrived and I went out and talked to him and then they came back and, ah, he said "You do understand that I have to give you a ticket."

I: So you didn't feel that you were treated with, um, very much respect and consideration?

R: No no to begin with I made the left turn so I'm guilty eh? Regardless of what happens. I understand that now to make the left hand turn regardless of what happens you're at you're at fault and there's no consideration given to you period. Whether she caused the accident or whatever happened. So it was like you go to court and you're you're guilty before you're proved innocent like.

I: Did you feel that that's why you were treated like that because you were at fault? Because you're senior?

R: Yes yes.

I: Did you talk with them about that at all? Did you make any sort of complaint?

R: No no. What's the use? Nobody listens anyway.

I: Is there anything else that you'd like to add to the whole interview? Any thoughts upon anything we talked about or something extra you want to say?

R: Well if I ever got involved in another accident I would want a little more than just, ah, the what you call it the [insurance fellow]. You're cut and dried when you go there.

I: You think they have the reports and they just take what they see on the reports then as . . .

R: Well that's all he did. He was a very nice man but he told me you haven't got a chance and I said why and part of it was I was a senior. And I had to ask I said well what's you see I had no relative or anyone with me I went there alone. I didn't know I'd never been through the routine and uh I should have taken I should have got somebody to . . .

I: Do you think it would have made a difference if you had someone with you?

R: Well I would have felt it would have made me feel better. Because he didn't want to talk about it he'd never even suggested it and I said I did stop I said they can lie all they like I said I don't have to lie I said I've tried to live my life all I've no reason to lie and he says oh well you wouldn't have a chance if you and I said what would I do well then he said you could go to I think Small Debts Court. . . . Well you know you haven't got a chance there either if you're a senior. [Female, sixty-five to seventy-four]

Police Officers at the Site of the Accident. When police officers attend a crash, they have three primary functions; to offer assistance where needed, to reconstruct the event, and to lay charges where warranted. Their versions are documented as official. Drivers' actions and intentions are compared to formal predetermined criteria of responsibility.

To arrive at a determination of law contravention and suggest absolute or relative fault, the police officers must converse with the drivers. Based in part on their explanations, law officers assign responsibility. To illustrate this thesis, excerpts from several discussions are provided:

1. I: Yeah well you're probably a lot more conscious of those things than a lot of people would be having driven all your life. How about the, ah, officials at the time of the accident? How were you treated?

R: Perfect, perfect I can't compliment the police enough. Know very well came up with the old question, he asked me "Did you have your seat belt on?" 'cause I was out of the car at the time. I said "Yes I did" and, ah, sat me in and I apologized. I said "It was my fault right off the bat." He said "Well I got to give you, ah, issue a ticket." I said "I realize this, no problems, I'm wrong so." As far as that part of it goes there was no problems, no hesitation no hold up or anything else. I was able to drive my car away.

I: You were?

R: Yes. [Male, fifty-five to sixty-four]

2. I: And how were you treated by the officials?

R: Very good, um, ya. Ah, ya, he was very good, you know. He took everything down and I just told him I wasn't very good at protecting myself, and you know. But, he really had a good look at it, and ah he realized that it sure wasn't all my fault. [Female, fifty-five to sixty-four]

3. I: How were you treated by the officials? Were the police at the scene?

R: And the police came after a while and, ah, he asked me if I had been drinking. I said "No." "Are you on drugs," I said "No I'm sixty years of age and I'm not going to start with drugs." And, ah, he asked me how it occurred, I told him exactly what I'm telling you and, ah, the ambulance came and then he asked me, my car was towed away and took me in to his car, the policeman. And he said, ah, "You know it's your fault?" I said "Well frankly I don't think it is my fault." He said "How so?" I said "Well I was driving and all of a sudden my car just all of a sudden, ah, my car went across the street," and I had two witnesses there. You know they saw how it happened. And, ah, he looked at my tires and said "Well you see you have a bald spot there," I said "How can I have a bald spot when I put those tires on in the springtime? I can assure you it couldn't be bald." And, ah, I said "I can get you the bill and everything." Anyway, ah, that is how it happened. It was my fault, my insurance went up to over $800 and that's all I can say about it. [Female, fifty-five to sixty-four]

In some cases, elderly drivers spoke at length about instances when they felt that police officers deliberately controlled the definition of the post-crash scene only to arrive at assessments based on predefined mind sets. This is not that surprising, since police officers' experiences show that most of the time responsibility for the crash lay with the elderly driver, confirmed in Chapter Five. The discussions with drivers were not considered to have been negotiations on the basis of shared awareness, rather they were like police interrogations intended to prove predetermined actualities of guilt. In these cases, whenever the elderly driver countered a police officer's assumptions it was rejected, or seriously questioned. Witness the following accounts:

1. I: How do you feel you were treated by officials after the accident? Did the police attend the accident?

R: Yup, the lady police was, ah, o.k. Um, she was rather new, being an ex-cop myself, I could feel for her. She didn't even, I could of got off this charge, she didn't even give me a ticket. I had to go back two or three days later and pick it up at the police station in Port Coquitlam, ah, but, um, and I should of taken it to court. Um, I was advised, ah, I better be careful how I say this. But, let me say somebody in the law enforcement authority, said that I stood a very good chance, if I would have taken it to court. Ah, but I just didn't have time at that time, I was too busy with other things, and I, but, ah, um, the, um, the second policeman that came on the scene, he was from the highway patrol and, um, I thought his manner was rather curt and, um, ungentlemanly. He didn't even ask me how I felt, simply because I had rammed into the back of the other car, he just assumed that I was in the wrong. And of course if you hit somebody from the rear in this province, automatically you're guilty, ah, for driving too closely, but there are extenuating circumstances for this, you know. And all he wanted to know was, "Have you been drinking?" in a very rough, curt voice and, ah, "Why you sitting on the driver's side?" So I said to him, "Well you see if you can get in on the, ah," oh, I'm sorry. "Why are you sitting on the passenger's side?" I said, "Find out by trying to open the door on the driver's side." I couldn't get the door open you see.

I: Um hum, so you were just on your way out of the car.

R: No no, I was sitting there, it was pouring with rain. There was nothing I could do. The ambulance was there looking after the two people in front, and . . .

I: Did the ambulance attendants look at you at all?

R: Not really, not really. I think they might have said, one might have said, "Are you o.k.?" and I said ya. [Male, sixty-five to seventy-four]

2. R: Oh, he wasn't bad, but he sort of had his own opinion, which I don't think he should have, eh?

I: And he felt quite plain to express that to you?

R: Ya, he sort of said well I could be in the wrong for not yielding the right of way on an incoming three way, but I had no chance in that situation, cause there was no way, no one could stop there.

I: Any other officials involved?

R: Just the tow truck, that was it. [Male, fifty-five to sixty-four]

3. I: You hit the windshield even with a seat belt on?

R: Yup twice and then the policeman he said, "Well by golly," he said, "Have you been drinking?" I said, "Yes I had a couple of little snifters of Scotch." "You did." Well of course there's no use you just have might of told him it was a bottle because God they're not going to believe that you see so gee whiz he said, "Well you don't look drunk," "I'm not drunk what the hell is the matter with you?" "Well," he said, "I'll give you a twenty-four hour suspension give me your keys." I said, "Here you can have them I don't think this car is going any place anymore." "Well" he said, "It looks all right only that it's crumpled up on the end the front end a little bit." And I signed the darn thing and he ripped off the slip and give it to me and, ah, he said, "You better get out of there." I said, "Yeah I'm thinking about that too." And just then up come another policeman, "What the hell goes on here?" he said. So the guy says he told him he says "He had a couple of drinks of Scotch and I sent him down for twenty-four hours." "No way," he says "No way," so he comes over with a clipboard and he's got papers as big as that and he's writing down there and he says "So you had a drink of Scotch?" and I said "Certainly I told the other officer," he said "I know I heard you." "All right" he said "So you were drunk?" "I was not" I said so he signs the doggone thing drunk driving. And I said "What did you write that on for?" "Well" he said "You are drinking aren't you or you wouldn't run into that pole?" I said "You're full of bullshit" I said "You don't know your job either. He maybe was a little lax but you don't know your job." He said "You want to tell me my job?" I said "Sure." "Well" he said "How come if you weren't drunk how come you run into that?" "Well I hate to admit" I said "But I was asleep without a doubt." "Yeah well" he said "Then you better get out of there" he said "Let me see you walk." So I said "Well you're gonna get a surprise there too I can't get out for one thing have you got a knife in your pocket?" "No" he said "We don't carry knives." "Well I got one in my pocket" I said "And if I can get my hand down in there I'd get it out and I'd cut this goddarn belt. And I get out of this car and let you know exactly the difference between a drunk man and a sober man." So he said "You want to fight eh?" "No that isn't it" I said. I said "You want to see me walk," so anyway oh boy when he got in and looked in there and he said "You're injured ain't you?" I said "Yes I'm injured" and he said "Well okay we'll get you out of there." So they phoned for an ambulance and, ah, then he asked me all these questions over again that the other fellow did and he said "Well" he realized then I wasn't drunk. [Male, seventy-five plus]

4. R: The police officer, she was quite rude, she said "What was your driving distance, what was your speed? On or below the speed limit and, uh, either too close or too fast and . . . To my feeling it wasn't too, whether it was my feeling or not, whether it was legal she said—either too fast or too slow, or too fast or too close by, you know, it was my choice. It was too close, let's say. I asked her if it could have been a condition of the road, wrong type of tires or something technical. I think if you rearend somebody it's always your fault. But I still feel and think that the fellow in front did something deliberate and he stopped and it was kind of a chain reaction. I don't know if there were any people behind me, I didn't notice if there were. [Male, sixty-five to seventy-four]

The predetermined assignment of blame, or for that matter, the final assessment of fault were the main ingredients of negative judgments interviewees assigned to their treatment by police officers. A supporting description is:

> Um well the police seemed to be ah well he was carrying on his duty trying to, ah, get information and so on and, ah, the firemen were very attentive very, ah,

considerate and, ah, they, ah, were concerned about my wife and they took command. They they came first and I thought that, ah, overall I was upset by the officiousness of the police after when he told me it was my fault because it, his manner toward me seemed to have changed. Because I was responsible and so on but again, um, being upset and, um, also shook up I could have been wrong. [Male, fifty-five to sixty-four]

Whereas some drivers assigned sinister plots to the attending police, others reported that the negotiation of fault and blame produced complimentary behavior and appropriate treatment. Several clear examples are provided:

1. I: Um, how were you treated after the accident by the officials? Like the police or [insurance].

   R: The policeman we had very very nice, really. And like I said, you know, well he was wondering about the fact that he was so far across the intersection already, by the time I hit him. He said well there is a I don't know whether he said it's two seconds, there is a hesitation anyway between my yellow light and his green light. And, he must have gone through it. The more I think about it, I know he had to, but at the time you see I never thought about it. I was more worried about people being hurt, and I was thankful that nobody really got hurt. Even my brother-in-law, it didn't really affect him. Which, I was glad about. And, they took my brother-in-law, the police took my brother-in-law home. He only lives about half a mile from where the accident happened. So, he was really nice, and he came back and waited until the wrecker came to pull my car.

   I: How about (the insurance company), were they?

   R: They never gave me no hassle. Like I got two points on it, so . . . [Female, fifty-five to sixty-four]

2. R: My car was a complete wreck and ah I got an allowance of $1,500 on that. It was a better car when I paid $4,500 for it to replace it. So it's, ah, it was one of those things. My neighbor next door here, ah, came over he said "I'm going," he has had the trouble with that corner for some time and he said "I'm going to take my car over and stop at the stop sign and at two or three places take pictures of the view from the left." Which he did and he said "If this comes to court as it might you will have these pictures." And that night I will say the police were leaning over backwards to be decent and nice about the whole thing.

   I: So you thought you were treated well then?

   R: Well in the evening well the day this happened I had a phone call from Staff Sergeant   I think his name was. I don't know him I never met him and as far as I know I have never seen him. He said "I just been looking over the reports for the day." And he said "I see you got caught on that awful corner," he said "I live not far from you," but he said "I've got into the habit of driving around two or three blocks if necessary instead of going through that corner." And he said "You have a chance to appear in court on this if you wish to, to dispute it." He says "If you will do that I will appear with you," and he said "We'll kill that charge." And when the time came I was to appear in court, the officer who appeared at the time of the accident, ah, phoned me he says "Well look if you want to appear all right but if you don't want to bother don't go," he says "I'm going in and I'm gonna kill the charge anyway." So I thought it was very very nice. You hear all sorts of remarks about the cruelty of the police but, ah, I thought that was . . .

I: Very decent.

R: Very very nice of them.

I: So you were charged with something then and?

R: I was charged with, ah, failing to grant right of way at a stop sign.

I: That was dropped then?

R: So that was all killed and I got my $10 back, huh huh. [Male, sixty-five to seventy-four]

While there may never be the ideal post-crash situation, after all, the elderly driver had just experienced an emotional and physically damaging drama, most elderly drivers appreciated their treatment by the police. At least, they were not displeased. Some liked it because of a few extra favors the police performed beyond the call of duty:

R: There was a police constable and he was just going off duty, and he came just right after the accident, just a couple of minutes after the accident, and he was very good. He got out of his car, helped push my car out of the way, and took my wife and the other person to the car and he was just an excellent person. In fact my wife phoned him and commended him for it. [Male, sixty-five to seventy-four]

R: Very, very well. I have absolutely no complaint. A policeman came. He was very helpful. Very polite. Of course, he was a young guy, so he was more interested in my granddaughter than in me [laughter]. [Male, sixty-five to seventy-four]

R: Oh, lovely. What was his name? It was a Scotch name. He was really nice. The policeman was really good. He said, "I'm awfully sorry but I have to give you a ticket and a few points." I still don't know how many points I got for that. [Female, sixty-five to seventy-four]

Other elderly drivers appreciated the treatment by police officers even though they were marked for blame. It was the tact police members used to negotiate fault that impressed them:

1. Very good, even though they ruled against me. He sympathized with me because there was no lines on the road. [Male, sixty-five to seventy-four]
2. Very good. Very good indeed, the officer was very good but he says, uh, he gave me the blue tag I still have it somewhere you realize he says you are at

fault because of the stop sign I says I realize that so I didn't fight it told me I could if I wished but I couldn't see the percentage it's my fault it still would be my fault but . . . [Female, fifty-five to sixty-four]

3. Very very well, ya, I was very impressed really because although I hadn't been in a lot of accidents, you know involved in traffic, and you know it tells you in the book what to do, get license numbers, names and addresses, but you're really not at your best to be doing things quietly and nor do you see environment conditions, and in this case, he suggested, look you don't need to worry. You know I started and I got a pencil and paper out and started doing some of those patterns, and license gathering, and he said don't worry about [?] when you follow up, which he did. He wrote it right up there, he gave us coffee. [Male, fifty-five to sixty-four]

In sum, satisfaction with police treatment was the commonly held appraisal. Were they cooperative? "Yes, they did their job" was a representative answer. Descriptors commonly offered included indications that police officers were pleasant, and treated the elderly drivers "very well," "very good," "excellently," or "just fine." The approximate ratio of positive to negative judgments was ten to one. Still, one elderly woman over seventy-five years of age provided the following extended version of her degrading experiences:

I: How were you treated by the officials after the accident?

R: I thought very unkindly.

I: Hmm.

R: Ah, for instance my car had to be towed away so the policeman did say "You go and sit in my car and I'll get details from you." Then we went up to the person who had hit me and he came back in a few minutes and, ah, he said he got into the car and he said "The other driver says you came right through the stop sign without stopping" and that just knocked the breath out of me. I said "That is ridiculous I was there for a minute and a half or two minutes before I saw an opening." And I told him what I'd seen. And, ah, I was sitting there shaking and I said "Look couldn't this be done at my house?" I said "I only live a short distance away" and I said "I'm feeling ill from shock." And he said "No we won't be long" and he went on and on with this what you call it? So, ah, I knew that I had to get out the car was stuffy and I said "Well I'll have to get out and phone to get some fresh air." He said "No you can't do that." I said "What do you mean, will you arrest me if I get out of your car?" He said "No but I'll have to restrain you." So I waited another little while finally he finished this report and the whole thing was he wanted to finish the report and give a copy to the other two people you see? Man it hit me.

I: Hmm.

R: As he opened the door and got out I opened my door and I walked home and, ah, about five minutes later he arrived at my door and gave me a blue ticket. Well I resented the whole thing.

I: What was that for, the blue ticket?

R: Because I was crossing a what you call it? And caused an accident according to how . . . So I did go down and complain to the police about it. I was being absolutely honest with him I thought, oh one thing I did say to him I said "Look I'm in shock if you can't see that I can assure you I am. So what if I had been damaged, physically damaged, what would you have done?" "Oh I would have taken you to the hospital immediately." And I said "Well," I said I forget now but I said "Then when would the report be done?" And he was filling out "Oh" he said "When you were able to do it." "Well" then I said "Why can't it be done later?" I couldn't move him. And I've never had any dealings with police and I didn't even know whether I had rights or not you know? But I would say that the whole business and his inability to understand that I was in a very bad state, ah, I was not myself a couple of months afterwards. But I don't think it was his intention I don't think he really understood. I don't I'm not saying he intended to be brutally unkind but he wasn't very understanding.

I: Not too sensitive?

R: Not too sensitive.

The vignettes that were on display portrayed the more common police-elderly driver circumstances. From all the presentations offered by a group of elderly drivers who had occasion to become directly involved with police officers at a dramatic time in their lives, no specific age bias could be detected. At the same time there was little evidence of anti-police feelings on the part of elderly drivers. The criticisms that were offered by some senior motorists featured unsatisfactory tact used by individual police officers, not any form of institutionally-supported negative stereotyping.

Insurance Negotiations. After the emotional experiences of an injury producing automobile crash comes a new concern; insurance. Economic interests surface. In British Columbia, every driver who is involved in a motor vehicle accident must negotiate with the Insurance Corporation of British Columbia, a public corporation representing all the motorists in the province.

Typically, the elderly driver's involvement with the insurance company involves assessment of fault and assessment of damage (metal and body). For a motorist, economic self-interest and regained health become important concerns. From the first focus, a competitive stance may result: the worth of the damaged automobile to the driver versus its value established by the insurer.

Often the elderly drivers did not receive the amount of money to which they felt entitled:

1. I: How about the [insurance] people, how were they?

   R: Well, I felt that they gypped me on my car, they didn't give me enough on my car.

   I: Is that right?

   R: My car was in a real good condition, yes it was, and I felt I should have gotten more for it.

I: I see.

R: Because I had kept it up and, ah, the other side was just like new, and I had new tires on, and a new battery in and, ah, things like that and, ah, it didn't make any difference. I showed them the bill, and there was nothing they could do about it, ah, so I felt I should have been given a little more than what I got.

I: Ya, o.k. [Female, sixty-five to seventy-four]

2. I: How were you treated by the officials?

R: Very good, the ambulance came. It was right by that fire hall they got oxygen out right away.

I: Yeah, the firemen came out did they?

R: Well this fellow that came across the road had first aid and whether they called across to the fire hall or not but they got an oxygen tent from there.

I: So the police were okay?

R: Very good.

I: How about ICBC?

R: Fine, a write-off car. Sure don't give you much of a write off though, terrible.

I: Yeah, you don't feel that it was fair.

R: Not really. The car was two years old, it cost $19,000 and they gave us $8,000, I don't really consider that too fair, a Thunderbird.

I: Two years old?

R: Yeah that's what they said, the book price. They just take it right out of their little black book.

I: Yeah, yeah.

R: There's no, there's no allowance for if it had an electronic dash in it and you know and all the computers and, ah, they don't consider that at all. That's your tough luck sort of thing.

I: Oh yeah.

R: I wasn't too happy about that, I can tell you. I said to them "Well let's fix the car, you guys rebuild the car," because it was a Thunderbird with not very much mileage on it. [Female, sixty-five to seventy-four]

3. R: On that is the, uh, the settlement that I got, uh, I believe the car was worth more than they gave me.

I: Than they gave you?

R: And, uh, the basis of that is that I had gone around and that particular vehicle, uh, I only some one in all of the car lots that I went to that was, uh, out for sale I looked through all of the books I could find and I could only find one in the books and when I talked to the, uh, assessor you know I said well you know how do you make the, uh, assessment on the car? Oh well they looked through this and that and the other and they get all kinds of information from different sources and they take an average I said well how can you take an average of one? But, uh, I gave up in the end, uh, you know I was not able to replace the car with the money I got which was basically. And the car was in excellent condition as you know when there is a vehicle condition there is usually bits of rust on the ground and so on there was no rust on the ground it was completely it was in first class condition.

I: Frustrating?

R: Yeah but but, uh, apart from that I had no problems. [Female, sixty-five to seventy-four]

As was previously mentioned, part of the insurance company's mandate is to assess the cost of injury. It is no surprise, therefore, that extent of injury and need and cost of therapy were noted objects of concern. Some elderly driver judgments on treatment provided by the Insurance Corporation were based on valuations of degree of satisfaction:

1. I: How about ICBC, how did they treat you?

   R: Oh fine, they're, ah, you know, it's still in the makings, I've been going to therapy, of course, you know, since my accident. I'm not going quite as often now.

   I: I don't know you've been going to therapy, you know, I don't know anything.

   R: No, but I have been, yes, I still am so, ah, and with some pain killers and I'm still, you know, so they have been very cooperative that way, yes.

   I: Are you feeling better?

   R: Oh yes some, it's coming along fine.

   I: Ya, that's not a very pleasant thing. I've never had it myself.

   R: No, well I didn't realize either whiplash until you know, I thought, "Oh it's much better." But then depends on what I do and how I do it, and then, you know, bang, there. Even this morning, my neck is sore, but I was at the fair yesterday and I guess too much looking around or something, it's surprising what little twists will you know, well it's just like a sprain in your foot you may say. It just takes so little it seems like, you know, even in the housework, you know, doing things, it's strange this whiplash but, ah, a sprain is a sprain, and sometimes I guess it can bother you too, most of your life I suppose. I hope not, but ha ha. [Female, fifty-five to sixty-four]

2. I: How about ICBC?

   R: Well ICBC they didn't give me a bad time. Ah, the girl that was my adjuster, what the devil was her name? I'd have it on a paper in there but, ah, when I told her about this here Voltaren [?] It's called [Clovenaxe] because that's the big word on the bottle and that was the first bottle I'd had eh and he [doctor] told me it he says it's the best darn pain reliever that the arthritic people have. "Well," I said "I don't have arthritis." "Yeah, she says, you got a little bit," he said. And now he said "This is why you have this pain." "I don't think so," I said. "Well," he said "We're gonna give you a thorough check up." And then when he gets the X-rays and he said "You know I can't understand this," he said, "You've been coming to me for twenty-five years," and he said "You were four and a half inches taller than you are now, what's wrong?" I said, "I don't know." [Male, seventy-five plus]

3. I: Have you been satisfied with ICBC?

R: No, not on this one. Absolutely not. And another thing about this ICBC woman here, I didn't get a copy of my, ah, what I signed. I got a copy the other day, it must be this one here. Is this yours here?

I: Um hum.

R: Well anyhow, I signed a thing here, and then after I signed it, she wrote something else on it. No I haven't 'cause she threatened that $1,000, she claimed me $1,000 to the accident. Well, for a whiplash and I bashed my shoulder on the steering wheel, and I hurt by back really good, and a permanent injury, and I settled for $3,500 because when she said that $1,000, it just freaked me out, I thought, "For what, what part of me is that $1,000 for?" So then, ah, she phoned me back a couple days afterward and then offered me $3,500, and I thought gee I'm sure getting lucky to get that much from them. And then she wrote on the thing, um, she said and the conditions under, um, section seven. So I thought what's section seven, it's supposed to be medical, so she wrote section seven on it and then put told June 30th, which I never signed, I had already signed the paper when she wrote it.

I: I see she added that on.

R: Yes, so after June 30th, and I never initialed or anything. So after June 30th, that's the end of that accident. I can't get any more pills or no more help on my back or anything. I was definitely not satisfied with that one. She made ICBC difficult on me. So now my family think I should of had a lawyer, or if I sign any more papers they're going to make sure that somebody is with me. On this next one, my sister is going to come with me and see what kind of ah, and it's going to be, ah, I'm going to make sure that I have, ah, like when my husband died, it was about twelve years ago, they figured on that, ah, that insurance, that a woman lives to be seventy-seven and a half years old. Well I'm sixty-six years old, so in and I've got ten more years, of a neck injury. So see I know that now, I learnt a little bit because I got. . . . [Female, sixty-five to seventy-four]

Health can be directly correlated to wage loss. When economics entered the health equation, several elderly drivers indicated signs of displeasure. A lengthy illustration, offered by a male between the age fifty-five to sixty-four, follows:

I: Okay. How were you treated by officials after the accident?

R: Ah, I have a grudge in my mind that ICBC people did not treat me very nice. When my son reached there he said "How are you?" I told him "I am feeling quite good. I don't know if I am very much hurt or not. But your mom is not okay." As the time went on, by the time he brought me home, brought us home, after some time he phoned the doctor and when the doctor gave us time we asked for a very immediate appointment. When we were on our way to that place I began to feel pains here. I'm going to tell you when I begin to began to feel it it was about half an hour of [?] and it went on increasingly. Sometimes when early in the morning when I woke up I felt it very difficult to especially to the left. It was painful to turn right but to turn left it was very painful. So for about two months I couldn't bend like this or I always felt pain except in during the day I was just walking or doing something here just or walk here, I got warmed up I was all right.

I: But in the morning after you were sleeping.

R: Yes, yes in the morning, yes. So we went to those people who gave us [heat] and when the girl applied the heat to the place and after that asked me "How, if I was all right?" I felt okay afterwards one or two hours it was all right. It was like this so you asked me the question. Those people totally refused to give me anything like [wage loss] or anything.

I: Anything like?

R: Anything like wage loss.

I: Oh I see yeah.

R: They paid some of it went to my wife, so they didn't pay me anything. I have not so far signed anything with them. When I asked them "Why are you not paying me?" They said "It was your fault." I said "Ask the Volkswagen people, we got the car fixed not by any some ordinary mechanic. We went right to the proper dealer."

I: Oh yeah, the Volkswagen dealer?

R: Yeah the Volkswagen. "And they'll tell you what was wrong." They towed the car from that place and they have a replaced the master cylinder and they are my witness that nothing was wrong with the car except that the master cylinder of the brake immediately all of a sudden went wrong when I applied it. I told them "I'm not at fault something out of my control happened. If I had some mistake of driving I was at fault." "So now you have paid the other lady out of our insurance that's right. Because she was not at fault at all it's my car's fault so my car has also been fixed but why don't you pay me wage loss. As for my reasons, ah, I think they are right not to pay me anything because I bought very few medicines, not more than I think $20 or $25 that I can [verify ?]. But they didn't give me any wage loss and they're even [?] that this was your fault. So when I go to some lawyer those people are [reluctant ?] because they know that we are going to get only some share of what he gets, what he will get because he never broke a leg, he never had any big injury."

The male driver was upset about the health payment, in part because he refuted responsibility or fault for the accident. This conflict became a routine discussion point. Consistent with their previously described refutations of blame, elderly drivers tended to approach the adjusters by denying absolute responsibility and hesitantly considering partial fault. These two discussions exemplify the thesis:

1. R: Even you see when I had to go to ICBC the lady who interviewed me she said "I know it's not your fault." She said "But the law says you have to be in control of your car at all times."

   I: Whether it's a mechanical error or whatever.

   R: So I just if somebody could tell me what I could have done I would appreciate it but nobody could tell me. Not even the policeman. [Female, fifty-five to sixty-four]

2. I: How were you treated by the officials, after the accident?

   R: Oh, very well.

   I: Was there police at the scene of the accident?

   R: Ah, there was an officer who came in because the taxi driver called him, and he just took notes of what I thought happened, and what the taxi driver information. But, when I went to ICBC, the adjuster there had a very difficult time to decide who was at fault. He said it was a really difficult one to figure out, because he just sort of seemed to me, and he was coming out of a side drive, and I was on the main road, King George. [Female, seventy-five plus]

The analysis of verbal data showed that aside from judgments, the insurance adjusting process was also a primary theme for appraising the treatment drivers were offered by insurance officials. One woman within the sixty-five to seventy-four year age bracket believed that she deserved the right to be part of the decision-making process:

R: I, ah, another point that I feel strong about. I should of had the right, as far as this is ICBC now, I should of had the right to see the car and decide whether I wanted to fix the body, because being hit by the back end, the motor wouldn't be damaged. I should of had the right to decide whether I wanted to spend $3,000 or $4,000 to fix the body of the car, or not. And, I wasn't given that choice. They just simply said that it was a write-off, and as I say, I should of had the right to decide that. If the motor is damaged then, or the frame, but it's the auto mechanic should have the right, or should tell me.

I: Anything else? You might never get another chance to get these things off your chest.

R: Well, as I say, there's some things I felt very strong about and, ah, I mentioned them. And as I say, I don't know, I have never looked at the laws of ICBC, but we do pay a lot of insurance and therefore we should have the right to decide what happens with our car.

I: With your car, ya. Well, o.k., great, thanks very much.

A male driver fifty-five to sixty-four questioned the institutional structure of the corporation and blamed the process of adjusting on that structure:

R: Yeah I've always looked at ICBC, well if you're having a problem you should be able to tell them and they should trust you. My personal feeling is that ICBC if they're on the other side they're offensive, they're not open, no they try to avoid you they try to stay from a distance so that the claim is lower and lower and lower. And that is to me is not the proper way it's I, I do know there is people take advantage of it but the majority should not suffer because of it.

I: Well I'm sure these are the kinds of things he wants to hear so if you got any other beefs or . . .

R: No that's about it I mean that's been one particular one I here again I, I personally couldn't say anything that held me at ICBC, ah, I notice every time when I wanted something I wanted to know something he had to go away and get the information so there's somewhere along the line, somebody higher up.

A tenet of life is that the institutional feature or process criticized by some people is worthy of praise by others. Witness the following accounts that display the fact that official estimates of some wrecked cars were judged to be satisfactory:

1. R: I like the truck very much, ya, and we got it rigged up for pulling a fifth wheel, and for going on trips.

   I: And it's as good as it ever was?

   R: Oh ya, it's in good shape, as far as I know it's A-1.

   I: I see, so you were happy about that?

   R: They put a new cab on, you see, and a new door on the driver's side, and they fixed, they even had to fix the other door on the opposite side, but like it just rammed right into the door in the bottom of the body frame, not the main frame you know, or nothing like that was hurt, but just the whole cab was shoved over. So, they put a whole new cab on, well like a second hand, a new cab. So I guess what happened, they got the $5,000 for fixing it up, I guess, you see, so I didn't have, we didn't have any trouble with ICBC or any you know. I've heard complaints about that, you know, getting, ah, well I did have a complaint, I wanted to get it fixed up, I didn't want to accept the $5,000 and write it off. [Male, sixty-five to seventy-four]

2. R: They gave me the value of what it is worth but it wouldn't be near the value because that car that car new is, ah, between $8,000 and $10,000 in that year.

   I: Yeah I hear this a lot you know that people . . .

R: But I got top price the lady, ah, Mrs. she she was a very, very, ah, she treated me more than right financially she gave me $2,500 that's that's the top price. That was the top price at that time.

I: Is that what they call a book value?

R: Or whatever is a book value, I never did see. So she gave me the top price so I had no complaints there. [Male, fifty-five to sixty-four]

Several elderly drivers were satisfied with the insurance affairs because they were able to negotiate their vehicles' values upwards. As one man within the sixty-five to seventy-four year old category described:

R: Yes, oh yes I have heard complaints, yes. But as far as I'm concerned, I have nothing to complain. Now this last one, I actually didn't have much to do with it because Body Shop right down here, they pretty well did the whole thing, you know. I wanted them to fix it in there. One thing about it, is that ICBC reached the with a first adjuster, or examiner whatever you call them, come out and he wanted to write it off, that was their first word. Well, I said no I didn't want to, because I'm equipped for pulling a fifth wheel trailer you see, and I got propane on, a big propane tank, and extra brakes, and all equipment that's on there now, and all the money involved, you know. I wanted to keep the same truck, as long as it was able to ah to fix it.

I: Oh I see.

R: So, ah, they had two or three inspectors down there, and finally they worked it through to get it repaired.

I: I see.

R: For $5,000. What they wanted to do was to pay me $5,000, and write it off, that was it. So the body shop did my dealing for me too, I actually had not much to do with it. [Male, sixty-five to seventy-four]

"Fairness" was a featured measuring device for victims' judgments and descriptions on post-crash treatment. The usual descriptions were cut and dry. Elderly drivers were either treated "fair" or they were not. Judgment of personal responsibility for the accident was the primary rule. Just as the former elderly driver was able to negotiate a "better deal" so did another fifty-five to sixty-four year old driver. For him the combination of the fairness of his settlement and the treatment by personnel were worthy of mention:

R: They come up with a figure and that's $2,500 and, ah, I managed to get it up to three and just what I said.

I: So you did bargain with them a bit?

R: A little bit and I got a little bit but I felt that I shouldn't because it was an accident I couldn't help it really and it should be fair I mean I know other people take them for a ride I didn't have no intention of this everything

> aboveboard I asked them "Just replace what I had that's all that I'm asking." But they don't do that, ah, they try to settle things but otherwise, ah, in the office I was treated well I can't say anything wrong there.

For one male driver, the difference between the Insurance Corporation's estimate of worth and his judgment was compensated for by the service:

> Very good. I was impressed with ICBC, I was, the service, the courtesy, I think, ah, as far as I'm concerned I have no complaints. I think the, ah, should have paid me about another $400 or $500 for the car but that's not serious. [Male, fifty-five to sixty-four]

In insurance affairs the front line personnel that attend to accident victims are the adjusters. Any discussion on service rendered implicates this group of employees. For one elderly driver the adjuster was "absolutely excellent":

> R: Oh, they were absolutely excellent. Yeah, that lady in charge Mrs. , you couldn't wish for a finer woman than that. She's really got something on the ball.
>
> I: She has?
>
> R: Oh, has she ever. I, I, I'll never forget her because she, she was an excellent woman you know what I mean? She was so, and thorough you knew everything but she had a personality more than that.
>
> I: She had it all going for her.
>
> R: Oh, she. . . .
>
> I: Knowledgeable.
>
> R: Oh, very knowledgeable. Oh, she was, she was excellent. You'd think you were working for ICBC but I bet she still is working for them. I don't know but I imagine she is but she was, I'll never forget her. She was just absolutely excellent. I told her so too I told her I told her she was one hell of, certainly been more than fair.
>
> I: And how were you treated by the officials afterwards?
>
> R: Oh, good, well we had to wait a half an hour for the police to come. I thought, they were right there you know their office is right there. But no problem I felt fine but I guess my reactions are slowing down a bit. [Male, sixty-five to seventy-four]

For another male driver, the adjuster was a know-it-all. She was considered to have been young and inexperienced:

> R: Well, I admitted right away, well, I says "Probably my fault because I left the stop sign" so I admitted it to him right there and then you see? I didn't argue the point but when I seen the way that my car was sitting and but took me a little while to consider and how he hit me just at a glancing blow from behind so I was figuring "Well you got a . . ."

I: How'd they treat you down at ICBC?

R: Well, I told that to the girl but she's only a little sixteen to eighteen year old something like that and she says, ah, she never makes a, she's a good driver you know very excellent driver "I never make a left turn I always just make right turns all the time."

I: This is what the girl at ICBC told you?

R: Yeah. I said huh huh huh, I thought I didn't even mention it but that would have looked funny if everybody just made right turns all the time. Nobody can make, nobody would make a left turn, why didn't they make that law?, I didn't tell her but I I figured there was no sense talking to her you know because . . .

I: Spend your life going around in circles wouldn't you?

R: Yeah, huh huh. I didn't even bother arguing the point, it's just anybody comes out with a statement like that it's no use to argue with them; they know everything. [Male, sixty-five to seventy-four]

Although the already mentioned examples serve as relevant themes freely and fully discussed by the elderly drivers, most of the senior claimants gave evaluative descriptions without lengthy retort. However, reading through the verbal data, it was found that the accounts included three outstanding themes: service, financial reimbursement, and fault:

1. There were no problems. It was pretty clear whose fault, who was at fault. [Female, fifty-five to sixty-four]
2. I thought very courteous due to the circumstances and all there was an intersection there and there was no reason for the accident really and I thought they were very businesslike. Yeah, I was quite happy with them. [Male, seventy-five plus]
3. Oh yes, very pleasant. That gentleman at ICBC was so nice. Most people are. [Female, sixty-five to seventy-four]
4. The insurance company sent me round a report and I filled it out and then I, everything was fine except the last one I don't figure that I should have full blame for it. [Male, sixty-five to seventy-four]
5. I think so yeah (got treated well). I got no complaints, ah, there was a lot of damage there and, ah, I always say I don't know you know I was just sitting there and you know that's a heavy car and this little Datsun. What would happen if I was sitting there in the Datsun and this one came? You know it makes you wonder. [Male, seventy-five plus]

Similar to the police treatment, the central orientation toward the insurance company involvement was acceptance; at times reluctantly stated, at other time readily expressed. "No complaints" was an answer often registered. The ratio between descriptions of adequate to inadequate treatment was about seven to one. Was there any evidence of stereotyping? Not one interviewee signalled that the insurance company personnel labelled the nature of the elderly driver based on age. Perhaps the following brief retort can be considered both a compliment and a social commentary:

> I: How were you treated by the police and ICBC after the accident?
>
> R: No different from anyone else, I guess. [Male, fifty-five to sixty-four]

The greatest number of criticisms about fair play and insurance were recorded by women. The men were more inclined to negotiate settlements, and be minimally satisfied with the interaction and settlement.

Spin-Off Learning from the Accident

A question asked of the elderly drivers was, "Some people think that even unpleasant things that happen to us can teach us something. Did you learn anything from your accident?":

> Learn? I learned not to take a sleeping pill that late at night. I've had so many accidents this year, lately I've . . . I went down to my husband's , I fell and split my head open and broke my wrist, just a couple of months later. Then I fell out of a car and I fell on my head and I thought I knocked myself out, I'm telling you it's just I'm always rushing though; I don't have time for anything. [Female, fifty-five to sixty-four]

The illustration, although real, was not part of any articulated pattern of thinking. Still, it underlines the fact that some residual learning can happen from dramatic episodes. Whether elderly drivers, in retrospect, interpreted their crashes as learning experiences indicates another stepping stone of how seniors perceive themselves as drivers.

Although some elderly drivers stated unequivocally that they learned "nothing" from their dramatic crashes, many reported that they did. Their lessons represent prevailing themes which provide a form of rationality to their driving behaviors.

I Learned To Be More Careful Making Turns at a Crossing. Needless to say, learning to make turns more carefully suggests some thought about the event in which elderly drivers considered themselves to be responsible or feel a little guilty. Take, for example, the left-hand turn. Statistics tell us this is a serious cause of accidents for which the elderly are usually held responsible. It requires good judgment, a critical eye and sound coordination. Above all it requires extra care:

> Yes I think so, ah, certainly on that particular corner I don't even turn left now without coming to a complete stop and if a car is turning left in front of me I don't care what happens he's gone and there is a clear road right down the way.

> So I certainly on left hand turns I will never ever ever turn left again without, without me being extra careful and being able to see. [Male, fifty-five to sixty-four]

One elderly driver was more precise when he discussed the lesson he learned about making left-hand turns. In the future he would not "inch" or edge the front of the car into the stream of oncoming traffic.

> It is a good idea if you are making a turn, and there's heavy traffic, fast traffic, that, um, that you should not point your wheels in the direction of your turn and until you are making, starting your turn. [Male, sixty-five to seventy-four]

One woman has "learned" not to make left-hand turns ever again:

> Yes, I sure learned. Don't make any left hand turns, and I don't do it very often anyway. But, I did take particular notice when I was driving, down, I was coming down 16th Avenue, at how many people that make a left hand turn there. And, down as I was coming along, like I had all, I could see that as plain as anything. There was no need for me to try and try to get around, just get around something like that. Driver's trying to get in front of me, the way her car was driving. [Female, fifty-five to sixty-four]

What about right-hand turns? Several elderly drivers learned to be more cautious while negotiating such maneuvers. Witness:

> I learned to, ah, be more cautious on those turns which I've done ever since but, ah, on the right hand turn especially, the left hand turn ain't too bad because you got the whole middle but in the meantime too you know you got to watch on the other side. There's an awful lot of things to watch you know but that's you do that automatic it's not a matter, ah, you do it every day it's just automatic for you to look in your mirror and watch your rear end. [Male, fifty-five to sixty-four]

I Learned to Be More Careful. Culturally speaking, great faith is placed in the ritualistic rule, "patience is a virtue." But, in traffic with so many stimuli hitting drivers every moment and with motorists trying to arrive at their destinations in acceptable periods of time, patience easily turns to impatience. Nevertheless patience, as a basic life construct, is typically interpreted differently by people.

Patience can be located within specific situations. Stop signs, for example, require patience for proper traffic assessment and wariness. After a person has a crash at a stop sign, reflections on patience may be inevitable. For one victim, the crash served as a refresher course:

> I'll take more time at, ah, a stop sign out of this. You bet. I generally always do, but it just happened that time, and well I don't know, it's just all excuses you

> know. Everybody can make lots of excuses but it's just an excuse, I was in a hurry to get going I guess, you know. But I didn't see him a bit, until I got out in the middle of the intersection, in fact, I didn't see him then because I was looking ahead, and wham right into the side of the door. [Male, sixty-five to seventy-four]

Entering a main artery from a side road also requires forebearance. It may demand so much that it can easily be exaggerated. Witness:

> Oh yeah, you see somebody coming you wait there even you have even if you have to wait there for half an hour. And that's what it comes to you know. [Female, fifty-five to sixty-four]

To be patient means not taking chances. This was a descriptor the elderly often used to describe themselves as drivers in Chapter Seven. It means making decisions on the basis of safe conditions. Learning to be more patient means taking even fewer chances than before. One elderly man reflected on his personal experience:

> Well, thinking, thinking the thing over I don't, ah, I only did what I, what I, I thought I was clear because I looked both ways and it's one of those stops where you that's, that's the thing you do you stop and wait. The only thing I would have done over that I learned by the accident is that, and I know that it would never happen again, is that I should have absolutely more patience. That's one thing I learned about it I learned that, ah, we all have to have a lot more patience. I know my daughter is far more patient than I am. But I guess it runs in the family but, ah, the thing is that's one thing I learned about it. [Male, sixty-five to seventy-four]

I Learned to Drive More Slowly. The generally accepted stereotype of elderly drivers as "slowpokes" makes it a little difficult to conceive of them as speeders. Whereas in focus groups over half of the elderly indicated that they are likely to speed, particularly on highways, the victims of serious crashes did not mention speeding per se. Rather they learned to slow down to more convenient speeds. Legal or maximum speed limits were not part of the conceptual apparatus interviewees used whenever they spoke about driving more slowly.

One interpretation of "slowing down" was the anticipation of a signal light about to change, or as a woman within the fifty-five to sixty-four year old age bracket announced, "I certainly will slow up when I figure there's going to be a yellow light."

Slowing down may also reflect the immediacy of driving conditions and the presence of signal lights. To illustrate:

> Well, I probably should have slowed up sooner. Well, I wasn't going fast, I mean I wasn't trying to gun it through the yellow light. But, I suppose maybe

> I should have been going slower because of the conditions. I don't know. I took the blame on it, but, ah, now I'm beginning to wonder whether I should of put some of the blame on the other fella too. And, they were asking me at ICBC about that, whether maybe the other guy was 25 percent at fault. I have to go and see about that yet. [Female, fifty-five to sixty-four]

So, as she revealed later, the woman learned to drive more slowly when approaching a traffic light that is turning or could be about to turn amber. Also, driving at reduced speeds in conditions such as "gravel roads" and rain was a lesson learned by her and other accident victims alike.

I Learned to Be More Alert. Alertness is a driver quality that cannot be sufficiently underscored as to its importance. One senior motorist learned to become more alert, that is, he learned to keep his wits about him during long trips:

> Well let's see. Well if I learned anything it would be to be more alert, it's possible you know. A person isn't always alert when they're driving you're driving along and you might go for miles and miles and be in a sort of trance. [Male, sixty-five to seventy-four]

Operating a motor vehicle requires a clear mind. This was a principle offered by some victims. If a driver's attention is not entirely directed at driving he is not considered to be alert. Alertness may be difficult to learn in light of the mind's constant wanderings:

> Well I think I learned to be a little more careful, and a little bit more alert. I think maybe, ah, sometimes you have something else on your mind that you, ah, I couldn't foresee it, and so, ah, you know it may hurt and take great lengths to keep looking both ways and always, you know, but, ah, even if I have to wait a little while, to cross over. Sometimes cars are coming so fast that, you know, you don't realize how fast they are coming. [Female, fifty-five to sixty-four]

or in terms of concentrating on other objects such as street signs or certain buildings.

I Learned to Be More Cautious and Careful. Caution and care were two factors prevalent in the verbal accounts. A review of the following response gives meaning to the claim:

> I can't say whether I learned anything or not. I think I've seen almost everything that happens on the road. If I had seen the accident coming, I probably could have learned something from it. The only thing that I could say is that you probably learn to be much more cautious and much more visually aware. I think that I was very aware of what was going on because I use the road quite often. [Male, sixty-five to seventy-four]

Regardless of how cautious elderly drivers felt they were before the crash, there was ample room to improve. They learned to be "a little more cautious" or "a little more careful." They now "look twice instead of once" and are more careful around "corners" and "stop signs." Intersections, also, were selected for extra treatment of care.

> Well, like I said, I am very cautious when I come up to a crossing now. Ah, also that I figure probably I'll think it over, right away before, ah, how much of the blame was mine, and how much was the other guy. Because, I took all the blame because I figured that I was in the wrong, not realizing that there is a difference in that light. [Female, fifty-five to sixty-four]

Some elderly driver claims about learning to be more cautious lay on a bedrock of meaning that they have always been cautious. It is their driving motif. Learning lessons from the accidents did not negate the original assumption held by most of the victims that they are basically cautious and careful drivers. Now they have become even more safe.

Among the volumes of comments were other strategic learning objects such as "leaving more space between cars," "watching the next guy all the time," "being more of a defensive driver," and "being more watchful."

The impact of learning is open to discussion. For one elderly man the learning was short term, six months to be exact:

> Oh yes. Well I did although I'm not so sure because I had one about six months later. However, when you're familiar with your own territory and, ah, you're inclined to relax and you're home now and, ah, the other one happened just turning in here eh? And I came down 20th and up on 51st to the Crescent and it's 200. And a young fellow had an idea he was, he saw the traffic and he was going to bypass it. He zoomed up on the inside. No, by the time you get your signal lights on and put your other signals lights on it was dusk too. And I didn't use my rear view mirror enough and in fact the bump is still on the car. So I was 75 percent to blame for that one. So the problem is yes you have, you must avoid left hand turns wherever possible. Go around the block. So I didn't feel bad about that and I don't feel that nervous. It makes my wife a little nervous though. [Male, sixty-five to seventy-four]

Life-Style Characteristics

That accidents are not isolated, single-cause events, has been stated so often that the message by now appears superfluous. This section explores the many subtle and visible features of life that are dramatically exhibited and that are possible preludes to the main event—driving, or driving toward an accident.

Use of the Automobile

Our society is a mobile one. Witness the planning of urban centers with their shopping parks, freeways and roadways, parking locations, and so forth.

Within such a society, personal independence is linked with personal mobility, which increases dependence on the automobile. This reality impacts the elderly. Witness the following comment:

> This is my transportation to Vancouver, unless I go on the Skytrain. But if I go on the Skytrain, I walk three or four blocks and I have to take the bus, the Skytrain and then another bus and then walk two blocks to where I'm going you know. [Male, fifty-five to sixty-four]

More specific to the elderly, retirement or preparation for retirement is a widely recognized event. It requires adjustments in coping with financial difficulties and leisure opportunities. Leisure, for the philosopher Plato, is an ideal where people free themselves of mundane, bothersome routines—from tedious physical labor. Intellectual and artistic pursuits are cultivated. However, the leisure status experienced by the elderly may not be one of free will, a decision strategically made. It is more likely the result of a drift, where they begin to plan their lives after having had their work lives cut. In short, the elderly learn leisure through the years, during which time the automobile is a vital component. Pleasure driving can be the modus operandi for leisure times. Witness:

1. I: What do you usually use your car for?

   R: Strictly pleasure and that's all I've got it insured for. No more back and forth to work. Now it's back and forth to the golf course.
2. Just for pleasure I might think. My wife drives it mostly too, I drive the pickup truck.
3. Purely personal driving. I'm retired so I don't go to work even.
4. Oh, oh just just for pleasure. And that particular day I was just taking it down to have the front end checked on it.

From work to retirement to leisure tends to be the chronology underlying people's senior years. Leisure, according to the senior motorists, includes activities such as driving for pleasure, visiting friends and family, engaging in organized hobbies or sport activities such as curling and golfing, going dancing and/or going fishing. The central factor that actualizes such possibilities is the availability and use of a car.

However, leisure or pleasure cannot replace the need to get things done. Elderly people cannot withdraw from the chores of shopping or doing household errands. The tedium of daily life necessitates use of a vehicle. Shopping, banking and running errands are functions routinely mentioned alongside pleasure:

1. I: What do you usually use your car for?

R: Just pleasure, running around getting groceries and stuff like that. [Female, fifty-five to sixty-four]

2. Just pleasure, shopping. The wife and I go across the line sometimes [U.S. border]. No long trips. [Male, sixty-five to seventy-four]

3. I: All right. What do you usually use your car for?

   R: Just to go curling and, ah, pick up groceries. [Male, sixty-five to seventy-four]

The conditions of life-span drift tend to be more prominent for elderly women than men. More women than men elaborated on the need to continue routine activities that entailed total involvement—beyond leisure or pleasure. They were more inclined to perceive themselves as doers—getting chores done. Retirement was not part of their lexicon. They had to:

1. Go grocery shopping, errands, going down to Guildford and pick up things. [Female, sixty-five to seventy-four]
2. Do regular chores. [Male, fifty-five to sixty-four]
3. Like, um, during school days I bring my, I get my granddaughter from school, and then when I go to church, and when I go to the hospital, and once in a while when I go visiting friends, I go and my sister lives in Burnaby, and all around. [Male, sixty-five to seventy-four]

That elderly women are inclined toward purposeful uses of the automobile was evident when women spoke of salient interests they had for the utility of the automobile. Three women over the age of seventy-five conversed:

1. Um, for errands such as going to the bank, getting my groceries and, ah, any calls that I might have to make on friends, not many of those, but I am using it every weekend to go to   , because my husband is in the hospital there.

2. I: What do you usually use your car for?

   R: Well it's just pleasure I use it, I guess more for I belong to the hospital auxiliary and I go to meetings and I take some a couple of the ladies with me and we have different things at the hospital that they put on for the patients.

   I: Uh huh.

   R: And uh so and then we meet at their homes every month and uh oh different things we do see them.

   I: Hmm.

   R: And that's my hobby something to do helping somebody.

   I: Helping somebody, great.

   R: And I visit I visit the hospital patients.

3. I'm not taking on as many things you see but I still take quite a number of friends pick them up and get them to the doctors and the hospital. The young lady who called me she just a moment ago she depends on me . . . and she and her sister who's not well. I take them wherever they wanted to go in other words I sort of taxi them and I've done quite a bit for a lot of people and, ah, I feel that I'm competent and capable to do it. When I feel I'm not believe me I'll be the first to stop. Because I don't want to get in an accident.

Age and activities thereof appear to be closely aligned. Women over the age of seventy-five are as involved in driving their cars for social participation as are elderly women in junior age groups. Witness some more sample comments:

1. Well I must have had a good day to go down and get my niece and take her shopping you know you don't do those things if you feel sad so I must have been pretty much all right. I go out every day up to the hospital to see my mother she's . . .
2. For private business, to see my friends take my friends or going to church.
3. Ah, well I guess most people call it pleasure, I go in to see my daughters, and I go over to Langley and, ah, and, ah, the Surrey shopping centres, and downtown White Rock. I've gone down to, ah, as far as Lynden with my car.
4. R: Ya, you know we find watches, and lots of lots of those cheap rings, that the kids have in popcorn boxes, and I found a wrist watch at, ah, a Timex, down at White Rock beach, well where we make the money is all the beer bottles and stuff we find. Sometimes a couple of dollars a day, in bottles and cash them in, and the money goes in the jar, so I use the car a lot for, um, driving into parks with a metal detector, and I go swimming over at Maple Ridge, a couple times a week.

   I: Well, that's quite a distance.

   R: Ya, I take the ferry at Fort Langley, it's 11 miles to the ferry from here to you know Fort Langley. I take the ferry across, up the hill and you're there. I do that a couple times a week. My son and I go to Golden Ears Park, ah, it just depends on how he feels whether he drives over, and I drive back. One usually drives over, and one comes back, so we hike up to . . .

While for some elderly people driving the automobile is considered to be the recreational goal, for the majority of the elderly the car is merely a means to another end. They use the vehicle for higher priority goals like engagement in pleasure-related events, involvement in shopping, running errands, participation in volunteer or charitable activities sponsored by churches or hospitals, assistance for other people and provisions for health care as in visiting doctors or dentists. Discontinued use of the car would limit elderly people's life-style possibilities. For, as one elderly man related, "it's my lifeline."

The assumption of a mobile society is that mobility or efficiency of mobility means availability of automobiles. Other than that, mobility means alternative transportation such as buses. The following is a case illustrating the thesis:

> I: And if you couldn't drive at all how would you manage your trip?
>
> R: Ah, well, I suppose I would have to get up about two hours earlier and take the bus, ah, for instance, ah, okay you take a place I worked at that's, ah, say on the corner of Willingdon and, oh, Canada Way now how do I get a bus from here to there?
>
> I: I have no idea.
>
> R: Well I would have to, ah, either take the, ah, bus from here pick up the LRT get off, ah, somewhere on around Kingsway and Willingdon and then try and find a bus that would take me down Willingdon and so on. Ah, if for instance I wanted to get to another place that I worked at which is the corner of Hastings and Boundary, ah, there is no direct bus route okay I would have to take a bus from here to Guildford and then take a bus from Guildford to Hastings. Now another place I worked at was in Coquitlam and there is no bus route from Surrey to Coquitlam, okay, and I can never understand why they don't put one in because I feel that there is a lot of people going over the Port Mann Bridge that would far prefer to go on a bus. But the only buses that go over the Port Mann Bridge they don't stop until they get to Hastings. So anybody who wanted to get into the Coquitlam area and that's building up there's a big industry over there, ah, there's no way they can do it on the public transport. [Male, fifty-five to sixty-four]

In modern society, self-help and individual effort are prime sources of social stability. The automobile figures in this design. People who have depended on a car for most of their lives and are in danger of losing their driving privileges would have to renegotiate life patterns. Previous possibilities or taken-for-granted social activities become tentative. The coordinates motorists use to map their personal terrains need to change. So, if or when the elderly drivers are threatened with the loss of their cars, how would they replot their life terrain? The question really is, How is life possible for elderly drivers who have lost their vehicles? This question is thoroughly addressed below.

Elderly Drivers' Attractions to Their Vehicles

The elderly drivers' attractions to their vehicles reflect social stratification. The attraction to, and purchase of, their present cars may be considered in terms of wealth. Some elderly drivers who have, or had at the time of purchase, no concern about finances chose more expensive cars like Oldsmobiles and Buicks. They bought them because:

1. . . . it certainly was a beautiful car, one of the top models. [Buick Skylark] [Male, fifty-five to sixty-four]

2. Well it just came in on the lot, and the salesman told me that's the car for me. [Oldsmobile] [Male, fifty-five to sixty-four]
3. I have two friends and they're my age one year two year difference and they both have one and, ah, they both told me how they just absolutely adore it you know and the, ah, the second one the first one she got hers for Christmas I guess the second one I got in her car and it was night and I said there's a lot of room in this car "I just love it" she said "I drove all the way down to Phoenix" and I don't do that and the same with—she said "I drove all the way up to my cabin." [Buick] [Female, fifty-five to sixty-four]
4. I: What attracted you to the car you own now?

   R: Well actually, I wanted to get a Chrysler V8. They're comfortable and what not. The thing that really attracted me to this one was, ah, it was different, I've got a computer.

   I: A computer?

   R: Ya, it tells you if your gas is getting low, and your oil is getting low, or a dozen of other things, door's ajar, and sometimes you get annoyed. [Female, sixty-five to seventy-four]

For most elderly drivers, however, there was a shared awareness that economics was and still is the primary variable that influenced the purchase or maintenance of their present cars. The criteria of attractive economics was purchase price. Witness:

1. The Ford. I guess price played a part. I got it for a good price. [Female, sixty-five to seventy-four]
2. Well, I got a pretty good deal on it. I got a good deal on my Mazda, which was three years old. I've been changing cars about every three years. In war times I could give it a piece of haywire, and wire them up. But, nowadays you can't do that. [Male, seventy-five plus]
3. It's something I've discussed a few times. Ah, the car, ah, well the fact that it was a stationwagon of course attracted me, the fact that it was the only car available, ah, that I could afford. Those two factors I think both of us had very little choice as far as color or size or anything. That is mostly determined by what we have in our wallets, huh huh. [Male, sixty-five to seventy-four]
4. They wanted eight and I offered them seven, or six I guess it was, and I went home and they, I wasn't home five minutes and they phoned me back and said "If that's what you want to give us you can have it for that," that's why I bought it. [Male, fifty-five to sixty-four]
5. We needed a new car and the price was right. It was new, left over from the year before so we got a good deal. [Female, fifty-five to sixty-four]

The flip side of economy, gas mileage, was a major factor a group of elderly accident victims considered relevant in their discussions on their present cars:

> It would be about, like I can go up to M____ and back for about $25 in the Honda, and my other car was $100. It makes quite a difference. [Male, seventy-five plus]

> Ah, I have driven bigger ones sure if you're going on a long trip the big one is a lot better. But for just driving around here and going shopping and, you know, going to work a small car I feel is a lot more economical. [Male, fifty-five to sixty-four]

> It's a good commuter car, easy on gas and pretty reliable. I go into Vancouver every day for work. [Male, fifty-five to sixty-four]

> . . . My husband, the gas mileage, the economy of it, it was his idea to buy it and not mine and now that we have it I love it, I wouldn't drive anything else. [Female, fifty-five to sixty-four]

Economy is change. Some interviewed participants who formerly drove large American cars such as Buicks, Oldsmobiles, or Chryslers have, in recent years switched to small Japanese cars because of economics. For some, the small foreign cars are thought of as:

> Reliable and really economical. I can drive, you know, a thousand miles for under $30. I mean these, these, Japanese cars are just so far ahead of the cars we had a few years back you know. Over the years some of the cars only had about 35,000 miles. You know the doors and the hinges didn't work right and the smoke. These cars today are good. [Female, sixty-five to seventy-four]

A Japanese van is considered more economical than an American one:

> Well I was, ah, the car I had before was a Dodge and a V8, and it used a lot of gas, that was one of the main reasons I switched to a smaller Japanese model because, ah, they were very economical and, ah, I liked the size of the van because it's, ah, it has a small cargo bay, and it's versatile. I can roll the back seat forward if I want to carry something a little larger, and the back seat is, ah, you know extra passengers if I want, or, so it's quite a versatile little vehicle, yet it's also economical to drive, it almost drives itself. I really enjoy that car. [Male, sixty-five to seventy-four]

Economy, plus versatility and engineering, produces a sum which makes the foreign subcompact an attractive alternative for some elderly discussants. The three benefits became major reasons why some drivers bought their present vehicles, and why they would in the near future hesitate in changing to an American model.

The transition from large to small car had its countertheme. Occasionally the trend was for senior motorists to change from small to large cars. Evidence from the interview data suggests that a small group of elderly drivers considered big cars to be safer than small cars. Large means solid, well-built vehicles with power to "get out of tight spots." Some meaningful discussion points raised were:

> It's a great, comfortable car and I guess if one wanted to look at it from the safety point of view, which I never really worried about in the past, anyway, it's a very solid car from the point of view of anybody hitting it or . . . [Male, sixty-five to seventy-four]

> Is the solidity, ah, it was solidly built, and the size of it. The distance between the, ah, the back of it and the cab, is you know, I guess rear-ending like that. The only two accidents I've ever had in my life have been two rear-enders, so we figure that that's, ah, this is a safety feature and, ah, that's why. [Male, sixty-five to seventy-four]

> Actually the car I own now my husband bought for himself. And I have a 1978 Oldsmobile. He wanted a heavier car. So I sold my car to one of my sons, and took my husband's car. I really like this car. It's easy and you feel really good while driving it. The car he just bought is a really heavy car, it's a 1988 Oldsmobile. While mine was getting fixed up I only had his car to drive. I noticed the difference in his car and my car but I got used to his car. It was a heavy car and as easy to manipulate. He says the new car is really easy to handle. He traded his old car in for this one. You feel confident in that car like in my car. [Female, sixty-five to seventy-four]

For the young, illness is looked upon as a transitory problem. For most people, becoming older means having health problems or physical ailments that stay. Based on health reasons, some elderly drivers selected certain cars. For example:

1. . . . the hospital, and I had a new hip in so I wasn't too mobile. That seemed easier to get in and out of than some of the other cars. It felt really comfortable, had an adjustable seat that I could you know a seat that you could? And I think that had a big bearing on it. A very very good friend of ours is a Chrysler dealer in Edmonton and he highly recommended that particular car. That had a bit of influence too. [Male, seventy-five plus]
2. Oh ya. I have I had a mastectomy too so I, and my arm gets sore so I had power steering and power everything in mine except power windows, I don't care about those. So I had to have power steering that was another thing that I wouldn't buy a car without it. [Female, sixty-five to seventy-four]
3. Well, it's hard to say, I would like to have a a sedan or something but now in my days they are so low built it's hard to get in and out. [Male, sixty-five to seventy-four]
4. I wanted a four door car because I don't like, you know, when you have, ah, my mother is still around so you have to have a car that older people are easy to get in and out of. [Female, fifty-five to sixty-four]
5. Ah, it's easy for parking it doesn't take much space it's cheap on gas, you know, and, ah, like four doors it's not that hard especially to close them when you get in the car like I used to have a one door before, ah, it used to be hard on me. [Male, fifty-five to sixty-four]
6. I'm restricted to automatics but not to glasses. I use my glasses but I don't really need them. My hearing is not too bad, except when I'm talking to people. [Female, sixty-five to seventy-four]

Other common features that attracted the elderly drivers' to their present vehicles was dependability, good visibility, nice looks, convenience (especially for small trucks and vans), ease of entry and handling. The latter was usually attributed to the convenience of automatic transmissions. Some elderly drivers prefer automatic transmissions because of poor health and lack of patience with manual gearshifts. Whereas a few would not drive cars with standard transmissions, others could not. So often the choice of car was made after having heard through word-of-mouth about a car's attractive features or through direct influence of a family member, most often a son or a close family friend. Allegiance was an attribute mentioned. Some senior motorists continued to deal with their previous car dealers because the latter had formerly sold the elderly cars that had the attractions they liked, needed, and appreciated.

Possibilities of a Next Car

Factors elderly drivers considered to be relevant for owning their present cars also appeared in the answers to the questions, "What kind of a car would you buy next time you buy one?" and "Why?" However, structures of answers showed some noticeable differences between groups. These central themes are designated by our three age groups.

Accident Victims Aged Fifty-Five to Sixty-Four. The first noticeable imprint in the data was that most drivers within this age group do contemplate purchasing another car. For some, however, it will be the last car:

> No, as a matter of fact I think, ah, we are on our last vehicles as far as, ah, depending on my health and my wife's health but, ah, I think we, the Buick, will certainly last us for just, ah, well we want to use it around here and you know and any trips that we might want to take in the Buick, ah.

But for the majority of drivers a new vehicle is definitely possible or probable. The major criteria for selection and purchase are staying with the same make of car whether it be large or small, changing to a smaller vehicle for economic purposes, or changing to a larger car for safety and protection. There was no uniformity in the responses. The interests of the fifty-five to sixty-four year old victims varied extensively.

Accident Victims Aged Sixty-Five to Seventy-Four. The most obvious difference between drivers within this age group and the younger age group is that many motorists now seriously consider their present car to be their last one. Economic stability, declining health, and progressive aging were prominent structures of reasoning for keeping the present car, allowing it to become the last car.

However, if the elderly could select a new automobile, they would consider brand name continuity as the major factor for making a decision. They would likely select the same vehicle they presently own. Moreover, some would make the selection on the basis of patriotism. American cars were often considered because they are "big, safe, and dependable," and as one interviewee felt, "I owe it to America to buy a North American car." Foreign compact cars, however, were still chosen most often as the new car—if there was a next time. As is self-evident by now, economics and dependability were the prominent reasons for deciding on a new car. But few people within this age bracket planned to shop for a new car. Their present models will serve them for the rest of their lives.

Accident Victims Aged Seventy-Five Plus. As might be expected, the "next" car for these people is likely to be the present car. For most drivers older than seventy-five, the car they presently own will last them. One of the reasons, besides recognition of age, is that because they do so little driving, the present car is and will stay in good shape. Many cars only have a few miles on them. So, why bother thinking about the next car? One elderly woman considered her present car to be:

> Such a nice one. Um, yes, I rather think that my days of driving are probably limited, and that my car will outlast me.

Others would choose the same model they are presently driving. The price of purchase is the key reason. A small group of very elderly drivers, although happy with their present car, would buy a new one. It is part of optimism for the future. To illustrate this theme, read the following colorful discussion:

> I: So you really didn't use it that much.
>
> R: No, once in a while I'll take it over town, well through town, 'cause I have a couple of sisters, one lives in Burnaby and the other lives out on Lake Road, and we'd drive over there.
>
> I: That's where we live in Burnaby. So you aren't thinking of buying another car next time? Um, you're not going to buy another car?
>
> R: Oh no, of course, ah, how old do you think I am?
>
> I: Well you don't look, um, well my father is seventy-three, he just had his birthday, maybe you're a little older than my dad.
>
> R: How much older do you think?
>
> I: O.k., I'll say seventy-five.
>
> R: Huh?
>
> I: I'll say seventy-five.
>
> R: I'm ninety-two tomorrow.
>
> I: Tomorrow's your birthday and you're ninety-two?
>
> R: Ya.

Losing the Car

Given the fact that the automobile is heavily used by elderly drivers for managing everyday routines, we could assume that removal of the car would create major disruptions in the elderly people's lives. Although faithful for some people, by and large the assumption is untenable. True, the automobile is a necessary part of life or even the elderly person's "friend." And, true again, the automobile is well used by elderly drivers. But the influential variable not considered in the equation is flexibility.

If we envision the elderly drivers' lives as theatrical performances, the car is an important prop for the drama. If we remove the present prop, the drama changes with new props. The organization of life around the car would mean a reorganized life-style. Certainly inconvenience and disgruntlement would result. And in some cases major life changes would be considered. However, the car, which the elderly along with other citizens hold in awe, often holds a condition of meaning that is not finite. The car is not an ontological structure. It is an object of meanings that can change when life circumstances change. To support this rule, a variety of cognitive styles found within interview discussions are delineated. Some correspond to the views expressed by the elderly in focus groups, while others show marked differences.

On the Buses, or Not. Buses or other forms of public transportation are considered by many to be viable alternatives to the automobile. In Chapter Seven, we reported that about 25 percent of the discussants would likely become bus riders if they were to lose their rights to drive. Moreover, 20 percent would relocate their homes closer to bus lines. The snag in comfortably using buses is geography/demography (where the person lives—rural, suburb, urban, etc.); timeliness (when the system operates); costs (how much the traveller pays); and routes/destinations (where the buses come from and go to). Most of our interviewees lived within the urban/suburban regions of Vancouver, where bus travel is available. But the extent to which it serves the needs of the elderly is questionable.

A conventional response to the probability of losing the car was to take the bus. Elderly drivers sensed that, with the loss of their vehicle, features of life would change; for example, not being able to visit certain people or to go certain places. Still, the elderly drivers could cope:

1. Well, I think, I think I'd be flexible that way, I'm quite sure that I could work in you know, I wouldn't mind catching the bus, I don't think so, but then like I say it would change my way of shopping and doing things I'm sure because, you know. [Female, fifty-five to sixty-four]
2. Ya, it is, you know, even like going visiting, you know, it would mean that you have to catch the bus and only transfer and, you know, it's I think but I'm sure you know if you have to do it you have to do it, and I think that I could cope with that too. [Female, fifty-five to sixty-four]

3. R: No, I mean if I didn't have transportation there is other ways of getting around, it doesn't bother me a bit about the price of gas, no.

   I: So you would take a bus?

   R: Oh sure I'd take a bus.

   I: Yeah, you're pretty versatile as far as transportation use?

   R: Yeah, I'm not that far away. I can get on the bus anytime from my house or from my work anytime. [Male, fifty-five to sixty-four]

4. No I don't suppose it would, it wouldn't make, except in bad weather because my, I suppose I'd learn to use a bus. Do you know I've never been on a bus since I came to Vancouver. [Female, seventy-five plus]

5. R: I probably would move out of here and get where I could be close to a bus line. Well, I prefer to be able to drive yes.

   I: But if you couldn't then you'd probably. . . .

   R: I'm adaptable. [Female, fifty-five to sixty-four]

6. R: Oh, well, I guess it would be a different style of life-style altogether, wouldn't it. Ha ha. I may have to depend on the bus, which I'm fortunate, I'm, you know, quite close to a bus stop here on Fraser Highway, but still I think it would be kinda hard because all my life, I've had that independence of taking the car going whenever I want, eh, and come whenever I want. So it would be, it would be quite a different life-style I think. I don't just how it would affect me, ha ha.

   I: How about getting on a bus, do you mind getting on a bus?

   R: No, I don't think I'd mind, but if I had to, you know, do all my shopping and be home, you know, some of the things that I have to shop for, it could, ah . . . [Female, sixty-five to seventy-four]

The degree to which the seniors would adapt to busing is a direct reflection of "where" the bus route is located and "when" the bus arrives and departs. Although the interviewees would consider taking public transportation, they do not wish to "wait for the silly buses." More restrictive yet is the time the last bus makes its run in the evening. To compensate, one elderly woman would consider moving closer to a bus line. Although it would be unsettling, still it would be more convenient:

R: Uh, if I continued to live here I couldn't go anywhere much at night without walking because the last bus goes out of here about quarter past six between here and White Rock where I can make the connection.

I: So if you moved then it would make not very much difference?

R: Yes it would. If I moved away from here I'd get on a bus line where I'd be close to a bus. [Female, fifty-five to sixty-four]

The frustration of depending on bus transportation was convincingly stated. The simple case of riding a bus as a mode of transportation was not the issue. It was the declared inconvenience. Witness:

1. Yeah, I use to when it was in Canada Way and Willingdon but when they moved over to Coquitlam it took an hour and a half and I, I had to walk, I had to walk. Well, at that time I was on 72nd on the other side of Scott Road. So I had to walk to Scott Road to get the first bus and even then I had to walk a distance. It would take an hour and a half and, ah, over there I can make it in twenty-five minutes. [Male, fifty-five to sixty-four]
2. Well I would have to, ah, either take the, ah, bus from here, pick up the LRT get off, ah, somewhere on around Kingsway and Willingdon and then try and find a bus that would take me down Willingdon and so on. Ah, if for instance I wanted to get to another place that I worked at which is the corner of Hastings and Boundary, ah, there is no direct bus route, okay. I would have to take a bus from here to Guildford and then take a bus from Guildford to Hastings. Now another place I worked at was in Coquitlam and there is no bus route from Surrey to Coquitlam, okay, and I can never understand why they don't put one in because I feel that there is a lot of people going over the Port Mann Bridge that would far prefer to go on a bus. But the only buses that go over the Port Mann Bridge they don't stop until they get to Hastings. So anybody who wanted to get into the Coquitlam area, and that's building up there's a big industry over there, ah, there's no way they can do it on the public transport. [Male, fifty-five to sixty-four]
3. Difference. Because distance first and transportation everyone depends on a car vehicle you know. I mean, you can walk a mile or something but distance and, you know, and buses and bus service is not so great around here that you can jump into a bus whenever you want to go somewhere. [Male, sixty-five to seventy-four]

For many, the bus is a definite alternative. For some it is preferred. For some it is considered. For a few it is out of the question. But when we consider how the transportation system is run and features accident victims attributed to buses, the alternative becomes less plausible. The quality of passengers ("vandals" and "rough, loud people"), or number of passengers on buses (overcrowding and standing) makes bus riding an experience described as "hated" and "dreaded." One man highlights the age difference between most passengers and the elderly:

> No, no somehow I, well, I've never used it in my life so somehow I went a couple of times to Vancouver and you get these bunch of kids in the back and then they start screaming, it's enough. Like once you get older you don't want to be with this, someone screaming at you all the time. You kind of want to be like semi-retired, you want to be left alone you don't want this. [Male, fifty-five to sixty-four]

A woman dislikes the possibility of having to stand on a bus:

> We have much better service than they had when I moved out here, many years ago. Much better service now but, ah, there are so many people commuting here, and they, I don't want to ride a bus if I have to stand. That, I can't do. [Female, fifty-five to sixty-four]

Busing is the least welcomed alternative for several people because, in their opinion, "there is no bus service" in their community. If there was, they would use it. But, as one man stated, "what is the sense of talking about something that is not there?"

Walking. Similar to busing, walking, as a plausible alternative to driving, depends on location. To facilitate continued day-by-day chores such as shopping, walking is considered within proximity of stores. Situational factors set limits on walking. For example distance and topography (hills) are environmental factors that seriously influence participation.

A second major limitation to walking as a necessary rather than voluntary mode of transportation is physiology. Some elderly drivers would like to walk to stores or to the bus stops, but:

> It would make a big difference because we don't have bus, ah, local transportation, you'd have to either walk down to St. Johns or up to [Como light?] and that is either uphill or downhill, like if you go downhill you've got to come back, and going uphill, well you know, and to catch a bus going at my age, that's not easy as that is the walk up a very [?] and, ah, ah, a very difficult time getting up this hill, there's a little place on the corner there, ah, he had a hard time getting up that hill, so it, ah, when I was younger I used to, you know, I used to walk it but now it would, ah, create a lot of difficulty unless we got a bus, some sort of bus service. [Male, sixty-five to seventy-four]

Others would be more motivated to become involved because, for reasons of health and exercise, they were told by doctors to walk. "I'm supposed to have a walk every day according to my doctor" was a comment heard in the interviews.

Although walking was a real option for some elderly motorists, it was not considered a total solution. For short excursions to the store, walking is indeed healthy and expedient. But for longer trips, alternative modes of transport must be arranged. Taxis were mentioned in tandem with walking. But more senior drivers were prone to arrange transportation with friends or family if the day came when they would no longer drive. Taxis are too expensive for most of the accident victims we talked to.

Working. For drivers within the fifty-five to sixty-four year old category, the possibility of not driving is more complex than for members of other age groups. They are still employed. Whereas the older groups can make allowances for everyday driving routines with respect to chores and leisure, members of the fifty-five to sixty-four year old group experience the pressure of being involved in the work force. Their employment reflects time schedules that demand access to a car. The resolution not to drive is a difficult one—nearly impossible.

Those who could would take the bus, even if it meant leaving earlier to arrive on time. Others, however, would feel pressured to move their household closer to the location of employment:

1. Well, M___ couldn't go to work, we would have to live in Coquitlam even if we did live there for twenty-three years. Umm. I go and get my kids. I don't know, I just use it. I can't imagine life without a car. I know someday it will come too. When you get older you can't drive but my mom is eighty-seven and she's still driving her car. [Female, fifty-five to sixty-four]
2. Well, I couldn't get to work unless we moved and I don't want that. [Male, fifty-five to sixty-four]
3. Well, I couldn't go to work or we'd have to move. A car's a necessity. [Male, fifty-five to sixty-four]

One motorist provided an extreme case. There is no reliable bus service near his home. His car is essential for work. Therefore, he believes that without a car his only option is to go on social welfare.

Freedom and Independence. To have and retain opportunities which provide personal outlets does much to improve an elderly person's emotional and social stability. It also can help lessen the stigma attached to aging and, in particular, retirement. The automobile is seen to be a vital ingredient for retaining forms of engagement. Or, decreased mobility of the elderly person fosters disengagement, which can be frustrating and injurious to good morale among the elderly.

The expressions "loss of freedom" and "loss of independence" furnished the background of elderly drivers' feelings about the loss of the automobile. As in the focus group interviewees in Chapter Seven, the two accounts became prevalent documentary themes. The forms of engagements that will have to be modified through loss of the car are hereby illustrated:

1. Um hum. And I belong to a treasure hunters club, which is over by Coquitlam, the West Coast Treasure Hunters Club, I go there all the time, and I belong to the gemology society. [Female, sixty-five to seventy-four]
2. Well he wouldn't, I mean he wouldn't be able to go places or do things you know. And, ah, um, we wouldn't be able to go shopping you know. You need a car for shopping. I mean it's a distance here from the bus. [Female, fifty-five to sixty-four]
3. Well I'd, ah, I'd ride a bus to work I think and, ah, I wouldn't be able to have a recreation vehicle and that would completely change my, ah, social life. And we travel distances from everything to square dancing and everything we do and we travel and use the car a lot, as I say, 20,000 miles a year and, ah, we don't use it, ah, unless there's somewhere where we're going for some interest or some pleasure. [Male, fifty-five to sixty-four]
4. R: I, ah, I don't know, I think that it would be, for me, it would be rather disastrous because I, I've travelled a long way in my car, I've been down

into Mexico and I've been, ah, up to Fort St. John in, ah, British Columbia and, ah, I have been up to, ah, Fort McMurray, beyond Fort McMurray up to, ah, Fort MacKay and, ah, in Northern Alberta and I've been right through to Newfoundland, ah, St. John's, Newfoundland and, ah, by way of [?] and, ah, around the islands and down into the, ah, [?] and then down into California two or three number of times.

I: Boy you really use your car, don't you?

R: And I, ah, do most of my, ah, moose hunting up in the neighborhood of, ah, of Eagle Creek and, ah, Hundred Mile House and Eagle Creek and up into Wells Grey Park and, ah, sometimes when I was going to Alberta, I would go, ah, the Yellowhead or [?] route and sometimes I would go way of Calgary, so I've covered a lot of country.

I: How about just your day to day activities when you're around here without a car. Could you get by without a car around here?

R: I wouldn't want to. I wouldn't want to. I would find it very onerous because the places that I go, ah, usually the bus service isn't very close. I do a lot of walking besides, but my car is a very essential part of my life, as you may well be aware, with over 18,000 kilometers on it on a short time that you can appreciate that I, ah, if I had to try to walk that, ah . . . [Male, sixty-five to seventy-four]

5. Well, even though I don't work, I still continue a great interest in instrumental music. I'm out about three times a week. I play trombone. I'm still very involved. [Male, sixty-five to seventy-four]
6. Yes, it would cut a lot of things down, because people are so, well, scattered, the family is scattered. You wouldn't be able to contact them except by phone. [Male, sixty-five to seventy-four]

According to interviewees, on the one hand some important life-style engagements considered to be necessary for daily life would have to be curtailed. On the other hand, a large group of elderly drivers considered freedom to do things with the car as convenience. And, as with other conveniences, they can be negotiated, altered or cancelled. Some representative comments follow:

1. No. Well, I shouldn't say that really, because you naturally miss the convenience of the car, to go and do your grocery shopping, you don't have to drag it home in that little go-cart or something, but there comes a time in your life if you have to do these things, then you have to do them, and I'm ready to settle, for which many many of my friends do not have cars, at their disposal. [Female, seventy-five plus]
2. No, I don't think so too much, because my husband is retired and, ah, until I learned to drive, I had to rely on him. I like the independence it gives me to have my own car, but no I don't think it would be too upsetting. Nope, it would be all right. [Female, sixty-five to seventy-four]
3. Well I don't know, ha ha, when you're used to this kind of life out here, I don't know if you'd want to, ah, you know, if the time comes, so a person

> would have to, well you'd just have to. But, ah, it would be a different life-style I'm sure, but I don't see why anybody couldn't cope with that, I mean you gotta be reasonable too, don't you? [Female, fifty-five to sixty-four]

4. Well, I would have to stay home more, because like you know, ah, the thing is that having a car, I can go out by myself, but I wouldn't be going out after dark by myself in order to catch a bus to go somewhere. [Female, sixty-five to seventy-four]
5. Well, well of course if I couldn't drive I'd be out of the bowling, that's the main bit of exercise . . . But otherwise the bus is only ninety feet from the door. [Male, seventy-five plus]

Losing the car is a very real possibility but not necessarily a probability for elderly drivers. They know and appreciate this. Many are prepared for the possibility. They are ready to move closer to a shopping center, bus line or workplace. They are prepared to give up certain liberties for the decision. But, it cannot be overemphasized that they would feel a sense of regret, a freedom lost. For some it is major restriction, for others it is entirely negotiable; not necessarily preferable but certainly possible. But one thing is for certain, loss of a car or license is final. It marks a station in life that is irreversible.

Becoming Older, and Changes in Driving Behavior

Everyone ages. Peoples' lives are a series of overlapping and interlocking stage scenes. Each scene represents an experience, the continuity of which makes up their life-histories. Life experiences provide everyone with a storehouse of insight and wisdom which help them traverse present reality and which are essential for planning the future.

As we wade through different experiences, views of self and circumstances are modified. New desires, situations, puzzle-solving solutions and dislikes replace old ones. Individuals evolve through their mind and body to come to terms with life. As one elderly driver said:

> Well, I think, ah, in a lot of respects I am (more careful) because, you know, experience is a good teacher isn't it, when you're driving so many years, you know you can have sort of an idea sometimes what some of these younger drivers are up to and you never know just what they're going to do, so I'm very cautious that way. But other than that, I don't really know what I could say about being more careful. [Male, seventy-five plus]

Continuous reappraisals of successes and failures are made according to "what was," "what is," "what shall be," and "what shall never be."

The behavioral episodes of special concern are the elements of adjustments people aged fifty-five plus have or have not made in driving. Not only are the normal age-changes relevant, but so are the recent experiences of dramatic injury-producing crashes.

Since change may be reflected in age, the data are dissected according to the age categories. Perhaps a trend will appear that will shed new light on the concept of adjustment and driving.

Changes in the Fifty-Five to Sixty-Four Year Olds. The male drivers who discussed driving adjustments concentrated on three prominent themes, not mutually exclusive but overlapping. The first relevant idea suggests that older drivers slow down. However, slowing down is defined according to a bench mark of meaning. For some elderly motorists, although they have slowed down, they still drive at a significant speed. Examine:

1. I: What about you in particular, have you noticed any changes in your driving over the past few years?

   R: A little slower.

   I: A little slower.

   R: A little more cautious, not slow, I still drive the speed limit, but I have a tendency to watch traffic all around me all the time.

   I: Have you always been much the same kind of driver?

   R: Ya. I was involved in a lot of racing at one time, and I built cars, but I wouldn't drive them.

   I: Car racing?

   R: Ya.

2. I: Have you actually noticed any changes in your own driving in the past few years?

   R: Not, ah, not really. I don't think, ah, well I have slowed down. I, ah, probably, ah, I think I'm more cautious than I was before but I certainly don't think I'm, you know, I never was much what you call a speed artist but, ah, I certainly, ah, like to get away but I don't do that anymore and actually I haven't done that for a number of years but, ah, it's just one of those things that this accident, ah, I, ah, just don't understand what went through my mind at the time and I saw green and my wife saw green and I just just don't understand it but, ah, as I said the evidence was against us and so I thought well I'm not going to dispute it at all. Just took my licks.

   I: Yeah. Hoped it wouldn't happen again. Is there anything that you'd like to add to what we've talked about or any comment that you'd like to make?

   R: I think you pretty well covered the total situation and, ah, I just, ah, as I said at the beginning it was quite traumatic and took a little while to get used to and, ah, but I feel quite comfortable driving I don't have any any qualms about it whatsoever and, ah, so.

3. I: And do you think you drive about the same as you did about fifteen or twenty years ago, do you drive about the same speed?

   R: Ah, not quite. I've slowed down a little bit. I used to drive, I used to drive at least, when the speed limit was 100 km an hour, I would drive about 110 you know, ah, now I'm just about, I'll stay at the limit.

   I: But you don't drive under the speed limit?

   R: Well ya, it depends on the conditions I will, ya, it doesn't bother me at all. One time that would bother me, I would travel 100, 110 when I would catch up to somebody I would get a little impatient, I would pull over and pass them, see, depending on the conditions I won't do that now. I'll do that if somebody, if I'm driving ninety-five, I'll never want to do eighty-five, and then there a lot of them passing you.

   I: So do you think you're a little more patient now?

   R: Ya, I'm a little bit more patient than I was when I was younger.

4. I: How about your driving in the past few years? Have you noticed any difference?

   R: Yeah, I've slowed down, I've slowed down. But I think I've slowed down basically because I'm always reminded that we don't have to go this fast. When I drove it was seventy miles an hour not fifty kms or what have you. I'm a little annoyed at that because I'm one of the old ones that have not gone into the metric system.

   I: It's difficult isn't it?

   R: It is, it is and, ah, I won't buy it you know and everybody laughs.

Others just drive more slowly or, stated otherwise, they "don't drive as fast as when they were young." In part they drive more slowly because, as one man said: "I don't think I'm as alert as I was when I was thirty-five or forty, that's for sure."

Driving more slowly was interpreted by another accident victim as driving more conservatively. Furthermore, driving more conservatively suggests increased caution, the second featured theme of change. According to some motorists, they are becoming more cautious drivers. One elderly driver stated:

> I'm a little more cautious that's all. I've never had that many accidents all the time anyhow. Maybe about four all the time I've been driving.

Cautious driving for some means taking fewer chances, while for others it means driving according to your wits. And, the interpretation of loss of wits is "like you put something away and you can't remember where you put it."

The third theme is an all-encompassing one. Some male drivers adjusted their driving behavior according to difficulties they now have which they did not have when they were younger. Consider the following excerpts about driving:

1. After dark I don't enjoy it anymore especially if it is raining. But it never used to bother me before.
2. Yeah I slow down quite a bit, ah, I have slowed. I can't say in my younger days that I was that good a driver. It was this sort of saying "I got size Charley, move" you know and, ah, that sort of thing but I think as time has gone on and then I'm converting from driving big cars to driving a small one. I think that also has something to do with it. Because in a big car you're a lot more at ease a lot more comfortable.
3. No, I think the one thing that makes me feel comfortable is when I'm driving on the freeway basically, ah, I watch other drivers doing things that could cause a serious accident like cutting in without signalling, ah, weaving in and out of traffic and, ah, I can't say I never did the same myself I did when I was younger. But now that I'm older I see the folly of it and, ah, how you are going to get the message across is a pretty hard thing to say. You know the old story is you owe it to preach to somebody but until something happens to him it isn't corrected.
4. No I guess I, um, I think I've become more patient with, ah, traffic I used to, ah, fifteen years ago I can recall when I started doing the same pattern driving from Langley then into the freeway over the Port Mann Bridge and there was always heavy traffic morning and night and, ah, I would be very impatient and, ah, then I started getting up and getting on the road fifteen minutes earlier and, ah, I noticed that made a big difference. And the traffic didn't seem to be slow at all. That was all. They try to cut the time too short.
5. Change I think. As one gets older, there's a tendency to get tired, there are times (same for me), when your eyes sort of, you have to blink and say, hey I better stop, I better pull over, have a cup of coffee or . . . But I know friends of mine who have fallen asleep at the wheel, on the freeway.

Other interviewees did not detail any changes in driving behavior. According to one motorist, driving "stabilizes and stays pretty much the same once you mature."

Discussions with the women drivers in this age group produced noticeably different points of view. Have there been any driving changes since they have become older? "No, none" was a near universal answer. If anything, some women suggested that they now drive more often, more comfortably, and more patiently. As a rule the latter two are generally considered to be positive driving behaviors.

Changes in the Sixty-Five to Seventy-Four Year Olds. Whereas the men aged fifty-five to sixty-four who were involved in injury-producing accidents stressed reduction in speed, increase in caution, and more attention to the traffic as central adjustments, men within the sixty-five to seventy-four year old group highlighted the amount of driving as the major change in their driving lives. Sixty-five is considered to be the traditional retirement age. So it is natural to assume that men who once travelled the roads to and from work now cease to do so. A review of the following representative excerpts from discussions stresses this idea:

1. Yeah. You see I only drive, ah, well maybe three, four hundred kilometers a month you see?, that's all I drive. Just to go get groceries and stuff and I can walk and it might be better for me anyway.
2. I haven't been driving as far or as long.
3. The only thing I don't, I'm not a driving fool or go along in the car all the time you know like young punks do, they gotta be behind the wheel all the time, you know. To me it's just, just for my own use, you know, for getting groceries, you know, stuff like that. As far as driving and going I used to drive all over the place, you know, all over the place. I worked in the mines for about fifteen years in B.C. and I always had a car and truck and in them days I used to like being on the road, you know, driving.

Less time spent as a driver may mean more time being a passenger. The man's spouse does the honor:

> Well granted, we don't drive as much now that we're elderly, I'm talking about myself. Now she drives the car a lot, and I just ride along, free of charge you see.

Others may also help chauffeur the elderly:

> No, I have noticed in the number of years when I have had students working for me who like to drive, I let them drive; I'm quite happy to be driven. I just say—do you want to drive? And I just give them the keys. It's tiring, and I've done a lot of driving. I no longer want to jump in the car just to go down to the corner store. I have times when I have long drives and you—you feel tired. There are certain times of the day when you're tired (when one feels more tired) especially after eating or . . . Conditions? That doesn't bother me, driving in the snow or rain or that, it doesn't bother me at all. It's not pleasant driving—it doesn't worry me; I'm not the kind of person whose worrying what's going to happen down the road.

Both of the above deliberations touch on voluntary reduction in driving and increasing time as passengers. Yet, how does an elderly person feel about enforced reduction in active driving due to age-related matters? The following segment of conversation provides much needed insight:

R: Well the thing is, ah, the, well I could have made a stink about it and what not, you know, with my, ah, my kids, my two or three sons are, I don't know, I guess they were all in on it. They didn't want me to drive any more.

I: No. Why was that?

R: Well on account of this accident.

I: Yeah, but. . . .

R: But, well I as far as I'm concerned I think I'm still an excellent driver and all the rest of it but it sure, ah, it hurt my ego completely and usually I take the car. I don't drive that much anyway anymore but I usually like to take the car from here and go down and have coffee and so forth and talk and what not. But it, ah, really hurt me in that respect.

I: Yeah, yeah. But don't you miss the car?

R: Oh certainly. I mean the thing is I, ah, that's something that hurt me worse worse of anything because, ah, you know, I mean, and in arguments with my wife and all the rest of it because, ah, that's something that . . .

I: Your wife drives?

R: Oh she drives, yeah.

I: Yeah.

R: Then, see, when I want to go somewhere I can't always go when I want to.

I: She doesn't want to go necessarily?

R: No, no. She doesn't necessarily want to go and so I, I mean that's the part that hurt me worse of anything out of the whole accident, that's why I wish it would never ever happened.

I: How's the transportation around here, I guess how is it? Not very good?

R: No it's not that good, no. And, ah, since I've, ah, on the circulatory system, since I've had, I've had a few operations so I mean the walking is, ah, I can only walk so far and then I, I've got to have more operations I don't know. See about having them soon but anyway that might overcome it.

I: Yeah, what is it—a problem with your knee?

R: Well no, no, it's not my, my knee it's the well for the, ah, the arteries in the legs like in this leg and in that leg and then I had an artery here it was clogged you know?

I: Oh I see.

R: So they, what they did here they just took and, ah, and, ah, pinched it, clamped it at each end like here and there it was about six-inches long and then they, ah, cut it open and scraped the artery and washed it out and sewed it up again.

Enforced adjustment is difficult because the elderly driver has not come to terms with his physical frailty and his altered daily schedule of activities which are heavily reliant on active use of the car.

Some of the men recognized their deteriorating physical state and have already adjusted accordingly. Poorer vision leads to less nighttime driving. Consider:

1. I: Have you noticed any changes in your driving over the past few years?

   R: My night vision isn't what it used to be, that makes a difference.

   I: Do you drive at night?

   R: Not much, we're usually home at night.

2. R: After I got older, past seventy, I felt a bit uncomfortable driving after dark.

   I: Have you always felt like that?

   R: No.

3. Well, actually when I think about it, the last number of years, we don't do too much driving at night hardly. You know as you get older you're a little more cautious I guess and stuff, yup. But I mean there's no problem as far as I know.

"There's no problem" could be considered as the central theme offered by elderly men in this age group. Certainly adjustments have to be made, but once they are made "there's no problem." For many men there never was a problem. There is no marked reduction in driving skill over the ages, only a few adjustments to keep the driving function "well-tuned." Some illustrations follow:

1. I would say in some cases that it's probably true, ah, although in my own particular case is I say I'm a little more defensive, so I think it's improved. Cause I'm a, you know, I'm more cautious probably or more, ah, aware of situations that could develop, even if they don't. But ya, I think that, ah, I can see situations that possibly could be a problem and then I take action to not become involved in that type of situation. But I do think that, ah, some cases, well, ah, but I don't think age is a, I've seen people who are older than us, well I have a sister-in-law who is an excellent driver and she's eighty, and she's an excellent, she doesn't walk too well, but she's an excellent driver. She's driven all of her life, and still drives with no problem. I've seen other people who will, you know, were obviously elderly, and they just look straight ahead, they don't look anywhere. I've watched them through the mirrors, and then I've seen young drivers who will swish in and out and, ah, you know, give you five inches of room when they cut in front of you, ah . . .
2. About the same. Reactions are pretty good yet and, ah, sight is good and, ah, this is mainly what you have to have. Judgment and that come with age. It comes with age. Young guys on the highway now with cars that are overpowered, you get a ticket if you drive too fast. But the cars are capable of speed now that some of them can't handle, their foot's heavy they tramp on it, you can hear it at night, you can hear it all over the city where they're squealing tires and everything else. Overpowering, you don't have to have it. Ah, if you're driving thirty miles an hour you'll get to your destination within minutes of somebody that takes chances at fifty or sixty.
3. I: Okay. What about you in particular. Have you noticed any changes or difference in your driving over the past few years?

   R: No, except that I know I'm getting older so I'm more careful. I like to watch, I know my hearing isn't as good as it used to be and my, ah. . . .

   I: You go a little slower maybe?

   R: Go a little slower, ah, I mean I've, if I was, if I was to feel that I've made any difference in my, to my driving, ah, I would just quit driving. I mean

> I wouldn't take a chance on driving but I don't have that trouble. I, we pulled a trailer and travelled, we've gone 9,000 miles this year travelling and, ah, we don't have any problems.

According to the elderly drivers, the driving adjustments they made were positive changes, enhancing the likelihood of good if not better performance. Taking fewer chances and becoming more cautious makes them better drivers because in their younger years they drove according to the expectations of that generation. In their youth they exceeded the speed limit, tailgated, weaved in traffic, and took chances. Now they are older and do not partake in these activities. As a result they are better drivers. In fact, many extended their judgments by proposing that not only were they improved drivers but they became better motorists than the general driving public. Witness:

> I: How about yourself in particular? Have you noticed any changes in your driving in the past few years?
>
> R: I don't think so, no. I don't think, ah, for instance I noticed today that there is a lot of bumper-riding, lot of cars are within feet of your rear end and I used to be the same when I was young but I don't do that now. And I always used to drive the fast lane when I was young. I don't do that now. So those are changes.
>
> Well, I think that your reactions are probably a bit slower. But I think that a wise person compensates for that by driving a little slower. I think I drive probably five miles an hour slower now than what I used to. Although I think that I can go on Vancouver streets and drive as well as anybody else but I know that on the highways probably fifty cars an hour pass me.

Others have images of being and always having been satisfactory drivers. There was no need to make changes before and there is no need now. A few illustrations clarify the thought:

1. Well it's a pretty, I'm being or judging myself so, ah, the thing is, ah, so, ah, I feel in my mind yes that I that I, I feel that I'm a satisfactory driver . . . haven't changed in particular.
2. Well, I'm going on to seventy-five now and I don't feel any different.
3. Well, I have a friend who's eighty-nine—he's still driving.

Concerning the female accident victims in this age group, their feelings were similar to those of their counterparts in the fifty-five to sixty-four year old age bracket. Few changed their driving behavior. They "don't feel any different behind the wheel":

1. No, I just drive as good as ever. I used to drive a tractor up at the farm and rake the hay. Do everything.

2. I really feel that I'm ready to drive. I wouldn't be if I weren't before.

Rather than adjust for age-related difficulties in driving, some women feel they are now better drivers than before. "I've got a bit more confidence in myself than I had before" answered one woman, while another outlined that after driving slowly for a while, "I'm back up to the right speed."

Compared to the women drivers in the fifty-five to sixty-four year old categories, the women sixty-five to seventy-four years of age were beginning to curtail their amount of driving. For some the decision was based on a judgment of driving capability, while for others it reflected proximity of children. As was said:

1. I: How about sixty-five or seventy?

   R: Well it's getting there, huh huh. I think that's pretty good too, huh huh. If you do things that you know you aren't capable of. . . . I don't think for one thing for myself I don't get in the car and drive like I used to. I used to you know get in my car and drive for five or six hours without even . . . you know but now once you knock over three or four miles you're tired.

   I: How about seventy-five or eighty?

   R: (It's really getting on there). Your reactions have to be slower don't they? And your eyes and your, I certainly see some people driving and I wouldn't want to drive with them and of course it's not always age either. They're no good drivers.

2. I: Hm, close to home?

   R: Yeah, I've curtailed my driving a bit of course there is no need for me to go any other where, because my son is in Richmond and, and does or anything at his place, well my daughter is going anyway so she comes over and we switch cars, huh huh.

   I: And she takes you along with her?

   R: And she takes her car and brings me back so she's good that way

3. Yup, my son lives in New West, and my daugher lives in White Rock. And usually I go up to Prince George, a couple times a year, and go to the lake and go fishing, I use the car there and go with them, and down to Vernon, and down to Montana. But this year I'm, I don't have the, I can't sit that long yet. And then with my second accident, um, my neck gets tired, if I, you know, drive it, like I haven't got the courage to try that far yet.

Others were more apprehensive. As one woman defines this:

I: O.k., what about you in particular, have you noticed any difference in your driving over the last few years?

R: Well, I found that I'm, I'm as I say, like, um, I'm, ah, far more apprehensive than what I used to be, you know, and, ah, I certainly don't take any chances. Sometimes like when you're younger, you think you know take them, but you don't do that anymore. Ha ha. Yup.

I: So you have noticed some difference in the last few years?

R: Well yes, yes. And, like I say, like there are places that I hesitate to go and, ah, because, ah, like I'm not too sure, you know. But sure I don't go whereas before it never bothered me.

For one elderly woman, being more careful means "I see him but I don't know, I think I'll let him come, I'm not in any rush." If a car is a block away she now waits because she has learned by experience to be safer. She has become more attentive:

> O.k., um, let me describe it this way. I think my driving now requires more concentration on the driving. You mentioned a while ago that people often do other things as they're driving, and I have to say myself, that I have to do less and less of that. Now my nature, I was always an individual who could keep 10 things going at once. Um, and I have noticed in the last three years anyway, less and less ability of personability along that line, in everything. Now translating that to driving, um, I need to keep myself more attentive to the subject of driving to the exclusion of other things, other thought processes and other conversations, distractions, etc. I consciously have to do that, try to do it, I think that has become necessary.

Although the women in the sixty-five to seventy-four year old age bracket are becoming more aware of driving adjustments, their predominant image of self as a good driver still has not changed. If any change did occur, it is, overall, for the better. The men were more precise about their adjustments but, similar to the women, most perceived their adjustments to have been made on the basis of strength, not weakness or shortcomings.

Changes in the Older-Than Seventy-Five Year Olds. For the men, a similar pattern of adjustment formulated by the elderly drivers between the age sixty-five to seventy-four held true. The only recognizable difference was the increased emphasis on slower driving and more caution. In fact this change predominated over the reduction in annual distance travelled and in amount of time behind the wheel. Several displays are illuminating:

1. R: No well I'd say I'm just a little more cautious at night.

   I: How about heavy traffic?

   R: Well, heavy traffic, I think you're safer. As long as somebody don't, ah, jump out and try to pass ten cars. Then there's liable to be a pile up at the end or someplace.

2. I: Hmm. Yeah, well what about you in particular? Do you have you noticed any difference in your driving in the last few years?

   R: No I haven't, no I just get in the car and go and doesn't bother me any. I do take more caution, especially since I've had the accident. Maybe I realize that, uh, the old peepers are not are not as good as they should be.

I: Yeah, still feel pretty comfortable?

R: Oh yes, yes and so does the wife. She's a good driver.

I: Hmm yeah.

3. R: Well, I think probably, ah, you have a tendency to slow up a little bit, you don't drive as fast. This is one thing that . . .

I: That you noticed that you did, ya.

R: That happens.

Implicit in the statements was the view shared by the oldest elderly drivers that they were still confident drivers. They considered their skills to be good. One elderly man drives a little more slowly now, but his "health is good and his nerves are excellent." Several men said they are now more cautious, and they believed that their reflexes are sharp, their abilities good and their physical condition excellent. Yet, later in the interviews, one of the same drivers revealed that he blacked out before the accident. Several others looked feeble and frail to the researchers. These drivers ignored their weak and vulnerable physical state. Instead, they complimented themselves about their facility for good driving. No major changes! More importantly, there was no hint or suggestion that they were untruthful or that they were exaggerating. Their view of self tended to mark an idealistic sense of self as a driver, one that was cast in their earlier years.

During the interviews several elderly drivers outlined that although their driving skills declined little due to aging, their trips were now defined according to necessity. Leisure driving has been reduced. The usual trips are to the "nursing home" or to go "shopping." Still they feel confident taking these short but important voyages.

For the women in this age bracket, the operative word is avoidance. Have they noticed any change in their driving ability over the last few years?

> You have to take care in conditions. Traffic is traffic though. I don't want to go into it now. If I got into an accident now it wouldn't make a difference whose fault it was. They'd blame it on me because of my age.

Yet how does she feel about driving a car?

> It's really the only thing that I have felt comfortable with. I've always been confident in driving.

Other examples of avoidance are:

1. I don't go to North Vancouver anymore because the accident happened there.
2. It's the time of day when the traffic is much heavier than other times, and certainly if there's any sign of ice or frost, older people shouldn't go out on the road, because they do not have the reflexes that the younger people have.

3. The fact that the glare, the glare at night bothers me that's another reason why I'll drive at night, um, I don't think I would to be honest I don't think I'd drive into Vancouver at night unless I had to an emergency.

Some newly acquired driving behaviors are described as being more sensible. One elderly woman related that "when you get older you get the sense to hold back. You don't try to challenge or anything." Another woman has become more aware of "difficulties that you have to face in driving." Nevertheless she classified herself as a confident driver.

Driving-Discomfort Generators

Elderly drivers who characterized their driving as confident and capable were further prodded as to what, if anything, made them feel uncomfortable about driving. Ambivalence was evident for some motorists while others were more definitive whenever they were prodded. The discomfort generators were not age or sex specific. For ease of reading, the most noticeable problematic driving features are reported according to prevailing categories.

Night Driving. Night driving creates "flashing headlights" which bother some motorists' eyes. Glare in heavy traffic situations is so distracting that many elderly try to avoid driving during this time. As one man explained, "My night vision isn't what it used to be."

Further problems arise when night driving is compounded by rain. For one woman, "It's hard to see. The windshield never seems to be clean enough." A man over the age of seventy-five combined dark and rainy conditions when he said:

> Well, then there's after dark, ah, when it's raining and dark, ah, well of course, I'm older, my eyes are not as good as yours so I have to be careful that I keep, that I can see the lines, or, of course it's fine if I'm behind, then I just assume, be in a heavy traffic when I'm, in that case, because then I can watch, follow the car ahead of me, more or less you see.

Night and rush-hour traffic appeared to be another focal point of discomfort. One woman (sixty-five to seventy-four) does not drive too much at night because:

> There's too many people out there, too many young people buzzing around causing accidents. I don't go usually in rush traffic.

Embedded in the accounts was the operative word "usually." Because nighttime driving was considered uncomfortable, attempts were made to "usually" avoid it. But, if we recall, the majority of accidents in which these drivers were involved happened at dusk—towards evening in rain conditions.

And, although avoidance of such driving circumstances are preferred by some senior motorists, if the need arises, the elderly are prepared to operate their cars in these conditions.

Other Drivers. A truism about traffic is that the roadway is a social environment. It is designed for mass movement of people. Other road users are a certainty. For a number of elderly drivers they make driving uncomfortable. More precisely, certain types of other drivers are problematic. They are speeders from whom elderly drivers "have to try to get out of the way," tailgaters who are "not leaving enough space" because they "want to get someplace in a hurry," lane changers or "lane snitchers switching back and forth," impatient drivers who "have no courtesy behind the seat or the wheel," risk takers or "drivers that take chances" and "idiots going like crazy . . . sliding and slipping" in the snow.

Rush-Hour or Heavy Traffic. Heavy traffic often brought with it the descriptor "hate." It is something many elderly drivers want to avoid at all cost. One woman does not feel relaxed when she "waits for traffic to go by, and if [she is] going to cross the street." A man does not "trust the other guy" in heavy traffic, while a woman finds it "nerve wracking."

To avoid heavy traffic, some elderly drivers organize their driving schedules around light traffic times. They don't want to "tangle" with people coming from work. One woman (aged sixty-five to seventy-four) said this about rush-hour traffic:

> No, if you don't have to, well why hold up some more of that kind of thing, because people are, I know most of the time, they're in a hurry to get home, and in a hurry to get to work. So if I don't have to drive, which most of the time I don't, unless I have an appointment, I will go, but I try to avoid it if I can.

To skirt heavy traffic on the highway, a possible strategy is to use secondary roads because the traffic is reduced and more evenly spaced. According to one senior driver:

> I'd rather take to a back road and go around because some of these drivers are very careless cutting in and out. That is one of the very dangerous things to do. [Male, seventy-five plus]

Inclement Weather. Poor driving conditions caused by inclement weather would be uncomfortable, for most people, regardless of age. On the Pacific Coast, rain is a fact of life. Not surprisingly, rain causing slippery road conditions is a discomfort generator. This does not mean, however, that elderly drivers necessarily try to avoid rainy driving conditions. Rather, they say they are just more careful.

Snow was mentioned by several elderly as was fog. From a safety perspective, both of these conditions are certainly dangerous.

Bridges. British Columbia's Lower Mainland has at least six major bridges that serve as its lifeline. A person who wishes to enter or leave Vancouver in any direction needs to cross a bridge. The Port Mann bridge, a long-span bridge serving Highway No. 1, was singled out by some victims as the major driving problem:

1. And I'm always, ah, I know when you're driving down on to the Port Mann Bridge and there's ice on it nobody can get stopped at fifty miles an hour if it really was an emergency. Other than that I, it never bothered me, the dark, and I've driven in all conditions. [Male, sixty-five to seventy-four]
2. Oh yeah, very certain about it. I don't like bridges first of all and, ah, especially that bridge. I don't like that one and if I sit up there and the traffic is stopped at the top it's just like being in a barrel, you're not going to get out, you know, I just start to sweat a bit. I just don't like bridges. [Female, seventy-five plus]
3. Ya, that's true. But my track over to Maple Ridge, again, I'm, I know it, I know where all the lights are, I turn left from Langley and go across the ferry, because I will not go on the Port Mann Bridge, which is shorter. [Male, fifty-five to sixty-four]

The Pattulo Bridge, serving Highway 99A, southeast of Vancouver, was mentioned by yet three more elderly drivers as a bothersome driving site.

Bridges connote danger. In particular, the narrow lanes bother one elderly man. As he described, "I try and make sure I'm dead on. That's about the only thing that I find that ever bothers me." Ice on the bridges bothers another man while the fast flow of traffic worries a third motorist.

It must be stressed that the discomfort factors provided by the elderly drivers were not offered freely. They were, by and large, teased out through a series of primary and secondary questions. Although, after rigorous discussion, many elderly drivers presented examples of problematic driving circumstances, they never wavered in their follow-up accounts that they were comfortable, competent drivers. A defensive stance could be detected.

View of Self as Driver

True, many of the elderly drivers involved in injury-producing crashes admitted to major driving discomforts. Still, while doing so, they had a view of self as driver that was positive. By and large, elderly motorists maintained that they were acceptable, if not exemplary, performers within the general parameters of driving capacities and limitations.

For numerous elderly drivers, the gap between the actual self and ideal self was small. They considered themselves to be comfortable and safe drivers. More importantly they yearned to be recognized as such. This, according to Krech et al. (1962), is an enhanced feeling of self esteem. Strengths are featured and weaknesses are devalued or denied in order to present a preferred sense of self.

So it should not be surprising to discover that, when the elderly drivers were asked whether they felt comfortable driving, a near universal yes was announced. They were comfortable at the time of the interviews and they had been comfortable all their lives. Witness:

1. When I'm driving a car, that's when I really feel comfortable. I'm at ease. I've driven almost all my life. [Male, sixty-five to seventy-four]
2. I've driven all my life. Always felt comfortable. The wife has never liked it, though. So I do the driving. [Male, seventy-five plus]
3. Yeah, I'm comfortable in the car, I'm used to it. For a number of years I used to, ah, drive up to . . . every week. Three and a half hours I had scheduled my time slot. Whether the radio is a distraction or not, perhaps it is, you don't think about your driving. [Male, sixty-five to seventy-four]
4. Yeah I've always been very comfortable with it, you almost say next to second nature. After growing up I was, I learned to drive on a '22 Chev so I mean that is fair experience. [Male, seventy-five plus]
5. I'm quite comfortable with driving. Yeah I drove back and forth for years and years. [Female, fifty-five to sixty-four]
6. Yes I do. I've driven ever since I was twelve years of age, and I was interested since this letter came, and, ah, um, since that accident, how when I start off, ah, sometimes before I get into the car, I think, ah, um, caution, or something. But, as soon as my car starts rolling, I feel as easy with it, it's a good car, I feel easy with it like I would in my rocking chair. And, ah, I have to be alert, I know I have to be quite alert, and, ah, try to make sure that, ha, my brakes off, and, ah, otherwise everything is going super. [Female, seventy-five plus]
7. Comfortable. I've been driving since I was twenty-three and I'm eighty-eight now. [Female, seventy-five plus]

Metaphors were offered to paint a picture of confidence. "It's home to me," "Forty-seven years on the road running an engine," "I just love driving . . . going by myself, nobody to tell me turn here, turn there," or "I can drive in between trucks or anything." An expanded answer to illustrate the image of self as a confident, capable driver follows:

> Oh yes, I always felt comfortable. I never was afraid to go in the traffic or go over bridges. What I want to mention, this was happened on 29th of October was it 29th? Anyway, no, it could have been in the beginning of November because my granddaughter from Germany who's, who was 26th on and she is driving herself. She visited me here and I drove her to North Vancouver to Squamish to the mountain up to Mount Seymour to the Island all around, on the Island everywhere, everywhere in the midst of a town to the Stanley Park and she, ah, said to me "Oma (she calls me Oma) I admire you your driving skill.

> You really are a good driver" she said and she was a driver herself and she felt very comfortable all the time. When I had people with me they all felt very comfortable. [Female, sixty-five to seventy-four]

The accidents in which this group of senior motorists were involved were serious. Injuries resulted. The events were dramatic. For several elderly women drivers the accidents left them feeling a little uncomfortable. But they soon recovered. Their actual selves again approached their ideal driver selves:

1. I: Hmm. Okay. Some people never feel really comfortable driving a car. Are you one of those people?

   R: After the accident I was. I had almost like a tight feeling but that's gone now.

   I: Hmm, so for a while as a result of the accident you felt nervous?

   R: Yes I felt very nervous.

   I: But normally you feel . . .?

   R: Oh, yeah I feel at home in the car, yes.

   I: Um, have you always felt comfortable driving?

   R: Yeah, yes well of course when I was learning I was a little nervous but, no, I feel, I feel quite at home in the car. I'm not afraid. [Female, sixty-five to seventy-four]

2. No, I was alone and I was comfortable and I was coming, ah, I was driving that way very often, and after the accident happened, I said, "Oh I don't think I can go that way again." And after, in fact the thought came across my mind, and I won't drive [?] either but then I thought, once I got the car replaced, I said, "Now look, that's not right. Get in that car and go. Get in that car and go." Because I said to myself, "I'm not nervous." It didn't make me nervous and I said another thing, "If I quit, I will be." [Female, fifty-five to sixty-four]

Elderly Drivers as Safe Drivers

The image of self as driver includes the factor of safety—in the commonsensical and not the epidemiological sense. Vehicle management is an offshoot of something basic in society—the "profiling" of people's conduct and character as safe motorists. You are only as safe a driver as your ability to avoid accidents and save your own and other people's lives.

Do elderly drivers envision themselves as safe drivers? Yes! Safe driver recognition is part of a continuum that follows from being a competent, comfortable, or cautious driver. That continuum was seldom broken by the accidents. They represented misadventures that elderly drivers rationalized as momentary lapses, anomalies, abnormal events that can happen to safe drivers.

1. Always try to be a cautious driver. No speeding, never talk to my wife; always watch the other guy—always. But this time, I'll tell you, was the first time I ever thought "leave a space always for the other guy—all the time—leave all the space and any time I see a guy comes between me and the other guy—I still keep my space. That was the first time [the accident]. [Male, fifty-five to sixty-four]

2. R: I think, ah, I've always been a cautious driver. I believe to be. I, I always have been. But that took me completely by surprise and I certainly enter into things much, much more cautiously and not only that, I certainly watch more people approaching and, you know, running, running a red light or an orange light or whatever. I take a double look when the light turns green but I always thought I did that for a long time but, ah, at that point I, I don't know what occurred that I saw green but I saw a green light. It's as, as I said, a complete surprise to both my wife and I in the hospital when . . .

   I: When you were told it wasn't green? Okay. Being a cautious driver, then, what kinds of things do you do that make you think that you are?

   R: Well, ah, I watch in the rear view mirror and I approach, well, the warning signal is ahead if it's on the road I approach it with caution and as I said before I look twice both ahead and each way before I start out and I double check the light. [Male, sixty-five to seventy-four]

3. I: Do you think you're a cautious driver?

   R: I'm a cautious driver, yes.

   I: Could you tell me what you do when you're driving to, ah, make you think that you're a cautious driver?

   R: Well I go on all that traffic roads and I'm not a fast driver and I keep my distance in front and, ah, I keep my eyes alert. [Male, seventy-five plus]

4. I: Do you think that you are a cautious driver?

   R: Yeah, I haven't had that many accidents. I had this one here, ah, I think before this one it must have been six or seven years since I had one.

   I: What kinds of things do you do when you're driving to make you think you're a cautious driver?

   R: Ah.

   I: Are you conscious of your speed and, ah, things like that?

   R: Ah, ya, I often watch my speed. Oh yeah, I watch my speed. I've never been caught for speeding. [Male, sixty-five to seventy-four]

The process of personal identification as a safe driver could be seen over and over again by all elderly drivers who were involved in injury-producing crashes. The interviewees left a set of marks or gauges by which they judged themselves. A list of these classification marks would be useful and enlightening.

I Am a Safe Driver Because I Am Watchful. The "I watch . . . " was a primary framework for judgment. Watching manifested itself in many different ways. Here are some: "You gotta watch for traffic coming up behind you and that ahead." "I certainly look right and left and ahead." "Watching other drivers, other people." "You always gotta watch the other guy because you don't know." "I always watch out for drivers behind me." "I've always watched the mirror."

I Am a Safe Driver Because I Never Speed or Hardly Ever Speed. "I never speed" was a definition of self as safe driver used with regularity. To add emphasis on the "never speed" theme, elderly drivers made sure that they "slow down at intersections" or always "stay in the slow lane on the highway." One elderly driver believed quite firmly that he does not speed "because of cops."

One elderly man within the sixty-five to seventy-four age bracket believed himself to be a safe, cautious driver because, among other things, he does not "speed very often." But his nonspeeding may, in the eyes of the police, be counter to safe driving. Read his explanation:

> I, ah, watch the, ah, I watch the traffic signs for the speed limit and I travel, I travel up to the speed limit, a good deal of the time, although I got a ticket one time up in the, ah, Cache Creek for not travelling up to the full, ah, up to the full speed, and I thought that that was a horrendous kind of a ticket to get. I was travelling between forty-five and fifty-five kilometers an hour and most of the time it was around fifty kilometers an hour speed, and the speed limit was ninety kilometers an hour, and the officer gave me a ticket because I was not travelling up to the full speed.

Speeding carries other meanings with regard to safety. Rather than offering a series of translations, the following verbatim accounts provide much more sharply the range of meanings assigned to speeding:

1. I drive slower than the average person. Very rarely do I go more than five or ten miles over the speed limit. Not like some people. I took the safe drivers' course. [Male, sixty-five to seventy-four]
2. R: Well, I drive within speed limits, ah, sometimes they honk you, if you drive less, around 196th speed limits on the sixty but the cars go flying past, you know, so if you like if you go that pace, it seems to me that you get pressured to go ahead, because you see the cars, you know, at your back, so you are pressured to, ah . . .

   I: To keep up.

   R: Ya, to keep up a little faster.

   I: But you try to stay within the speed limits.

   R: Ya.

   I: Anything else?

   R: Well, I really drive, I don't really drive too fast, because sometimes I bring my grandchildren with me, so it makes me . . . [Female, sixty-five to seventy-four]

3. You mean for speeding? I sort of go with the flow with traffic like when we're coming home at night, you know, I mean I'll never get over into the right hand lane and go eighty kilometers I'll stay with the traffic in this lane doing 105 or 110. [Female, fifty-five to sixty-four]
4. Well I've always been that way. I'm not a fast driver I, ah, in town here if it says thirty miles an hour I go twenty-five if it says forty I go thirty-five I go under the speed limit all the time and, ah, when I go up hunting and that I never go over the speed limit. If it says sixty I drive sixty or under eh? I drive within the speed limit all the time that's why when you say that I don't know if the wife was laughing at me when I said that or not but I I think I'm a cautious driver. [Male, sixty-five to seventy-four]
5. Ah, I'm careful. I never drive fast, ah, the only time that I had a speeding ticket was a particular job where there was a lot of pressure to go, go, go, from one place to the other. That's the only time I had speeding ticket, I haven't had it for years. [Male, seventy-five plus]

I Am a Safe Driver Because I Keep an Appropriate Distance between Cars. For some elderly drivers, the image of self as a safe driver hinges on the space they leave between themselves and the cars in front of them. They "try to keep a good distance." For the car behind them, they look in the rear view mirror to see "how far the guy behind [them] is."

What is a safe distance between cars? That appears to be a judgment call. One woman driver (aged fifty-five to sixty-four) said:

> Well you're supposed to leave about, at least three lengths, aren't you? Three or four lengths. You know it all depends on how fast you're driving, but, if you leave too good a bit of space, he'll get in there. But I like leaving a decent space if you possibly can. You're supposed to leave about three spaces aren't you?

Another clarified:

> Well I've always believed that you should drive two vehicles, the fellow that's in front of you and your own or the fellow that's behind you and your own. I've had problems especially on the freeway. I like to keep about three car lengths ahead of, and it seems no matter if you go the speed limit and you leave that three, somebody is going to cut in front of you so if you lag back you always get some jerk who starts blowing his horn and, ah, I let them blow their horn because, ah, all I'm doing is maybe cutting back about five miles an hour so the other fellow can get up ahead again and, ah, I never fall behind a truck because especially those big freight trucks 'cause you can't see a thing you can't see on either side of you so what I do with them I usually lag back and lag back until I get two or three cars in front of me and if possible I'll pass them but, ah, I think, ah, if you're, ah, a defensive driver and, ah . . . [Male, sixty-five to seventy-four]

I'm a Safe Driver Because I Drive Defensively. To be safe means to be a defensive driver. This view was shared by some of the elderly. Several motorists used the catch-all metaphor "defensive" driving to clarify their views. For them, the meaning was self evident. For others, a definition was offered. To illustrate:

1. Ah, I drove, I took and believe in defensive driving. Ah, don't depend on what the other guy is going to do, you do the things that are right. I took my driving lessons from a driving school, and my hubby used to laugh at me. They always said, they say you have to come to what they call, a four wheel stop. And nothing else, but a four wheel stop, is a stop. And, I firmly believe in that. When you come to a stop sign, you stop. You don't just slow down, with 95 percent of the people do. Especially out here in a small local area like this. They just slow down, rather than stop. And, ah, I give the other guy, I wait to see what the other guy is going to do, before I would move, and I wasn't a fast driver, I would drive the speed limit. I don't believe in being, you know, dragging your feet sort of speak and holding the other guy back. [Female, sixty-five to seventy-four]
2. I think I drive defensively, I think I always have. I think I always drive a number of cars ahead of and I don't drive where I am, I drive in a situation ahead, and always have and you know they say you should and I, ah, so in that respect if that's caution, I'm cautious. I wouldn't call it caution, but if you understand it. That's just good driving. [Female, sixty-five to seventy-four]

I'm a Safe Driver Because of My Successful Driving History. For a group of elderly drivers, to be accident free or relatively accident free, and/or ticket free reflects the image of a safe driver. By not having experienced legal problems, they considered themselves to be unequivocally safe. Two senior drivers explained it their way:

1. Well I think that I always was pretty cautious. I mean the fact that I've never had an accident in forty-two years of driving, and you have to understand my job is driving, you know, I don't just drive to work, and then park my car for eight hours, and then drive home, I'm driving all day long, and you know, I drive in extreme situations like the Canyon, the Caribou, I used to in those days anyway. Um, but um, I think I'm a courteous driver, I don't cut people off, um, I don't make turns which are unreasonable or unnatural. You see that all the time, and it's the most ridiculous thing I've ever seen. It's too bad there aren't more police around to give them tickets for lane changes, just come back from Vancouver any night, those lanes are solid, 'cause these idiots, backwards and forwards, lane to lane. They don't get anywhere. [Male, fifty-five to sixty-four]
2. I: Do you consider yourself a cautious driver?

   R: Yes I certainly do consider myself that. I've been driving for nearly forty years and I've had no problems. None at all. No problems whatsoever.

   I: How do you mean you've had no problems?

   R: No tickets, no accidents to speak of until this one. [Male, sixty-five to seventy-four]

3. Well I've got a clean record, if that's what you mean. I've been driving since I was fifteen. [Male, fifty-five to sixty-four]

I'm a Safe Driver Because I Obey Traffic Signs. "Laws are meant to be broken," so the popular cliché states. The police would certainly disagree, as would some elderly drivers. Their attentiveness to the traffic laws implies safety. So they are safe drivers because:

1. I always stop at stop signs.
2. I don't speed. I follow the rules of the road.
3. I signal early.
4. I always come to a full stop.

Coming to a full stop at stop signs was routinely mentioned as a characteristic of a safe driver. Implied in this theme is that other drivers do not stop:

> That's right. I really do because being in, I've seen in so many places and being in the situation where it says stop, and I'll stop and at a four way stop well this here fella won't stop, you know. You'll find those drivers they just don't stop. I don't know if they just don't see it or if they're not thinking, or you know how it is. Some of these people are not that cautious I guess. [Female, sixty-five to seventy-four]

I'm a Safe Driver Because I Keep My Car in Good Shape. Attention to the vehicle means attention to safety and caution. The mechanical condition of the car suggests the degree to which the owner is a safe driver:

1. Well, I would like to think that my car is always in first class shape. I wouldn't drive a vehicle unless I knew what was [?]. Well those sort of things, my brakes, my tires and the lights and so on, I always feel I have to have in tip top shape. [Male, fifty-five to sixty-four]
2. Ah, I always look when I go into an intersection, um, well now I make sure [?] because before we didn't have to, but you know, and, ah, I make sure my windshields are clean, and my headlights are clean. I clean my windshields, I clean my headlights, and, ah . . . [Male, fifty-five to sixty-four]
3. I keep the car in perfect order, I have a good mechanic who twice a year goes over my car thoroughly. He checks everything out and he's excellent. Right now I have a little thing that needs fixing but I'll attend to that right away. [Male, seventy-five plus]

I'm a Safe Driver Because I Don't Like In-Car Activities. Doing two things at a time is considered dangerous. Therefore, if a driver's spouse begins to chat the driver says "hush." An all-encompassing thought was shared by a male driver within the fifty-five to sixty-four year old category:

> Yes, yes, yes. Well the other thing is, ah, generally I even, I even, of course my son who is a very experienced driver over here. He is about thirty-five, I always ask the driver "don't talk." I never talk when I drive even if my wife is there or somebody is there along with me and they try to talk I tell them "Don't talk, we'll talk when we get there." I never talk. Sometimes I never even [hear ?] somebody talking when he is driving. One thing is, we shouldn't talk. The other is whatever is on my mind whether I'm very happy or whether I have some sad thoughts, leave them there. I have a practice to leave everything there, I can go to sleep within ten minutes if I have a bad [?] and we sit here. I'll take my [?] I go to bed, I go to sleep, they're all wondering and they ask me "How you do it?" I tell them "I learned it to control my mind for some time and ask him to leave everything else, now I want to sleep." You can tell your mind like this and you can practice it but that's yoga and you can do it. In my life there have been so many sad happenings I lost my very dear sister and there were other happenings, I have never spent a single night without sleep. Except when I had once I had malaria over there and once or twice I had flu, not this flu, Asian flu is very dangerous. Then it won't let me sleep otherwise if I am well whatever happens I'll decide with me for today the things are gone I'll take it up tomorrow, let me go to sleep. I control myself and that's how I drive.

I'm a Safe Driver Because of the Many Activities in Which I Engage. Safety and caution mean constant roadway vigilance. Attention must be paid to a variety of roadway obstacles, driver behaviors and traffic circumstances. The sum of the activities makes for an evaluation of self as a safe or cautious driver. Examine:

1. Well, first of all you got to watch your your traffic coming up behind you and that ahead of course. To make sure things are moving properly, don't over speed over drive. If you're driving at night you take it slower, I try to keep a fair distance between me and the car ahead so that if I have to stop I know that I can stop in time. Generally just watching traffic and I find that with this van that I've got now I can see traffic for miles. [Male, fifty-five to sixty-four]
2. I keep speed limits, I watch the traffic, and I mean just because it says stop, I don't depend on the other guy to say stop, because you know when there is a four, I always, I'm very careful that way because you never know about drivers. [Female, sixty-five to seventy-four]
3. I always keep with the speed limit. I watch my turns. I always check carefully the distance between other cars. I know lots of people who are always in a rush, but I take my time. You can't go wrong if you do the right thing. [Female, fifty-five to sixty-four]
4. Watch for other traffic, keep the proper distance. All those sort of things. I don't over-travel my vision, that's for sure. [Male, fifty-five to sixty-four]

An abbreviated review of the elderly drivers' accounts leaves an impression that their self-esteem is very high indeed. At first glance one would not think that all of the drivers had recently experienced serious crashes, and that most of the crashes were the fault of these same drivers. Perhaps the close correspondence between the elderly drivers' actual and ideal selves is the conceptual rationale that supports the positive images which the elderly drivers have. Negative factors are negated. Responsibility, confidence, comfort, safety, and caution are cognitive resources elderly drivers used to define themselves with great regularity.

Driving Experience

People tend to frame their present and plan their future according to their past. Experiences are the raw materials used to define individuals' perceptions of reality. It cannot be otherwise. People common-sensically know it and all branches of the social sciences substantiate it.

The savoir-faire of elderly driver experiences was "success." Elderly drivers routinely described their driving histories as flawless ones. They then introduced their unblemished pasts as atonements for their present crashes. By implication or explicit reasoning, the accidents were new experiences, unexplainable in light of the elderly drivers' successful driving lives.

A central theme that explained away fault for the injury-producing crash was "I never had an accident . . . in . . . years." This form of reasoning allowed elderly drivers to retain their face or image as competent drivers for all practical purposes. Witness:

1. R: I never had an accident in Quebec. I used to drive from Quebec up to Montreal and on to Toronto. I've never had a serious accident. I've also been to Norway and driven there and crossed the border into Sweden and driven there without any accidents and that's on the other side of the road.

   I: And this was in your own back yard.

   R: This was in my own back yard after about fifty odd years of driving. Now I know I'm seventy-nine but I still feel capable, my sight is good. So that's all I can tell you. [Female, seventy-five plus]
2. No, no, no. I've done a lot of driving. I had twelve years truck driving and I never had one accident and I probably have way over a million miles, city, freeway driving and, well not that much city driving exactly, but I drive in the city, I drive in San Francisco or Los Angeles or . . . [Male, sixty-five to seventy-four]
3. Well, you know when you refer to my accident, you're hitting a sensitive chord. I've never in my life, I've driven since I was about sixteen seventeen, and I've never in my life had an accident for which I was to blame outside of the one that where I hit black ice and I can explain that in detail, it simply was not my fault. Unavoidable situation. [Male, seventy-five plus]
4. I have been driving for years and I've never rear-ended anyone before. I don't know how long the other driver's been driving. I wouldn't say he's a youngster, I would say he was probably in his thirties, but how long he's been in this country and been driving here, I don't know. [Female, sixty-five to seventy-four]

Similar in meaning but slightly different in form were the many extended answers elderly drivers gave outlining successful driving in bad or very bad driving conditions:

1. R: When I was driving in the dark nothing bothered me, I did not, I drove and I could see in the rain nothing bothered me, ah, even the snow and ice I was always I had to drive to the hospital one time to Port Moody you know what that means?

   I: Yes.

   R: From Lion's Gate to Port Moody in the snow in the winter or snow from all the cars were lying on the side. I was driving nicely. And, ah, even on icy roads I always knew what I had to do. I always reacted in the right moment. My reaction was always very good. [Female, seventy-five plus]
2. Me? Sure I've driven practically, well I've been in Canada sixty-three years now, and I've driven sixty of them and, uh, when I mean driving I mean driving in the old days was not like driving today. In some ways it was worse, we had heavy winters, we had no tires no chains. The first chains to come in was the overall things that went over the wheel, before that we used ropes so I mean you name it I've done it. [Male, seventy-five plus]
3. Doesn't bother me, no it doesn't bother me. If I, ah, in driving in traffic doesn't particularly bother me, ah, I've driven on the California freeways and so on and, ah, sometimes the traffic gets pretty sticky there, and you can get into, ah, problems with, through no fault of your own. Like one problem I had when I was on vacation in that we were in California, we had been in Los Angeles and we gone to [?] beach and were on our way home and, ah, we come under the, ah, from, ah, what's the name of town, ah . . . but anyway you go under the freeway and then you turn left alongside of the freeway and come up on a ramp up onto the Los Angeles freeway and, ah, I was travelling along in the second lane and then, ah, the turnoff came at the San Diego freeway and I glanced in my mirror, and there's another car coming up doing about, oh, about ten miles an hour or fifteen miles an hour faster than I was going, and he's right on my tail and the two lanes turn off. I have no choice, I was peeled off onto, with the other traffic right behind, I had no choice, I had to turn off, and that was an experience with heavy traffic. Other than that, if I'm going to turn off, I try to work my way over to the left hand lane, or the right hand lane rather, so that I'm not going to get caught. That was an experience, I learned a lesson. [Male, sixty-five to seventy-four]

For some motorists the substantive element of an honorable driving history is that they were employed as motor vehicle operators. They said:

1. Well, ah, I think I'm a I'm a cautious driver I, I think I'm a good driver, I, ah, I drove as professional driver for, ah, quite a few years in the Air Force. I spent a lifetime in the R.C.A. and, ah, I taught safety and safe driving to my employees and at a regular basis. I took safety courses and I was very safety-conscious and, ah, always telling the other people how how to drive and, ah, but I always, ah, drove defensively and, ah, always anticipating what the other person might do. [Male, fifty-five to sixty-four]

2. I've been a professional driver for twenty years. I drove a van (furniture truck) and I always drive carefully. Also (my wife) always makes sure I have my seat belt on before I start the car; she's very aware of that. She makes sure . . . [Male, sixty-five to seventy-four]

The code of relating driving biographies is to define one's history according to a standard of interpretation which expresses competence and skill. These are some examples of storytelling: the time of learning to drive which often began in the 1920s, 1930s, or 1940s; the location of learning, being on farms or in small towns; the rigor of driving experienced in rain, snow, and dark; their records of driving which were accident and citation free. These productions served as a corrective process, providing the interviewers a model to help them interpret the elderly drivers' historical position vis-a-vis the crash, and to establish a present level of competence. Salvaging and sustaining the image was a primary motive.

Pet Peeves

Pet peeves is an appropriate metaphor to feature the "oh, by the way" comments elderly drivers offered toward the conclusion of the interviews. Their unsolicited presentations provided a series of "behavioral" tendencies to further develop a portrait of elderly driving conduct.

The peeves given by elderly drivers form a sense of ontology. They begin with the question, "What exists?" And "what exists" is viewed as a fundamental, ongoing traffic/driving problem. It is a relationship characterized by action of official and unofficial parties upon each other.

An example of the intersection will serve to illustrate the constitutive relationships. The intersection is constituted by builders and engineers, by different groups of drivers who travel in it, and by the law enforcers that patrol it. All or some of these basic constitutive elements were highlighted by the accident victims as major complaints, or pet peeves.

The most evident complaint shared by elderly drivers is other drivers. Responsibility for forms of bad or hazardous problematic driving was consistently imputed to them. Fortuitous consequences were projected because other drivers were reckless, inconsiderate, unsafe, irresponsible, and so forth. The other-driver-as-pet-peeve rule was repeatedly evoked with emotion and firm stance. Other drivers were considered offensive to the elderly. They needed to be treated with expedience to clear the streets.

They do silly things, so often that it becomes the norm. Furthermore, the other drivers were often grouped as the majority of motorists. Implicitly, or at times explicitly, elderly drivers stood aside from the other driver actions, to signify they are not part of the troublesome picture out there. Consider the following verbatim accounts:

1. Now I know when there is a damn red light and I stop, if I make a right turn I stop whether there is anybody in the intersection or not and make damn sure that there's nothing coming and then make my signal and, ah, make the turn in a proper way in the right hand lane. God, we see people all the time pull up to a red light and they don't even stop—they go right through or down the left on making a right turn. I don't know why there is not more accidents than there are. And another thing that contributes to a lot of the accidents is poor policing, very poor policing. In fact there is hardly anybody going by at the legal speed and that darn rubber and screeching tires in and all night. [Male, fifty-five to sixty-four]

2. No that's the only thing I'd say in B.C. They have a hell of a lot of bad drivers. But they don't give no signals and that's a thing as soon as they get on they never put a signal light on until they're about three feet from where they are going to turn. Not twenty or thirty feet back where you should be or more. Put your signal on and let the people know what you're doing, they don't do that here. But, ah, that's a thing that I found out here and you know how far you have to go to stop one of those cranes. It takes a lot of territory, if you're doing thirty miles an hour and not even on a dry day how they know when they're going to swing in front of me and there's a car right out in front of them he's not going to stop. I mean there's nothing I can do about it. [Male, sixty-five to seventy-four]

3. R: I feel fine. I find that other drivers seem to be in such a hurry it's like coming off on to 200 the other night and then there's traffic coming right. And likewise a lot of the cars don't seem to stop they seem to go right straight on and I mean to me this is, oh my God.

   I: And just barely making it in front of the cars that are coming.

   R: Right in between two cars, you see, and I always sort of brake again and look again and if there's cars coming I wait until they go by and then I start. And the fellow behind me of course he's in such a hurry and of course he pulls to the right of me and I think, well he's going to go down 88th but no he cuts me off and I mean there's where you get your accidents, you know I mean, it was when I saw him I thought oh he's going 88th and then he just pulled in front of me. Frustration.

   I: So impatience and that kind of thing?

   R: That's right. It's more or less "come on lady—get going." We were talking about this the other day going to, ah, work and I said well I don't like going in the left hand lane because there's so much traffic like at 152nd coming off and 176th coming on to the freeway and I always find that they never yield they just barrel on so I stay in my sort of in the left lane and then once I get past the last, you know, the Coquitlam one? Because . . . [Female, seventy-five plus]

Several readings of the transcripts showed an intensity behind the elderly drivers' views about other road users. They were routinely stereotyped according to race, age, sex and/or perceived socioeconomic status. It seems that a group, like the elderly, whose members may suffer the brunt of societal stereotyping, themselves stereotype.

One classic stereotypical group of "other drivers" which are noticed and critiqued by numerous elderly drivers are the young drivers. They are typed as individuals who willfully speed, run lights, cut in front, or whip around. They are considered to be irresponsible. The following sample transcriptions verify the interpretations:

1. R: Yes, yes I'm quite comfortable. Ah, ah, as I said, I mainly watch out for the youngsters that, ah, just put their foot down on that pedal and go regardless, and I watch out for them.

   I: O.k.

   R: 'Cause one day we were driving up towards Guildford, and, um, we were on the inside lane, and there was a car on the left of us, and we came close to a driveway, um, that led into a parking lot, and this car came from the left, with some young fellows in it, and whipped right in on front of us into the driveway. Never should he have crossed right in front of my car from the left, but if it hadn't been for quick thinking and slamming on the brakes. . . . So it was the old person again, who was the cautious one, right? [Female, seventy-five plus]

2. I have a pet peeve. There's too many young people driving too fast, ah, today. They're driving over the speed limit in here where it's congested where they should be more careful eh? That's about the only peeve I have, ah, these young people seem to be irresponsible. I'm not saying they're not careful drivers but they drive too fast. Many a time I'm driving the speed limit down the street here and I'm not driving fast every day I go out on the road. They got to pass, they got to pass and they only go two three blocks and they turn off or you know and things like that I think "What the hell is the matter with them. Couldn't they wait? Can't they just stay in line they got to take a chance and go around?" That's the way they operate. [Male, fifty-five to sixty-four]

3. R: We were just talking at work and I says "Heh, when I first started driving a car the age was twenty-one, and you see all these little heads just popping, they got to look underneath the steering wheel. There's no way.

   I: Hmm you figure that's too young, sixteen?

   R: Oh yeah should be nineteen at least. I mean it's a runaway from home like I mean sixteen, they tell the parents what to do because they can jump in the car and just pack the kids and . . . [Male, sixty-five to seventy-four]

4. R: But, ah, I, ah, no I don't think so, I don't know. But, ah, well it's made a difference too, because you see my, ah, now, like, ah, my husband passed away a few years ago, and I'm driving all the time, and I think that, ah, that, ah, the, ah, well not so much in the driving, but ah, the, ah, I found that, ah, especially young people and especially if they see an older woman, well you know they they, they sometimes dare you to do things, like they'll pass you, and they try to push you over and things like that, and that, I found that, ah . . .

   I: That fact is simply because you're older.

   R: Older, I feel ya, because I felt this because they say, "Oh well here's an old woman." Ha ha. But, because I never experienced that before, you

> know, but I have quite often in the last year or so about the young people and they cut in front of you and you have to slam on your brakes and, you know, things like that, now that to me I found disturbing, so I watch. So, as I say, I never speed but I have control then, you know. [Female, sixty-five to seventy-four]

Young drivers were the featured group senior motorists identified as culprits on the road. However, the descriptor "young" was rarely defined. Young, to a seventy year old motorist could be anywhere from age sixteen to forty or older. Young encompassed anyone who is not old. But it did not stop there. Women drivers were also identified by both male and female elderly drivers as pet peeves. To prove:

> Ninety-five percent it's true when you have a ridiculous driver in front of you and I make it a point to look and it's usually a female. And speeding, I just moved in this area and this is the road to the hospital I know it's close to the hospital but they speed here terrible. This is the main access road to the hospital and it's, you see the hospital is right there up on the hill. [Male, sixty-five to seventy-four]
>
> You know, I find people with small cars, and a small powerful car, you know, they seem to be aggressive, very aggressive, and I find a lot of women drivers are very very aggressive. Much more so sometimes than the young men drivers. [Female, sixty-five to seventy-four]

Certain ethnic groups or "foreigners" who could not speak English became the objects of complaints. They were considered to be problems on the road because they are unable to read road signs and they cannot communicate with other drivers in the case of a crash.

An example of a dialectic turnaround was extracted from the transcription data. A reading of the conversation begged the question, "who really are the elderly?" A woman approaching seventy-four is considered to be elderly. She articulated that the elderly drivers are problems. So, by implication is she a problem? She did not say, but there is an implicit assumption she is not. It's the other elderly drivers:

> R: They think that they have the right to make a very slow, right turn, you know when they turn off the road, when they're coming down the highway, they very slowly make their turn, whereas no matter how many traffic, or how much traffic, how close the traffic is behind them, they still take their good time to make their turns. I think.
>
> I: Why do you think that is?
>
> R: Because I think they've probably lived their day, and were maybe doctors or lawyers or somebody that has lots of money, and they've always had their own way, and they were the boss. And, ah, they can just go ahead and do their own driving and nobody is going to say "Hurry up old man, there's all us young guys driving."

I: So you think that most of the old people driving had fairly high positions when they were younger.

R: I don't know why I think that but, ah, the way they drive, and they have no more right to drive slow, than the young people. You've got your driver's right, everybody has the same right.

I: Do you think it has anything to do with their alertness, or their reactions, or . . .

R: Not really because, ah, I always prefer my kids to drive because I think that my son, especially young guys, I think young guys are really the sharpest drivers. They can zoom in there, and do things that I never would do. Which is wrong for them to do, but they do it. Cause they get away with it, and they know what they're doing, they're very sharp, the young men I think are very sharp in the way they are driving.

With so many "poor" other drivers on the road, some elderly would like to see more police vigilance. In fact, their peeve was that there is insufficient law enforcement for obvious law breakers. More speed traps, ticketing of violations and enforcement at stop signs was urged. A handful of motorists went so far as to suggest personal involvement in monitoring traffic violations. The following suggestion has a definite flavor of vigilante action:

> Older men who have retired who would be willing to give it a couple of weeks, go round in their own cars. Now from a legal point I don't know if it would work, any car that he saw speeding, take his license number and pass it over to the police. But would his word be any good 'cause he's not a policeman? If we could have two weeks of that all around and catch some of these people who are dashing madly back and forth I think they'd begin to realize they're not going to get away with it. A number of accidents just here, you know up here, you can hear them. Somebody forgets the stop sign or somebody dashes through as somebody's moved through the stop sign. Something must be done but I, they can't afford to have an extra police to police the traffic. What about taking on, ah, conscientious citizens for a short time and see what would come of it. [Female, seventy-five plus]

Another side to increased police involvement was noted. The laws should be enforced uniformly and expeditiously. Some elderly drivers requested increased police vigilance. Yet they themselves should be immune to it, because they are not the "real" speeders or crazy drivers. The following excerpt displays the irony candidly:

> I think maybe I'd like to comment on something else. For example, one of the things that the, ah, our traffic rules and laws regulations, etc., and our views by very often the police and I would like to give you just one out of a several examples that I could give you. I was living in Edmonton, lived in Edmonton for three years after leaving Toronto, just prior to my return to Vancouver, and on a Sunday morning, my wife and I were simply driving to the church. We're odd-

balls, we go to church on Sunday. So we were driving to church on Sunday, and on a downhill grade, with both sides of the roads were cement, probably twelve, fifteen feet and there was no crosswalks, and a downhill grade, and I caught myself driving possible eight or maybe ten miles an hour exceeding the speed limit, and lo and behold at the bottom, if you can believe it, there are five police cars. Five of them, and when the officer stopped me with radar, and went to work, I sized up the situation and I was angry, and I said, "You know, I would think that you'd have something more sensible, something more constructive to do, than to have five of you policemen, five police cars sitting here not solving crime, and pinching people early Sunday morning on their way to church." I said, "That seems quite ridiculous." And you know, the policeman said to me, "You know what?" He says, "I agree totally." [Male, sixty-five to seventy-four]

Another road user class that became the target of some elderly drivers' complaints was that of bicyclists. The criticisms were twofold: reckless driving and driving on the sidewalk. The two major peeves are outlined:

1. R: And another thing is, like in even bicycles when they're starting off driving bike they should be, because it seems like the way they drive the bike that's the way they drive their car after they get in a car.

   I: Yep that's interesting.

   R: You know like you go down the road and you'll see a kid on a ten speed, he's got his hands on his side and he's pedalling away and you don't know should I pass him is he going to slip what's gonna happen? And then the next thing you know he's going like this and he's right across the road. He's crossing the street in between the cars as if he, as if he's running eh? (Male, fifty-five to sixty-four)

2. Well like, ah, giving bicycles more road room so they don't have to be on the sidewalks or else do like they do in Europe divide the sidewalks in half. I don't know how many times in Vancouver that I haven't just about been hit by a bicycle on a sidewalk and yet the bylaw here "No bicycles on the sidewalk allowed" but then again they don't give them any place to ride a bicycle and I'm not a heavy biker for [?]. I'm not into bikes, I know in Europe I rode a few kms on bikes, ah, but I'm not really into the bike line but, ah, it's a vehicle for transportation, it's a vehicle for economy. [Male, fifty-five to sixty-four]

From a completely different perspective, yet entirely relevant to driving, were peeves about road designers, planners, or engineers. Intersections were poorly designed. Street signs were inadequate. There were either too many traffic lights per street or not enough. Narrow lanes were bothersome. Double-lane roadways converging into single lanes were candidates for complaint. Notice:

1. R: But the only explanation from my side, you know, concerning the accident I had, was that the intersection is poorly designed for the situation or for the circumstances there, you know. I think that I was not familiar with the place, you know. I used to go through the place many years ago

when we used to go to the Princess Park and maybe the stop sign was the other way, you know, but actually Wellington is the through street going from one place to some place, but that just ends, you know about a couple blocks up that intersection, you know, so I, what I think is that what they should have done is they changed this stop sign, and put it, make a four way stop sign you know.

I: Ya, I've heard that before, people obey it more when it's a four way.

R: But this is, it looks like a major intersection in that you know, so it wasn't marked you know, like there was only, I checked it after, there was only the stop sign, but there was no lines, you know, like you could have seen lines for a stop, but there was nothing, and beside that, beside the stop sign there were some shrubs or bushes, you know. I'm not sure that it wasn't, ah, you know, we went there after, and it was all trimmed after, you know. [Female, fifty-five to sixty-four]

2. R: It's a speed lane that's all it is you know I know that for sure. Because I go there practically every day and then I know that everybody complains about the speeding there and then you see coming from Cloverdale you coming this way now this lane all of a sudden it comes to a dead end here so they have to turn into this lane that's is how far they fixed the road. This is double here and all of a sudden the right hand lane is cut off maybe you noticed that.

I: Yeah they merge into the lane.

R: Now this bloody lane here is going at a hell of a speed all the time to try and beat the speed lane and they will have cut off here before you you see? You drive there three four times and you'll notice it yourself or anybody else for that matter. But they're always going at a hell of a speed to try and get to that little cutoff here where . . .

I: You normally drive in the center lane do you?

R: Well sure, I always drive in that lane you see? [Male, sixty-five to seventy-four]

Finally, for several elderly drivers, small cars were upsetting. Drivers were not mentioned. From the interviewees' perspectives the little cars "can't stay in their lanes," "drive from one side to another," or "speed and cut in."

To Summarize

An attempt was made to portray a sense of structure, and an appreciation of the nature of serious crashes in which elderly drivers were involved. But beyond that, we tried to exhibit the way elderly people think, reason, and rationalize the multifaceted components of driving, aging, and accident involvement.

First let us note that the motorists' own self-confidence in their abilities to drive pervades the thinking of the elderly drivers involved in injury-producing crashes. The all-consuming image left by the accident victims was that they were cautious, good drivers even though they experienced dramatic crashes for which many were officially charged or that they are a greater risk measured by exposure than other drivers. They described themselves as watchful, and slow, keeping appropriate distances between cars, driving defensively, having safe driving histories, obeying traffic signs, keeping the cars in good running order, and disliking in-car distractions. These self-evaluations tend to be at odds with accident statistics. In their view, the accidents were anomalies that happen to good drivers. The "real" blame lay with the other drivers, the condition of the roadway environment and/or foul weather.

The crashes occurred while the seniors were travelling for such reasons as shopping, visiting friends or family, running errands, attending health care appointments, enjoying recreation events, or participating in church- or hospital-related volunteer work. The car is undoubtedly the elderly person's lifeline.

Significantly, more crashes occurred going toward, rather than away from, home. The anticipation of returning to familiar surroundings and becoming involved in home-related activities may have contributed to the elderly's misadventures. Yet the trips during which the accidents happened were commonly judged to be routine and normal. Little out-of-the-ordinary happened before the elderly sat behind the wheel of their vehicles. However it was noted that for some accident victims the day leading up to the crash was problematic because of irritations, personal problems, medical concerns or arguments.

As a rule, the accident victims disliked driving during rainy nights because of the glaring lights and during rush-hour or heavy traffic because of impatient, careless drivers. But, if a trip was considered necessary, the motorists would be prepared to drive during these times. Proof of this take-charge attitude lay in the numbers. The majority of crashes in which the 130 elderly drivers were involved occurred at dusk or at night, many in rainy conditions. The victims considered these trips to have been important enough to take risks and they felt competent to counter hazardous conditions. Interestingly, these same drivers may in fact be exemplary motorists during ideal driving conditions as suggested by statistical analysis.

The accident focus became clearer when we established that just before the crash some of the drivers were attentive to things other than immediate driving chores. They were searching for certain markers such as signs, houses, street exits, or stores; speaking to passengers; thinking about issues removed from driving; or day dreaming. But, the accident-involved drivers consistently stated that they were driving normally. It was the other drivers or the conditions of the road that were abnormal. Not surprisingly, discussion about the possible prevention of the crashes focused continuously on the critical behaviors of other drivers or invisible experts such as traffic engineers who failed to adequately design or maintain the roadway.

The accident-involved seniors repeatedly stereotyped young or younger drivers as being impatient, unsafe, and reckless. Although they personally experienced other people's accusations of being slow and dangerous, they generally did not believe that members of the police department or the Insurance Corporation participated in stigmatization. Any concern about treatment by insurance company personnel was based on disagreement about the worth of the wrecked vehicle.

It became obvious that the elderly lived in constant fear about the possibility or probability of forever losing their driving privileges. A conventional response to such an eventuality was to take the bus. As things are today, this alternative is not without problems because of limited bus routes and inconvenient scheduling. This limitation is especially relevant to the younger elderly drivers who are still working. For others, walking can replace driving. The catch, however, is that the stores must be located near the elderly persons' homes or within their walking perimeter. Taxis are too expensive. Receiving rides from other people may be expedient and welcomed, but may also be too inconvenient, unless the chauffeur is willing to be flexible with his or her time. Overall, the impact of losing the car can be suitably phrased as the loss of freedom and independence and curtailment of life-style.

Over the years, the accident victims have learned to compensate for age-related weaknesses by being more patient and driving more slowly and more cautiously—being more conservative. This they believe makes them good drivers—better than most. Their positive self-esteem is built on a bedrock of successful driving experiences which were portrayed as respectable, including few crashes or traffic violations.

The general tenor of this chapter was intended to be upbeat. Sections dealt with how and what elderly drivers consider to be normal, not how they should be admonished for their shortcomings. The extent to which the features described constitute prime criteria for follow-up, without entering the halls of stigmatization, is noteworthy for further consideration.

References

Connidis, I. 1987. "Life in Older Age: The View from the Top." In V. Marshall (Ed.), *Aging in Canada: Social Perspectives* (2nd ed.). Toronto: Fitzhenry and Whiteside, pp. 424-50.

Goffman, E. 1967. *Interaction Ritual*. New York: Anchor Books.

Krech, D., R. Crutchfield, and E. Ballachey. 1962. *Individual In Society*. Tokyo: McGraw-Hill Koga Kusha Ltd.

Marsh, P., and P. Collett. 1986. *Driving Passion: The Psychology of the Car*. London: Jonathan Cape.

Schutz, A. 1970. *On Phenomenology And Social Relations*. Chicago: University of Chicago Press.

Stone, L., and S. Fletcher. 1987. "The Hypothesis of Age Patterns In Living Arrangement Passages." In V.W. Marshall (Ed.), *Aging in Canada: Social Perspectives*. Markham, ON: Fitzhenry and Whiteside.

9

Windows of Change: Transitions, Predictions and Eventualities

B. de Vries

For I dipt into the future, as far as the human eye could see,
Saw the vision of the world, and all the wonder that would be;

Saw the heavens fill with commerce, argosies of magic sails,
Pilots of the purple twilight, dropping down with costly bales;

Heard the heavens fill with shouting, and there rained a ghastly dew
From the nation's airy navies grappling in the central blue;

Far along the world-wide whisper of the south-wind rushing warm,
With the standards of the peoples plunging through the thunder-storm;

Till the war-drum throbbed no longer, and the battle flags were furled
In the Parliament of man, the Federation of the world.

There the common sense of most shall hold a fretful realm in awe,
And the kindly earth shall slumber, lapt in universal law.

So I triumphed ere my passion sweeping through me left me dry,
Left me with the palsied heart, and left me with the jaundiced eye;

Eye, to which all order festers, all things here are out of joint:
Science moves, but slowly slowly, creeping on from point to point:

Slowly comes a hungry people, as a lion creeping nigher,
Glares at one that nods and winks behind a slowly-dying fire.

Yet I doubt not through the ages one increasing purpose runs,
And the thoughts of men are widened with the process of the suns.

What is that to him that reaps not harvest for his youthful joys,
Though the deep heart of existence beat for ever like a boy's?

Knowledge comes, but wisdom lingers, and I linger on the shore,
And the individual withers, and the world is more and more.

Knowledge comes, but wisdom lingers, and he bears a laden breast,
Full of sad experience, moving toward the stillness of his rest.

(Lord Tennyson, "Loksley Hall")

In order to make the "what is" description of elderly drivers more meaningful, interest should be placed on the interaction between present and future. Given the reality of today, we need to watch unashamedly the blurred vision of the future become more defined and crystallized. As the hues take on sharpness, it will become easier for us to evaluate possible or probable consequences of time and social change.

A broad array of literature pertaining to the existential, medical, legal, social, demographic, and economic dimensions of aging was analyzed. The real and/or perceived trends and concepts that were unearthed were then related to the world of driving. The synthesis of the two led to this chapter. It encourages the reader to sit back and carefully reflect on what may come. It shakes us out of our tendencies of entropy—trust in institutional states—to retain the life structures of today.

The first issue that comes to mind is that people in western society have a love affair with the automobile. It is an absorbing love of a curious sort. Marsh and Corbett (1986) claimed that our culture and even our private lives are dominated by the complex and multifaceted relationship we have with cars. The automobile has permeated the most intimate spheres of existence: our homes, our families, ourselves.

The car is granted a position of prominence and celebration in front of the family residence and is accorded a dwelling of its own that would be the envy of many Third World families. To get from our easy chair in front of the television to our comfortable seat in front of the steering wheel need not require going out of doors. The automobile has been advertised as a "living room on wheels" (Marsh and Corbett 1986) providing us with the opportunity to take "our homes" with us when we travel.

The personalization of the car has gone even further. A widespread number of motorists have symbolically included their motor vehicle in the family unit. For example, Marsh and Corbett (1986) reported that in a recent poll commissioned in Great Britain, over 750,000 people have personified their vehicles by naming their current or former car "Betsy," "Bessie," or other names. We speak to our cars: we coax them when they stall and reinforce or stroke them when they start; we scold them when they hesitate and comfort them when they've been injured.

Automobiles are forms of prestige and distinctions. They reflect our personalities. They become statements of our being through their name, color, power, shape, and size. They feed our egos and provide us with opportunities for control and mastery. They form the boundaries of our personal space and provide us with the illusion of privacy and anonymity in public places.

The automobile has become the vehicle (in every sense of the word) that satisfies a whole constellation of personal needs. In urban settings, shops and services are located at distances that mandate the continued and increased use of the automobile which, in turn, provides the ingredients that enable "urban sprawl" to flourish. We drive to shopping centers to fulfill our most basic needs—food and clothing. We access our personal and social relationships, health and recreational services, and even our education by way of the automobile. In short, the car has essentially restructured the organization of society. It has changed our concept of home and community, the organization of our lives and social activities, and our views on self and local, national or even international environments.

Notwithstanding this intriguing and pervasive psychological relationship between person and car, the simple and significant fact remains that the automobile is the way by which the vast majority of North Americans transport themselves. The reliance on the automobile for autonomy, independence, and even survival has remained constant over many years (Winter 1984)—a reliance that knows no age boundaries and cuts across cohort effects. Although today's seniors may have grown up during a time when the automobile played a less prominent role (i.e., more of a luxury, more of an oddity), the elderly like all other age groups, consider the automobile to be a necessity. We need only to reread Chapters Six, Seven, and Eight to become aware of the vital role the car plays in elderly people's lives. Furthermore, Brainin (1980) reported that elderly individuals without vehicles are displeased with their transportation mode and options and find walking and public transportation difficult. It is unlikely that other means of transportation will emerge in the near future to satisfy the continuing and continually expanding transportation needs of the elderly. This serves as a short preview of the elderly and driving.

Previous chapters in this volume presented the theoretical and empirical context for an examination of the elderly driver. The aim of this chapter is to move beyond the other sections and provide a platform from which a perspective on the future might be afforded. This entails a recapturing of "where we've been" and "where we are" to provide the conceptual backdrop against which an evaluation can be made of "where we're going." However, a task that proposes to chart all of the "waters known" and some that have yet to be "discovered" is doomed to failure and defeat unless certain constraints and conditions are made explicit at the outset. The content domains covered in this chapter are therefore selective rather than exhaustive. Their inclusion is intended to represent the most important and significant issues. They highlight facets of the plethora of elderly needs that involve, and are met, by the use of the automobile.

The basic assumption upon which the selected content rests is that to understand aging, we need to understand life span. After all, old age and aging are expressions of relativity. This notion was introduced earlier in Chapter Two and is further discussed here in demographic terms. Inseparable from the demographic concerns of the population aging are issues of health and welfare. Typically longevity is at least partially predicated upon a modicum of health.

Patterns of social activity are equally important in the concept of life span. For example, who we see, and the frequency of contact are implicated in morale, life satisfaction and ratings of health (Riley and Foner 1968). The role of sociality in a life span perspective becomes vital in terms of the elderly care-giving, support, and social mobility.

The mobility and patterns of social interaction are particularly salient, as they lie at the core of the ground swelling of social and political activity by seniors. Politically, vocal groups are letting their voices be heard and their "clout" be felt, especially in the presence of the formation of potential cleavages between young and old and in defense of the economically disadvantaged (e.g., older women).

The areas/issues mentioned so far are not inseparable from one another. They all have a bearing on the transportation needs of the elderly—the aging driver and the use of the automobile. For example, at the most fundamental level, there is a growing number of seniors. Their proportions of population "pyramids" are expanding. As reported in Chapter Three, parallel to the elderly population growth is the increasing percentage of elderly drivers and their continued use of the automobile.

Positive health (in part) promotes this population growth. But it also facilitates social activity, social mobility, and financial well-being, which in turn promote positive health. This inherent dialectic/chain of mutual influence contributes to continued and increased transportation needs. Factors such as population numbers, health, social activity, and finances come together to make age a salient political issue and to create an environment by which seniors are more prepared to effectively voice their concerns.

These are but a smattering of the myriad of integral and integrated issues that speak to the elderly driver and form the basis of discussion. Following a brief description of the historical roots, current trends, and future prospects of relevant issues, the notion of how the automobile filters through these issues will be discussed.

The Demography of Aging

There are probably as many definitions and examples of aging as there are individuals; everyone has an idea of what it means. For most people, however, an aging population signifies an increasingly large number of older individuals, especially those sixty-five years of age and older. With growing percentages of older individuals, a population is said to be aging. This view is supported by the United Nations, which considers a population as "aged" when more than 7 percent of it is over sixty-five years old (McDaniels 1986).

There is nothing magical or sacred, however, about the age sixty-five; it was first introduced in 1882 by Bismarck as the age for Germans to retire, when the average life span was forty-five years. During the 1935 Depression, the United States adopted the sixty-five year old bench mark primarily because it was believed that young men supporting families should have a higher priority for scarce jobs than should older persons (Kimmel 1974).

There is an inherent cultural bias in the adoption of a specific year of life as the entry point into old age. As McDaniels (1986) suggested, it might be that populations in Third World countries such as those in Africa or South America are actually older than have been acknowledged. If, in such countries, the average life expectancy is fifty, and a significant proportion of the population is forty years of age or over, then this population would be considered old (or aging) even though it had very few representatives in the sixty-five and older age group. Thus, "to say that a nation's population . . . is aging is to say little about either the absolute or the relative numbers of elderly persons found in that society at a particular point in time" (Myles and Boyd 1982:259). It is nevertheless the case that most of the worldwide statistics on old age rely on this conventional, Western measure and definition.

There is another problem contained in an analysis of an aging population when proportions of individuals over and under some specific age are considered. In particular, the age-precise "packaging" strategy promotes the view that there exist distinct groups of people—"old" and "young." This reflects relativism. It is our contention that an understanding of an aging population entails a recognition of changes at all ages, not just those that occur in any particular sector (e.g., the sixty-five and older group). In the 1970s, the proportion of people over the age of sixty-five in Canada grew by 35.3 percent. During the same decade, the proportion of people between the ages of twenty and thirty-four grew by 37.3 percent, while the proportion of those between the ages of five and fourteen decreased by 19 percent (Statistics Canada 1984). Thus, the aging of the Canadian population during the 1970s was a result of not only a swelling of the numbers in the older age groups, but also the entry into adulthood of the "baby boom" generation (i.e., those who were born in the late 1940s and 1950s) and, more importantly, the decline in the numbers of the youngest group (McDaniels 1986). The overall effect is an increase in the general average age. It is the sort of Gestalt approach that is mandated in an analysis of population aging.

Population Aging: Some Relevant Factors

In the literature, several factors have been identified as contributing to an aging population. One that has received a great deal of press and attention has been the linkage of population aging with increased life longevity and/or decreased mortality. This is usually attributed to the advancements in medical technology. However, in the overall process, medical advancements played somewhat of a "supporting" role in population aging.

Although older persons have benefited from medical advances, they do not do so to the same extent as younger persons and particularly infants. The diseases and accidents that plague and have plagued elderly individuals continue to persist and are typically more resistant to medical intervention. For example, elderly-prone accidents, such as falls, account for a large proportion of hospital visits. Major chronic diseases such as arteriosclerosis, cancer, emphysema, diabetes, cirrhosis, and osteoarthritis continue to strike the elderly (Simmons-Tropea and Osborn 1987). Even those diseases that have been treated successfully have had the effect of allowing a greater number of individuals to attain "old age." They do not necessarily stretch out the life span, defined by Stone and Fletcher (1986) as the age to which the hardiest one tenth of 1 percent (one in 1,000) of a birth cohort will survive. The real advances in medical technology have meant that more infants survive childbirth and childhood diseases, live successful lives and eventually reproduce. The process has the long-term effect of rejuvenating a population.

There has been some debate, however, about the length of effective human life span. It has recently been suggested that the human life span may be between ninety-five and 100 years of age. For example, Stone and Fletcher (1986) reported that in 1941, women eighty years of age had less than a 10 percent chance of reaching age ninety-two, and a 6 percent chance of becoming ninety-four. In 1971, eighty year old women had a 20 percent chance of reaching ninety-two, and a 12 percent chance of reaching ninety-four. After this age, survival rates decreased rapidly. Men have not enjoyed the same sorts of increments in survival chances, neither throughout the life span, nor at age eighty. However, some 70 percent of the men and above 80 percent of the women who will be in the seventy-five to seventy-nine age range in 2016 will live to become eighty to eighty-four years of age by 2021. There is no reason to believe that the aging trend differs greatly in the United States. In both countries the incremental survival chances point to the need for support service demands of a population segment above the age of eighty-five.

At the center of the life-span discussion is Fries' (1983) theory of the compression of morbidity. This theory suggests that times of ill health and disability in old age can be compressed. As the onset of the symptoms of disease is delayed longer than the rate to which life expectancy is increased, people will be in poor health for a shorter period of time at a later stage in life. But with compression can come poorer health based on the cumulative effects of disease. Therefore, there arises a greater need for medical intervention and even hospitalization in later life. Schneider and Brody (1983) reported that over the years symptom onset of disease has remained fairly stable, while prevalence of disease has increased in the face of longer life. The result is that a greater number of seniors are afflicted by chronic diseases for a greater length of time. Because of the compression factor, the elderly will be in poorer health at a later period in their lives. But their lives are extended. Early mortality has declined.

Concomitant with the declining elderly mortality rate is a documented increase in positive attitude towards their physical fitness. During the years 1976 to 1981—a period marked by intensive advertising about the benefits associated with physical fitness—seniors, especially those in the early years of retirement, recorded a greater increase in the portion of performing regular exercise than any other age group. Moreover, the nonsmoking rates rise with age peaking in the "eighty-and-over" group, where more than three-quarters are nonsmokers. Similarly, the regular consumption of alcohol declines with age. Attention to health status and related concerns seems to be an important aspect of aging which may manifest itself in a diminishing of the diseases to which the elderly have previously been sensitive.

A second factor contributing to an aging population is immigration. As the West was being opened in the early 1900s and again in the time immediately following World War II, North America welcomed large numbers of new citizens. McDaniels (1986) points out that the new arrivals during these periods of time were mostly young people. They presently swell the ranks of the elderly population, as endorsed by the observation that more than one-third of those over the age of sixty-five, at least in 1971, were born outside of Canada (Statistics Canada 1976). However, the immigration factor wields a double-edged sword. Today's high rates of immigration by younger people contribute to making Canada more youthful. It is an interesting observation that government immigration policies and practices have pronounced effects on the relative aging of its population.

The most important and consistent factor contributing to the aging of the Canadian population, however, is the seemingly neglected impact of the declining rates of fertility. In fact, Gee (1982:61) has claimed that "population aging is the unplanned by-product of planned parenthood." Declining fertility rates reduce the proportion of individuals in the youngest age group relative to the total population. This serves to increase the proportions held by older age groups. Thus, as McDaniels (1986:6) has written, "declining fertility causes the population to age, even if the absolute numbers of older people remains the same." The major fall in the birth rate has occurred since 1960: the post "baby boom" or the "baby bust" generation. In 1986, the Canadian fertility rate was 1.6, less than half of the fertility rate of 3.5 experienced in 1946.

Population aging, then, is a consequence of many factors, the most notable being the declining rate of fertility. These factors, however, do not operate in isolation and are probably inseparable from the social and economic forces which also contribute to population aging. For example, immigration trends vary with the economy. There are waves of migration (both immigration and emigration) in relation to the variation of available resources. That is, a buoyant job market attracts immigrants; a depressed job market detracts or discourages potential immigrants and may even encourage emigration. Birth rates, too, are at least a partial function of the recognition of the economic and social instrumentality of smaller families. In fact, it can be said that population aging is both a sign and a product of the relative affluence of an industrialized nation.

Of interest is that aging populations can be controlled by governments who manipulate the defined factors. Governments may target certain health areas in their funding with the aim of promoting research and the eventual treatments of the diseases and disorders to which seniors are particularly vulnerable. Campaigns (not unlike the successful Fitness Canada appeal) can identify issues of health and welfare relevant to seniors and to aging in general. A country's immigration policies may be set with an eye toward the future. As well, tax credits and benefits may be allocated with fertility rates in mind. The quality of life and the shapes of population pyramids can all be affected and to a large extent determined by acts of legislation.

The Canadian Context

Whereas the foregoing discussion focused on factors associated with demographic or population aging, the following account examines the Canadian population and its aging status in relation to other countries and in relation to itself. There are varying degrees of "aged" populations throughout the world in adherence to the United Nations definition provided earlier. In 1980, six percent of the population of the world was at least sixty-five years of age (United Nations 1984). Presently, of all continental regions, Europe has the greatest percentage of population over the age of sixty-five, followed by North America and the USSR. Africa has the smallest percentage, slightly less than Latin America and Asia (United Nations 1984). In the economically developed countries, 11.1 percent of the population is over sixty-five; in the economically developing countries, 4 percent are of this age. It has been predicted by Siegel (1981) that these percentages will rise to 12.6 percent and 4.4 percent, respectively, by the year 2000.

Among the countries in the world with the most aged—West Germany, Belgium, France, Hungary, Switzerland, the Scandinavian countries, the United Kingdom and the United States—Canada is probably the least old. It has the largest proportion of people younger than fourteen, the largest proportion of citizens between the ages of sixteen and sixty-four (the labor-force age range), and the smallest proportion of inhabitants older than age sixty-five (McDaniels 1986). We should add that a significant reason for the European countries having large proportions of elderly people is that they suffered enormous loss of life—young men primarily—during World War II. This contributed to their present-day aging status.

Currently in Canada those over sixty-five years of age account for 10.3 percent of all Canadians. By the year 2000, this should rise to 13.5 percent; by the year 2006, this figure is projected to be 14.2 percent; and by 2031, approximately 24 percent of the Canadian population will be sixty-five years of age and older (D'Arcy 1987). Relatively speaking, Canada stands in good stead, particularly economically, given the proportion of the Canadian population in the labor-force and pre-labor-force age range. This is a favorable climate that will likely persist well into the twenty-first century.

It is a commonly held view that an aging population is in an economic "crisis" state (McDaniels 1986). The "crisis" has typically been assumed to take the form of a society no longer productive or creative by virtue of its aged population. Innovations and creative energy are thought to fall under the relatively strict purview of the young, as a consequence of "diminishing capacities" with advanced age. It is also feared that further problems would develop from the inability of a country's social system to provide pensions and health care to an expanding older population.

But, an examination of aging shows that none of Canada's contemporary countries experienced the anticipated crisis. In part that is because upwardly spiralling national debts and economic recessions seem to run orthogonally or independently and not consequentially to population aging. "To claim that today's economic problems are caused by population aging . . . seems too simplistic in light of the fact that economic problems have preceded the advent of an actual acceleration in population aging" (McDaniels 1986:49).

Although Canada is less old than other industrialized countries, nevertheless it still is aging. From 1851, the time of the first census, to 1981, the median age or midpoint of a population where 50 percent is older and 50 percent is younger has steadily increased from 17.2 to 29.5 years (Foot 1982). Traditionally, median age of thirty or greater is considered old, while a median age of twenty or lower is considered young (Shrylock and Siegel 1975). In the same time interval, the percentage of the population sixty-five years and older has risen from about 2.7 to 10. Of course, these two trends are highly related and not quite as linear as portrayed here. On the one hand, during the Depression years, there were substantial leaps in both the median age and the proportion of elderly reflecting low birth rates and little immigration. On the other hand, during the "baby boom" years, which was also a time of high immigration, there were slight decrements in both of these measures indicating a rejuvenation of the population. The decades following, however, have since revealed the lowest birthrates in Canadian history (McDaniels 1986).

It is perhaps this accelerated pattern of aging that has generated the greatest concern and fueled an "aging crisis" fire. We do not propose that some concern is not warranted; we do suggest, however, that an aging "crisis" is not (yet) upon us nor is it necessarily imminent. We, both as a society and as aging individuals, have the opportunity and the time to prepare ourselves and our environments for an ever-increasing aging population. We may begin this preparation by examining our peers and the other Western countries who are more aged, yet continue to produce, be creative, and grow. We may also examine our history and chart our own aging across time and recognize that this is neither something old nor evil. We must, however, also examine our values of, and our perspectives on, aging: we must deal with our ageism—our stereotyping and discrimination of people as a consequence of their age. Age is a convenient and standardized metric or yardstick; it is not, nor should it be, a value judgment.

Health and Well-Being

An Insider's Perspective on Health and Well-Being

One of the largest growth groups within the elderly population is the old-old: increasing numbers of individuals eighty-five years of age and older are beginning to fulfill their life-span potential. Medical/social advances have facilitated this temporal extension, but speak little to the issue of quality of life. Northcott (1982) conducted a study of 440 Canadians of all ages and found that older individuals generally felt less stressed and more satisfied with their lives than did younger persons, with the sole exception of health. It was a significant stressor for more older adults. Even within this context, Matthews et al. (1984) found that the majority of senior Canadians (aged sixty-five and over) reported sufficiently good health to perform their usual activities; the vast majority lived independently in the community, and had incomes above the poverty line (when taken as a whole). This "hidden" group of seniors is of greatest relevance for the present analysis.

Several community studies have been activated to examine health status as a function of age. For the most part, the major dependent measures have been partial or total assistance needed for the following five activities of daily living (ADL) items: rising and going to bed, daily personal hygiene, walking around inside the house, bathing, and shopping in summer. Results from investigations in provinces such as British Columbia, Manitoba, Ontario, and

Quebec are surprisingly consistent: the proportion reporting a need for some assistance with at least one of these activities ranged from 5 to 16 percent for those aged sixty-five to sixty-nine, rising to 33 to 35 percent for those aged seventy-five and over (Marshall 1987). As Marshall stated, if it is a male who reports assistance, the chances are reasonably good that it is being provided by a spouse. If a female reports this need for aid, the chances are that no husband is alive to provide it, and assistance must come from some other source. When questioned about any physical condition, illness, or health problem that is "presently bothersome," the proportion of males responding affirmatively rose from 38 percent of men in their forties to 64 percent of men over age eighty. For females, the corresponding percentages were 44 and 85, respectively (Marshall 1987).

Connidis (1987) conducted a study with 400 community-dwelling seniors examining their likes, dislikes, and worries about further aging: a "view from the top." Only 12 percent of the respondents had used community services at some time in the past and 7 percent were using some form of community services at the time of the interview. These percentages probably underestimate the actual need for service. The researcher overlooked regional differences in availability of services and respondent differences such as knowledge of available services and initiative taken to retain independence or search out service agencies such as public health nurses, meals-on-wheels, homemaker services, and library facilities. When asked about their need for additional help, respondents focused on the salience of basic support services, highlighting the importance of receiving assistance for routine needs such as household chores, grocery shopping, and medical care.

In response to features elderlies liked or disliked about their "stage of life," 90 percent of the respondents were able to mention something they liked, whereas 10 percent claimed to like nothing about their age. The likes of older age included greater freedom and fewer worries (often with respect to work and family), old age pension and financial security, good health, and respect from others. The dislikes of older age included physical limitations on activity, poor health, concerns about widowhood, dependency on others, shorter remaining time to live, and treatment by others. It is interesting to note that similar domains were perceived to be likes by some and dislikes by others.

Moving from dislikes to worries or major concerns about older age, health and dependency or, more specifically, institutionalization and loss of home and autonomy predominated. It appears that the largest proportion of older adults, as reported by Connidis (1987), liked certain parts of their age, but tempered this with an awareness of negative aspects. Connidis summarized the reality for us when he wrote, "In short, older people tend to combine a positive view of their stage of life with a realistic grasp of its detriments" (Connidis 1987:468).

The British Columbia Medical Association (BCMA) has elucidated some of these detriments. They reported, for example, that the elderly require and use more health services per capita than any other age group. Approximately 10 percent of the population over the age of sixty-five accounts for over one-third of the patient days in hospitals per year with most of the medical costs generated during the last six months of life. Such a claim seems to substantiate the compression of morbidity hypothesis described earlier. The health care system is, however, designed more for the treatment of acute than of chronic or degenerative conditions. Seniors are over represented among those who suffer from one or more chronic illness (Harris 1978). The availability of medical care also varies from community to community with rural areas and the inner cores of metropolitan centers often lacking physicians and the facilities required to adequately serve an aging population. It is only recently, and still relatively infrequently, that "medical personnel at any level are trained for, or specialize in, the care of older patients" (McPherson 1983:185).

Despite the presence of diagnosed acute or chronic ailments, the majority of seniors subjectively report that their health is good or excellent (McPherson 1983). This finding was also evident in our survey and focus group interview results. Self-evaluations of good health appear to be especially true for those elderly who have higher levels of education and income (Graney and Zimmerman 1980) and certain ethnic groups (Graney and Zimmerman 1980). For example, over 62 percent of elderly Americans who were members of a racial or ethnic minority group related their health as fair or poor, whereas the corresponding percentage for elderly white Americans was only 37 percent (Harris 1981). Similar to age in this respect, health may be socially defined, contingent upon levels of health expectations for persons of particular age and ethnic groups and the "functional adequacy" of the limiting conditions (Hickey 1980).

Transportation and Health and Well-Being

Reasonable access to transportation may well play a pivotal role in both the actual and the perceived health and well-being of a senior population. From the Connidis study described previously, a central factor underlying some of the dislikes of one's present age and concerns about one's future aging is related to issues of mobility (limits/restrictions on activity), independence, and autonomy. The removal of one's license (or restrictions placed thereupon) calls into play such concerns. Cutler (1975), for example, found a very strong and consistent relationship between access to transportation and life satisfaction among seniors. This was especially true with private as opposed to public transportation.

An even more direct link between health and access to transportation is clearly evidenced in an analysis of elderly members of minority groups.

McPherson (1983) has described the inherent double-bind of elderly Indians living on reservations. As a consequence of their disadvantaged economic position and their geographic location (i.e., reservations beyond the borders of metropolitan areas), these seniors have neither their own vehicles nor ready access to public transportation. Such a situation contributes to poor health in that professional treatment is not sought (owing, in part, to the complicated "seeking" process) and/or emergency treatments that are set at distances that may well be health-jeopardizing. Moreover, when such individuals are hospitalized in city facilities, visits from friends and relatives, a consistent factor in morale and, hence, health promotion are often constrained by the same factors as those mediating the initial medical contact/treatment.

Health is both a reason for, and a reason for not, driving. That is, vehicles are used in the provision of access to the health care system for oneself and/or significant others. It is also the case that upon failing/diminishing health, licenses to operate these same vehicles are removed or qualified (e.g., restriction placed upon them). Public transportation does not always fill in the remaining gaps. Rural areas are predominantly excluded. Even where public transportation does exist, several barriers to its effective utilization by elderly people may also be present. These may take the form of unavailable or inconvenient bus routes, overly expensive fares, psychological factors such as fear of crime or victimization at bus/metro stations, and physical restraints such as large crowds or intimidating flights of stairs. Transportation and primarily the use of the automobile may, in some very important and seemingly unusual ways, form a bridge or a link between the individual and his/her own health. In such a sense, driving is more than just a means of transportation, it is a need in and of itself, and the ways by which other needs (particularly health) are met and serviced. And, looking at present and future trends in transportation planning, the situation will likely continue in the near future. In fact, the significance of health-related automobile travel is more likely to grow than it is to diminish. It is a fact that needs to be addressed by policy makers, legislators, and planners.

Housing Environments

Reiterating a relevant point, the aging of the Canada's population will become most evident in the growth of those over eighty-five years of age—the highest utilizers of health services. This is an important point, given that the institutionalization of the elderly in Canada is high compared to any other jurisdiction in the world, with the exception of the Netherlands (Marshall 1987). Large (1981) reported that 8 percent of the Canadian population sixty-five years of age and older is, at any one time, institutionalized, and this rises to 39 percent of those over age eighty-five. Children are not always available.

For example, almost 20 percent of people over the age of sixty-five have no children alive, or if available, not always willing or able to provide a home for an aged parent.

Nevertheless, the greatest percentage of elderly do live at home where the family is currently the provider of much support. Several American studies reported that 70 to 80 percent of the assistance received by the elderly does not come from the formal service sector; it comes from family, friends, and neighbors (e.g., Maddox 1979). As Rosenthal (1987) suggested, it is unlikely that the family represents an untapped resource whose exploitation could relieve governments of the costs of service provision. Furthermore, while families do provide care, there are limitations on their ability to do so. Some limitations have to do with family structure. We are presently experiencing the beginnings of two generations in retirement, an old-old group and a young-old sector. This creates a situation where "families will have a fragile structure in terms of ability to provide support" (Marshall 1987:478). Some limitations to provide assistance stem from broader social change factors. For example, there are currently more middle-aged women in the paid labor force, which reduces their ability to provide care to older family members. Any social policy that promotes family care may serve to make older individuals dependent on their children, a situation that most older people themselves wish to avoid.

Most importantly, however, the inherent mobility of our culture/society may preclude a significant proportion of the face-to-face delivery of services offered to aging parents by their children. Gutman (1986), for example, has reported that in each of the census years 1961, 1971, 1976, and 1981, approximately *half* of the population five years of age and older were living at a different address than five years earlier. There is also high mobility among those sixty-five years and over. During the same census period, the percentages of seniors who changed residences were between 26 and 31. The overwhelming majority of these moves is from urban to urban setting, independent of provincial boundaries (Longino 1980). This is not surprising given that most of the Canadian population, including seniors, live in metropolitan areas, closer to social care facilities and life-sustaining conveniences.

There exist several reasons to explain why elderly people move from one location or region to another. Economics may play a role, although probably less so than among those in the labor force who move in response to differential employment opportunities and wage rates. Return migration or a return to one's place of birth after a period of residency elsewhere is often thought to be a critical factor in elderly moves. Serow (1978) has examined the rates of such migration for the United States population over the periods of 1955-60 and 1965-70. He found peaks at ages five to nine and twenty-five to twenty-nine, followed by a continuous decline after age thirty, with an upturn in the sixty-five to seventy-four age group. This pattern of movement may represent a "nostalgic attempt" to recapture some of the feelings of security associated with the family home or an attempt to increase the likelihood of accessing kin for the provision of assistance (Gutman 1986). Correspondingly, Wiseman (1980) suggested that some seniors move in either recognition or anticipation of a need for assistance due to declining health status. Biggar (1980), for example, reported that of elderly migrants, 6.3 percent were living in the home of their children and 4.5 percent with siblings. The corresponding percentages for nonmigrants were 3.2 and 2.6, respectively. Shulman and Drass (1979) found that 20 percent of their sample of Canadian seniors moved in order to be closer to kin and/or friends.

Environmental conditions also play a role. The changing demographics of a neighborhood, the desire for better housing, and related environmental reasons such as cleanliness, safety, and proximity to amenities have also been cited as prompting relocation (primarily for local moves). Furthermore, the needs of a senior population are not static across later life. Changing physical and social circumstances often necessitate movement. Most living arrangements become less adequate with advancing age and most house furnishings are incompatible with physical limitations (Harbert and Ginsberg 1979).

Temperature, or the climatic conditions more generally, is a significant determinant of migration. Longino and Biggar (1981) reported that over 20 percent of those sixty years and older presently residing in Florida and Arizona had moved into these states over a preceding five-year period. Statistics Canada (1984) reported that the West Coast consistently attracts the greatest number of seniors in interprovincial moves. The pull of warmer climates on retired individuals has often been reported, but it should also be noted that climatic correlates such as heating costs and health concerns might be important considerations themselves.

More specific to housing, discussion usually revolves around age-segregated and age-integrated housing options for the elderly. The theoretical antecedents of these two housing options are found in disengagement theory and activity theory, respectively. The former describes the voluntary and inevitable withdrawal of the individual from society and society from the individual, while with the latter proclaims that successful aging and satisfaction in later life are predicated upon maintenance of social activity and role enactment. Currently, seniors appear to favor age-segregated housing (with some qualifications), including such options as trailer parks, private and public housing complexes, and retirement communities.

Several age-segregated communities have recently emerged, loosely modelled after senior urban centers in Arizona (e.g., Fun City) and California (e.g., Leisure World). Such developments are heralded as facilitating social interaction and providing ready-made potential social networks. Smaller scale "communities" such as the large buildings housing seniors in Vancouver's West End, however, have often been criticized and labeled by residents themselves, as "senior's ghettos." The homogeneity or lack of diversity contained in these buildings is perceived by many elderly residents as sterilizing, promoting age segregation and stereotyping in the broader community. Such was the problem in the model community built upon the newly reclaimed territory of Noord-Oost Polder in the Netherlands. This city was constructed for the explicit inhabitation of young families—a supposed paragon of family living. It failed, however, as more and more of these young families tried to return to the cities from whence they came in search of intergenerational interaction for both emotional and instrumental (i.e., care-giving, child support) reasons.

Housing Environments and Transportation

The segregation housing concept is relevant to an interesting community developing in northern Ontario. Elliot Lake was formerly a mining town and nearly abandoned with the closure of the mine. It is currently promoted as a community for seniors, providing affordable housing while injecting new life and money into the depressed area. Both the needs of the community and of the seniors are being met. Its northern location and its fairly homogeneous population, however, may well precipitate (on the basis of the preceding example) frequent travel in and out of the community, and this has obvious transportation implications. Its distance from large urban centers mandates the continued use of the automobile. This use reflects great distances and longer exposure on the roads. Fun City, for example, has been labeled by some (e.g., McPherson 1983) as "isolated," referring to its lack of public transportation and its distance from medical, cultural, shopping, and entertainment centers. The automobile, in such instances (and, in many ways, Fun City has become the paragon of age-segregated housing), will not only continue to be the predominant mode of transportation but will continue to grow in both use and importance as it represents the link between the aging individual and her/his familial ties and other social-medical resources.

If the trend continues to age-segregated housing, the usage of the vehicle for basic necessities such as shopping may decline. However, the decrease in travel could be more than offset by long trip uses. If the elderly search for family and friends contact beyond where they live, then it is quite likely that they will take more frequent long trips, increasing their exposure to high speed, long duration traffic.

Similarly, a North American economic phenomenon is the single industry town. As industries such as mining or logging decline, new economic ventures are sought. Two prominent ones are tourism and retirement. With respect to the latter, towns cater to a quality of life for the elderly. Affordable housing, accommodating climate or environmental features and proximity to facilities like shopping and recreation, and organization of events enjoyed by the elderly are marketing devices used to motivate the elderly to move.

Although the communities are not age segregated as such, still they are distant from major urban centers and other destinations where elderly people's children and friends live. Again, increased highway travel is anticipated for meeting the real need to visit family and friends. A trip through the Okanagan Valley in British Columbia demonstrates the visibly large number of elderly drivers travelling to or from centers such as Vancouver, Calgary, or Edmonton.

Social Relations

A central theme in the health and mobility issues is the role of significant other people in the lives of elderly individuals. As previously described, some of the concerns the elderly had about aging were dependency and the loss of a spouse; some of the reasons for migration were the nearness of kin and support networks. Although popular culture suggests that youth is a time of high sociability, and that old age is a time of loneliness, there are several large-scale surveys that challenge this belief (see, for example, Rubenstein and Shaver 1982). In fact, self-reports of loneliness appear to be the highest among adolescents and decrease with age. While it is true that the amount of social contact declines with age (e.g., Riley and Foner 1968), it may also be the case that the desired level of contact drops as rapidly as the actual level of contact. This congruence may preclude loneliness. It has also been reported (e.g., Revenson and Johnson 1984) that seniors rated the quality of their relationship as higher than did younger people, a factor once again associated with lower levels of loneliness. A possible exception to this pattern of decline, however, is some evidence that among the old-old, loneliness is very common (Perlman, in press).

Several correlates of loneliness among the elderly have been presented in the literature. For example, studies have generally found an association between poor health and greater loneliness (e.g., Kivett 1979), perhaps mediated by restricted mobility. Research also suggests that limited access to transportation is related to loneliness (Perlman et al. 1978). The evidence on the association between income and loneliness is inconclusive (Perlman, in press). Shulz (1976) provided an experimental demonstration of the importance of controlling social relations and its impact on loneliness. College students visited residents of a retirement home for a two-month period. In half of the cases, the seniors could decide on the frequency and duration of the visits; in the other half of the cases, they did not have this control. Even though the total contact was the same in both conditions, seniors who could decide on the parameters of these contacts reported themselves as lower in loneliness and higher in hope and happiness. It has also been found that adults who live alone are generally more lonely than those who live with others (see, for example, Revenson and Johnson 1984), although this is not exclusively true among seniors (Gubrium 1975).

While it is true that not all seniors are lonely (and are probably less lonely than adolescents, at least), loneliness in old age is associated with poor health, difficulties getting transportation, lack of perceived control, and living alone. All of these may be age-related "causes" of loneliness, but all of these are also associated with loneliness at other stages of the life cycle. Furthermore, the direction of causality has yet to be unequivocally established. What is clear is the inherent dialectic of factors associated with aging.

Loneliness and Transportation

Transportation in general, and the automobile in particular, is a key instrument in the social lives of a senior population preventing/reducing loneliness, fostering social interaction through social mobility, enriching physical health and psychological well-being. It exaggerates the instances of dysfunction and increases the probability of adjustment.

On one level, well-being comes from the knowledge/recognition that one's mobility is not restricted. The perception of control over one's social environment (and perhaps orthogonal to the actual amount of control), as demonstrated by Shulz (1976), leads to significant decrements in loneliness and increments in hope and happiness. This may well account for the strengthening of the association between an elderly person's access to transportation and life satisfaction with private as opposed to public transportation (i.e., choosing one's time of departure/route of voyage). Cape (1987) suggested that, especially for retired farm couples, driving is a regular source of companionship where a significant proportion of time is spent on "motor junkets, euphemistically known as 'going shopping.'" As long as there is a pull toward social relations, and attempts to move away from loneliness, the automobile plays and will continue to play a vital role. Furthermore, the automobile opens the doors to the much-used health care system of an aging population and the supportive relationships of friends and family, at varying distances. In fact, a sizable proportion of the variance contained in the pathways between increasing age and decreasing health, and decreasing health and increasing loneliness may well be accounted for by access to transportation.

Interwoven into the social fabric of a senior population is accessible transportation. The automobile has become sufficiently integrated into their lives and worlds that it is no longer possible to extract it as a single factor (independent from the rest) for examination. It need not only be a means to an end, the ways by which their needs are met, but it may be an end in itself to the extent that driving is a form of relaxation, a way of earning a living, a measure of satisfaction. These ends were certainly evident in the discussion of Chapters Seven and Eight.

The Politics of Aging

An awareness of the aging population brings with it a recognition of potentially significant political, social, and economic implications. As Dobson (1983:124) wrote, "On the basis of sheer numbers, there is little doubt that the elderly have the potential to play a significant political role, just as laborers and blacks have done in this century." The extent to which this role may be effectively played out has been of recent empirical interest, and is described herein.

Age and Political Participation

A series of cross-sectional, cross-cultural studies (e.g., Nie et al. 1974) has examined the relationship between age and political participation or involvement such as voting. The general pattern of involvement approximates an inverted "U." Participation rates are the lowest among the youngest voters (individuals in their late teens and early twenties) constantly rising through middle age and then slightly declining among those fifty to sixty years of age and older. Subsequent investigations, however, have found that in controlling for (or holding constant) sex and level of educational attainment, there was no longer any evidence of downturn of political participation in the later years. In fact, under such conditions, Glenn and Grimes (1968) reported that levels of political interest typically increased from young adulthood to old age; people slowly but steadily became more attuned to current events as they matured from young adulthood to old age (Glenn 1969). Cutler (1978) reported that large proportions of the older population are involved in voluntary associations, and it appears to be the case that organizational involvement itself, even in nonpolitical congregations, serves to heighten political awareness and activity.

Consider an individual who engages in voluntary work in a drop-in, referral, or service delivery organization for seniors. When governmental cutbacks affect the availability and the sorts of resources to which she (older volunteers are primarily women) is able to direct her clientele, the impact of the cutback is made both salient and immediate. Volunteers are consequently more vigilant of, and sensitive to, these relevant governmental moves. Such a dynamic underlined the recent quick and decisive action taken by seniors in opposition to the British Columbian government's increase in "rent" in long-term care facilities. Although the decision was not reversed, additional monies were found to provide seniors with the necessary funds required to cover this increased expenditure. Similar quick action was taken in opposition to the introduction of user fees in Medicare payments (although a favorable response from the government has not yet been reached).

Political participation seems to be related to a number of individual differences in the sociodemographic characteristics of various age cohorts (including education). If the inverted "U" is, in part, a function of the contemporary elderly, then the gradual replacement of this cohort with a group that has had greater accessibility to higher education should function to increase the rates of political participation by the future elderly (Dobson 1983). Along such lines, Cutler (1978) reported that in 1952, 19 percent of the sixty-five-and-older age group had completed high school, whereas, in 1972 the corresponding percentage was 30. The estimates are that by the year 2015, the cohort which was in its early twenties in 1972 will have approximately 85 percent of its members having at least completed high school. Neugarten (1974) adds to this the proposition that "tomorrow's" elderly will also be younger (if elderly is defined as post-retirement and the trend of increased voluntary retirement at ages younger than sixty-five continues) and therefore different from the elderly of today. She suggested that the future "young-old" will be healthier, wealthier, better educated, and politically more interested, experienced, and skilled than older persons of the past.

Such factors will serve to promote future political activity and participation of the elderly. Their early retirement and relative youthfulness will offer them the time and the energy required in the devotion to relevant causes (e.g., social and/or economic). Their health and relative wealth will provide them with the resources to sustain this activity and "purchase" political clout. They will be able to support (socially, morally, and economically) candidates who are willing and capable of voicing their concerns (and with these expanding numbers, there are likely to be many candidates courting this vote). Their higher levels of education will promote such political activity as a life-long pattern and underscore its importance in later life. They are likely to have had a history of political involvement (to varying degrees) and are unlikely to settle for less in retirement years.

Age and Political Attitude

Questions arise revolving around the types of attitudes associated with those seniors who are likely to be participants in political activities. There has been a tendency to stereotype the elderly as conservative, opponents to change (Ward 1984). A sizable body of research exists that substantiates this position (e.g., Cutler and Kaufman 1975; Riley and Foner 1972). More recently, however, this claim has met with some dispute. For example, with particular reference to the issue of abortion, Cutler (1980) found that older persons changed their attitudes over time to the same extent as younger persons and in the same direction. That is, seniors were characterized by neither a lesser change nor change in a direction differing from that of younger persons. A comparison of flexibility in the United States presidential voting also revealed that older voters were no less flexible than younger voters in supporting a candidate of the "other side" (opposite of their own party identification). Furthermore, there has also been some discussion that the elderly are *more* liberal (or at least more active) on issues involving self-interest (e.g., social welfare programs and mandatory retirement). Some other suggestions are that older age is associated with increased attitudinal support for the federal role in medical care financing and that there is a general trend toward a pro-federal orientation (e.g., Dobson 1983). This, too, has interesting potential ramifications. The senior support for increases in the federal role (of any number of social programs) is at loggerheads with recent governmental trends toward privatization. This asymmetry may well breed discontent, promote potential cleavages, and foster increased political activity on the part of seniors.

Another line of research has examined the aging-conservativism hypothesis from a partisanship perspective. Studies conducted in the United States (see Dobson 1983) reported that older persons were more likely than younger persons to identify themselves as Republicans. Given that the Republican party is generally assumed to be more conservative than the Democratic party, this association was interpreted as further evidence for increased conservatism with age. Apart from the cautionary flags waved in the interpretation of cross-sectional data as evidence of age differences, another interesting issue is raised by such an investigation. The values expounded by political parties are not static and can change over time. Glenn and Hefner (1972:38) have suggested that the "social definitions of the politics of people in the aging cohorts probably changed a great deal even though party identification changed little . . . suggest[ing] that many young liberals have become old conservatives without experiencing appreciable changes in attitudes and values."

A Canadian equivalent may be found in the recent free-trade accord negotiated by the Progressive Conservative party with the United States (opposed by the Liberals and the New Democratic party, although not exclusively so). Although the parameters and dynamics of the deals may differ, free trade was once an initiative of the Liberal party, and opposed by the Conservatives. What may remain stable is party affiliation; what may gradually shift or change is party position. Age per se, then, appears to have no systematic relationship with political preference. This implies, of course, that more than a single party will be called upon to respond to the senior's cry; the advocacy of senior's demands will not reside in some fringe element. The corollary of this is that, out of necessity, all political parties will have to speak to the concerns voiced by seniors.

Age and Political Voice

Is there the potential for the elderly to coalesce and form a unified political force? There is some significant discussion on this issue. Strieb (1968), for example, has noted that the elderly are a heterogenous, diverse group and encompass a broad range of needs, attitudes, and values—a sort of pluralism that may preclude effective social movement. In fact, social forces (e.g., ageism) function to inhibit seniors from identifying themselves as "old" (a necessary if not sufficient requirement for social movement) potentially precluding vocal advocacy of senior-relevant issues. ("Middle-age" appears to be a less pejorative, less threatening, more preferable label.) The elderly also consistently interact with other generations (e.g., intrafamilial ties) which serves to weaken the commitment to a single age-based group (McPherson 1983). Moreover, the courting of the senior vote by all political parties (as described above) may well serve to diffuse any "critical mass" necessary for a social movement.

Nevertheless, Cain (1975) and Ragan and Dowd (1974) advocated the potential for the development of age-based cleavages formed, in part, by the pressures exerted on the economic system by a growing elderly population and on the weakening of kinship ties (as a consequence of the geographic mobility of adult children and their elderly parents). Rose (1965) has discussed the development of a "subculture" of the age based on demographic and social forces such as the numbers of older persons and their improved health, the development of "age-segregated" housing and retirement communities, and social programs providing the vehicle for increased interaction among the elderly.

A potential cleavage between older and younger age groups that might seek expression is of an economic nature hinged upon the assumption that an increase in the proportion of seniors imposes an increased burden upon those in the labor force. Discussions of dependency ratios (e.g., the percentage of those sixty-five and over in relation to the percentage of those between eighteen and sixty-four) typically point to the uninterrupted (observed and anticipated) increase in this ratio from the 1930s through 2050 as evidence of forthcoming economic alarm: the "crisis view." Such a focus on old-age dependency, however, fails to consider that the dependency burden (the proportion of those who are dependent) necessarily consists of the young as well as the old (McDaniels 1986). Ridler (1979) suggested that increases in the proportion of old people are likely to be offset by decreases in the proportion of young people. Moreover, owing to the facts of declining birth rates and increasing longevity, in the early decades of the twenty-first century, the skills and services of a senior population may be in high demand and even required to meet the needs of the labor force of the day (McPherson 1983).

A caveat to the foregoing conclusion, however, rests in a consideration of the types of costs associated with care for the young versus care for the old. The position has been articulated that the economic costs of supporting a dependent child are largely individualized; that is, one pays the debts associated with the rearing of one's own children. The costs of support for an older population are supposedly more collectivized (presumably based on the high use of public medical/social facilities by seniors). Calvert (1977) argued that the crucial or relevant ratio is that referring to the older population vis-à-vis the working aged population.

Inherent in such a position is the tenuous assumption that all people over the age of sixty-five are economically dependent on public services and that all people of working age are active contributors to some central pool. There are many older people (especially in the young-old category) who continue to work (at least part time), many of whom are financially independent and many of whom are cared for by private pensions and/or kinship resources. Correspondingly, many people of working age do not actually contribute. Even more implicit in this position, however, is the assumption of declining productivity and creativity in an aging population: older people are nonproductive and depress the creative spirit and energy of a society. Many examples exist in blatant disproof of this. Consider, for example, individuals such as Bertrand Russell or Albert Einstein or a nation such as West Germany which has one of the highest proportions of its population over the age of sixty-five. It continues to be productive and respected internationally. (McDaniels 1986). Thus, the proposed economic cleavages "waiting in the wings" are necessarily qualified by a host of other factors such as world tensions, the instability of currency, and industrial and trade policies which have more immediate and severe effects on a nation's economy.

Nevertheless, there are said to be cross-cutting pressures at work to heighten age solidarity and increase the probability for age conflict (Dobson 1983). Foner (1975:153) has written:

> Individuals of like age move together through a particular environment. Unlike members of a given social class or ethnic group who have lived varying periods of time and have been exposed to diverse historical experiences, age peers share a common past and face a common future, and this commonality cuts across other lines of stratification.

The common base is not age, per se, but shared experiences in the political and social realm. As Ragan and Dowd (1974) have said, the distinction is really one between a simple age cohort and a political generation.

According to Mannheim (1952), a generation is more than just a group of people born during the same time period (which is what the term "cohort" is meant to represent); a generation is a group of people who have experienced and reacted to particular political, social, or historical events in the same way (McPherson 1983). The result of this is a shared historical consciousness (unique from other generations) promoting a particular social meaning for their lives. An example of such a generation is one in which people had just entered, or were about to enter, the labor force at the onset of the Depression in 1929; this generation "has generally been consistently willing to work hard for low wages" (McPherson 1983:233). Similarly, the "baby boom" generation was exceptionally large, given its situation between two periods of relatively low fertility rates, and has been well publicized: it has been associated with a history of social change.

This wave of individuals has had a similar impact on the other institutions which it has touched. They have experienced crowded schools (facilities which were originally designed to meet the needs of the prior and much smaller cohorts—see Cutler 1978) and crowded job markets and have faced competition throughout their lives (both from within and from other generations). A third generation identified by McPherson (1983) is that of the "counter culture": the student protest groups of the 1960s. He suggested that this generation may always be more outspoken and critical of political, social, and economic conditions than generations preceding or following it.

The recognition of these generations has had the general effect of promoting "age" as a social and political issue which may have the subsequent effect of fostering the development of an age consciousness or an age awareness. Aligned with the increments in levels of education and health status are these generational effects which, in many ways, ensure future political activity on the part (and the behalf) of seniors. The "Depression generation" will continue to seek employment: their often inadequate pensions and their dedicated work history reinforce this. As a result, we can be assured of significant numbers of elderly driving to and from work during such high-risk times as rush hour. Overall, the question of work involvement will continue to make mandatory retirement an issue of contention and maintain the competition for employment and the other circumscribed resources that must be shared. The British Columbia Medical Association's stance on mandatory retirement at the age of sixty-five reflects the importance of the issue.

Institutions such as care and recreation facilities and support services will continue to expand to meet the requirements of this bulge in the population. The numbers involved and the tradition established mandate this expansion and change. Following this generation of competitors lies the "generation of critics" who, at the very least, will ensure that any changes made are not transient and temporary. In many ways, they have become the gatekeepers of human rights.

Political Movements

In the United States, there exist many organizations run by seniors whose raison d'être is to act as the guardian of the rights and concerns of the elderly. Among the largest of these are the American Association of Retired Persons (AARP), the National Council of Senior Citizens (NCSC), and the Gray Panthers, whose aggregated total membership numbers into the tens of millions of people. (The AARP alone boasts a membership of over twenty- five million people.) There are also several membership bodies composed of retirees in certain occupations such as the National Retired Teachers Association (NRTA, a sister organization of AARP), and the National Association of Retired Federal Employees (NARFE).

Similarly, there are organizations whose mandate it is to address the needs of particular seniors such as the National Council of the Black Aged, the National Association for Spanish-Speaking Elderly, and the National Indian Council on the Aging, as well as many others on statewide and municipal levels. Furthermore, interest groups also exist focusing on the needs and aspirations of the elderly, but not necessarily by the elderly such as the National Council on the Aging (NCOA) and the Gerontological Society of America (GSA). AARP has reported that "there are currently around one thousand separately organized senior citizen's groups in the United States at the local, state, and national levels [excluding the] . . . local chapters of national organizations, the total of which for AARP and NCSC alone is in excess of five thousand" [Pratt 1983:146].

Canada, too, has several active political organizations of interest to, and/or administered by, senior citizens. The first senior's organizations at the municipal and provincial levels were established in the 1930s; the first national body was chartered in 1954 (Canadian Governmental Report on Aging 1982). Presently, all provinces have organizations; there are also several national bodies (primarily comprising retired employees of such industries as telephone and transportation). There is a National Advisory Council on Aging to advise the Minister of National Health and Welfare and some provincial governments have similar bodies to provide advice on matters pertaining to issues of aging and the aged at provincial levels. All of these councils include senior citizens in their membership.

At several junctures over the past years, senior citizen's organizations have made themselves visible and have exerted pressure on governments to effect change. Perhaps the most recent and graphic example was the 1985 march on

Parliament Hill by thousands of seniors in protest of the government's decision to de-index federal pensions. Their statement was loud and clear and its effect was strong and immediate. An issue that touched the very core of senior's lives, as attested to by the high proportions of seniors whose primary or sole income is derived from federal sources and had gerrymandered with an impact of sufficient strength so as to highlight the commonalities among diverse groups. That is, pensions are apparently superordinate to ethnic, regional, or even provincial differences and it is this "broader" quality that contributed to the eventual success of the senior's protest. The march was the culmination of intensive lobbying efforts and provided for the rest of Canada a demonstration of force which surprised many, including seniors themselves.

The stereotypic portrayal of aging and the elderly in the popular media has recently fallen under the careful scrutiny of media watch groups, including members of the Gray Panthers and the National Council on Aging. These organizations have posed a series of questions and have provided a list of guidelines for the prevention of fact distortion and the promotion of positive images of older persons. (Included in such lists are cautions against portraying the elderly as inflexible, unproductive, meddling, senile, and sexless.) The aim is not to present a "whitewashed" view of aging; rather, the aim is to ensure a balanced and realistic portrayal. Just as finding humor in the plights of handicapped, alcohol abusers, and members of ethnic and racial minorities is no longer acceptable, so too, is it becoming unacceptable to use the elderly as a forum for humor.

These broader appeals, and issues of economics in particular, have a higher probability of rallying and creating support and eventual successful resolutions than more local and specific suits. Provincial campaigns, to varying degrees, often fail to mobilize the "critical mass" necessary for reform in part because of the reduced, absolute population base from which it can draw, but also because of the perceived heterogeneity within provincial bounds. The implication is that national efforts, for the most part, will be the most effective ways for promoting change.

Such an example serves to highlight the potential political clout wielded by the elderly. Organizations of senior citizens, however, are not a sudden and mysterious phenomenon. In fact, Pratt (1983) has described the Townsend Clubs, which were formed and organized in the early 1930s by a sixty-six year old practicing physician in California, Dr. Francis Townsend. Dr. Townsend witnessed three poorly dressed elderly women scrounging for food in a garbage dump and was apparently so moved that he developed and initiated the "Townsend Plan" which called for a pension of two hundred dollars per month for persons of sixty-five years of age or older. The only condition attached was that the entire amount of money be spent in the United States in the month following its receipt. He envisaged the plan as revitalizing a depressed economy and providing aid/restoring esteem to a hard-hit elderly population. The Townsend movement subsided as the post-Depression economy flourished, but the seeds had clearly been planted for the development of future senior citizen organizations.

The organizations born in the time following the Townsend movement were, for the most part, constructed around a single issue, not unlike the Canadian march, or around a single leader (not unlike the Townsend movement itself) (Pratt 1983). The resolution of the issue or the death of the leader thus brought about the demise of the group. In the United States, however, there are currently a growing number of bureaucratically arranged, modern organizations concerned with a range of sociopolitical issues (Cutler 1978). They are financed by membership dues and external sources and advocacy of the political positions of the elderly is but one of several services offered to their membership. Their advocacy, however, is full and committed. The AARP, for example, has a Washington, D.C., staff of approximately 400 people, a national lobbying staff of nine, and has made between thirty-five and forty congressional appearances. Similarly, the NCSC has a Washington staff of eighteen, a national lobbying staff of four, and has made between twenty and thirty congressional appearances (Pratt 1983). Canadian seniors have yet to organize themselves in parallel ways, although the potential is clearly present. "Squinting our eyes" and looking southward may offer us a glimpse of our aging future, politically.

It is also worth noting, however, that the extent to which the elderly voice is "heard" is at least partly dependent upon the government's willingness to listen (and their perspectives on the target group). This is an important point. What view does the government take on aging and the elderly? The answer to this question has obvious ramifications for future political directions. Currently, at least according to one political commentator on television, "the elderly are to federal politics what yuppies are to BMW sales." The elderly vote is actively courted and publicly cherished. If, in this case, the government is responding to the elderly as a unified and effective political force to be reckoned with (as suggested by Cutler 1978), then such government-elderly interactions should likely persist. Alternatively, as described by Dobson (1983), if the government is responding to the elderly in terms of welfare consideration (i.e., a group disadvantaged by the concomitants of their place in the life cycle, such as low income, poor health), then inflation and the rising costs of social programs might preclude such interactions in the future. Should this latter alternative represent the more dominant picture, then one might speculate that the former alternative would emerge in response. Once again, recall the recent march on Parliament Hill. At least in the Canadian context, neglecting the concerns of the elderly might well create an environment through which better organized and more politically powerful elderly groups would flourish.

Age has "arrived" as a social and political issue and will undoubtedly continue to spark controversies at all levels of government in the years ahead, especially as seniors come to realize their own political potential. The advent of age as an issue is largely a function of the "baby boomers," a well-recognized bulge in the population which has had discernible effects on the institutions of society with which it has come in contact. This group has made "generation" a common word in the vocabulary of many promoting an age consciousness or an age awareness. The awareness is crossed with a number of sociodemographic characteristics such as education, income, and health. That is, the youth of today and the seniors of tomorrow are, generally speaking, better educated, healthier, and wealthier than any other cohort in history. There are factors which have been shown to be associated with increased political participation. Together, these indicators suggest that the seniors of tomorrow will not only be more politically active, but active in age-relevant ways (i.e., in ways that acknowledge population parameters). As those who are elected and those who do the electing recognize and play these roles, politics and age will become familiar bedfellows.

In a very significant way, political involvement or activity brackets discussions of aging and health/well-being, housing environments, and social relations. That is, it is through political action that changes in any or all of these areas can be effected. Along such lines, recall the political action taken in response to the de-indexing of the Canadian Pension Plan. Similar action was taken in opposition to the introduction of various user fees in Medicare services. It is not a substantial leap in logic to suggest that insufficient or ineffectual services or the curtailment of same in any of those sectors which are directly relevant to a senior population may precipitate action of an inherently political nature.

Politics and Transportation

Transportation is one service that reflects the political agenda of the elderly. Transportation, however, like income, is a compounding/mediating factor for seniors (Harbert and Ginsberg 1979). It is the way by which the doors to the health care system are opened, the way by which social relations (e.g., support networks) unfold and proceed, and a decisive factor in housing choices and options. It is also the way by which effective participation in the political process is facilitated. Nevertheless, transportation is a frequently cited problem for older adults. As we already described, there are economic and physical barriers to adequate public transportation, and access is substantially contingent upon urban setting. Harbert and Ginsberg (1979:39) have concluded that public transportation "seems to be designed for the strongest, heartiest [sic], and most agile riders." The private automobile truly reigns supreme influencing highway construction, zoning patterns, and all but a small proportion of public transportation funds (Harbert and Ginsberg 1979). Owning a car, however, is not always an option for seniors: low incomes under already high strain often do not allow for the high cost of auto maintenance and repair.

The automobile has produced a host of economic and social changes including the near-destruction of public transit systems in many cities (e.g., Los Angeles). Harbert and Ginsberg (1979) have described the circular dilemma this raises for seniors and other "have-not" groups in the following way. The default mode of transportation is the automobile. In its absence (and usually as a function of finances) people take public transit; when people can afford cars, ridership decreases. This decrease hits at the life source of transit systems which respond by increasing fares to recover expenses which further discourages service users. Routes change, are deleted, equipment deteriorates, and nobody wins.

Such a vicious cycle is fertile ground for the promotion of politically active seniors. This is perhaps especially true because of the compounding and pervasive nature of transportation in later life. There has been some recent discussion of the drivers' licenses as fundamental rights of individuals contained within the Charter of Rights in the new Canadian Constitution. But just as driving is a basic issue in itself, so, too, is it a basis of many of the other central issues of later life. New and further "senior-friendly" forms of public transit need to be explored. These may vary from public transit timetables that cater to groups other than rush-hour commuters to improvements in the design and function of bus steps, exit doors, and sheltered bus stops with seating provided. Discounted fares during non-rush-hour periods and the "Handy Dart, Dial-A-Ride" programs are important and valuable adjuncts to the transportation needs of, for example, Vancouver seniors.

Furthermore, as the elderly become more politically attuned, they may well confront governments or issues as mandatory driver tests for the aged. In Chapters Seven and Eight, we learned that the majority of elderly drivers are not against tests. They are opposed to tests based on age. They feel this is discriminatory because of their own evaluations as being responsible, competent, safe drivers. Their belief is that mandatory testing should be undertaken for all drivers after a number of years.

As the baby boomers progress into later years, so will undoubtedly the consumer market. Certain seating arrangements, door designs, lighting and the like in cars will undoubtedly be planned to please the elderly drivers. As we move into the new century, engineering changes will follow pace with the market, and the market will be the elderly.

On a practical level, small "p" political involvement such as community volunteer work requires continued use of the automobile. As shown in Chapter Eight, a number of crashes involved elderly drivers who were involved with volunteer services. Also, with the high educational levels of elderly, increased involvement in community affairs will certainly follow. Again, usage of the automobile will be required. Any suggestion of possible censure of elderly driving rights will likely meet a lobbying response led by well-educated, community networking elderly.

Women and Aging

One "ominous development" (as Stone and Fletcher 1980, have called it), that may have a substantial impact on public and economic policy is the proportion of women (and particularly widows) in the older population. As reported in Chapter Three, there is a significant imbalance on the distribution of the sexes in older age groups. This is predominant because women outlive men, exacerbated by the propensity of women to marry men slightly older than themselves. Stone and Fletcher (1986) reported that for every 100 men between the ages of sixty-five and sixty-nine there were 125 women, for every 100 men aged eighty to eighty-four, there were 175 women, and for every 100 men ninety years of age or older, there were 267 women.

There are several important ramifications of this imbalance in ratio. One, in particular, aligns itself with the current cohort of seniors. Women in this cohort were born during or prior to the early 1920s and were, for the most part, socialized into "traditional" sex roles. That is, the primary responsibility for the home and child care resided with these women, many of whom did not work outside of the home. When they chose or were able to find paid employment, it was frequently for minimal wages in low-prestige and often temporary jobs reducing their earning potential and disqualifying them from private pensions as workers. Most women were therefore seen as dependent on their husband's income and would often experience the discontinuance of his pension upon his death (McDaniels 1986). Statistics Canada (1982) outlined that approximately 30 percent of the contributors to public pension plans and over 70 percent of the contributors to private pension plans have made no provisions for pension benefits to go to the surviving spouse upon the death of the paying member. The transfer of these payments is not automatic and often requires the completion of several forms, which many women are either unaware of or uncomfortable in seeking out. Recall that the bulk of the financial responsibilities for these "traditional" couples resided with the primary wage-earner: the man/husband.

These are the types of reasons that underlie the statistics describing the incidence of poverty and aged women. Warlick (1983), for example, wrote that in 1978, one out of every six women aged sixty-five or over had an income below the official poverty line. Furthermore, women were twice as likely as men to experience poverty during old age. Poverty was the rule for one out of every five women living without a spouse, and the probability that a woman would be without a spouse in old age was 63 percent (i.e., widowed, separated/divorced, or never married) (Warlick 1983). Although the rise in labor force participation among females of all ages over the past several decades has been dramatic, there has not been an accompanying increase in the average job status (and hence income) of women vis-a-vis men or in the proportion of women entitled to private and/or public pension plans (Warlick 1983). Women often fail to meet the eligibility requirements of private pension plans which are predicated upon a continuous minimal work history or a minimal level of earnings. Moreover, when plans do pay benefits to women, they are often less than those paid to men, given that payment is based on actuarial tables usually calculated separately for men and women because of the different life expectancies. That is, women supposedly collect benefits for a longer time period than do men so that the same amount of money, should that ever be the case, is spread over a longer time period.

These problems facing older women are unlikely to subside; they require legislative and attitudinal shifts, neither of which is associated with rapid change. Until action is taken, however, these issues are likely to intensify and grow with the aging population. The grassroots movements of seniors' organizations need to be joined by those in both the public and the private sector to redress this economic imbalance and effect change. Historically, women have been unwelcomed in voting places; in the more recent past (and perhaps consequently), women have been reticent in voicing political opinions and even in voting. Men have largely assumed this "right." The women's movement has been struggling to change this and has been greeted with great success. Much like the description of factors associated with volunteer work in this regard, the women's movement functions to increase an individual's political acuity. Participation facilitates an increased awareness of the relevant issues and a greater hesitance in conforming to conventional sex-role expectations. Further cohorts of women, therefore, are likely to play more active and central roles in the decisions and the decision-making processes affecting their lives. Economics has already become a significant factor with the inherently rational argument of equal pay for work of equal value.

Women, Aging, and Driving

The current cohort of senior women are in a more precarious position, wedged between the women's movement and age consciousness on the one hand, and a history of traditional sex roles on the other. Perhaps nowhere is this more obvious than in the increasing numbers of older women who are just learning how to drive. Particularly in rural settings, but perhaps more generally as well, elderly women have "found themselves committed to a life-style that was largely dependent upon the health and vigor of their husbands" (Cape 1987:92). Many of these women are now widows finding themselves in the position of having to claim responsibility for a wider spectrum of their needs, including transportation. Apart from the traumatic emotional experience of widowhood, these women also have to cope with physical and social immobility rooted in the loss of their "husband-chauffeur" (Cape 1987). This lack of transportation creates barriers to the social construction of a new identity and life-style in widowhood (Martin-Matthews 1987).

Winter (1984) has enumerated some of the concerns of elderly women drivers which include a fear of driving on freeways, driving at night, and mention of visual problems which interfere with driving. Special educational and/or training programs for beginning elderly drivers would certainly be of some utility and benefit. These concerns need to be addressed as increasing numbers of elderly women assume primary responsibility for their transportation needs. And, the outlook is not only that greater numbers of elderly women will be driving in the future, but they will also be driving for more reasons.

Concluding Comments

Previous chapters in this and other volumes have attempted to present an image of aging in the context of the life span. After all, aging is a process that has its origins at birth—it is not some disconnected and mysterious period or aspect of life. The common comparison of old versus young has had the unfortunate effect of creating the false impression that there exist distinct and independent groups of people, imposing a dichotomy onto what is, in essence, a continuum. Perhaps nowhere is this more clearly articulated than in the analysis and understanding of an aging population. Populations age as a function of conditions (e.g., increased longevity, patterns of migration, rates of fertility) which may target or highlight particular age groups but which effect and result in changes in all age groups (and thus the population in general). It is not unlike the Hermeneutic circle of text and context: text can only be fully understood within its context and context can only be derived from the text. Similarly, an analysis of any one particular age group only makes sense within the context of the life span and the life span can only be understood by the various age groups comprised therein. This is the backdrop against which this chapter (and, in fact, this book) is to be evaluated. To study the elderly is to take a snapshot of a moving target.

Concomitant with this life-span perspective is the inherent multidimensionality and multidisciplinary nature of the study of aging. An analysis of aging and/or the elderly does not fall under the strict purview of any one particular discipline. For example, aging is more than a psychological process—it is equally a social phenomenon woven into our culture, life-style expectations, attitudes, and attributions. This sort of multidimensionality rose to the surface in the discussions of the interactive factors relevant to, and represented in, the transportation use and patterns of an aging population.

These factors really represent the fundamental or concentric needs of a (senior) population ranging from the more basic to the more over-arching—from physical and mental health through shelter and social welfare to paradigms, politics, and worldviews. It is especially interesting to note how prominently the automobile figures in even the most basic of these needs; it is indeed a telling comment on our twentieth century consciousness that the automobile provides a structure on which an analysis of personal needs may be supported.

It is highly doubtful that the automobile will diminish in importance or be "toppled" from its position of prominence in our lives in the years to come. As a society, we persistently organize ourselves in ways that mandate the continued and increased usage of the automobile. We often pay only lip service to public transportation in urban centers; we don't even consider such services in rural settings. We've chiselled away at passenger rail service such that it is presently a faint and fading shadow of what it once was.

It is without doubt, however, that population parameters are shifting: what was once a country of the young is becoming a country of the old. The charting of the median age over time provides a testimony to this. Corresponding to these dynamic parameters are profiles and patterns of traffic and driving unlike many seen before. Recall Winter's (1984) estimate that by the year 2050, 39 percent of all drivers will be at least fifty-five years of age (as opposed to the approximate 25 percent of drivers today). A growing number of North American cities may assume the form of southern California where the start, finish, and direction of rush hour becomes increasingly unpredictable as the hours "9" and "5" become increasingly irrelevant to many.

The automobile will continue to be the lifeline for the seniors of tomorrow. As described above, it is the key that opens the door to the health care system, and this becomes especially true as health care becomes increasingly centralized. The costs associated with medical technology have risen dramatically and are therefore housed in fewer facilities. Hospitals continue to construct additional wings, and physicians continue to congregate in medical centers. Access to these services is at least partially facilitated by, and often requires, the use of the automobile.

These sorts of reasons and rationales for driving are highly related to age and therefore bound to increase. Driving, and even owning a car, are commonplace among today's youth and tomorrow's seniors. The reliance on the automobile is almost a part of the socialization process. North Americans are also frequent movers, and as families and social networks span the country, face-to-face interaction is predicated upon a variety of transportation modes, not the least of which is the automobile. The movement to rural areas and retirement communities falls into this same arena. As described before, these seniors' communities are not necessarily at the core of senior-relevant worlds. The automobile is the bridge to the medical, cultural, shopping, and entertainment centers.

Morale and social welfare are also contingent upon unrestricted access to transportation. Recall the high, positive association between life satisfaction and private transportation (Cutler 1978; 1980) perhaps mediated by a sense of autonomy and personal control. The automobile is not only the means by which we uncover our social (and support) networks, it also provides us with a social setting (a forum for companionship) in and of itself (e.g., Cape 1987).

Accessible and adequate transportation in general, and the automobile in particular, is an essential/integral thread in the fabric of well-being of a senior population. The preceding discussion has attempted to demonstrate how transportation is not only a need in and of itself, it is also the way by which other needs (including health) are presently met and serviced, and will continue to do so. These hierarchical needs are bracketed by paradigms and political perspectives. Future cohorts and generations of politically active and informed seniors will certainly resonate to this fact and speak to such issues with strength and conviction. Transportation may well be the ground upon which the political clout of a senior population is recognized by both the expanding senior elector and the advisedly responsive elected.

References

Aiken, L.R. 1982. *Later Life* (2nd ed.). New York: Holt, Rinehart and Winston.

Biggar, J.C. 1980. Who Moved among the Elderly, 1965 to 1970: A Comparison of Types of Older Movers. *Research on Aging*, 2(1), pp. 73-92.

Brainin, P. 1980. *Safety and Mobility Issues in Licensing and Education of Older Drivers*. Washington, DC: U.S. Department of Transportation.

Cain, L. 1975. "The Young and the Old: Coalition or Conflict Ahead?" *American Behavioral Scientist*, 19, pp. 166-75.

Calvert, G.N. 1977. *Pensions and Survival: The Coming Crisis of Money and Retirement*. Toronto: Financial Post.

Cape, E. 1987. "Aging Women in Rural Settings." In V. Marshall (Ed.), *Aging in Canada: Social Perspectives* (2nd ed.). Toronto: Fitzhenry & Whiteside, pp. 84-99.

Connidis, I. 1987. "Life in Older Age: The View from the Top." In V. Marshall (Ed.), *Aging in Canada: Social Perspectives* (2nd ed.). Toronto: Fitzhenry & Whiteside, pp. 424-50.

Cutler, N. 1978. "The Consequences of Population Dynamics for Political Gerontology." In M.E. Kraft and M. Schneider (Eds.), *Population Policy Analysis*. New York: Lexington Books, pp. 27-36.

Cutler, S. 1980. "Aging and Conservatism: Cohort Changes in Attitudes about Legalized Abortion." *Journal of Gerontology*, 35, pp. 115-23.

Cutler, S.J., and R.L. Kaufman. 1975. Cohort Changes in Political Attitudes: Tolerance of Ideological Nonconformity. *Public Opinion Quarterly*, 39, pp. 65-70.

D'Arcy, C. 1987. Aging and Mental Health. In V. Marshall (Ed.), *Aging in Canada: Social Perspectives* (2nd ed.). Toronto: Fitzhenry & Whiteside, pp. 424-50.

de Vries, B. 1988. *The Concept of Self in a Life Span, Life Event Context*. Unpublished doctoral dissertation, The University of British Columbia.

Dobson, D. 1983. The Elderly as a Political Force. In W.P. Browne and L.K. Olson (Eds.), *Aging and Public Policy: The Politics of Growing Old in America*. Westport, CT: Greenwood Press, pp. 123-44.

Foot, D.K. 1982. *Canada's Population Outlook: Demographic Future and Economic Challenges*. Toronto: Lorimar.

Foner, A. 1975. "Age and Society: Structure and Change." *American Behavioral Scientist*, 19, pp. 114-65.

Fries, J.F. 1983. "The Compression of Morbidity." *Milbank Memorial Fund Quarterly*, 61(3), pp. 397-419.

Gee, E. 1982. "Discussion of John F. Myles' 'Social Implications of a Changing Age Structure.'" In G. Gutman (Ed.), *Canada's Changing Age Structure: Implications for the Future*. Burnaby, BC: Simon Fraser University Publications, pp. 59-66.

Glenn, N.D. 1969. "Aging, Disengagement and Opinionation." *Public Opinion Quarterly*, 33, pp. 17-33.

Glenn, N.D., and M. Grimes. 1968. "Aging, Voting, and Political Interest." *American Sociological Review*, 33, pp. 563-75.

Glenn, N.D., and T. Hefner. 1972. "Further Evidence on Aging and Party Identification." *Public Opinion Quarterly*, 36, pp. 36-48.

Graney, M., and R. Zimmerman. 1980. "Health Self-report Correlates among Older People in National Random Sample Data." *Mid-American Review of Sociology*, 5(2), pp. 47-59.

Gubrium, J. 1975. "Being Single in Old Age." *Aging and Human Development*, 6, pp. 29-41.

Gutman, G.M. 1986. "Migration and the Elderly: An Overview." In G. Gutman and N. Blackie (Eds.), *Aging in Place: Housing Adaptations and Options for Remaining in the Community*. Burnaby, BC: Gerontology Research Centre, Simon Fraser University, pp. 71-90.

Harbert, A., and L. Ginsberg. 1979. *Human Services for Older Adults: Concepts and Skills*. Belmont, CA: Wadsworth.

Harris, C. 1978. *Fact Book on Aging: A Profile of America's Older Population*. Washington, DC: National Council on the Aging.

Harris, C. 1981. *Aging in the Eighties: America in Transition*. Washington, DC: National Council on the Aging.

Hickey, T. 1980. *Health and Aging*. Monterey, CA: Brooks/Cole Publishing Co.

Kimmel, D.C. 1974. *Adulthood and Aging: An Interdisciplinary Developmental View*. New York: Wiley & Sons.

Kivett, V. 1979. "Discriminators of Loneliness among the Rural Elderly." *Gerontologist*, pp. 108-15.

Kogan, N. 1979. "Beliefs, Attitudes and Stereotypes about Old People." *Research on Aging*, 1, pp. 11-36.

Large, M. 1981. "Services For the Elderly." *Ontario Medical Review*, pp. 38-41.

Longino, C.F. 1980. "Residential Relocation of Older People: Metropolitan and Nonmetropolitan." *Research on Aging*, 2(2), pp. 205-16.

Longino, C.F., and J.C. Biggar. 1981. "The Impact of Retirement Migration on the South." *Gerontologist*, 21(3), pp. 283-90.

Maddox, G. 1979. "Sociology of Later Life." *Annual Review of Sociology*, 5, pp. 113-35.

Mannheim, K. 1952. *Essays in the Sociology of Knowledge*. London: Routledge and Keegan Paul.

Marsh, P., and P. Corbett. 1986. *Driving Passion: The Psychology of the Car*. London: Jonathan Cape.

Marshall, V. 1987. "The Health of Very Old People as a Concern of Their Children." In V. Marshall (Ed.), *Aging in Canada: Social Perspectives* (2nd ed.). Toronto: Fitzhenry & Whiteside, pp. 473-85.

Martin-Matthews, A. 1987. "Widowhood as an Expectable Life Event." In V. Marshall (Ed.), *Aging in Canada: Social Perspectives*. Toronto: Fitzhenry and Whiteside, pp. 343-66.

Martin-Matthews, A., J.A. Tindale, and J.E. Norris. 1984. "The Facts on Aging Quiz: A Canadian Validation and Cross-cultural Comparison." *Canadian Journal on Aging*, 3, pp. 165-74.

McDaniels, S.A. 1986. *Canada's Aging Population*. Toronto: Buttersworth.

McPherson, B.D. 1983. *Aging as a Social Process*. Toronto: Buttersworth.

Myles, J.F., and M. Boyd. 1982. "Population Aging and the Elderly." In D. Forcese and S. Richer (Eds.), *Social Issues: Sociological Views of Canada*. Scarborough, ON: Prentice-Hall, pp. 258-85.

Neugarten, B.L. 1974. "Age Groups in American Society and the Rise of the Young-Old." *Annals of the American Academy of Political and Social Science*, 415, pp. 187-98.

Nie, N.H., S. Verba, and J. Kim. 1974. "Participation and the Life Cycle." *Comparative Politics*, pp. 324-40.

Nishio, H.K., and H. Lank. 1987. "Patterns of Labour Participation of Older Female Workers." In V. Marshall (Ed.), *Aging in Canada: Social Perspectives* (2nd ed.). Markham, ON: Fitzhenry & Whiteside, pp. 228-44.

Northcott, H.C. 1982. "The Best Years of Your Life." *Canadian Journal on Aging*, 1(3/4), pp. 72-78.

Palmore, E. 1980. "The Facts on Aging Quiz: Part Two." *Gerontologist*, 21, pp. 431-37.

Palmore, E. 1982. "Attitudes Toward the Aged: What We Know and What We Need to Know." *Research on Aging*, 4, pp. 333-48.

Pratt, H.J. 1983. "National Interest Groups among the Elderly: Consolidation and Constraint." In W.P. Browne and L.K. Olson (Eds.), *Aging and Public Policy: The Politics of Growing Old in America*. Westport, CT: Greenwood Press, pp. 145-79.

Perlman, D. (in press). "Loneliness: A Life Span Family Perspective." In R. Milardo (Ed.), *Families and Social Networks*. Beverly Hills, CA: Sage.

Perlman, D., A. Gerson, and B. Spinner. 1978. "Loneliness among Senior Citizens: An Empirical Report." *Essence*, 2, pp. 239-48.

Public Affairs Directorate. 1982. *Canadian Governmental Report on Aging*. Ottawa: Minister of Supply and Services.

Ragan, P.K., and J.J. Dowd. 1974. "The Emerging Political Consciousness of the Aged: A Generational Interpretation." *Journal of Social Issues*, 39, pp. 137-46.

Revenson, T., and J. Johnson. 1984. "Social and Demographic Correlates of Loneliness in Later Life." *American Journal of Community Psychology*, 12, pp. 71-85.

Ridler, N.B. 1979. "Some Economic Implications of the Projected Age Structure of Canada." *Canadian Public Policy*, 5, pp. 533-41.

Ridley, M.W., and A. Foner. 1968. *Aging and Society: An Inventory of Research Findings*. New York: Russell Sage Foundation.

Rose, A. 1965. "The Subculture of Aging: A Framework for Research in Social Gerontology." In A. Rose and W. Peterson (Eds.), *Older People and their Social World*. Philadelphia: Davis, pp. 3-16.

Rosenthal, C., 1987. "Aging and Intergenerational Relations in Canada." In V. Marshall (Ed.), *Aging in Canada: Social Perspectives* (2nd ed.). Toronto: Fitzhenry & Whiteside, pp. 311-42.

Rubenstein, C., and P. Shaver. 1982. *In Search of Intimacy*. New York: Delacorte Press.

Schneider, E.L., and J.A. Brody. 1983. "Aging, Natural Death and the Compression of Morbidity: Another View." *New England Journal of Medicine*, 309, pp. 854-56.

Serow, W.G. 1978. "Return Migration of the Elderly in the USA: 1955-1960 and 1965-1970." *Journal of Gerontology*, 33(2), pp. 288-95.

Shrylock, H.S., and J.S. Siegel. 1975. *The Methods and Materials of Demography*. Washington, DC: Bureau of the Census.

Shulman, N., and R.E. Drass. 1979. "Motives and Modes of Internal Migration: Relocation in a Canadian City." *Canadian Review of Sociology and Anthropology*, 2(2), pp. 333-42.

Shulz, R. 1976. "The Effects of Control and Predictability on the Physical and Psychological Well-Being of the Institutionalized Aged." *Journal of Personality and Social Psychology*, 33, pp. 563–73.

Siegel, J.S. 1981. "Demographic Background for International Gerontological Studies." *Journal of Gerontology*, 36, pp. 93-102.

Simmons-Tropea, D., and R. Osborn. 1987. "Disease, Survival and Death: The Health Status of Canada's Elderly." In V. Marshall (Ed.), *Aging in Canada: Social Perspectives* (2nd ed.). Toronto: Fitzhenry & Whiteside, pp. 399-423.

Snider, E.L., 1980. "Explaining Life Satisfaction: It's the Elderly's Attitudes that Count." *Social Science Quarterly*, 61, pp. 253-63.

Statistics Canada. 1976. *1971 Census of Canada, Profile Studies: The Age Structure of Canada's Population* (Vol. 1, Part 1). Ottawa, Minister of Supply and Services.

Statistics Canada. 1982. *Pension Plans in Canada, 1980* (Catalogue No. 74-401). Ottawa, Minister of Supply and Services.

Statistics Canada. 1984. *Current Demographic Analysis, Fertility in Canada: From Baby Boom to Baby Bust* (written by A. Romaniuc) (Catalogue No. 91-524E). Ottawa: Minister of Supply and Services.

Stoddart, K. 1987. "Erfahrung of Young Drivers." In P. Rothe (Ed.), *Rethinking Young Drivers*. North Vancouver, BC: Insurance Corporation of British Columbia, pp. 131-98.

Stone, L.O., and S. Fletcher. 1980. *A Profile of Canada's Older Population*. Montreal, PQ: Institute for Research on Public Policy.

Stone, L.O., and S. Fletcher. 1986. *The Seniors Boom: Dramatic Increases in Longevity and Prospects for Better Health*. Ottawa: Ministry of Supply and Services Canada.

Stone, L.O., and S. Fletcher. 1986. *The Seniors Boom: Dramatic Increases in Longevity and Prospects for Better Health*. Ottawa: Statistics Canada, Population Studies Division.

Strieb, G.F. 1968. Are the Aged a Minority Group? In B.L. Neugarten (Ed.), *Middle Age and Aging*. Chicago: University of Chicago Press, pp. 35-46.

United Nations. 1984. *Demographic Yearbook, 1982*. New York: United Nations.

Ward, R.A. 1984. *The Aging Experience: An Introduction to Social Gerontology* (2nd ed.). New York: Harper & Row Publishers.

Warlick, J.L. 1983. "Aged Women in Poverty: A Problem Without a Solution."In W.P. Browne and L.K. Olson (Eds.), *Aging and Public Policy: The Politics of Growing Old in America*. Westport, CT: Greenwood Press, pp. 35-66.

Winter, D.J. 1984. "Needs and Problems of Older Drivers and Pedestrians: An Exploratory Study with Teaching/Learning Implications." *Educational Gerontology*, 10, pp. 135-46.

Wiseman, R.G. 1980. "Why Older People Move: Theoretical Issues." *Research on Aging*, 2, pp. 141-54.

10

Recommendations

To deprive elderly people of their bogeys is as bad as snatching from babies their big stuffed bears.

(Logan Pearsall Smith, *Afterthoughts*)

Whenever a serious problem arises in society, whether it has to do with personal, social, or physical relations, someone insists on a single cause. This has become almost a fetish, a fixed source, a deterministic stance. It pursues a definition of a fixed and permanent reality, one that characterizes the empirical world.

According to Dewey (1939), the individual and the social milieu cannot be kept apart by abstractions. So it is with elderly drivers. There is a reality behind their appearances that needs to be satisfied before we can confidently grasp the pragmatic and conceptual nature of their behavior. The commonplace of the elderly of tomorrow is the adventure of today, and that is what we were engaged in. We were not interested in elderly driver behavior as individual pathology. To get at the content of elderly drivers we searched the dimensions of self in social transactions bringing to the eye a certain coherence which we attempted to portray in this monograph.

In traffic safety, before research findings become instruments for action, they have to be instruments for preparation. For that, specific areas are involved. The preparatory suggestions we provide are not to be interpreted as a loose-leaf notebook of microwave cooking. They represent an understanding of a group of people based on tolerance, excitement, and integrity. After all, what we recommend waits ahead of us.

Education

The opportunity exists for professionals to engage in an educational venture for the elderly that begins with "felt needs" and problems and is concerned with life adjustment, freedom, social change, technical innovations, and legalities. The data support the need for such education and the good reception such a program would receive from the elderly. We recommend therefore: That an educational traffic safety/driving program be developed that focuses on defensive driving, the physical nature of aging, myths about elderly drivers, self esteem, knowledge on traffic laws and an awareness of automobile features and technology.

The program should be comprehensive enough to allow the elderly to become thoroughly acquainted with driving and to be able to entertain a changing world and new ideas and technology. For most elderly motorists, driving was learned about a half century ago. Major changes have occurred since then. Also, the elderly drivers' self-assessments of confidence and competence may be appropriate platforms for education initiatives. A broad understanding of changes, self-images and capabilities, and their driving risks should help elderly people become more aware of themselves.

Public Awareness

We know that the elderly use three major channels of communication for keeping abreast with changes. These are newspapers, radio/television, and word-of-mouth. The elderly are attuned to lifelong learning through convenient sources. On this basis we suggest: That ongoing media ads are developed for the elderly that are simple, honest and direct.

The ads may take the form of public service announcements and they should be regular fixtures ingrained into the media's schedules.

Since word-of-mouth is also a dominant process for keeping informed, it could also be turned into a potential for increasing awareness of traffic. We propose: That elderly-interest organizations or other relevant institutions plan regular seminars on traffic safety for senior communities large or small.

The latter proposal may be adopted by community service groups, churches or school board adult education departments.

Messages

We have just proposed a strategy to increase awareness. In other words, we pointed to possible messengers. We now need to express more precisely the kind of messages that would be most acceptable to elderly drivers.

Based on the research, there appears to be a need for messages that address the fact that routine activities in which elderly drivers engage and which they consider to be problem-free do entail risk. More specifically we challenge traffic safety educators to develop messages:

1. That outline accident responsibilities assigned to elderly people making

turns at intersections, not yielding the right-of-way and leaving a stop sign without due caution.
2. That specify the legal parameters in traffic and its changing nature.
3. That define elderly driver accident involvement in terms of exposure on the road.
4. That define distracting features in the car such as daydreaming or general inattention to traffic, looking for directions, etc.

The messages must be more than reflections or photo galleries of loosely defined issues. They must deal with the facts, and come to grips with the many problems that beset the elderly.

Reexamination

Reexamination is a policy decision that should be carefully reviewed by provincial or state motor vehicle departments. But it should be considered on the highest possible ethical standards. More precisely we recommend: That motor vehicle departments consider conducting vision tests and coordination tests at regular time intervals from about age fifty-five onwards.

Age as a sole criterion for mandatory reexamination is believed to be, by many, a reactionary prejudicial demand. We know that eyesight and reaction time decline with age. Also, we know that the majority of elderly do not believe that they have problems with these, and that they would not mind being tested. Therefore routine testing with license renewal or stipulated time periods could be seen as a progressive action.

Licensure

An extension of reexamination is licensure. We know that the vehicle is a key feature in the elderly's quality of life. In fact it is linked with psychological, social, and physical well being. We also know that the elderly recognize that the day may come when they cannot drive any longer.

Based on the research, we consider the following recommendations to be forward-looking and sensitive:

1. Based on reexamination results and driving records of an elderly person, the individual's family doctor and a doctor appointed by the motor vehicle department do separate physical examinations and decide with the elderly person the extent to which he or she is still able to drive safely.
2. If there is no consensus between the doctors, the Superintendent of Motor Vehicles should, after an interview with family members and an in-depth review of medical findings, make the final decision on licensure.

The elderly trust, first and foremost, their doctors. According to the research participants, driving-related decisions should be made by a medical doctor and the elderly person. Other possible parties that are trusted enough to contribute are family members and the Superintendent of Motor Vehicles.

Based on all available data, the basis of a license decision should be the result of unbiased eyesight tests, other medically related exams, and knowledge tests.

With the possibility of losing a license, the elderly person's life is in a turmoil. Elderly people need accessible transportation to carry on a full life which they believe is their inherent right. To help do this we offer the following recommendation: That social and service agencies, and community interest groups, organize volunteer chauffeur programs so that the elderly can engage in activities free of transportation worries.

As the elderly population seventy-five years old plus is increasing, it would be a wise move by public transit officials to establish routes and schedules to make transportation more accessible to neighborhoods that comprise a significant elderly population.

Engineering and Urban Planning

Besides using the automobile, the elderly walk or take the bus. Use of such transportation alternatives is sure to increase in the future. We should prepare for that probability by seriously considering the following recommendations:

1. That the design of traffic control devices be sensitive to the needs and capabilities of elderly pedestrians, especially in communities or neighborhoods containing significant elderly populations.
2. That in communities supporting a significant elderly population, bus routes and trip schedules be planned in accordance with the needs of the elderly.
3. That the service of special buses for the disabled and/or elderly be implemented at a level consistent with the increasing elderly population.
4. That means for enhancing oncoming vehicle visibility, such as mandating daytime headlight use, be considered as a way to improve elderly driver assessment of maneuver opportunities.

Any preparation for action we take should incorporate the elderly people's views. Their perceptions of safety, caution, other drivers, personal abilities, relationships with others, and involvement in driving behaviors considered to be risky and dangerous are vital ingredients. They should form the platform upon which intervention strategies are built.

Conclusion

By now, the reader will have a grasp of the basic problems of aging and operating a motor vehicle. Both are interrelated problems. First, the research data are often not clear-cut. Second, even when they are, their interpretation is usually distorted by traditional research pressures which have influenced or shaped the definition of the problem. In the final analysis, the many psychological, social and physical elements have been poorly articulated to those who bear the label of elderly.

The monograph was designed to help reduce the sense of frustration which often overwhelms the elderly when they are faced with discussions on driving and traffic safety. We hope that an understanding of the broad yet deep nature of the subject matter will result in shifting public focus on the elderly driver away from the narrowly defined empirical to the more open multiperspective, where it clearly belongs.

We are aware that we can motivate the elderly to make some changes in their personal driving habits that may significantly reduce their chances of becoming a fatality. But the possibilities are measured. That is, we need to first find out the extent to which the elderly are firmly locked in their particular worldviews. Canada, and we hazard to say the United States, offers elderly people limited opportunity to choose freely where to live and how to travel. The lack of convenient mass transit routes and schedules, increasing urban sprawl, shortage of rural medical health and other care facilities, and inattention to other viable transportation possibilities force the elderly to accept the automobile as a fundamental tool for retaining a desired life-style.

We must be willing to accept the fact that a significant change in traffic behavior starts by clarifying the many factors that impact the overall interests and welfare of the elderly. We need a balance between the statistical configuration of elderly driver accident involvement and the personal/social circumstances that impact on it. A review of the book should make this more obvious.

The ability for the elderly to protect themselves and become partners in prevention rather than treatment is ever present. They need to be encouraged to partake collectively in education and understanding of safety problems, particularly in high-risk circumstances. At the same time we must guarantee them that any monitoring of driving-related hazards is not a reflection of mainstream political expedient discrimination. The victory will be realized when the elderly drivers become a lower accident-risk group without losing their independence, life-style and self-esteem. If our book contributes to the advancement of this goal, we have taken a significant step forward.

Reference

Dewey, J. 1939. *The Philosophy of John Dewey*. New York: Tudor Publishing Company.

APPENDIXES

APPENDIX A

Appendix to Chapter 2: The Elderly Under the Conceptual Microscope Tables A–1 to A–5

Demographic Data on Adults over the Age of Sixty-Five for the Province of British Columbia

Tables A-1 to A-5 are taken from data reported in Fact Book on Aging in British Columbia compiled by The Gerontology Research Centre, Simon Fraser University (1986). These data represent the currently available figures or projected estimates from Statistics Canada. Sources of these data are various and the Fact Book on Aging in British Columbia should be checked for these details.

The total population of those aged sixty-five and older in British Columbia in 1981 was 298,200, which was 10.9 percent of the total population. It is estimated that by 1991 the total population of those aged sixty-five and older will total 410,500, which is projected to be 12.7 percent of the total population.

Currently (1986), within this sixty-five-plus age cohort, those aged eighty are the fastest growing segment representing over 20 percent of those over the age of sixty-five. There are considerable differences to be noted on important social indicators that are used to describe a population as the following tables suggest. Where possible we have presented the data for the following subcohorts sixty-five years of age or older: sixty-five to sixty-nine; seventy to seventy-four; seventy-five to seventy-nine; eighty to eighty-four; and eighty-five and older.

TABLE A-1
Age Structure and Sex Ratio
of the Population Aged 65+ (1981)*

Age	Sex Ratio Male/Female**	Total Number	% of Total
65 - 69	87/100	108,000	36.2%
70 - 74	85/100	78,500	26.3
75 - 79	82/100	53,000	17.8
80 - 84	64/100	31,400	10.5
85+	51/100	27,100	9.1
Total		298,000	100.0%

*(Table 1.2; Table 2.1)

**Calculated at age 65+ the sex ratio is 79 males per 100 females; at age 80+ the sex ratio is 58 males per 100 females.

TABLE A-2
Marital Status of the Population Aged 65+ (1981)*

Age		Married Number	Married %	Widowed Number	Widowed %	Single or Divorced Number	Single or Divorced %
65-69	(M)	42,575	84.5%	3,035	6.0%	4,750	9.8%
	(F)	35,585	61.7	16,710	29.0	5,380	9.3
70-74	(M)	28,990	80.6	3,455	9.6	3,525	9.8
	(F)	21,060	49.6	17,565	41.3	3,870	9.1
75-79	(M)	17,845	74.3	3,646	15.2	2,515	10.5
	(F)	10,070	34.5	16,660	57.1	2,465	8.5
80-84	(M)	7,905	64.6	2,955	24.2	1,440	11.3
	(F)	4,025	21.0	13,710	71.5	1,425	7.4
85+	(M)	4,475	48.3	3,850	41.6	935	10.1
	(F)	1,670	9.4	14,920	83.7	1,245	6.9

*(Table 4.1)

TABLE A-3
Urban/Rural Distribution of Population Aged 65+ (1981)*

Centers with Populations	Number	% of Total
500,000 and larger	130,435	43.7%
100,000 - 499,999	36,440	12.2
30,000 - 99,999	37,335	12.5
10,000 - 29,999	24,995	8.4
5,000 - 9,999	9,390	3.1
2,500 - 4,999	8,535	2.9
1,000 - 2,999	4,690	1.6
999 - Farm, Non-Farm	46,395	15.6
Totals	298,215	100.0%

*(Table 5.2)

TABLE A-4
Living Arrangements of Population Aged 65+ (1981)*

Type of Arrangement	Male Number	Male %	Female Number	Female %
Persons in Private Households:				
Family Households	99,225	75.6%	82,065	49.6%
Nonfamily Households				
with someone	4,095	3.1	9,305	5.6
living alone	18,785	14.2	58,570	35.2
Persons in Collective Dwellings:				
Nursing, Chronic Care, hotels, hospitals, religious homes, etc.	9,110	6.9	15,545	9.3
Totals	131,215	100.0%	165,485	100.0%

*(Table 7.1)

TABLE A-5
Educational Attainment of Population Aged 65+ (1981)*

Highest Level of Schooling Reported**	Male Number	Male %	Female Number	Female %
Less than Grade 9	51,025	40.9%	55,475	36.6%
Grades 9 - 13	43,100	34.6	58,535	38.6
Some Post-secondary	23,315	18.7	33,120	21.9
University degree	7,290	5.8	4,360	2.9
Totals	124,730	100.0%	151,490	100.0%

*(Table 9.1)
**Education "Not Reported" is 21,950 or 7.4% of total population aged 65+.

APPENDIX B

Appendix to Chapter 6: Interview Survey Trends, Factors, and Patterns

Methodology

Introduction

The purpose of this study was to determine trends on how senior drivers view their own driving practices and attitudes. The face-to-face structured interviews used in this study were developed on the basis of the results of the Focus Group Study and questionnaires used in two other surveys of senior drivers (Planek et al. 1968; Yee 1985).

Subjects. Nine hundred and four (904) licensed drivers fifty-five years of age and older were interviewed using a structured interview schedule. Subjects were selected on the basis of age groupings, sex, and place of residence. These selection factors were chosen to insure that a representative sample of elderly drivers was interviewed.

There were three age categories from which subjects were chosen: fifty-five to sixty-four, sixty-five to seventy-four and seventy-five and older. The division of older persons into these three age categories is according to accepted gerontological practice. The fifty-five to sixty-four year old group tends to be active and in reasonably good health. During the years between sixty-five and seventy-four, there is a high probability of psychological, physical, and social transitions occurring. The seventy-five-and-over group tends to be more restricted in life activities and to manifest more physical disabilities.

Sex was used as a selection variable as it was speculated that the driving practices and attitudes of men and women may be different, due to sex differences in social roles and marital status distribution.

The 904 subjects were drawn from three areas in British Columbia: Vancouver, Victoria and the Okanagan. Within each area, communities were selected that have a high percentage of senior citizens and provide a good representation of the types of communities, neighborhoods, roads, and highway, in which seniors live and drive.

Subjects were recruited through articles in community newspapers, radio interviews and public service announcements, a postal drop, random telephoning, notices in senior centers, and lists of senior drivers obtained through community associations.

The Structured Interview Setting. All subjects were individually interviewed by a trained interviewer at a time and place convenient to the subject. This was usually at the subject's home. The interviews lasted between forty-five and seventy-five minutes. Prior to beginning the interview, the purpose of the study was explained to the subjects and an informed consent signed. Interviewers were instructed to: speak slowly and clearly, enunciate well, speak up but not too loudly, not to rush the respondent's answers, and if the subject seemed tired, to take a break. The interviewers' introductory comments, instructions to subjects and the order in which the questions were asked were standardized for all subjects and all interviewers. Interviewers read the questions to the subjects and all answers were immediately coded according to fixed response categories on the survey instruments. The question was repeated when the interviewer felt that there may have been some difficulty with comprehension or hearing.

The structured interview consisted of sixty-one questions (some questions had multiple parts) grouped into ten sections. The sections in the order in which they were asked are: demographic information, driving history, characteristics of vehicles driven, driving patterns, opinions about driving, driving difficulties, licensure, driving education, changes over time, and difficult driving maneuvers.

References

Planek, T.W., M.E. Condon, and R.C. Fowler. 1968. "An Investigation of the Problems and Opinions of the Aged Driver." National Safety Council.

Yee, Darlene. 1985. A Survey of the Traffic Safety Needs and Problems of Drivers Age 55 and Over. In *Needs and Problems of Older Drivers: Survey Results and Recommendations*. Proceedings of the Older Driver Colloquium, Orlando, FL. Sponsored by AAA Foundation for Traffic Safety, pp. 96-125.

Subject's ID 1 9

INTERVIEW SCHEDULE
OLDER DRIVERS STUDY

Gerontology Research Centre
Simon Fraser University

Respondent's Name: ______________________________

Street Address: ______________________________

City: ______________________________

Telephone No: ____________________

Date of Interview: ____________________

Interview began at: ____________________

Interview ended at: ____________________

				Column
Subject's I.D.	1	9		1-6
Sex: Male		1		7
Female		2		

I DEMOGRAPHIC INFORMATION

Since we need to be able to describe the people who took part in this study, I'm going to begin by asking you some questions about yourself and your household. First of all:

1. How old were you on your last birthday? ____________ 8-9

2. What is your present marital status?

		Column
married	1	10
separated or divorced	2	
widowed or	3	
single	4	
[D.K./no response]	5	

*3. With whom do you live?

	Y	N	DK/NR	Column
alone	1	2	9	11
with mate or spouse	1	2	9	12
with children	1	2	9	13
with other relative(s)	1	2	9	14
with non-relative(s)	1	2	9	15
other (specify) ____________	1	2	9	16

4. Now I'd like to ask some questions about your employment experience and education.

(a) What is your present employment status?

		Column
work full-time	1	17
work part-time	2	
retired	3	
unemployed	4	
never worked outside the home	5	
[D.K./no response]	9	

(b) What kind of work have you done most of your adult life? Tell me what kind of work it was - for example, an accountant, bus driver, housewife?

____________________ 18-19

(c) What was the highest level of education you completed?

		Column
primary school	1	20
some secondary school	2	
secondary school graduation	3	
technical school	4	
some college or university	5	
university degree	6	
graduate or professional degree	7	
[D.K./no response]	9	

*For all questions with an asterisk, you may check more than one category.

	Y	N	DK/ NR	Column
5. Turning now to some questions about financial status				
*(a) Do you presently receive:				
The federal Old Age Pension or Spouse's Allowance	1	2	9	21
Full or Partial Guaranteed Income Supplement	1	2	9	22
The Provincial Guaranteed Annual Income for Need Supplement	1	2	9	23
War Veteran's Allowance	1	2	9	24
(b) What was your *and your spouse's (if married)* total annual income in 1986? Would you say:				
0-$4,999	1			25
$5,000-9,999	2			
$10,000-19,999	3			
$20,000-29,999	4			
$30,000-39,999	5			
$40,000 or more?	6			
[D.K./no response]	9			
6. I'd now like to ask you a few questions about your health.				
(a) First of all, how would you rate your health at the present time? Would you say it's:				
excellent	1			26
good	2			
fair, or	3			
poor?	4			
[D.K./no response]	9			
(b) How would you describe your vision with glasses if you wear glasses when driving? Would you say it's:				
excellent	1			27
good	2			
fair, or	3			
poor?	4			
[D.K./no response]	9			
(c) How would you describe your hearing ability? Would you say it's:				
excellent	1			28
good	2			
fair, or	3			
poor?	4			
[D.K./no response]	9			

II DRIVING HISTORY

I'd now like to ask you some questions about your driving history.

7. How many years ago did you learn to drive?

		Column
less than 5	1	29
5-9	2	
10-19	3	
20-29	4	
30-39	5	
40-49	6	
50 or more	7	
[D.K./no response]	9	

8. Have you ever completed a formal Driver Education or training course?

		Column
yes	1	30
no	2	
[D.K./no response]	9	

9. How did you originally learn to drive?

		Column
Self taught	1	31
Parent taught	2	
Friend/relative taught	3	
School course	4	
Driving school	5	
[D.K./no response]	9	

10. In the last 5 years have you had an accident when you were driving:

(a) that involved no other vehicle or person?

		Column
yes	1	32
no	2	
[D.K./no response]	9	

(b) that involved another vehicle?

		Column
yes	1	33
no	2	
[D.K./no response]	9	

(c) in which someone was injured?

		Column
yes	1	34
no	2	
[D.K./no response]	9	

(d) that involved a pedestrian?

		Column
yes	1	34
no	2	
[D.K./no response]	9	

*11. In the last 5 years, have you received a ticket for:

	Y	N	DK/ NR	Column
Failure to yield	1	2	9	36
Speeding	1	2	9	37
Going too slowly	1	2	9	38
Not heeding traffic lights	1	2	9	39
Not heeding traffic signs	1	2	9	40

				Column
Improper passing	1	2	9	41
Improper turning	1	2	9	42
Reckless driving	1	2	9	43
Tailgating	1	2	9	44
Other (specify) ____________	1	2	9	45

III CHARACTERISTICS OF VEHICLES DRIVEN

Now I'd like to ask you some questions about the vehicles you drive.

12. How many vehicles do you and/or other members of your household own? — 46
    [D.K./no response] 9
13. How many of these vehicles do you, personally, drive? — 47
    [D.K./no response] 9

IV DRIVING PATTERNS

Now I'd like to ask you about your driving experiences.

14. In an average week, how many days do you usually drive? — 48
    (If less than once a week, code as 8; if never drives, code as zero and ask "Do you plan to resume driving"? If answer is YES, continue but modify all questions so that when questions asked about current driving practice, difficulty, etc., you modify and ask when you drove, etc. If answer is NO, skip to final question and terminate interview with that question.)
    [D.K./no response] 9
15. In an average week, how many days do you usually drive during the morning or evening rush hour? — 49
    (If less than once a week, code as 8; if never, code as zero.)
    [D.K./no response] 9
16. In an average week, on how many days do you usually drive after dark? — 50
    (If less than once a week, code as 8; if never, code as zero.)
    [D.K./no response] 9
17. When do you usually do most of your driving:
    (Only read 1-3, but if answer is 4-7 code accordingly.)

		Column
morning	1	51
afternoon or	2	
evening	3	
morning and afternoon	4	
morning and evening	5	
afternoon and evening	6	
3 equally	7	
[D.K./no response]	9	

18. Do you usually drive:

		Column
weekdays only	1	52
weekends only or	2	
on both weekdays and the weekend	3	
[D.K./no response]	9	

				Column
19. Approximately how many miles do you drive a year? Would you say:				
less than 5,000 miles	1			53
5,000-7,999 miles	2			
8,000-11,999 miles	3			
12,000 or more miles or	4			
do not drive at the present time	5			
[D.K./no response]	9			
Kilometres ______________________				
Kilometre Conversion				
5,000M = 8,000K				
8,000M = 13,000K				
12,000M = 19,500K				
20. Do you usually drive as frequently in the winter months (November to March) as you do in other months?				
yes	1			54
no	2			
[D.K./no response]	9			
*21. (a) Who often rides with you when you drive:	Y	N	DK/ NR	
Mate or spouse	1	2	9	55
Children	1	2	9	56
Grandchildren	1	2	9	57
Other relatives (e.g., brothers, sisters, nieces, nephews)	1	2	9	58
Friends or	1	2	9	59
Neighbours	1	2	9	60
No one	1	2	9	61
Other (specify) ______________________	1	2	9	62
______________________________				
(b) In general, how do you feel about having passengers when you drive. Would you say:				
very comfortable	1			63
comfortable, or	2			
uncomfortable	3			
[D.K./no response]	9			
*22. In a typical week, other than driving there yourself, how do you get places:	Y	N	DK/ NR	
walk	1	2	9	64
bus	1	2	9	65
others drive me	1	2	9	66
bicycle	1	2	9	67
taxi	1	2	9	68
other (specify) ______________________	1	2	9	69
______________________________				

				Column
Subject's I.D.	2 9			1-6

*23. People use their cars for a number of purposes. Do you use your car for:

	Y	N	DK/ NR	
shopping	1	2	9	7
driving for pleasure	1	2	9	8
visiting family or friends	1	2	9	9
going to church	1	2	9	10
vacation travel	1	2	9	11
attend social or cultural events or entertainment	1	2	9	12
engage in sports (e.g., golf) or attend a sporting event (e.g., football game)	1	2	9	13
health care service	1	2	9	14
volunteer activity	1	2	9	15
attend meetings	1	2	9	16
getting to/from work	1	2	9	17
other (specify) ____________________	1	2	9	18

____

V OPTIONS ABOUT DRIVING

24. How would your life change if you could no longer drive: Would you:

	Y	N	DK/ NR	
rely on other forms of transportation	1	2	9	19
have to move (near to transit)	1	2	9	20
be less independent/free	1	2	9	21
stay close to home	1	2	9	22
be less social	1	2	9	23
have to change your lifestyle	1	2	9	24
be less mobile	1	2	9	25
other (specify) ____________________	1	2	9	26

____

25. How do you feel about the way you drive? Do you think you are:

more able than the average driver	1	27
about as good as the average driver	2	
less able than the average driver	3	
[D.K./no response]	9	

26. When you are driving, how do passengers affect your ability to attend to driving:

distracts me very much	1	28
distracts me a little	2	
does not distract me at all	3	
[D.K./no response]	9	

27. How do you usually feel when other drivers are discourteous or drive carelessly:

Angry	1	29
Annoyed	2	
Tense	3	

		Column
Frightened	4	
Not bothered	5	
[D.K./no response]	9	

28. When the driving behavior of other drivers annoys you, how are you most likely to respond:

Drive more aggressively	1	30
Slow down and block them	2	
Move out of the way	3	
Do nothing	4	
Other (specify) ____________________	5	
______________________________		
[D.K./no response]	9	

29. When you are personally upset about something unrelated to driving, do you usually:

Avoid driving	1	31
Take extra care when driving	2	
Drive as usual	3	
Take less care driving	4	
Use the car to work out your feelings . . .	5	
[D.K./no response]	9	

30. What does your family think about you as a driver? Do they think you are:

an excellent driver	1	32
a good driver	2	
an average driver	3	
a poor driver	4	
a very poor driver	5	
[D.K./no response]	9	

31. (a) Do you think you drive differently now than when you were younger?

yes	1	33
no (SKIP TO QUESTION 32)	2	
[D.K./no response]	9	

(b) In what ways do you drive differently now?

____

____

____

____

32. How do you usually feel about driving:

(a) like it	1	34
neutral, that is, it's okay	2	
don't like it	3	
[D.K./no response]	9	
(b) confident	1	35
comfortable	2	
anxious	3	
distressed	4	
[D.K./no response]	9	

				Column
33. What age group do you think cause the most problems on the road:				
16-20	1			36
21-30	2			
30-55	3			
56-75	4			
76+	5			
[D.K./no response]	9			

VI DRIVING DIFFICULTIES

I would now like to ask you about difficulties that some people say they experience.

34. Do you have difficulty with the ______ of traffic signs on streets or highways:				
(a)	Y	N	DK/ NR	
placement	1	2	9	37
size of sign	1	2	9	38
shape of sign	1	2	9	39
colors	1	2	9	40
size of lettering	1	2	9	41
clarity of lettering	1	2	9	42
message	1	2	9	43

If answer to all is NO, skip to Question 37.
If answer is YES to any of the above, ask
(b) Are there any signs in particular that you have difficulty with, for example, stop, yield, etc.

____

____

____

35. Do you think your difficulty with signs or signals is due to: (only read 1-3, but if answer is 4-7, code accordingly)		
your vision	1	44
your reaction time or	2	
the sign itself?	3	
1 and 2	4	
1 and 3	5	
2 and 3	6	
1, 2 and 3	7	
[D.K./no response]	9	

*36. On what type roads to you have difficulty with traffic signs: (only read 1-3, but if answer is 4-8, code accordingly.)		
freeways	1	45
two-lane/rural roads, or	2	
city streets?	3	
1 and 2	4	
1 and 3	5	
2 and 3	6	

		Column
1, 2 and 3	7	
other (Specify) ________________________	8	
[D.K./no response]	9	

37. Do you usually have difficulty seeing at night when you drive?

yes	1	46
no	2	
[D.K./no response]	9	

38. Does oncoming headlight glare at night usually bother you?

yes	1	47
no	2	
[D.K./no response]	9	

39. Does daytime glare from either oncoming headlights, the sun or its reflection usually bother you?

yes	1	48
no	2	
[D.K./no response]	9	

40. How difficult is it for you to turn your head to look back over your shoulder when driving or backing up:

Very difficult	1	49
Somewhat difficult	2	
Not very difficult, or	3	
Not at all difficult?	4	
[D.K./no response]	9	

41. (a) I'm going to read you a list of common driving faults people often make. Please tell me which you make most often:

Drive too fast for conditions	01
Speeding	02
Fail to yield right of way	03
Failure to come to complete stop at stop sign	04
Run a red light	05
Run a yellow light	06
Drive left of centre	07
Make an improper pass	08
Make an improper turn	09
Follow too closely	10
Drive too slow for the traffic flow	11
Fail to signal	12
[D.K./no response]	99

(b) and (c) I'm going to read the list again, now tell which you make second and third most often.

(a)	__________	50-51
(b)	__________	52-53
(c)	__________	54-55

				Column
42. How fast do you usually drive in comparison with the general flow of traffic:				
faster	1			56
about the same or	2			
slower?	3			
[D.K./no response]	9			
43. How often do you "nod off" when you are driving an automobile?				
frequently	1			57
sometimes	2			
seldom or	3			
never	4			
[D.K./no response]	9			

VII LICENSURE

I now have some questions about licensing.

44. Which of these reasons might cause you to decide to stop driving in the future:	Y	N	DK/ NR	
poor health	1	2	9	58
poor vision	1	2	9	59
causing a bad accident or narrow escape . .	1	2	9	60
physical impairment	1	2	9	61
knowledge that skill slipping	1	2	9	62
can't afford it	1	2	9	63
other (specify) ____________________ ____________________	1	2	9	64

*45. Who should make the decision about when it is time to give up driving:	Y	N	DK/ NR	
the driver	1	2	9	65
family members	1	2	9	66
a doctor	1	2	9	67
the Motor Vehicle Licence Department . .	1	2	9	68
ICBC or	1	2	9	69
the Police department	1	2	9	70
other (specify) ____________________ ____________________	1	2	9	71

Subject's I.D. 3 9 1-6

*46. What things would you consider in determining whether you should give up driving:	Y	N	DK/ NR	
health	1	2	9	7
accident record	1	2	9	8
need for mobility	1	2	9	9
other available transportation	1	2	9	10
road test	1	2	9	11

				Column
written test	1	2	9	12
other (specify) ____________	1	2	9	13

____

____

47. Do you think reexamination should be required before a person's licence is renewed?
    (a) If no, skip to Question 48
    (b) If yes, at what age?

			Column
No	0	0	14-15
All ages	1	1	
Other			

*48. What kind of periodic driver reexamination would you favour for older drivers:

	Y	N	DK/ NR	Column
an eye test?	1	2	9	16
total physical examination?	1	2	9	17
a written test?	1	2	9	18
a driving (road) test?	1	2	9	19
no reexamination?	1	2	9	20

49. Would periodic reexamination make you feel nervous or threatened?

		Column
yes	1	21
no	2	
[D.K./no response]	9	

VIII EDUCATION

50. When did you last attend a driver education, training or retraining course?

		Column
never	1	22
less than 5 years ago	2	
5-9 years ago	3	
10-19 years ago	4	
20+ years ago	5	
[D.K./no response]	9	

51. Do you keep current (up to date) about changes in traffic regulations, signage and road markings? If you keep current, how do you do so?

	Y	N	DK/ NR	Column
Keep current	1	2	9	23
Department of Motor Vehicle mailings . . .	1	2	9	24
Pick up material from Licence office	1	2	9	25
Pick up material from Insurance Agent . .	1	2	9	26
Newspaper	1	2	9	27
Radio or T.V.	1	2	9	28
Word of Mouth	1	2	9	29

Column

IX CHANGES OVER TIME

52. Under certain conditions, some older people feel they drive better than they used to, some feel they drive the same as they used to while others feel they don't drive as well. I'm going to read you a list of 12 different driving conditions. For each condition I read, please tell me whether you feel you drive better, the same or worse than you did at age 35-45:

	Better	Same	Not as Well	DK/ NR	
Night driving	1	2	3	9	30
Coping with headlight glare	1	2	3	9	31
Winter driving	1	2	3	9	32
Driving in rain and fog	1	2	3	9	33
Driving in snow, sleet or slush	1	2	3	9	34
Freeway driving	1	2	3	9	35
Driving on city streets	1	2	3	9	36
Driving during rush hour	1	2	3	9	37
Driving when tired or upset	1	2	3	9	38
Driving after drinking	1	2	3	9	39
Driving after medication	1	2	3	9	40
Holiday/vacation driving	1	2	3	9	41

Comments ____

____

____

*53. Some people have told us that they now ______ than they used to. Is this true for you?

	Y	N	DK/ NR	
drive more cautiously	1	2	9	42
drive more defensively	1	2	9	43
drive slower	1	2	9	44
get less upset	1	2	9	45

*54. What are your greatest concerns about your own driving:

	Y	N	DK/ NR	
loss of attention or concentration	1	2	9	46
losing licence or having to quit driving	1	2	9	47
getting hit	1	2	9	48
injuring a pedestrian	1	2	9	49
losing my driving abilities	1	2	9	50
hitting another car	1	2	9	51
other (specify) ______________	1	2	9	52

____

Column

X DIFFICULT DRIVING MANOEUVRES

55. There are various types of driving manoeuvres that some people find difficult. I'm going to read you a list of these and for each one I mention, please tell me how frequently you, personally, find it troublesome.
Do you frequently, sometimes, seldom or never find it troublesome to:

	Freq.	Some	Sel-dom	Never	DK/NR	
(a) Change lanes	1	2	3	4	9	53
(b) Steer your car	1	2	3	4	9	54
(c) Read traffic signs	1	2	3	4	9	55
(d) Make right turn	1	2	3	4	9	56
(e) Make left turn at controlled intersection	1	2	3	4	9	57
(f) Make left turn at uncontrolled intersection	1	2	3	4	9	58
(g) Keep up with traffic	1	2	3	4	9	59
(h) Park your car	1	2	3	4	9	60
(i) Pass other cars	1	2	3	4	9	61
(j) Back your car	1	2	3	4	9	62
(k) Enter stream of city traffic	1	2	3	4	9	63
(l) Enter uncontrolled intersection . . .	1	2	3	4	9	64
(m) Enter controlled intersection . . .	1	2	3	4	9	65
(n) Enter freeway	1	2	3	4	9	66
(o) Keep the car in its lane	1	2	3	4	9	67
(p) Judge distances	1	2	3	4	9	68
(q) Keep an appropriate distance . . .	1	2	3	4	9	69

Subject's I.D. 4 9 1-6

56. I'm going to read you a list of conditions under which some people don't drive or try to avoid driving. Please tell me whether this is a condition you either try to avoid driving in or don't drive in:

	Try to Avoid	Don't Drive in	Do Drive	DK/NR	
At night	1	2	3	9	7
In rain	1	2	3	9	8
In Fog	1	2	3	9	9
In show, sleet or slush	1	2	3	9	10
On freeways	1	2	3	9	11
In rush hour	1	2	3	9	12
In heavy traffic areas (e.g., bridges, tunnel, congested)	1	2	3	9	13
In heavy holiday traffic	1	2	3	9	14
Other (specify) ____________________	1	2	3	9	15

____

	Y	N	DK/ NR	Column
*57. What personal factors, characteristics or impairments make driving difficult for you?				
poor hearing	1	2	9	16
poor vision	1	2	9	17
poor night vision	1	2	9	18
rain	1	2	9	19
glare	1	2	9	20
can't turn head	1	2	9	21
fatigue	1	2	9	22
none	1	2	9	23
Other ______________________________	1	2	9	24

____

		Column
58. Statistics show that a fair number of people drink and drive. Do you currently drink and drive?		
(a) yes	1	25
no	2	
[D.K./no response]	9	
(b) If no, why not:		
Unsafe to do so	1	26
Scared I will be stopped by police . .	2	
Someone deters me	3	
Don't drink	4	
Other ______________________________	5	
______________________________		
If yes to (a), mark [D.K./no response] . . .	9	
59. Have you had dealings with ICBC in the last five years?		
(a) yes	1	27
no	2	
[D.K./no response]	9	
(b) If yes, were you treated or dealt with:		
Fairly	1	28
Unfairly	2	
If no to (a), mark [D.K./no response]	9	
(c) In a courteous way	1	29
In a noncourteous way	2	
If no to (a), mark [D.K./no response]	9	

60. Is there anything that we have not discussed that you find important:

____

____

____

Column

ONLY ASK IF PERSON DOES NOT DRIVE AND DOES NOT PLAN TO DRIVE AGAIN.

61. (a) How long ago did you stop driving? (Code in months)__________ 30-32
    (b) Why did you stop driving? ______________________________
    ____
    ____
    (c) Why will you not start driving again?
    ____
    ____

Interviewer's number 33-34

Tables B-1 to B-48

Statistical Tables

Based on Survey

Findings

TABLE B-1
Self-reported Sociodemographic Characteristics of Survey Participants

	Age Group				
	55-64 (n=247)	65-74 (n=490)	75+ (n=167)	Missing Data	Total (n=904)
Mean age	60.6	69.2	78.8	5	68.6
% Male	44.9	48.8	56.3	2	49.1
% Married	71.7	65.2	61.1	2	66.2
% working					
full-time	20.0	1.4	1.2	4	6.4
part-time	13.9	5.1	3.6		7.2
% in receipt of OAS or SA	10.1	97.8	98.8	2	73.9
% receiving an income supplement:					
GIS	3.6	10.7	15.1	3	9.5
GAIN	.4	2.1	4.8	6	2.1
War Veterans Supp.	5.7	5.3	7.2	4	5.8
Total Family Annual Income (%)					
$ 0 - $ 4,999	4.3	1.4	2.1	137	2.3
$ 5,000 - $ 9,999	5.7	5.5	7.7		6.0
$10,000 - $19,999	18.7	33.4	42.3		31.0
$20,000 - $29,999	20.6	27.4	27.5		25.6
$30,000 - $39,999	20.1	15.9	10.6		16.0
$40,000+	30.6	16.3	9.9		19.0
Primary Life Occupation (%)				1	
Professional	21.5	20.7	28.1		22.3
Managerial	17.4	15.5	11.4		15.3
Clerical	12.1	12.7	9.6		12.0
Sales	8.1	7.6	9.0		8.0
Service	5.2	7.8	3.6		6.3
Skilled:					
White Collar	5.3	7.4	8.4		7.0
Blue Collar	6.5	7.2	10.8		7.6
Semi- or unskilled	4.9	4.5	3.6		4.4
Farmer	1.6	2.0	2.4		2.0
Housewife	15.4	12.5	7.8		12.4
Retired	0.0	0.0	0.6		0.1
Other	1.6	2.0	3.0		2.1
Living Arrangement (%)					
Alone	19.8	32.0	37.1	1	29.6
Mate/Spouse	70.9	63.7	58.1	0	64.6
Children	21.1	4.7	0.6	0	8.4
Other relatives	5.3	2.0	1.8	0	2.9
Non-relatives	4.5	1.6	0.6	0	2.2
Other	1.6	0.2	1.2	0	0.8

TABLE B-1 (Continued)
Self-reported Sociodemographic Characteristics of Survey Participants

	Age Group				
	55-64 (n=247)	65-74 (n=490)	75+ (n=167)	Missing Data	Total (n=904)
Level of Education (%)				1	
Primary/Some Secondary	23.9	26.3	30.7		26.5
Secondary grad.	26.7	28.2	2.9		26.8
Some college/university	40.9	37.5	40.4		38.9
Technical school	8.5	8.0	6.0		7.8

TABLE B-2
Percentage of Age Groups Reporting Health, Vision and Hearing Ratings

	Age Group				
	55-64	65-74	75+	Missing Data	Total (n=904)
	(n=247)	(n=490)	(n=167)		
Overall Health Rating				0	
Excellent	40.9%*	33.3	29.3		34.6
Good	47.8	57.3	58.7		55.0
Fair	9.7	8.2	8.4		8.6
Poor	1.6	1.2	3.6		1.8
	(n=235)	(n=461)	(n=156)		
Vision Rating				52	
Excellent	42.6	38.6	30.8		38.3
Good	55.3	59.0	61.5		58.5
Fair	2.1	2.2	7.1		3.1
Poor	0.0	0.2	0.6		0.2
	(n=247)	(n=490)	(n=167)		
Hearing Rating				0	
Excellent	38.5	32.4	26.3		33.0
Good	52.6	55.7	49.7		53.8
Fair	8.5	11.0	23.4		12.6
Poor	1.4	0.8	0.6		0.7

*All percentages reported in this table and all succeeding tables are column percentages.

TABLE B-3
Percentage of Age Groups Reporting Years Since Learning To Drive

	Age Group 55-64 (n=246)	65-74 (n=488)	75+ (n=165)	Total (n=899)
<20 Years ago	3.3	2.9	2.4	2.9
20-29 Years ago	9.8	6.1	3.6	6.7
30-39 Years ago	31.3	15.8	8.5	18.7
40-49 Years ago	51.2	22.7	9.7	28.1
50+ Years ago	4.5	52.5	75.8	43.6

TABLE B-4
Percentage of Males/Females Reporting Years Since Learning to Drive

	Male (n=440)	Female (n=457)	Total (n=897)
<20 Years ago	0.7	5.0	2.9
20-29 Years ago	0.9	12.3	6.7
30-39 Years ago	7.7	28.9	18.5
40-49 Years ago	32.0	24.5	28.2
50+ Years ago	58.6	29.3	43.7

TABLE B-5
Percentage of Males/Females Keeping Current about Traffic Regulation Changes

	Male (n=430)	Female (n=442)	Total (n=872)
Yes	91.2	91.0	91.1
No	8.8	9.0	8.9

TABLE B-6
Percentage of Males/Females Reporting How They Keep Current about Traffic Regulation Changes

	Male	Female	Missing Data	Total (n=904)
Newspaper	59.9	58.1	29	59.0*
Radio or T.V.	34.7	37.2	29	36.0
Word of Mouth	19.9	29.9	26	24.9
Dept. of Motor Vehicle Mailings	19.4	14.4	27	16.9
Insurance agent material	15.8	12.6	26	14.4
Pick up material from DMV office	26.2	12.3	26	14.2

*Each row represents column percentages for discrete items which do not add up to 100% as respondents could respond to more than one item.

TABLE B-7
Percentage of Age Groups Reporting How They Originally Learned to Drive

	Age Group			
	55-64 (n=247)	65-74 (n=486)	75+ (n=165)	Total (n=898)
Friend taught	42.1	37.7	31.5	37.8
Self-taught	17.8	25.1	32.7	24.5
Parent taught	18.2	18.7	20.6	18.9
Driving course	21.2	16.7	15.2	17.6
School course	0.8	1.9	0.0	1.2

TABLE B-8
Percentage of Males/Females Reporting How They Originally Learned to Drive

	Male (n=441)	Female (n=455)	Total (n=896)
Friend taught	27.4	47.9	37.8
Self-taught	40.6	9.0	24.6
Parent taught	22.4	15.6	19.0
Driving course	7.7	26.8	17.4
School course	1.8	0.7	1.2

TABLE B-9
Percentage of Age Groups Reporting Completion of Driver Education Course

	Age Group			
	55-64 (n=247)	65-74 (n=490)	75+ (n=166)	Total (n=903)
Yes	42.5	42.7	32.5	40.8
No	57.5	57.3	67.5	59.2

TABLE B-10
Percentage of Age Groups Reporting Accidents During the Last Five Years

	Age Group				
	55-64	65-74	75+	Missing Data	Total (n=904)
	(n=246)	(n=479)	(n=166)		
Involved other vehicle	18.7	22.8	21.7	13	21.4*
	(n=246)	(n=485)	(n=166)		
No other vehicle	6.1	7.6	7.2	7	7.1
	(n=246)	(n=478)	(n=166)		
Injury occurred	1.2	3.3	5.4	14	3.1
	(n=246)	(n=478)	(n=166)		
Involved a pedestrian	0.8	0.8	0.0	14	0.7

*Each row represents column percentages for discrete items which do not add up to 100% as respondents could respond to more than one item.

TABLE B-11
Percentage of Male/Female Drivers Reporting Accidents During the Last Five Years

	Male	Female	Missing Data	Total (n=904)
	(n=436)	(n=453)		
Involved other vehicle	23.2	19.6	15	21.4*
	(n=437)	(n=458)		
No other vehicle	7.1	7.0	9	7.2
	(n=435)	(n=453)		
Injury occurred	3.4	2.9	16	3.2
	(n=435)	(n=453)		
Involved a pedestrian	0.7	0.7	16	0.7

*Each row represents column percentages for discrete items which do not add up to 100% as respondents could respond to more than one item.

TABLE B-12
Self-reported Moving Violations During the Last Five Years by Age

	Age Group				
	55-64 (n=247)	65-74 (n=490)	75+ (n=167)	Missing Data	Total (n=904)
Speeding	22.7	11.8	12.0	0	14.8*
Other	4.5	4.3	6.6	0	4.8
Not heeding traffic signs	2.8	2.2	3.0	0	2.5
Improper turning	3.2	1.6	2.4	0	2.2
Not heeding traffic lights	2.8	0.8	1.8	0	1.5
Failure to yield	0.8	0.4	1.8	0	0.8
Improper passing	0.8	0.2	0.0	0	0.3
Going too slowly	0.0	0.4	0.0	0	0.2
Reckless driving	0.0	0.0	0.0	0	0.0
Tailgating	0.0	0.0	0.0	0	0.0

*Each row represents column percentages for discrete items which do not add up to 100% as respondents could respond to more than one item.

TABLE B-13
Self-reported Moving Violations During the Last Five Years by Gender

	Age Group			
	Male (n=443)	Female (n=459)	Missing Data	Total (n=904)
Speeding	18.3	11.3	2	14.9*
Other	5.2	4.4	0	4.8
Not heeding traffic signs	3.2	2.0	2	2.5
Improper turning	3.2	1.3	2	2.2
Not heeding traffic lights	2.7	0.4	2	1.6
Failure to yield	1.4	0.2	2	0.8
Improper passing	0.5	0.2	2	0.3
Going too slowly	0.2	0.2	2	0.2
Reckless driving	0.0	0.0	0	0.0
Tailgating	0.0	0.0	0	0.0

*Each row represents column percentages for discrete items which do not add up to 100% as respondents could respond to more than one item.

TABLE B-14
Self-reported Mean Number of Days Driven per Week by Age

	Age Group			
	55-64	65-74	75+	Total
Days driven	5.6	5.2	4.8	5.3
After dark	2.1	1.7	1.3	1.6
Rush hour	1.9	1.3	1.2	1.5

TABLE B-15
Self-reported Mean Number of Days Driven per Week by Gender

	Male	Female	Total
Days driven	5.6	4.9	5.3
After dark	1.9	1.5	1.7
Rush hour	1.6	1.3	1.5

TABLE B-16
Percentage of Age Groups Reporting Time of Most Driving

	Age Group			
	55-64 (n=247)	65-74 (n=486)	75+ (n=162)	Total (n=895)
Morning and Afternoon	45.7	43.2	43.2	43.9
Morning	10.9	17.9	18.5	16.1
Afternoon	14.2	15.0	19.1	15.5
Afternoon and Evening	2.8	3.5	4.3	3.5
Morning and Evening	2.8	1.4	0.0	1.6
Evening	2.4	0.6	1.2	1.2

TABLE B-17
Percentage of Age Groups Reporting When They Usually Drive in the Week

	Age Group			
	55-64 (n=247)	65-74 (n=486)	75+ (n=162)	Total (n=895)
Weekdays only	7.3	10.7	17.3	10.9
Weekends only	1.6	0.2	1.9	0.9
Both	91.1	89.1	80.9	88.2

TABLE B-18
Percentage of Driver Age Groups Reporting on Winter Driving

	Age Group			
	55-64 (n=246)	65-74 (n=486)	75+ (n=162)	Total (n=894)
Do you usually drive as frequently in the winter months as you do in other months?				
Yes	77.2	72.4	66.7	72.7
No	22.8	27.6	33.3	27.3

TABLE B-19
Percentage of Driver Age Groups Reporting Approximate Annual Miles Driven

	Age Group			
	55-64 (n=244)	65-74 (n=483)	75+ (n=161)	Total (n=888)
<5,000 Miles*	32.8	37.5	62.7	40.8
5,000- 7,999 Miles	24.6	30.4	20.5	27.0
8,000-11,999 Miles	21.3	21.9	11.8	19.9
12,000+Miles	21.3	10.1	5.0	12.3

TABLE B-20
Percentage of Males/Females Reporting Approximate Annual Miles Driven

	Male (n=439)	Female (n=447)	Total (n=886)
<5,000 Miles*	22.3	58.8	40.7
5,000- 7,999 Miles	28.5	25.5	27.0
8,000-11,999 Miles	28.9	11.2	20.0
12,000+Miles	20.3	4.5	12.3

*Kilometer Conversion: 5,000 miles = 8,000 kilometers
8,000 miles = 13,000 kilometers
12,000 miles = 19,500 kilometers

TABLE B-21
Percentage of Driver Age Groups' Feelings about Having Passengers

	Age Group			
	55-64 (n=246)	65-74 (n=485)	75+ (n=161)	Total (n=892)
Very Comfortable	49.2	44.1	38.5	44.5
Comfortable	48.0	52.0	57.8	51.9
Uncomfortable	2.8	3.9	3.7	3.6

TABLE B-22
Percentage of Male/Female Drivers' Feelings about Having Passengers

	Male (n=438)	Female (n=452)	Total (n=890)
Very Comfortable	50.0	39.4	44.6
Comfortable	48.6	54.9	51.8
Uncomfortable	1.4	5.8	3.6

TABLE B-23
Percentage of Age Groups Reporting Who Most Often Rides with Them

	Age Group				
	55-64	65-74	75+	Missing Data	Total (n=904)
No one	74.0	69.8	65.4	10	70.1*
Mate or spouse	16.2	19.7	25.3	8	19.8
Friends	10.5	11.1	17.9	8	12.2
Grandchildren	4.1	6.0	5.6	9	5.4
Other relatives	3.2	3.7	1.9	8	3.2
Neighbours	3.6	3.3	8.6	8	4.4
Children	4.9	1.8	3.1	8	2.9
Other	0.8	0.2	1.2	8	0.6

*Each row represents column percentages for discrete items which do not add up to 100% as respondents could respond to more than one item.

TABLE B-24
Percentage of Age Groups Reporting Trip Purpose

	Age Group 55-64	65-74	75+	Missing Data	Total (n=904)
Shopping	96.8	96.7	94.4	9	96.3*
Visiting Family or Friends	96.8	95.9	93.8	9	95.8
Social/Cultural/Entertainment	93.9	90.3	84.6	11	90.3
Pleasure	85.0	85.1	84.0	11	84.9
Health Care	78.9	77.9	75.6	12	77.8
Meetings	73.3	70.8	61.7	9	69.8
Vacation Travel	77.1	69.5	54.0	12	68.8
Attend/Engage in Sports	55.1	52.3	46.3	11	52.0
Volunteer Activity	52.5	52.8	45.3	14	51.3
Church	38.8	43.1	43.2	10	41.9
To/From Work	24.3	6.4	3.8	14	10.9
Other	11.4	7.0	6.8	10	8.2

*Each row represents column percentages for discrete items which do not add up to 100% as respondents could respond to more than one item.

TABLE B-25
Percentage of Males/Females Reporting Trip Purpose

	Male	Female	Missing Data	Total (n=904)
Shopping	95.0	97.8	11	96.4*
Visiting Family or Friends	95.9	95.6	11	95.7
Social/Cultural/Entertainment	90.2	90.3	13	90.2
Pleasure	89.1	80.7	13	84.8
Health Care	76.4	79.2	14	77.9
Meetings	68.4	71.1	11	69.8
Vacation Travel	81.3	56.6	14	68.8
Attend/Engage in Sports	61.4	42.8	13	52.0
Volunteer Activity	45.4	56.8	16	51.2
Church	38.1	45.6	12	41.9
To/From Work	15.1	6.9	16	10.9
Other	8.9	7.5	12	8.2

*Each row represents column percentages for discrete items which do not add up to 100% as respondents could respond to more than one item.

TABLE B-26
Percentage of Age Groups Reporting Use of Alternate Transportation Other Than Driving

	Age Group				
	55-64	65-74	75+	Missing Data	Total (n=904)
Walking	57.5	63.9	63.6	8	62.1*
Other drives me	35.2	33.1	32.9	9	33.6
Bus	15.4	29.2	30.2	8	25.6
Bicycle	12.1	8.0	4.3	8	8.5
Other	4.5	2.9	5.6	10	3.8
Taxi	2.0	2.1	4.9	10	2.6

*Each row represents column percentages for discrete items which do not add up to 100% as respondents could respond to more than one item.

TABLE B-27
Percentage of Males/Females Reporting Use of Alternate Transportation Other Than Driving

	Male	Female	Missing Data	Total (n=904)
Walking	66.8	57.5	10	62.1*
Others drive me	20.9	46.1	11	33.7
Bus	23.0	28.2	10	25.6
Bicycle	11.8	5.3	10	8.5
Other	4.3	3.3	12	3.8
Taxi	1.8	3.3	12	2.6

*Each row represents column percentages for discrete items which do not add up to 100% as respondents could respond to more than one item.

TABLE B-28
Percentage of Age Groups Reporting Life Changes if They Stopped Driving

	Age Group				
	55-64	65-74	75+	Missing Data	Total (n=904)
Rely on other modes of transportation	95.9	96.3	95.5	19	96.0*
Be less mobile	86.5	81.0	87.3	24	83.6
Less independent/free	82.0	83.6	78.6	18	82.3
Change lifestyle	72.1	63.5	59.7	26	65.1
Stay close to home	55.4	54.4	67.8	54	57.1
Be less social	51.1	47.3	45.5	37	48.0
Other	31.6	28.2	26.7	10	28.9
Have to move (near to transit)	20.2	17.7	14.7	27	17.9

*Each row represents column percentages for discrete items which do not add up to 100% as respondents could respond to more than one item.

TABLE B-29
Percentage of Males/Females Reporting Life Changes if They Stopped Driving

	Male	Female	Missing Data	Total (n=904)
Rely on other modes of transportation	95.9	96.2	21	96.0*
Be less mobile	85.4	81.9	26	83.6
Less independent/free	82.6	81.9	20	82.2
Change lifestyle	64.8	65.3	28	65.1
Stay close to home	64.5	49.9	56	57.1
Be less social	50.6	45.5	39	48.0
Other	28.1	29.7	12	28.9
Have to move (near to transit)	16.7	19.1	29	17.9

*Each row represents column percentages for discrete items which do not add up to 100% as respondents could respond to more than one item.

TABLE B-30
Percentage of Age Groups Reporting Driving Ability

	Age Group			
	55-64 (n=245)	65-74 (n=483)	75+ (n=161)	Total (n=889)
Better than average	43.3	42.4	35.4	41.4
As good as average	55.9	56.9	61.5	57.5
Less able than average	0.8	0.6	3.1	1.1

TABLE B-31
Percentage of Males/Females Reporting Driving Ability

	Male (n=435)	Female (n=452)	Total (n=887)
Better than average	47.1	35.8	41.4
As good as average	51.7	63.1	57.5
Less able than average	1.1	1.1	1.1

TABLE B-32
Percentage of Males/Females Reporting Family Assessments of Their Driving Ability

	Male (n=418)	Female (n=427)	Total (n=845)
Excellent	23.4	16.4	19.9
Good	58.4	63.9	61.2
Average	16.3	18.3	17.3
Poor	1.4	1.4	1.4
Very poor	0.5	0.0	0.2

TABLE B-33
Percentage of Age Groups Reporting Feelings about Driving

	Age Group			
	55-64 (n=247)	65-74 (n=487)	75+ (n=162)	Total (n=896)
Like it	70.0	76.8	77.2	75.0
Neutral/It's Okay	24.7	20.9	21.6	22.1
Don't like it	5.3	2.3	1.2	2.9
	55-64 (n=241)	65-74 (n=472)	75+ (n=158)	Total (n=871)
Confident	53.5	54.2	38.6	51.2
Comfortable	45.2	43.6	59.5	47.0
Anxious	1.2	2.1	1.9	1.8

TABLE B-34
Percentage of Males/Females Reporting Feelings about Driving

	Male (n=440)	Female (n=454)	Total (n=894)
Like it	74.5	75.3	74.9
Neutral	23.4	20.9	22.1
Don't like it	2.0	3.7	2.9
	Male (n=430)	Female (n=439)	Total (n=869)
Confident	55.8	46.7	51.2
Comfortable	43.7	50.1	47.0
Anxious	0.5	3.2	1.8

TABLE B-35
Percentage of Age Groups Reporting Feelings When Other Drivers are Discourteous or Drive Carelessly

	Age Group			
	55-64 (n=246)	65-74 (n=482)	75+ (n=158)	Total (n=886)
Annoyed	59.3	64.3	61.4	62.4
Not Bothered	22.0	19.3	25.3	21.1
Angry	15.0	10.6	8.2	11.4
Tense	2.0	3.9	2.5	3.2
Frightened	1.6	1.9	2.5	1.9

TABLE B-36
Percentage of Age Groups Reporting Driving Response to Other Driver Annoyances

	Age Group			
	55-64 (n=242)	65-74 (n=478)	75+ (n=158)	Total (n=878)
Move out of the way	42.1	44.4	49.4	44.6
Nothing	30.6	34.1	32.3	32.8
Other	24.4	18.8	17.1	20.0
More aggressive	1.7	1.9	0.6	1.6
Slow down	1.2	0.8	0.6	0.9

TABLE B-37
Percentage of Males/Females Reporting Driving Response to Other Driver Annoyances

	Male (n=432)	Female (n=444)	Total (n=876)
Move out of the way	42.6	46.6	44.6
Do nothing	33.6	32.0	32.8
Other	20.8	19.4	20.1
More Aggressive	1.9	1.3	1.6
Slow down	1.2	0.7	0.9

TABLE B-38
Percentage of Males/Females Reporting Reactions to Being Personally Upset

	Male (n=432)	Female (n=444)	Total (n=876)
Drive as usual	63.0	40.6	51.5
Take extra care	25.2	33.1	29.3
Avoid driving	8.5	23.7	16.3
Take less care driving	2.7	1.8	2.2
Use car to work out feelings	0.7	0.7	0.7

TABLE B-39
Percentage of Age Groups Reporting Changes in Driving

	Age Group				
	55-64	65-74	75+	Missing Data	Total (n=904)
Drive more defensively	87.4	87.2	85.7	13	87.0*
Drive more cautiously	75.1	79.3	82.6	14	78.8
Get less upset	51.0	47.4	38.7	55	46.9
Drive slower	31.3	34.4	37.5	15	34.1

*Each row represents column percentages for discrete items which do not add up to 100% as respondents could respond to more than one item.

TABLE B-40
Percentage of Males/Females Reporting on Drinking and Driving

	Male (n=438)	Female (n=453)	Total (n=891)
Do you currently drink and drive?			
Yes	22.1	7.9	14.9
No	77.9	92.1	85.1
	Male (n=342)	**Female (n=415)**	**Total (n=757)***
Why not drink and drive?			
Unsafe to do so	54.1	51.3	52.6
Don't drink	36.5	43.4	40.3
Police may stop	5.6	3.1	4.2
Other	3.2	2.2	2.6
Someone deters me	0.6	0.0	0.3

*Missing Data = 147

TABLE B-41
Percentage of Age Groups Reporting Difficulty with Traffic Signs

	Age Group				
	55-64	65-74	75+	Missing Data	Total (n=904)
Placement	41.7	45.3	39.1	10	43.2*
Size of sign	16.1	19.8	21.6	10	19.2
Size of lettering	15.8	18.4	19.1	10	17.8
Message	11.7	13.4	8.6	10	12.1
Clarity of lettering	8.1	10.3	13.0	8	10.2
Colours	6.5	7.4	7.5	12	7.2
Shape of sign	0.8	2.5	1.2	11	1.8

*Each row represents column percentages for discrete items which do not add up to 100% as respondents could respond to more than one item.

TABLE B-42
Percentage of Age Groups Reporting Difficulties with Dangerous Visual Conditions

	Age Group				
	55-64	65-74	75+	Missing Data	Total (n=904)
Bothered by night headlight glare	33.7	41.2	45.8	25	39.9*
Bothered by daytime glare of headlights or sun	26.3	24.6	28.1	14	25.7
Difficulty seeing at night	20.5	22.2	32.2	30	23.5

*Each row represents column percentages for discrete items which do not add up to 100% as respondents could respond to more than one item.

TABLE B-43
Percentage of Age Groups Avoiding or Not Driving in Dangerous Traffic Conditions

	Age Group				
	55-64	**65-74**	**75+**	**Missing Data**	**Total (n=904)**
In fog:				20	
Try to avoid	61.6	69.7	62.5		66.2
Don't drive	6.5	8.4	12.5		8.6
Do drive	31.8	21.9	25.0		25.2
In heavy holiday traffic:				29	
Try to avoid	57.7	59.5	54.8		58.2
Don't drive	6.6	6.9	15.9		8.5
Do drive	35.7	33.5	29.3		33.4
In snow, sleet, slush:				15	
Try to avoid	56.5	57.7	54.0		56.7
Don't drive	6.5	10.4	11.2		9.4
Do drive	37.0	32.0	34.8		33.9
In rush hour:				13	
Try to avoid	48.2	50.1	51.6		49.8
Don't drive	2.4	5.2	9.3		5.2
Do drive	49.4	44.7	39.1		45.0
At night:				13	
Try to avoid	25.2	36.8	46.6		35.4
Don't drive	1.6	3.5	9.9		4.2
Do drive	73.2	59.7	43.5		60.5
In heavy traffic areas (bridges, tunnels, etc.):				15	
Try to avoid	33.6	33.4	36.3		34.0
Don't drive	1.6	2.3	5.0		2.6
Do drive	64.8	64.3	58.8		63.4
In rain:				10	
Try to avoid	13.4	17.5	31.7		18.9
Don't drive	0.4	0.0	0.6		0.2
Do drive	31.8	21.9	25.0		25.2
On freeways:				24	
Try to avoid	6.1	8.4	9.5		8.0
Don't drive	1.2	2.5	6.3		2.8
Do drive	92.6	89.1	84.2		89.2
Other:				672	
Try to avoid	76.7	85.2	70.0		79.7
Don't drive	20.0	11.5	22.0		15.9
Do drive	3.3	3.3	8.0		4.3

TABLE B-44
Percentage of Age Groups Reporting Driving Fault Most Often Made

	Age Group			
	55-64 (n=190)	65-74 (n=336)	75+ (n=99)	Total (n=625)
Run yellow light	38.9	39.6	50.5	41.1
Fail to stop completely at stop sign	16.8	21.4	18.2	19.5
Speeding	22.6	16.7	9.1	17.3
Drive too slow for traffic flow	6.8	9.8	10.1	9.0
Follow too closely	4.2	5.7	4.0	5.0
Fail to signal	5.8	1.8	1.0	2.9
Fail to yield right of way	0.5	1.8	2.0	1.4
Drive too fast	1.6	1.8	0.0	1.4
Make improper turn	1.6	0.9	2.0	1.3
Drive left of center	1.1	0.0	1.0	0.5
Make improper pass	0.0	0.6	1.0	0.5
Run red light	0.0	0.0	1.0	0.2

TABLE B-45
Percentage of Age Groups Reporting Difficult Driving Maneuvers

	Age Groups			Missing	Total
	55-64	65-74	75+	Data	(n=904)
Do you find it troublesome to:					
Change lanes?				11	
Frequently	2.8	2.3	1.9		2.4
Sometimes	21.9	22.1	21.0		21.8
Seldom	16.2	11.4	13.6		13.1
Never	59.1	64.3	63.6		62.7
Make a left turn at uncontrolled intersection?				13	
Frequently	3.6	3.5	3.8		3.6
Sometimes	17.8	19.8	24.4		20.1
Seldom	8.9	10.5	13.1		10.5
Never	69.6	66.1	58.8		65.8
Enter uncontrolled intersection?				11	
Frequently	1.6	1.2	1.2		1.3
Sometimes	14.2	16.1	15.4		15.5
Seldom	6.1	7.9	13.6		8.4
Never	78.1	74.8	69.8		74.8
Enter stream of city traffic?				13	
Frequently	3.2	0.6	1.9		1.6
Sometimes	11.7	13.0	20.5		14.0
Seldom	6.5	6.8	9.9		7.3
Never	78.5	79.5	67.7		77.1
Enter freeway?				37	
Frequently	0.4	1.1	0.6		0.8
Sometimes	15.4	13.4	11.6		13.6
Seldom	8.3	6.2	9.7		7.4
Never	75.9	79.4	78.1		78.2
Back up your car?				9	
Frequently	1.2	2.5	5.6		2.7
Sometimes	9.3	10.1	17.9		11.3
Seldom	4.5	6.4	8.0		6.1
Never	85.0	81.1	68.5		79.9
Read traffic signs?				9	
Frequently	0.4	0.6	0.0		0.4
Sometimes	13.8	12.8	14.2		13.3
Seldom	6.1	9.5	10.5		8.7
Never	79.8	77.2	75.3		77.5
Park your car?				10	
Frequently	2.0	1.6	2.5		1.9
Sometimes	9.3	11.3	13.0		11.1
Seldom	5.7	6.6	8.6		6.7
Never	82.9	80.5	75.9		80.3

TABLE B-46
Percentage of Males/Females Reporting Difficult Driving Maneuvers

	Male	Female	Missing Data	Total (n=904)
Do you find it troublesome to:				
Change lanes?			13	
Frequently	1.8	2.9		2.4
Sometimes	16.6	27.0		21.9
Seldom	11.6	14.6		13.1
Never	69.9	55.5		62.6
Make a left turn at uncontrolled intersection?			15	
Frequently	2.7	4.4		3.6
Sometimes	16.2	23.9		20.1
Seldom	11.9	9.3		10.6
Never	69.1	62.4		65.7
Enter uncontrolled intersection?			13	
Frequently	0.7	2.0		1.3
Sometimes	11.9	19.0		15.5
Seldom	9.8	7.1		8.4
Never	77.6	72.0		74.7
Enter stream of city traffic?			15	
Frequently	1.1	2.0		1.6
Sometimes	11.4	16.7		14.1
Seldom	7.5	7.1		7.3
Never	80.0	74.2		77.1
Enter freeway?			39	
Frequently	0.5	1.2		0.8
Sometimes	9.3	18.1		13.6
Seldom	8.2	6.6		7.4
Never	82.0	74.2		78.2
Back up your car?			11	
Frequently	2.0	3.3		2.7
Sometimes	8.9	13.2		11.1
Seldom	4.8	7.5		6.2
Never	84.3	75.9		80.1
Read traffic signs?			11	
Frequently	0.7	0.2		0.4
Sometimes	14.8	11.7		13.2
Seldom	9.8	7.7		8.7
Never	74.8	80.4		77.6
Park your car?			12	
Frequently	0.9	2.9		1.9
Sometimes	6.4	15.5		11.0
Seldom	5.2	8.2		6.7
Never	87.5	73.5		80.4

TABLE B-47
Percentage of Age Groups Reporting Factors They Would Consider in Determining Whether They Would Stop Driving

	Age Group				
	55-64	65-74	75+	Missing Data	Total (n=904)
Health	97.6	98.3	98.7	19	98.2*
Accident record	89.6	86.2	87.4	49	87.4
Road test	89.3	81.8	77.0	38	83.0
Other available transportation	67.5	71.9	69.5	37	70.2
Written test	53.6	49.6	46.4	54	50.1
Need for mobility	54.0	43.8	45.0	68	46.9
Other	17.1	17.6	16.3	15	17.2

*Each row represents column percentages for discrete items which do not add up to 100% as respondents could respond to more than one item.

TABLE B-48
Percentage of Respondent Age Groups in Favor of Driver Reexamination at License Renewal

	Age Group			
	55-64 (n=245)	65-74 (n=480)	75+ (n=156)	Total (n=881)
At no age	31.4	23.8	34.6	27.8
At all ages	35.9	36.5	30.1	35.2
Specific ages	24.5	58.6	16.9	37.0
	(n=80)	(n=191)	(n=55)	(n=326)
At 65 years	28.8	20.9	18.2	22.4
At 70 years	36.3	34.6	36.4	35.3
At 75 years	12.5	18.3	14.5	16.3
At 80 years	2.5	15.7	20.0	13.2

APPENDIX C:

Appendix to Chapter 7: Focus Group Discussions Face to Face

Methodology

Overview of the Research Design

The structure of the focus groups was based on a 5 x 3 x 2 factorial design. It involved five geographic locations, three age groupings and both male and female drivers. The five locations in British Columbia were: West Vancouver, White Rock, Victoria, Oak Bay, and the Okanagan Valley. The three age groups were fifty-five to sixty-four, sixty-five to seventy-four and seventy-five plus. In total, thirty-one focus group sessions with a mean size of 5.2 persons were conducted: seven in West Vancouver and six in each of the other four locations.

The entire focus group process included 162 elderly participants. Of these, ninety-nine were males and sixty-three were females ranging in age from fifty-six to eighty-six. Forty-six percent were aged fifty-five to sixty-four, 36 percent were aged sixty-five to seventy-four, and 18 percent were aged seventy-five and over.

The three age groupings were chosen to encompass the pre-retired and the already retired, and among the already retired, the young-old and the old-old. These latter groups are known to differ considerably in terms of health status and life-style. The unequal age and sex distribution represented a deliberate attempt to approximate the 1984-85 age-sex distribution of licensed drivers in British Columbia. The five geographic locations were selected because each one has a high percentage of seniors (15 to 28 percent) and because together they provide a good representation of the variety of communities in which seniors live and drive.

Specific Procedures

Recruitment of Elderly Interviewees. The elderly who participated in this research were recruited through articles written in community newspapers, radio public service announcements, on-air interviews, random digit dialing, and notices in senior centers. Persons fifty-five or older, holding a valid driver's license and living in the designated communities, were asked to call or write the Gerontology Research Centre, Simon Fraser University, if they were willing "to share [their] views on such topics as reasons for driving, driving habits, attitudes, concerns, and expectations about licensing." The potential interviewees were informed that about two hours of their time would be required. They were also told that the information would be gathered through small group discussions at a central location in their community or through a personal interview in their home. The first persons to respond who met the age, sex, and geographic requirements of the focus group study were scheduled to participate.

Conduct of the Focus Group

When participants first arrived at the focus group location, each was asked to sign an informed consent form and complete a participant information form. On the latter document the elderly drivers were requested to provide some personal, yet relevant information on their:

1. Age.
2. Sex.
3. Marital status.
4. Present employment status.
5. Highest level of education completed.
6. Major (pre-retirement) occupation.
7. Whether they were in receipt of Old Age Security Pension (OAS), Guaranteed Income Supplement (GAIN), or War Veteran's Allowance.
8. Self-perceived health status.
9. Self rating of present vision and hearing.
10. Present level of alcohol use.
11. Level of consumption and name of regularly used prescription and over-the-counter medications.
12. Make and year of automobile usually driven.
13. Estimated distance driven in an average year.
14. Accident history over the past five years.
15. History of traffic violations over the past five years.

After these forms were completed, the group leader introduced herself and the other study staff, described the purpose of the study, emphasized the confidentiality of comments/names of participants and indicated that all comments were welcome. The respondents were notified that there were no right or wrong answers. The purpose of the exercise was to uncover all points of view. The group leader then proceeded to ask, in the order specified, each question listed in the Focus Group Discussion Guide. Spontaneous responses were welcomed. However, when there were no replies forthcoming to a question, the group was prompted by a series of possible or plausible responses listed in the discussion guide. They were answer types presented earlier by other groups.

Response Recording. All sessions were tape recorded. Two trained observer-coders attended each session. Their role was to record, on partially precoded forms, all responses from all participants, including comments that did not relate to the specific questions asked but which were important to the general topic (these were recorded as close to verbatim as possible). Nonverbal behavior such as nodding agreement with another participant was also coded. Each observer was responsible for coding responses for one-half of the group.

The precoded responses on the recording form were derived from the elderly driver literature and from three pilot sessions conducted before commencement of the actual study. These sessions constituted an important part of the training given to the group leaders and to the six observer-coders.

The coding strategy was designed to help manage the tremendous amount of information that sixty hours of interaction provided. Such a process had positive strengths and weaknesses. The major strength was that a whole plethora of data could be categorized and analyzed. Its major weakness was that in the process of categorization some of the rich text was lost. To compensate for the latter, the interview tapes were individually reviewed. Commentaries that exemplified meanings of certain categories were included in the write-up.

Focus Group Methodology. To deal with such potential problems as the leader failing to cover all relevant issues and concerns, injecting her biases into the wording of the questions, possibly forgetting or misinterpreting group comments or issues, or inferring consensus when, in fact, there was none, the group discussions were organized accordingly:

1. A list of specific questions were developed for group leaders. The leaders were not restricted to this list. They were encouraged to probe responses and ask additional questions. However, it was essential that the listed questions were asked. This procedure ensured that all questions of critical interest were presented to all groups in a consistent manner, using wording that had been pretested to ensure clarity and comprehension. It also ensured that key areas of elderly driver lives were covered.
2. Two observer-coders attended each session and recorded, on a partially precoded form, all comments made by focus groups participants as they occurred. As well the observer-coders were instructed to record nonverbal responses such as members shaking their heads in disagreement when other participants presented their points of view.
3. Each individual's responses in the group were recorded separately. This

> enabled us to identify, with considerable precision, the extent to which there was consensus within any one group and across the various groups in the study. We consider this to be a key innovation that guards against the possibility of leaders highlighting, in their reports, what may be essentially idiosyncratic viewpoints, spectacular, but unsupported by others.

Additionally, an abundance of personal data from focus group participants was gathered through the information sheet. They were summarized and cross-tabulated by age, since age was a primary variable of interest.

Focus Group Discussion Guide and Tables C-1 to C-25 Based on Focus Group Findings

SFU Gerontology Research Centre
Focus Group Study of Older Drivers

Discussion Guide

(Introduce by saying our first topic is, or our next topic is)

TOPIC 1: Driving Pattern	*Response Categories*
1.1Q For what purposes or types of activities do you use a car. That is, what things do you do that involve use of a car?	Business, commuting to and from work, pleasure, shopping, to go to entertainment, to go to sporting events, family visits, visiting friends, to health care practitioner or centre, social events, meals, meetings, volunteer work
1.2Q When and under what conditions do you try to avoid driving?	(a) Don't avoid anything (b) Day/night, morning/afternoon/ evening, weekdays/weekends (c) Winter/fall/summer (d) Good/bad weather (e) Rush hour/quiet times (f) City/highway, familiar/unfamiliar (g) Poorly lit roads
1.3Q When you drive others, what types of people tend to be passengers in your car?	Alone, mate, friend, children, grandchildren, other family members, other seniors, younger people, work associates, business contacts, parents, neighbours
1.4Q How often do you usually drive?	Daily, weekly, several times per week, monthly, several times a month, a few times a year, almost never, never
1.5Q In a typical week, other than driving there yourself, how do you get places?	Others drive me, bus, taxi, bicycle, handidart, walk

TOPIC 2: Attitudes and Beliefs	*Response Categories*
2.1Q How do you feel about driving:	Like/don't like, bored, anxious, excited, nervous, comfortable, uncomfortable, confident, annoyed, impatient, intolerant
2.2Q What do you think about *other older drivers*?	Safe/unsafe, cautious, law abiding, accident prone, good/bad, average, better/worse/same as younger/ older/others, slower, all different, should be retested
2.3Q What do you think *most people* think about older drivers?	Safe/unsafe, cautious, law abiding, accident prone, good/bad, average, better than younger/older/others, worse than younger/older/others, same as younger/older/others, slower, all different, should be retested

2.4Q What does your family think about *you* as a driver?	Safe/unsafe, cautious, law abiding, accident prone, good/bad, average, better/worse/same as younger/ older/others, never liked my driving, think I should stop driving, think I drive OK
2.5Q How do you think the police feel about and treat older drivers?	Safe, unsafe, cautious, law abiding, accident prone, good/bad, average, better/worse/same as younger/others Fairly/unfairly, blame them unjustly, give the benefit of doubt, condescending, like other drivers, helpful, with respect
2.6Q Do you drive differently now than when you were younger and if so, in what ways?	Yes/No Drive more now, slower/faster, avoid heavy traffic, less night driving, avoid bad weather, limit self to familiar routes, more cautious/less cautious, better/ worse, drive more defensively, more aware/less aware of things, less recklessly, avoid stressful situations
2.7Q What are the characteristics of a good driver?	Competent, experienced, courteous, alert, patient, aware of things, considerate of others, concentrate on driving
2.8Q What annoys you about other drivers?	Lack of courtesy, aggressiveness
2.9Q What do you think are the major causes of accidents among older drivers?	Alcohol, unsafe drivers, weather, night driving, discourteous drivers, other drivers, speed, unsafe cars, misjudgement of other vehicles and drivers, difficulty reading/seeing signs and signals, slower reactions, less attentive, confusion, roads more complex now, driving patterns different now
2.10Q How would your life change if you could no longer drive?	Less independent, less mobile, less social, fewer vacations, couldn't work, stay closer to home, take longer to get places, become public transit user
2.11Q What values does your car symbolize for you?	Convenience, freedom, independence, "macho," rejuvenation, comfort, adventure, expense, necessity, relaxation, memories, pleasure

TOPIC 3: Driving Difficulties	*Response Categories*
3.1Q What are the driving manoeuvres that you find difficult?	Changing lanes, turning, going fast, steering, parking, keeping up with traffic, backing up, joining a stream of traffic entering a highway, keeping in the lane, judging distance, keeping a good following distance, reading street signs, reading instructional signs

3.2Q What type of roads do you find difficult?	Limited access highways/highways/city streets, narrow roads, gravel roads, one-way roads/two-way roads, intersections
3.3Q What personal factors, characteristics or impairments make driving difficult for you?	Fatigue, poor vision, stress, poor reaction time, poor health, drugs, alcohol, information overload, glare, always a poor driver, mobility impairment, poor judgment
3.4Q What are your greatest concerns about *your own* driving?	Hitting another car, losing licence, getting hit, becoming ill while driving, injuring a pedestrian, losing concentration/attention, being a danger to others

TOPIC 4: Design	*Response Categories*
4.1Q What changes in road or highway design or in traffic signs or signals would make it easier for you to drive?	More one-way streets, controlled access highways, left turn lanes and signals, stop lights, stop signs, better lighting, lower speed limits, larger signs, more advance warning about exits
4.2Q What changes in pedestrian signals, crossings or rules would make it easier for you as a driver?	Push button signals should activate faster

TOPIC 5: Licensure	*Response Categories*
5.1Q Should people be required to give up their driver's licence when they reach a certain age and if so, at what age?	Yes/No 50-54, 55-59, 60-64, 65-69, 70-74, 75-79, 80-84, 85-89, 90-95, 95+
5.2Q What factors should be considered in deciding if someone should be retested?	Age, good health, specific illness, vision problems, accident occurrence, violation
5.3Q If older drivers were required to be retested before their licence was renewed, at what age should this happen?	50-54, 55-59, 60-64, 65-69, 70-74, 75-79, 80-84, 85-89, 90-95, 95+
5.4Q Should a medical checkup, fitness test, eyesight test, road test or written test be a condition of your licence renewal?	Medical checkup, fitness test, age test, written test, road test
5.5Q What do you think about the need for vehicle testing?	
5.6Q What things in the future might cause you to stop driving?	Hazard to others Unsafe for self Poor health Poor vision Slower response time Poor hearing

5.7Q Who should decide when you should stop driving?	Self Family Doctor Police Licence Department ICBC Unbiased test
5.8Q The Motor Vehicle Act requires physicians to notify them about drivers who have some impairment that may affect driving. What do you think about this?	Appeal should be possible, more than one doctor's opinion should be used
5.9Q Sometimes issues of discrimination come up. Does retesting of older drivers discriminate against them? (Probe for reasons why)	Yes, No

TOPIC 6: Education	*Response Categories*
6.1Q If a course were to be developed for older drivers, who should take it?	Violators, people who fail the road test, people who have had accidents, people referred by the doctor
6.2Q What do you think should be included:	Handling the vehicle Distance judgement Laws and regulations Courtesy Driving in heavy traffic Bad road conditions driving Bad weather conditions driving

TOPIC 7: Violations	*Response Categories*
7.1Q From time to time almost all of us commit some traffic violation. What type of violations do you most frequently commit?	Speeding, going through a yellow or red light, illegal turn, illegal passing, not wearing a seat belt, not signalling, going through a stop sign, failure to yield right of way, follow too close, drinking and driving
7.2Q Do you have any suggestions for revision of our driving regulations?	
7.3Q Do you usually travel the speed limit or go with the flow of traffic?	Speed limit, flow, both

TOPIC 8: Medication Effects	*Response Categories*
8.1Q Have you or anyone you know had the experience of medication affecting driving? If so, what were the effects?	Yes/No Sleepiness, nausea, blurred vision, dizziness, tremor, muscle weakness

8.2Q What were the drugs?	Pain killers, tranquillizers, anti-depressants, heart medication, cancer drugs, anti-histamines, anti-coagulants

TOPIC 9: Other

9.1Q In the five minutes we have left, is there anything else about driving and the older person that you think we and ICBC should know or be concerned about?

CLOSING

After general discussion (TOPIC 9)

THANK PARTICIPANTS BY SAYING -

On behalf of the SFU Gerontology Research Centre and ICBC, I really want to thank you for taking the time to come and share your ideas and opinions with us today.

If you would like a summary of the findings, please put your name and address on one of these envelopes and leave it with us. Since the study will take us some time to complete, you will not hear from us until sometime in the new year but be assured, you *will* hear from us.

HAND OUT PARKING/GAS REBATE AND SAY-

In *this* envelope you will find $5 to help cover your transportation costs. Please sign this receipt form as we need it for our records.

Tables C-1 to C-25

Based on Focus Group Findings

TABLE C-1
Sociodemographic Characteristics of Focus Group Participants

	55-64 (n=74)	65-74 (n=59)	75+ (n=29)	Missing Data	Total (n=162)
% male	52.7	67.8	69.0	0	61.1
% married	75.7	81.4	69.0	0	76.5
% working					
full-time	17.6	1.7	0	1	8.7
part-time	12.2	8.6	0		8.7
% in receipt of OAS or SA	8.1	96.6	89.7	0	54.9
% receiving an income supplement					
GIS	0	8.5	0	0	3.1
GAIN	0	1.7	3.4	0	1.2
War Veterans Allowance	1.4	5.1	3.4	0	3.1
*Primary Life Occupation (%)				11	
Professional	19.4	14.3	32.1		19.9
Manager—large	14.9	12.5	10.7		13.2
Semi-professional	7.5	7.1	10.7		7.9
Manager—small	9.0	8.9	21.4		11.3
Clerical	23.9	16.1	0		16.6
Skilled	10.4	8.9	3.6		8.6
Semi-skilled	4.5	8.9	14.3		7.9
Unskilled	0	3.6	0		1.3
Not in labor force	10.4	19.6	7.1		13.2
% with a degree or some college or university training	55.5	49.2	55.1	0	53.0

*Categories from Pineo and Porter (1967)

TABLE C-2
Self-reported Health Status, Medication and Alcohol Use and Vision and Hearing Ratings of Focus Group Participants

	55-64 (n=74)	65-74 (n=59)	75+ (n=29)	Missing Data	Total (n=162)
	%	%	%		%
Overall Health Rating					
Excellent	58.1	36.2	41.4	1	47.2
Good	39.2	55.2	55.2		47.8
Fair	2.7	6.9	3.4		4.3
Poor	0	1.7	0		0.6
No. of Prescription Medications Used Regularly					
0	63.5	55.9	51.7	0	58.6
1	23.0	28.8	27.6		25.9
2	9.5	13.6	13.8		11.7
3	4.1	1.7	3.4		3.1
4+	0	0	3.4		0.6
No. of Over-counter Medications Used Regularly					
0	60.8	50.8	58.6	0	56.8
1	29.7	40.7	34.5		34.6
2	6.8	6.8	6.9		6.8
3	1.4	1.7	0		1.2
4+	1.4	0	0		0.6
Frequency of Alcohol Use					
Daily	10.8	16.9	17.2	0	14.2
Several times a week	25.7	23.7	13.8		22.8
Weekly	17.6	16.9	24.1		18.5
Monthly	18.9	20.3	13.8		18.5
Nonuser	27.0	22.0	31.0		25.9
Vision Rating					
Excellent	21.9	40.7	27.6	1	29.8
Good	72.6	54.2	69.0		65.2
Fair	4.1	5.1	3.4		4.3
Poor	1.4	0	0		0.6
Hearing Rating					
Excellent	37.0	33.9	21.4	2	33.1
Good	46.6	47.5	64.3		50.0
Fair	15.0	16.9	10.7		15.0
Poor	1.4	1.7	3.6		1.9

TABLE C-3
Driving Purposes and Activities*

	55-64 (n=72)	65-74 (n=58)	75+ (n=29)	Total (n=159)
	%	%	%	%
Shopping	70.8	67.2	72.4	69.8
Pleasure	69.4	67.2	51.7	65.4
Visiting Family/Friends	51.4	29.3	69.0	46.5
Vacation Travel	44.4	37.9	37.9	40.9
Social & Cultural Events/Entertainment	30.6	25.9	34.5	29.6
Sports/Sporting Events	12.5	25.9	6.9	16.4
Driving Others	15.3	13.8	0	11.9
Commuting to/from work	20.8	5.2	0	11.3
Health Care	6.9	6.9	17.2	8.8
Volunteer Work	5.6	13.8	0	7.5
Meetings	2.8	10.3	13.8	7.5
Business	11.1	5.2	0	6.9
Other	2.8	8.6	3.4	5.0

*In this and all subsequent tables unless otherwise indicated column percentages do not add up to 100 percent as subjects frequently gave more than one response.

TABLE C-4
How Their Life Would Change if They Could no Longer Drive

	55-64 (n=72)	65-74 (n=58)	75+ (n=29)	Total (n=159)
	%	%	%	%
Devastated, shocked, heart broken, unhappy, awful, frustrated, traumatic, like losing my right arm, frightening, would die	29.2	44.8	31.0	35.2
Become public transit user	23.6	24.1	31.0	25.2
Have to move (e.g., nearer bus)	19.4	29.3	10.3	21.4
Less independent/free	22.2	17.2	0	16.4
Stay closer to home	12.5	6.9	27.6	13.2
Less mobile	16.7	10.3	10.3	13.2
Inconvenient, disappointed but I'd learn to live with it	13.9	12.1	13.8	13.2
Less social	12.5	10.3	13.8	11.9
It would change my life-style	9.7	6.9	20.7	10.7
Take longer to get places	11.1	6.9	0	7.5
Save money	8.3	6.9	6.9	7.5
It would restrict my activities	8.3	3.4	6.9	6.3
Take taxis	2.8	8.6	10.3	6.3

TABLE C-5
Symbolic Value of Their Car

	55-64 (n=67)	65-74 (n=54)	75+ (n=29)	Total (n=150)
	%	%	%	%
Independence	31.3	35.2	17.2	30.0
Freedom	26.9	29.6	34.5	29.3
Mobility/flexibility	19.4	20.4	41.4	24.0
Transportation	19.4	22.2	13.8	19.3
Convenient, quick	13.4	14.8	10.3	13.3
Pleasure, enjoyment/mental health	11.9	13.0	6.9	11.3
Status/class/pride	7.5	11.1	13.8	10.0
Important/means a lot	6.0	9.3	17.2	9.3
Necessity/essential	6.0	13.0	6.9	8.7
Part of life/trusted friend/mode of life	9.0	9.3	6.9	8.7

TABLE C-6
Conditions Under Which Respondents Avoid Driving

	55-64 (n=71)	65-74 (n=59)	75+ (n=27)	Total (n=157)
	%	%	%	%
None	25.4	18.6	18.5	21.7
Bad weather	100.0	100.0	100.0	100.0
Nights (especially rainy nights)	28.2	49.2	55.6	40.8
Rush Hours	25.4	32.2	29.6	28.7
Heavy traffic areas (bridges, tunnels, congested areas)	7.0	10.2	0	7.0
Heavy holiday traffic	5.6	5.1	3.7	5.1
Weekends	7.0	1.7	0	3.8
Poorly lit roads	1.4	0	3.7	1.3

TABLE C-7
Types of Passengers Typically Carried

	55-64 (n=70)	65-74 (n=57)	75+ (n=29)	Total (n=156)
	%	%	%	%
None	10.0	3.5	6.9	7.1
Friends	37.1	35.1	55.2	39.7
Other seniors	25.7	40.4	51.7	35.9
Grandchildren	34.3	26.3	34.5	31.4
Mate	27.1	35.1	20.7	28.8
Other family	34.3	21.1	31.0	28.8
Children	18.6	14.0	0	13.5
Business contacts	10.0	0	0	4.5
Work/activity associates	5.7	3.5	6.9	5.1
Neighbors	2.9	5.3	10.3	5.1
Hitchhikers	4.3	7.0	0	4.5
Visitors & tourists	4.3	3.5	3.4	3.8

TABLE C-8
Frequency of Driving

	55-64 (n=72)	65-74 (n=59)	75+ (n=29)	Total (n=160)
	%	%	%	%
Daily	81.9	74.6	86.2	80.0
Several times a week	13.9	22.0	13.8	16.9
Once a week	4.2	1.7	0	2.5
Holidays only	0	1.7	0	0.6
Total	100.0	100.0	100.0	100.0

TABLE C-9
Estimated Kilometers Driven per Year

	55-64 (n=74)	65-74 (n=58)	75+ (n=27)	Total (n=159)
	%	%	%	%
Not driving at present time	0	1.9	0	0.6
800- 6,999 km.	21.6	19.0	48.1	25.2
7,000-11,999 km.	27.0	25.9	11.1	23.9
12,000-18,999 km.	21.6	27.6	33.3	25.8
19,000+	29.7	25.9	7.4	24.5
Total	100.0	100.0	100.0	100.0

TABLE C-10
Age of Auto Usually Driven

	55-64 (n=73)	65-74 (n=59)	75+ (n=29)	Total (n=161)
	%	%	%	%
Less than 2 years (1986-87)	26.0	16.9	13.8	20.5
2- 4 years (1983-85)	26.0	37.3	24.1	29.8
5- 8 years (1979-82)	26.0	22.0	24.1	24.2
9-21 years (1966-78)	21.9	23.7	37.9	25.5
Total	100.0	100.0	100.0	100.0

TABLE C-11
Other Transportation Used

	55-64 (n=61)	65-74 (n=56)	75+ (n=27)	Total (n=144)
	%	%	%	%
None	19.7	10.7	25.9	17.4
Walk	47.5	53.6	44.4	49.3
Bus	23.0	33.9	22.2	27.1
Others drive me	18.0	10.7	22.2	16.0
Bicycle	13.1	10.7	0	9.7
Taxi	3.3	5.4	0	3.5
Other	1.6	1.8	0	1.4

TABLE C-12
Feelings about Driving

	55-64 (n=71)	65-74 (n=59)	75+ (n=29)	Total (n=159)
	%	%	%	%
Positive				
Like/enjoy it	73.2	64.4	93.1	73.6
Comfortable	8.5	27.1	24.1	18.2
Confident	4.2	6.8	6.9	5.7
Negative				
Feel nervous/stressed/anxious	5.6	8.5	0	5.7
Don't like it	9.9	3.4	0	5.7
Concerned about other drivers/cars	1.4	5.1	17.2	5.7
Neutral				
It's a convenience/means of transportation	16.9	13.6	3.4	13.2
Neutral/acceptance	4.2	10.2	6.9	6.9
Other				
Rather be a passenger	4.2	0	0	1.9
Nervous/uncomfortable as a passenger	4.2	3.4	0	3.1

TABLE C-13
Perceptions of Older Drivers

	55-64	65-74	75+	Total
	%	%	%	%
a) What do *you* think about other older drivers?				
	(n=70)	(n=57)	(n=28)	(n=155)
Cautious	32.9	38.6	21.4	32.9
Slower	38.6	22.8	25.0	30.3
All different	24.3	12.3	7.1	16.8
Average/same as others	7.1	10.5	28.6	12.3
Not aware of other drivers unpredictable/don't signal	21.4	1.8	10.7	12.3
Better than others/younger people	4.3	10.5	25.0	10.3
Worse than others/younger people	15.7	5.3	0	9.0
Unsafe/Look out for them	14.2	5.3	0	8.4
Fine, pretty good	2.9	12.3	10.7	7.7
Some are terrible/should be off road	7.1	10.5	3.6	7.7
Law abiding	4.3	8.8	3.6	5.8
Courteous/considerate	4.3	8.8	3.6	5.8
b) What do *most* people think about older drivers?				
	(n=60)	(n=55)	(n=26)	(n=141)
They are slow	31.7	38.2	26.9	33.3
Resent/are critical of/have little patience for etc.	18.3	34.5	26.9	26.2
Think they are worse than other drivers	23.3	3.6	34.6	17.7
Feel they should stop driving	11.7	3.6	23.1	10.6
Cautious	6.7	7.3	19.2	9.2
Unpredictable/erratic	8.3	7.3	7.7	7.8
Law abiding	1.7	10.9	11.5	7.1
c) How do you think the *police* feel about and treat older drivers?				
	(n=67)	(n=56)	(n=26)	(n=149)
With respect	52.2	48.2	38.5	48.3
Don't know	25.4	25.0	26.9	25.5
Fairly	22.4	25.0	15.4	22.1
Like others	16.4	12.5	26.9	16.8
Give them benefit of the doubt	14.9	8.9	0	10.1
Helpful	6.0	14.3	7.7	9.4

TABLE C-14
Their Families' Perceptions of Them as a Driver

	55-64 (n=70)	65-74 (n=57)	75+ (n=28)	Total (n=155)
	%	%	%	%
Good/excellent driver	27.1	40.4	39.3	34.2
Think I drive OK/no complaint	25.7	42.1	25.0	31.6
Are critical/don't like my driving	20.0	10.5	7.1	14.2
Think I drive too fast	17.1	12.3	7.1	13.5
Spouse critical/nervous/won't let me drive	5.7	8.8	7.1	7.1
Bad/unsafe/worse than others	8.6	5.3	3.6	6.5

TABLE C-15
Changes in Driving Behavior

	55-64 (n=71)	65-74 (n=59)	75+ (n=28)	Total (n=158)
	%	%	%	%
a) Do you drive differently now than when you were younger?				
Yes	52.1	57.6	67.9	57.0
No	16.9	35.6	21.4	24.7
b) How?				
More cautiously/less reckless	39.4	30.5	50.0	38.0
More defensively	36.6	20.3	25.0	28.5
Slower	18.3	22.0	25.0	20.9
Better	9.9	13.6	14.3	12.0
Not as easily upset/less stressed	15.5	6.8	7.1	10.8
More conscientious/serious	4.2	10.2	10.7	7.6

TABLE C-16
Characteristics of a Good Driver

	55-64 (n=70)	65-74 (n=58)	75+ (n=25)	Total (n=153)
	%	%	%	%
Courteous	37.1	34.5	32.0	35.3
Considerate	38.6	24.1	44.0	34.0
Defensive driving	35.7	37.9	8.0	32.0
Patient	11.4	31.0	36.0	22.9
Alert	20.0	24.1	20.0	21.6
Law abiding	15.7	22.4	20.0	19.0
Know car and route	27.1	10.3	8.0	17.6
Aware	15.7	22.4	8.0	17.0
Concentrate	15.7	12.1	8.0	13.1
Competent	11.4	12.1	4.0	10.5
Good vision, reactions	5.7	15.5	8.0	9.8
Steady, not in fits & starts	5.7	10.3	16.0	9.2
Experienced	7.1	10.3	8.0	8.5
Keeps car in good shape	12.9	1.7	8.0	7.8

TABLE C-17
Traffic Violations

	55-64	65-74	75+	Total
	%	%	%	%
a) From time to time, almost all of us commit some traffic violation. What types of violations do you most frequently commit?				
	(n=71)	(n=47)	(n=26)	(n=144)
Speeding	66.2	72.3	50.0	65.3
Running light	16.9	12.8	23.1	16.7
Rolling stop	12.7	12.8	0	10.4
No seat belt	14.1	6.4	11.5	11.1
Missing Data=18				
b) Do you travel the speed limit or go with the flow of traffic?				
	(n=70)	(n=52)	(n=28)	(n=150)
Flow	70.0	63.5	50.0	64.0
Speed limit	12.9	9.6	17.9	12.7
Both	11.4	25.0	25.0	18.7
Missing Data=12				
c) Do you have any suggestions for revising our driving regulations?				
	(n=58)	(n=40)	(n=15)	(n=113)
Better enforcement	17.2	35.0	13.3	23.0
More punishment for violators (especially drinking)	34.5	2.5	13.3	20.4
Raise speed limit	22.4	20.0	0	18.6
Missing Data=49				

TABLE C-18
Driving Difficulties

	55-64	65-74	75+	Total
	%	%	%	%
a) What are the driving maneuvers that you find difficult?				
	(n=42)	(n=37)	(n=13)	(n=92)
Parking	50.0	45.9	46.2	47.8
Backing up	19.0	24.3	23.1	21.7
Checking over shoulder	21.4	8.1	7.7	14.1
Missing Data=70				
b) What type roads do you find difficult?				
	(n=54)	(n=44)	(n=16)	(n=114)
Icy, snowy, wet	35.2	29.5	6.3	28.9
Gravel roads, unpaved	24.1	29.5	18.8	25.4
Bumpy ruts, washboard, pot-holes	13.0	11.4	37.5	15.8
Narrow roads	7.4	13.6	43.8	14.9
Winding, curvy, blind corners	7.4	13.6	18.8	11.4
Multi-lane highways	11.1	9.1	6.3	9.6
Dark surface at night	5.6	11.4	0	7.0
Missing Data=48				
c) What personal factors, characteristics or impairments make driving difficult for you?				
	(n=43)	(n=30)	(n=15)	(n=88)
Poor vision	44.2	30.0	20.0	35.2
Poor night vision, highway, rain	27.9	20.0	20.0	23.9
Glare (from sun, at night)	18.6	16.7	40.0	21.6
Can't turn head (arthritis, stiff neck)	14.0	23.3	13.3	17.0
Fatigue	11.6	16.7	13.3	13.6
Poor hearing	2.3	10.0	20.0	8.0
Missing Data=74				
d) What are your greatest concerns about your own driving?				
	(n=57)	(n=42)	(n=20)	(n=119)
Losing attention/concentration	28.1	40.5	40.0	34.5
Losing license/having to quit driving	24.6	31.0	20.0	26.1
Getting hit (esp. by drunks, careless drivers)	17.5	16.7	20.0	17.6
Injuring pedestrian	17.5	16.7	5.0	15.1
Losing abilities/health problems which interfere with driving, e.g., arthritis	14.0	9.5	20.0	13.4
Hitting another car	15.8	4.8	10.0	10.9
Missing Data=43				

TABLE C-19
Recommended Road and Traffic Sign Changes to Make Driving Easier/Avoid Pedestrians

	55-64	65-74	75+	Total
	%	%	%	%
a) What changes in road or highway design or in traffic signs or signals would make it easier for you to drive?				
	(n=72)	(n=54)	(n=23)	(n=149)
Larger signs, bigger letters	34.7	38.9	43.5	37.6
More left turn lanes	34.7	37.0	43.5	36.9
Standardization of placement, style of signs and lights	18.1	37.0	34.8	27.5
More advance warning about exits	22.2	24.1	30.4	24.2
Lines, cats eyes, reflectors, etc.	23.6	20.4	0	18.8
Unobstructed signs/lights/signs in center of intersection	19.4	9.3	17.4	15.4
Unambiguous signs	6.9	7.4	17.4	8.7
Better lighting	8.3	13.0	0	8.7
Missing Data = 13				
b) What changes in pedestrian signals, crossings or rules would make it easier for you as a driver?				
	(n=65)	(n=46)	(n=16)	(n=127)
Pedestrians obeying rules, being more responsible, cautious	29.2	45.7	56.3	38.6
Crossings better lit, better marked	29.2	21.7	18.8	25.2
Police enforce rules (e.g., J-walking)	20.0	8.7	18.8	15.7
Warning of X-walk ahead (e.g., flashing lights)	15.4	10.9	31.3	15.7
Longer "walk" time to cross	12.3	15.2	12.5	13.4
Pedestrian should point	6.2	13.0	6.3	8.7
Missing Data = 35				

TABLE C-20
Perceived Cause of Accidents in Older Drivers

	55-64 (n=69)	65-74 (n=55)	75+ (n=27)	Total (n=151)
	%	%	%	%
Less attentive	43.5	40.0	37.0	41.1
Slower reactions	34.8	36.4	59.3	39.7
Difficulty seeing/reading signs, signals/poor vision	26.1	20.0	40.7	26.5
Physical degradation/medical problem	14.5	10.9	18.5	13.9
Driving too slow/cautious	13.0	9.1	0	9.3
Misjudgment of other vehicles/ drivers	8.7	7.3	7.4	7.9
Unsafe drivers/beyond capabilities/ lack of experience	7.2	7.3	11.1	7.9
Poor perception	13.0	0	3.7	6.6

TABLE C-21
Annoying Behaviors of Other Drivers

	55-64	65-74	75+	Total
a) What annoys you about other drivers?				
	(n=72)	(n=59)	(n=28)	(n=159)
Don't signal/late signal	30.6	30.5	42.9	32.7
Tailgaters	29.2	32.2	21.4	28.9
Pass & cut you off/cut in then turn	18.1	22.0	21.4	20.1
Lack of courtesy/consideration	22.2	8.5	10.7	15.1
Too slow/weekend drivers/in wrong lane	15.3	15.3	10.7	14.5
Lane hoppers	9.7	16.9	21.4	14.5
Don't obey rules of road/signs	9.7	5.1	10.7	8.2
Too courteous/hesitant/indecisive	11.1	0	7.1	6.3
Aggressiveness	4.2	6.8	7.1	5.7
Loud radio/Walkman	2.8	11.9	0	5.7
Motorcycles in & out/bikes	2.8	6.8	7.1	5.0
Horn honkers	1.4	1.7	21.4	5.0
b) Action when annoyed				
	(n=68)	(n=54)	(n=26)	(n=148)
Slow down/let them have their way	25.0	24.1	15.4	23.0
Sigh/talk to self/shake head	17.6	18.5	30.8	20.3
Ignore	19.1	18.5	15.4	18.2
Swear/shout at them	20.6	7.4	15.4	14.9
Accept/don't let it bother me	10.3	16.7	7.7	12.2
Honk	13.2	11.1	0	10.1
Get tense/frightened/stressed/ end up annoyed/angry	10.3	3.7	15.4	8.8
Do nothing	8.8	3.7	3.8	6.1
Back off	2.9	11.1	0	5.4

TABLE C-22
Reasons/Age for Retiring Drivers

	55-64	65-74	75+	Total
	%	%	%	%
a) What factors should be considered in deciding if someone should be retested?				
	(n=68)	**(n=57)**	**(n=25)**	**(n=150)**
Health	44.1	54.4	56.0	50.0
Violations/driving record	38.2	31.6	44.0	36.7
Age	36.8	35.1	16.0	32.7
Accidents (with fault)	25.0	24.6	20.0	24.0
Vision problems	20.6	31.6	0	21.3
Specific illness (e.g., stroke, epilepsy, heart problems or physical impairment)	25.0	8.8	36.0	20.7
Hearing problems	10.3	17.5	0	11.3
Psychological test scores	7.4	10.5	8.0	8.7
Missing Data=12				
b) If older drivers were required to be retested before their license was renewed, at what age should this happen?				
	(n=78)	**(n=52)**	**(n=30)**	**(n=160)**
55-59 years	2.6	0	0	1.3
60-64	5.1	0	0	2.5
65-69	21.8	19.2	6.7	18.1
70-74	30.8	17.3	16.7	23.8
75-79	3.8	13.5	16.7	9.4
80 and over	1.3	3.8	6.7	3.1
No specific age but must be additional reason	20.5	32.7	43.3	28.8
Everyone should be retested	6.4	1.9	6.7	5.0
Missing Data=2				

TABLE C-23
Criteria for License Renewal

	55-64 (n=71)	65-74 (n=54)	75+ (n=26)	Total (n=151)
	%	%	%	%
Passing an:				
Eyesight test	71.8	53.7	34.6	58.9
Medical checkup	62.0	61.1	42.3	58.3
Road test	59.2	57.4	38.5	55.0
Fitness test	52.1	38.9	30.8	43.7
Written test	47.9	38.9	15.4	39.1
All tests for renewal for everyone	9.9	13.0	34.6	15.2
Missing Data = 11				

TABLE C-24
Cessation of Driving

	55-64	65-74	75+	Total
	%	%	%	%
a) What things in the future might cause you to stop driving?				
	(n=71)	(n=50)	(n=27)	(n=148)
Poor health, medical condition (heart attack, trouble breathing)	56.3	72.0	63.0	62.8
Poor vision	19.7	10.0	22.2	16.9
Bad accident, narrow escape, making mistakes	14.1	24.0	11.1	16.9
Physical impairment, handicap	8.5	24.0	22.2	16.2
Hazard to self/know I'm slipping	15.5	14.0	14.8	14.9
Can't afford to, economics	18.3	8.0	7.4	12.8
Hazard to others	14.1	10.0	7.4	11.5
Mental impairment	1.4	20.0	14.8	10.1
Missing Data=14				
b) Who should decide when you should stop driving?				
	(n=72)	(n=53)	(n=29)	(n=154)
Doctor	37.5	56.6	55.2	47.4
Self	37.5	28.3	55.2	37.7
Unbiased test	31.9	39.6	31.0	34.4
License Dept.	27.8	24.5	10.3	23.4
Family	22.2	13.2	3.4	15.6
Panel of experts	11.1	1.9	10.3	7.8
Appeal process should be possible	18.1	16.4	3.6	14.8
Missing Data=8				
c) The Motor Vehicle Act requires physicians to notify them about drivers who have some impairment that may affect driving. What do you think about this?				
	(n=72)	(n=55)	(n=28)	(n=155)
Good idea/should be obliged to report	90.3	92.7	89.3	91.0
Only after discussion with patient	5.6	5.5	0	4.5
Doctors have too much authority now	1.4	5.5	0	2.6
Qualifiers				
Appeal/opportunity to get a second opinion	23.6	21.8	3.6	19.4
Missing Data=7				

TABLE C-25
Driver Education

	55-64	65-74	75+	Total
	%	%	%	%
a) If a course were to be developed for older drivers, who should take it?				
	(n=68)	**(n=45)**	**(n=25)**	**(n=138)**
All drivers, not by age	35.3	33.3	4.0	29.0
Violators	35.3	20.0	24.0	28.3
Optional, people who want to brush up	13.2	22.2	24.0	18.1
Everyone "older"	7.4	28.9	20.0	16.7
People who have had accidents	13.2	13.3	12.0	13.0
Missing Data = 24				
b) What should be included?				
	(n=63)	**(n=37)**	**(n=20)**	**(n=120)**
Defensive driving	38.1	45.9	40.0	40.8
Laws and regulations	12.7	27.0	35.0	20.8
Bad roads/weather	6.3	16.2	15.0	10.8
Missing Data = 42				

APPENDIX D

Appendix to Chapter 8
Victims of Serious Crashes

Methodology

Data-Gathering

The data upon which this chapter is based were obtained via a program of intensive unstructured discussion using an interview guide. Areas probed for detailed information included the nature of the injury-producing crash, the events that led up to the accident, the context in which the accident occurred, the role of the automobile in the elderly driver's life-style and the driver's understanding of himself and other age mates.

The interview team consisted of four persons: three female registered nurses in their middle years and a male in the same age group as the interviewees. The need for empathy on the part of the interviewers was considered to be crucial. The selection of middle-aged female nurses and a senior male who had interview experience in medical or personnel contexts proved valuable for trust and understanding.

The pool of elderly drivers who were involved in injury-producing crashes was provided by the British Columbia Motor Vehicle Department. Its staff searched department files for individuals who met the study's criteria: drivers aged fifty-five or over, drivers living within the urban areas of British Columbia, and drivers who were involved in a documented injury-producing accident during 1986 while operating noncommercial vehicles. The files were then forwarded to the study team. Over 700 names were received. We reviewed these, largely to eliminate crashes that appeared too traumatic to recall and ones too minor to discuss. Eligible files were returned to the Department of Motor Vehicles.

Upon receipt, the Superintendent of Motor Vehicles mailed each eligible motorist a letter urging him or her to participate in the study. In addition the study team sent a letter outlining its special interest in the elderly person's involvement. Both letters asserted the confidentiality of the study, assuring potential participants that their names or any other identifiers would not be attached to the interview material that they might provide.

Potential elderly driver participants were contacted by telephone. At this time the interviewer introduced him or herself, explained the purpose of the interviews, answered any queries the participant might have, and if all was satisfactory, arranged a time and place for the interview. There was considerable enthusiasm for the study. There were a few times when elderly drivers refused to participate in the study. The refusals were based on lack of time or the fact of ongoing litigation rather than suspiciousness or hostility. Such instances were rare.

The Questions

The interviews that were undertaken could best be described as semistructured. Topics for discussion were selected in advance. In a nutshell the questioning was based on the following four principles:

1. Persons interviewed were known to have been involved in an injury-producing accident.
2. Significant elements, patterns, processes and total structure of the accident were analyzed by the researcher.
3. Major areas of inquiry, and criteria of relevance for the data to be obtained were planned.
4. Focus on the subjective experiences of the elderly exposed to the pre-analyzed situation was established to ascertain the respondents' definitions of the situation.

To overcome the occurrences of vague or general answers, no answer at all, or statements that the elderly drivers do not know, probes, or follow-up questions were used. The chief function of the probes was to lead the elderly driver to answer more fully and accurately, or at least to provide a minimally acceptable answer beyond a simple yes or no. The second reason for using probes was to help structure the elderly drivers' responses and make sure that the topics of interest to the interviewer were covered and the amount of irrelevant information minimized.

The following queries were asked of each interviewee:

I The Accident. In as much detail as possible, please tell me how the accident happened.

Could you see the accident coming or was it a complete surprise?

Some accidents just happen. Was yours one of these or was there something that you or the other driver could have done to prevent it?

What could have been done?

Do you think the accident could have been prevented if either you or the other driver had been more skilled?

What were your first thoughts after the accident?

Some people think that even the unpleasant things that happen to us can teach us something. Did you learn anything from your accident?

Do you think of yourself as a cautious driver? What kind of things do you do to rate yourself as a cautious driver?

II Prior Events. Where were you going to or coming from when the accident happened?

What was the last activity you engaged in before you got into the car to make the trip that ended up as an accident?

Most people do things while they're driving, like talking to passengers, looking at billboards, listening to music, smoking. What were you doing in the car just before the accident happened?

Do you think that what you were doing might have distracted you and perhaps contributed to the accident?

How?

III Event Context. Some people never really feel comfortable driving a car. Are you one of those people?

What is it about driving that makes you feel uncomfortable?

Have you always felt like that?

Most people feel uncomfortable driving in certain conditions, like in the snow or rain, or in heavy traffic, or even after dark. Are there any conditions that you like to avoid?

Why?

Have you always felt like that?

Were any of these conditions present on the day of the accident?

Why did you drive in conditions that made you uncomfortable?

Have you driven in similar conditions since the accident?

Why?

If you're like most people, you have your good days and bad days. Do you remember what kind of day you were having before the accident?

How were you treated by officials after the accident?

IV Role Of The Car And Driving. What do you usually use your car for?

Was the accident trip part of this pattern or was it a relatively unique event?

In some European countries, the price of gasoline is so high that only the wealthy can afford to operate a car. Imagine that situation happening here and you found yourself unable to drive. Would it make much difference in your life?

What kind of difference?

What kind of car do you think you'll buy next time?

Why would you choose one like that?

What attracted you to the car you own now?

V Self Image. Some people think that a person's driving ability starts to fall off or diminish after they get past, say, fifty-five or sixty. What do you think about this?

Why?

What about after sixty-five or seventy?

Why?

What about seventy-five or eighty?

Why?

What about you in particular? Have you noticed any changes in your driving over the past few years?

What are they?

Data Analysis

The intent of the analysis was to locate principal thought structures, not establish correspondence with pre-determined categories: concern was wholly with discovery, not documentation of what is already known. Perhaps the best metaphor to describe the general format of the analysis, at least in its earliest phases, is "a scavenger hunt without a list." We proceeded, armed only with the notion that any encountered particular may later prove to be relevant. From our perspective, relevancies were to be revealed, not located and imputed.

The scavenger hunt metaphor was actualized in the first reading of the transcripts. Every interviewee response was assigned an individual code number and explanation. It was then refined several times to locate specific clues as to why certain thought structures prevailed.

Index